ESSAYS ON MENTAL INCAPACITY AND CRIMINAL CONDUCT

Publication Number 683
AMERICAN LECTURE SERIES®

A Monograph in

The BANNERSTONE DIVISION *of*
AMERICAN LECTURES IN BEHAVIORAL SCIENCE AND LAW

Edited by

RALPH SLOVENKO, LL.B., M.A., Ph.D.

Professor of Law
University of Kansas School of Law
Lawrence, Kansas
The Menninger Foundation
Topeka, Kansas

Essays on

MENTAL INCAPACITY
and
CRIMINAL CONDUCT

By

HELEN SILVING
Professor of Law
University of Puerto Rico
Rio Piedras, Puerto Rico

CHARLES C THOMAS • PUBLISHER
Springfield • Illinois • U.S.A.

Published and Distributed Throughout the World by
CHARLES C THOMAS • PUBLISHER
BANNERSTONE HOUSE
301-327 East Lawrence Avenue, Springfield, Illinois, U.S.A.
NATCHEZ PLANTATION HOUSE
735 North Atlantic Boulevard, Fort Lauderdale, Florida, U.S.A.

© 1967, by CHARLES C THOMAS • PUBLISHER
Library of Congress Catalog Card Number: 67-13064

With THOMAS BOOKS *careful attention is given to all details of
manufacturing and design. It is the Publisher's desire to present books
that are satisfactory as to their physical qualities and artistic possibilities
and appropriate for their particular use.* THOMAS BOOKS *will be true
to those laws of quality that assure a good name and good will.*

Printed in the United States of America
X-2

To
Judith and Milton Kestenberg

PREFACE

W HOM DO we punish? Whom do we treat? Can we classify people on the basis of the type of act they commit? Behavior, depending on its etiology or consequences, is viewed as either "bad" or "sick" and disposition follows accordingly. Disposition is usually carried out in a stick-to-the-book rigid manner. The rules have been a long time in evolution, and perhaps we have given more attention to the rules than to the substance. The rules have become so technical, and so removed from people, that as a consequence, we have heard it said by the most eminent authorities that we should forget about rules or principles, and just do the "right thing."

Mental illness, leprosy and venereal disease were all at one time thought to be problems of morality and therefore criminal. In 1962, the United States Supreme Court reasoned that narcotic addiction is in the same category as those other "diseases." The Court said that a State may not constitutionally inflict punishment for an illness, whether the illness be narcotics addiction or the common cold. The Supreme Court must have reflected on Samuel Butler's biting satire, *Erewhon* (nowhere), where the sick were punished for being sick, that is, for "being" rather than for "doing." In *Erewhon,* a person having "pulmonary consumption" was sentenced to "imprisonment, with hard labor, for the rest of your miserable existence," and the judge reproached him in his oral opinion:

> "It is intolerable that an example of such terrible enormity should be allowed to go at large unpunished. Your presence in the society of respectable people would lead the less able-bodied to think more lightly of all forms of illness; neither can it be permitted that you should have the chance of corrupting unborn beings who might hereafter pester you . . . But I will enlarge no further upon things that are themselves so obvious.

You may say that it is not your fault . . . I answer that whether your being in a consumption is your fault or not, it is a fault in you, and it is my duty to see that against such faults as this the commonwealth shall be protected. You may say that it is your misfortune to be criminal; I answer that it is your crime to be unfortunate."

There has been much writing on the subject of mental incapacity and criminal conduct. Indeed, probably no topic in behavioral science or law has been given comparable attention. Yet the issues remain obscure and we are nowhere near a happy solution.

In a manner that has made her prominent around the world, Professor Helen Silving in these essays brings a much needed perceptiveness. She is a student of criminal justice in the grand old European manner, and she has been rightly regarded as the "First Lady of American Criminal Law." In these essays she seeks to overcome the ontological approach to language. In her very rational manner, she is guided by a consistent general idea of modern criminal justice, rather than by a mixture of ad hoc decisions concerning incoherently isolated issues.

Professor Silving believes strongly that the direction of penal reform should be determined by a conscious choice of a philosophy of justice. Professor Silving maintains that in a free society, certain constitutional principles govern the choice of definition of "legal insanity" or "mental incapacity" (as the author calls it), the rules on evidence and proof of this condition, the types of disposition of persons acquitted by reason of insanity, as of any other rules. Among these constitutional principles, realism or orientation to the facts and laws of human life, as found by the so-called "sciences of man," must figure prominently. Professor Silving states, however, that this does not imply indiscriminate authorization of all scientifically "rational" types of disposition at criminal law. Disposition as well as accusation and trial is subject to constitutional limitations.

Similarly, Professor Silving maintains, the issue of the significance to be attributed to coincidence of alcoholism, drug addiction or acute intoxication with criminal conduct is in a free society a matter of rational policy conceived in the light of scientific insight into these phenomena and of constitutional limitations.

In all these contexts there is need in modern law for discarding obsolete, often magical notions. Indeed, there is need for ridding law of the encumbrance of belief in an inherent fixed reality of mental phenomena and for orienting it to the contemporary image of a universe in motion and dynamic psychology. Professor Silving analyzes concepts such as "responsibility," "guilt," "insanity," and "dangerousness" with a view to determining their social and legal meaning and the "meaning of their meaning."

This book presents, in addition, a critical evaluation of various conceptions and tests of "legal insanity" available in comparative law patterns, as well as various comparative law approaches to the treatment of the criminality of persons affected by use or abuse of alcohol and narcotic drugs. It suggests new approaches for adoption in penal codes.

RALPH SLOVENKO

Editor, American Lectures
in Behavioral Science and Law

ACKNOWLEDGMENTS

I HAVE been an Adviser to the Legislative Penal Reform Commission of the Commonwealth of Puerto Rico and to the Commonwealth Department of Justice. It is hence important to stress that the opinions expressed in this book are exclusively my own; they should not be attributed to any Branch, Department or Agency of the Commonwealth.

I wish to recognize my great indebtedness to Professor Paul K. Ryu of Seoul National University, Seoul, Korea, who formulated the theory of causation which has served as the point of departure for the basic concepts developed in this book. Ryu, Causation in Criminal Law, 106 University of Pennsylvania Law Review 773 (1958). The theory of "responsibility" submitted in this book is based on that formulated in Professor Ryu's "Korean Culture and Criminal Responsibility" (Yale Thesis 1958, on file at the Library of Yale Law School). The justification of the exemption for mental incapacity advanced in this book is based on the rationale of punishment developed in Ryu and Silving, Error Juris: A Comparative Study, 24 University of Chicago Law Review 421 (1957).

The term "impairment of integrative functioning" in the test of mental incapacity was suggested by Dr. Angel Miranda.

I am indebted to Professor Ralph Slovenko for most valuable suggestions and criticisms.

I am grateful to Dr. David M. Helfeld, Dean of the Law School of the University of Puerto Rico, for constant encouragement and support in my research and writing.

I also wish to recognize the valuable assistance offered by Professor Max Persche, Librarian, and by the Personnel and Staff, of the Library of the University of Puerto Rico School of Law.

The Toronto University Press, the Journal of Criminal Law, Criminology and Police Science, and the University of Puerto

Rico Law Review have graciously given permission to repro-
duce in this book the following essays:

"Mental Incapacity in Criminal Law," which appeared in CUR-
RENT LAW AND SOCIAL PROBLEMS, Vol. II (Macdonald ed.,
University of Toronto Press 1961);

"The Criminal Law of Mental Incapacity," which appeared in Vol.
53, No. 2, *Journal of Criminal Law, Criminology and Police Science*,
Copyright ©1962 by the Northwestern University School of Law;

"Psychoanalysis and the Criminal Law," which appeared in Vol.
51, No. 1, *Journal of Criminal Law, Criminology and Police Science*,
Copyright ©1960 by the Northwestern University School of Law;

" 'Guilt': A Methodological Study," which appeared in Vol. 32, No.
1, of the University of Puerto Rico Law Review (1963).

HELEN SILVING

CONTENTS

                                                                Page

Preface vii

Acknowledgments xi

INTRODUCTION 3

Problems of Interdisciplinary Communication 5

Meaning of Ascertaining "Meaning" 9

"Responsibility" 15

"Guilt" 23

"Dangerousness" 45

"Rule by Labels" and Terminology 48

MENTAL INCAPACITY IN CRIMINAL LAW 51

The Purpose of Punishment and the Area to
    Which It Is Inapplicable 56

  A. Guilt as Directive in Punishment: Mental Incapacity
      Exemption Conceived As a Quality Excluding Guilt 57

     1. Guilt as Intent 58

     2. Guilt as Blameworthiness 61

        A. Manifestation of Community Judgment 62

        B. Formation of Community Judgment 70

     3. Guilt in the Light of Phenomenological Thought 71

     4. Guilt as Interpreted by the Writer 72

  B. Punishment as a Functional Means of Deterrence:
      Mental Incapacity as "Nondeterrability" or Unfitness
      to Serve as Means of Deterring Others 74

  C. Punishment as a Means of Reformation: Mental In-
      capacity as an Inability to Be Reformed 76

  D. Punishment as Law Assertion: Mental Incapacity
      Exemption Where Punishment Is Not Law Assertive 77

  Summary 78

Page

Available Mental Incapacity Tests 79

Total Exemption Tests: A. M'Naghten's Case, Irresistible
Impulse, Model Code Tests, German Test 80

   1. M'Naghten 80

   2. Irresistible Impulse 93

   3. The Model Penal Code Tests 94

   4. German Tests 101

      A. The Philosophy of the "Incapacity" Concept 102

      B. So-Called "Mixed System" 103

      C. Critique of the Incapacity Formula 104

      D. The So-Called Biological Basis 107

      Recent Reform Drafts 111

Total Exemption Tests: B. The New Hampshire Test, The
Durham Rule, The Spanish Test 113

   1. The New Hampshire Test 113

   2. The Durham Test 116

   3. The Spanish Test 120

Partial Exemption Tests 125

   1. Partial Responsibility 126

   2. Diminished Responsibilty 128

Summary 130

Recommended Test 134

Summary 139

Conclusion 140

THE CRIMINAL LAW OF MENTAL INCAPACITY 141

I. Problems Pertaining to the "Trial Stage" 146

   A. Procedure to Determine Mental Incapacity Related
   to Engagement in the Criminal Conduct 146

      1. Who May Raise the Mental Incapacity Issue? 146

      2. Bases of Doubt Regarding Mental Capacity or
      Fitness to Proceed 151

      3. Evidence of Mental Incapacity Pertinent to the
      Act Charged 157

Page

4. Disposition and Remedies in Cases of Mental
   Incapacity 161
B. Determination of Fitness to Proceed; Measures Im-
   posed Upon the Unfit; Remedies 161
   1. Selecting the Proper Test 161
   2. Objective Trial 168
   3. Measures Imposed Upon Persons Unfit to Proceed 169
II. The Scheme of Measures Applicable in Cases of Acquittal
   by Reason of Mental Incapacity 171
   A. Substantive Provisions 179
      1. Test of "Dangerousness" 179
         a. The Criminal "Act" as Indicium of
            "Dangerousness" 180
         b. The Mental Element in "Mental Incapacity" Cases ..187
         c. Plurality of Criminal Conduct 191
         d. Miscellaneous Indicia of "Dangerousness":
            Personality Evaluation 195
      2. Principle of Proportionality of Measure to Danger 196
      3. Special Categories of the Mentally Incapacitated:
         The "Habitual Offender" and the "Offender Not
         Susceptible to Punishment 199
         a. The "Habitual Offender" 199
         b. The "Offender Not Susceptible to Punishment" 202
   B. Constitutional and Procedural Problems 207
III. Conclusion 213
INTOXICANTS AND CRIMINAL CONDUCT 214
   I. Alcoholism and Drug Addiction Qualifying for the
      General Mental Incapacity Exemption 232
   II. Intoxication As Basis of Special Mental Incapacity
      Exemption 250
      Lessons to Be Learned from Scientific Insight...................251
      Attitudes to Alcohol Reflected in Legal Development 256
      Recommendation for Adoption of the Principle of
      Exemption 262

Page

Actio Libera in Causa 264

   Intoxication for the Purpose of Crime Commission 264

   Intention to Commit Crime and Alcohol Consumption
     (or Drug Use) in Knowledge of Intoxicating Effect 270

   Reckless Actio Libera in Causa and Miscellaneous Other
     Situations 272

   Section 330a of the German Penal Code 278

   Draft of a New Penal Code of Germany of 1962 286

   Evaluation of Our Study of Section 330a and the
     Draft Version 289

   Basic Suggestions 290

   Italian Draft 1949-50 293

   Evaluation of the Doctrine of the Italian Draft 298

   Final Policy Scheme 299

III. Measures Applicable in Cases of Acquittal by Reason of
Mental Incapacity Connected with Alcoholism or Drug
Addiction or by Reason of Intoxication 302

   Bases of Measures 302

   Title 1: Measures Applicable in Cases of Alcoholism and
     Drug Addiction Qualifying for the General Mental
     Incapacity Exemption 307

   Title 2: Measures for Persons who Commit Crime When
     in a State of Acute Intoxication 314

IV. Specific Crimes Created by Narcotics and Alcohol
Legislation 318

Conclusion 328

CONCLUSION 338

*Table of Penal Codes, Penal Code Drafts, Statutes and Other
General Sources* 355

Table of Cases 363

Index of Cited Authors 367

Subject Index 371

ESSAYS ON MENTAL INCAPACITY AND CRIMINAL CONDUCT

INTRODUCTION*

THE ESSAYS presented in this collection deal with the problem of designating the mental states which in a rational system of law ought to qualify an offender for exemption from punitive responsibility and for potential treatment by nonpunitive preventive and protective penal law sanctions.

The object of the first essay, "Mental Incapacity in Criminal Law," is to show what should not be read into the so-called "defense of insanity" and how an exemption for the mentally "abnormal" should be formulated. The second essay, entitled "The Criminal Law of Mental Incapacity," deals with the treatment of persons exempted on the ground of "mental incapacity," as well as with matters of procedure and proof. The third essay, on "Intoxicants and Criminal Conduct," deals with offenders whose total life conduct is affected by commitment to intoxicants and with acutely drunken offenders. A final section of this essay is devoted to discussion of specific crimes which feature alcohol or drug consumption, particularly their constitutional aspects.

The choice of these topics for a collection on *Mental Incapacity and Criminal Conduct* should not be taken to imply that other so-called "exemption grounds" might not as well be properly included. I have in mind particularly the "defense of error" which shares with the above-enumerated topics the foundation of the exempting quality upon an inadequacy in the "mental element of crime." This does not apply equally to other exemption grounds such as self-defense and necessity, although penal

---

*Portions of this Introduction are reprinted from my article, *Psychoanalysis and the Criminal Law*, 51 JOURNAL OF CRIMINAL LAW, CRIMINOLOGY AND POLICE SCIENCE 19, at 20-24 (1960), by special permission, Copyright © 1960 by the Northwestern University School of Law, Vol. 51, No. 1. Other portions are reprinted from my article *"Guilt"; A Methodological Study*, 32 REVISTA JURÍDICA DE LA UNIVERSIDAD DE PUERTO RICO 11 (1963), by special permission.

codes generally predicate applicability of these exemptions upon the presence of a mental factor. While in them it is required that the actor know that he is being attacked or that a state of necessity obtains, such requisite in contemporary laws adds but a "moralizing" modicum to a situation which is on independent objective grounds believed to be exempting. This psychological qualification in self-defense and necessity should be jettisoned. There is no valid reason for penalizing a man for saving his own life, even though "unconsciously."[1]

While it would be proper to extend the scope of this collection to the treatment of error, tangential with mental incapacity, a full discussion of all allied topics would require further elaboration of the general issue of the so-called "mental element." To limit this volume to a reasonable length, it is necessary, as it always is when complex situations are discussed, to adopt a standard of selection. The reason for selecting the above-mentioned topics for separate treatment is that they are generally, though often inarticulately, assumed to be connected, even where alcoholism and addiction are expressly denied qualification as "mental disease" and acute intoxication is held irrelevant. Error is seldom discussed in context with "insanity," although the most current "insanity" test (*M'Naghten*)[2] is in the last analysis a test of "error."

To convey the extent of this inquiry, it is necessary to describe the methodological approach to be followed. The aim is to introduce a new orientation into the philosophy of the "mental incapacity exemption"—the so-called "defense of insanity"—and a new approach to the treatment of "criminal conduct" connected with use of intoxicants. This implies "purging conventional symbols" which reflect outdated and obscure criminal law philosophies and assigning to them a clear meaning, adjusted to modern rational criminal law demands. The conventional terminology has been mostly retained while the referent is substantially reformulated. The reason for maintaining existing terms, of course,

---

[1]Compare SILVING, CONSTITUENT ELEMENTS OF CRIME—(Thomas, ed. Slovenko 1966).

[2](1843)10 C. & F. 200 (H.L.).

is not an aim at disguising the change but precisely an endeavor to point it up more sharply. Introducing new terminology carries the risk that discarded ancient concepts would infiltrate as matters of pretended self-evident validity.

PROBLEMS OF INTERDISCIPLINARY COMMUNICATION

Purging symbols, said Whitehead,[3] is the first task of reason. However, such purging has a different import in so-called "normative" and in so-called "descriptive" disciplines. In the latter, a symbol which does not symbolize anything but merely provokes emotional responses related to unconscious associations with unidentified and not readily identifiable past experiences is "senseless," though it may be "sensibly" (intelligently) exploited. By contrast, in normative disciplines and particularly in law, a "descriptively senseless" symbol may have the quality of "imposing meaning."

Thus, assuming that the term *insanity* occurs in a given law, a psychologist or psychiatrist consulted as to its meaning may very well say that it does not mean anything; but when a lawyer is asked the same question, he may at best say that this concept is vague, and when he says that it is "senseless," the rational import of his statement is that the reservoir of its potential meanings is so broad that the choice among them of its "proper meaning" by a future decision-maker will be legally "arbitrary." Apart from constitutional issues which use of such term may raise, decisional interpretations may endow it with increasingly definite "meaning"; such process of endowing an initially "senseless" term with "sense" may be essentially legislative; but unless challenged as violative of the principle of separation of powers or due process, it is attended by a "normative effect" obliterating perhaps the mark of its origin.

"Normativization" of a concept is often not a conscious process. A legislator or a judge may well use a term in the mistaken belief that it has been defined previously by a given science; if he attaches legal consequences to an authoritative finding that

---

[3]WHITEHEAD, SYMBOLISM, ITS MEANING AND EFFECT (1927).

such term is appropriate in a more or less concrete situation, he may unwittingly guide future use. Thus, the "scientifically senseless" term acquires "legal meaning." Often also, despite such "normativization," decision-makers continue to use it in a manner and in the belief as though it were still referring to a descriptive scientific category. Sometimes, "normative" and "descriptive" connotations are confused. Moreover, lawyers may mistakenly use an accepted "scientific term" in a sense different from that attributed to it by the respective science. Such use creates further, more complex misunderstanding between lawyers and men of science.

Psychiatrists, on the other hand, often distort the meaning of terms used by lawyers, ascribing to "legal" terms of art a connotation which for purposes of psychiatric expert judgment they are not purported to convey. When this happens and when, in addition, lawyers are not methodologically prepared to articulate their own position properly, the "double-talk" assumes new dimensions. Thus, for example when a psychiatrist is asked whether within the *M'Naghten* "insanity test"[4] the accused knew that his conduct was "wrong," and the expert objects to being called upon to resolve a "moral issue of right and wrong" which is "scientifically unanswerable" and which, as a psychiatrist, he is not equipped to answer, lawyers assume an attitude of *peccavi* as if, indeed, they were asking for performance of an impossible task.[5] Actually, whatever the shortcoming of *M'Naghten*, this is not one of them. In such instances, the expert is not called upon to choose between "right and wrong" or to determine whether

---

[4]The English test formulated in 1843, *supra*, still dominates the vast majority of jurisdictions of the common law world. It is colloquially called the "right-wrong test" and takes defendant's knowledge that his conduct is wrong as proof of his sanity.

[5]In United States v. Freeman, 357 F.2d 606 (2d Cir. 1966), Judge Kaufman, delivering the majority opinion, whereby for the federal courts within the Second Circuit the M'Naghten test was replaced by the American Law Institute Model Code test, cited with apparent approval a statement of Dr. Lawrence Kolb, Director of the New York Psychiatric Institute, Professor and Chairman of the Department of Psychiatry at Columbia University, declaring that "answers supplied by a psychiatrist in regard to questions of rightness or wrongness of an act or 'knowing' its nature constitute a professional perjury." *Supra*, at 619.

the accused's conduct was "wrong"; the law or community standards have already passed on the question of "criminality" or
"wrongfulness"; the expert has no choice whatever in the matter.
His objection is inapposite. The question asked of him is strictly
limited in scope: "You may take it that that which the accused
did, if indeed he did it, is 'legally [whether directly by legal
fiat or by community judgment adopted by law] wrong'; now,
tell the jury whether the accused knew this."

Of course, a psychiatrist might rejoin that he does not like
the total premise of the law, its punitive approach, its orientation to "right and wrong." If he refuses cooperation on this
ground, his position is comparable to that of a conscientious ob-
jector. It is not, however, implicit in "psychiatric" insight, though
it may be inferred from some standard of ethics which derives,
or is believed by him to derive, support from psychiatric insight.
In fact, when speaking of the "superego"—and this is a category
in the intradisciplinary discourse of psychiatrists—the latter
posit the existence of social and legal judgments as to what is
"right" and as to what is "wrong." This does not require the
psychiatrist to share the prevailing judgment, and he hardly
ever assumes that it does. What then is the reason for his disavowal of such "objectivity" when it comes to cooperating with
representatives of the legal profession?

One gains the impression that the source of the misunderstanding in principle between lawyers and psychiatrists is not so much
a failure of mutual intellectual communication as it is a bias
against each other's "moral" attitudes. The need of our age is
not solely to bring about intellectual comprehension between
lawyers and psychiatrists but also to create a sense of cooperation
that would facilitate development of a new "juridicopsychiatric
social morality" which, in turn, would afford the proper background for acceptance of a genuine reform of criminal law and
procedure as instruments of justice. This, I submit, requires integration of psychiatrists into the decisional process as equal participants with jurists, as independent "judges" in a true sense
of the term, sitting on the bench together with jurists from the
very beginning of proceedings until their termination and beyond, and not merely as expert witnesses or members of more or

less "quasi-judicial" boards. Psychiatrists must learn that they can no longer wash their hands of social responsibilities, and lawyers must learn that they can no longer use psychiatrists as cloaks.

Referring to a legal usage of a term as "incorrect" should not be taken to mean that it points to something that does not exist or is not attended by legal consequences. "Incorrect" may mean rather that such usage suggests a distorted image of the nature of legal or other normative operations, for example, by creating the impression as though a scientifically correct proposition were also necessarily legally valid, indeed, "law" itself. The fact is that the law is not a science, though it may and should formulate its policy in the light of scientific findings. However, belief in the "normative force" of scientific findings may in the course of judicial practice develop a rule that the concrete findings are binding or, indeed, a rule that science in general has this effect. But such incidental consequences of initially "incorrect" legal opinion are in principle not desirable, since legal decision-making should be a conscious rational process and judges should know exactly what are the operational results of their actions.

Similarly, one might call "incorrect" a usage which conveys the notion as though any consciously or unconsciously desired result or other normative feature were by the same token a present actuality of fact or of valid law. On the other hand, this should not be taken to exclude adoption of, for example, a "natural law" standard, so long as such adoption is based on conscious choice.

True, a usage is often said to be "incorrect" when, considering the "proper ends" of criminal law, established in the light of a chosen philosophy of such law—herein, the political philosophy of a "free society"—such usage reflects an undesirable criminal law philosophy. But such application of the term "incorrect" may be misleading, since it confuses "undesirable" aim with "incorrect" meaning, which is methodologically fallacious. However, "incorrect" may be properly used to indicate that actual or legitimate postulates of a political ideology are misrepresented, confused or not represented at all.

Generally, when manipulating legal terminology, it is most

important to be aware of the methodological import of its use in a given context. Before facing the problem of the "meaning" of legal or social terms, decision-makers ought to face the initial problem of what ascertaining the "meaning" of such terms signifies. This question of the meaning of ascertaining "meaning" is thus a preliminary one in all legal-sociological-psychological discourse. We must face it. The subject merits discussion under a separate heading.

I shall, thereafter, devote special sections in this introduction to problems of the "correct usage" of the term *responsibility* and the extent to which, in a free society, *responsibility* may and should be affected by scientific findings, of the meaning of *guilt* and the place of *dangerousness* in democratic law. Two final sections will deal with "rule by labels" and "terminology."

MEANING OF ASCERTAINING "MEANING"

The very formulation of the question, What is meant by ascertainment of the "meaning" of terms such as "responsibility" or "guilt"?—key words in the criminal law vocabulary, on whose meaning depends the place of "insanity" in such law—seems to suggest the idea as though the term came first and its meaning came second, while we might expect meaning to be the primary, and terminology but a secondary, matter. The fact is, however, that our life and actions are only partially governed by meaning, in the sense of rational meaning. As the Bible suggests, the Word came before Creation. Words, their sound and the unconscious associations attached to them, govern us, often beyond our control. Belief in the magic of words is said to be characteristic of primitive people. Actually, modern civilized men are by no means free of a similar tendency to attribute to words an impact beyond the scope of consciously realized meaning. We thus frequently use a word as though its meaning were obvious; yet, when asked what exactly that word means, we are puzzled to find that we are not prepared clearly to formulate that which it stands for. We might have some fuzzy notion of that which it is supposed to symbolize, but that notion is not consciously conceptualized in our minds, and is so laden with emotions that purging it, in the sense in which Whitehead recommends the "purging of symbols," presents a major task. For this reason we often feel when searching for the meaning of a term such as "responsibility" or "guilt" as though we were engaged in an exploratory expedition into a reality beyond the rational sense of a "word."

For scientific purposes such search would seem superfluous. Men of science—one might argue—would do best if they proceeded from "meaning" and assigned to each meaning a term chosen by arbitrary fiat to serve the purpose of convenient scientific communication, preferably a number or an otherwise formal symbol, such as a letter of the alphabet. Confusion of meanings could be avoided thus. But this method, though it might be appropriate in mathematical sciences, is not appropriate in the social sciences. Actually, it is not even used in the former; e.g., notions of mechanics, such as "force" and "mass," have been derived from the common language and then endowed by physicists with a specific scientific meaning, distinct from that attributed to them in everyday life.[6] Certainly, in the social sciences, such arbitrary assignment of a term to a meaning would miss an essential purpose of these sciences, namely, that of clarification of meaning of social usage. In the social sciences the symbol assigned to a meaning itself constitutes a meaningful issue. Thus, for example, the very fact that in social usage a term has a particular dual meaning, referring to two apparently distinct realities, may point to a connection assumed in the given society to exist between these two realities. Terminology is a social factor having a significance beyond that of a mere designation of specific meanings. In law the ascertainment of the meaning of terms performs not only a scientific but also a specifically legal social function. Although legal interpretation is now known to be a highly creative task of lawmaking, it undoubtedly also includes a "finding" of social meaning.

While the meaning of a social term may not be at all settled, such term may be deemed to carry extremely significant social consequences, which it may be practically impossible to disso-

---

[6] On this see FRANK, PHILOSOPHY OF SCIENCE, Introduction XVI, XVII (1957).

ciate from that term and associate with another, new term. For such consequences are taken to attach to that term regardless of changes in the scope of its meaning. Perhaps no better example of this phenomenon can be found than is afforded by the history of the terms "guilt" and "insanity."

In cases where the defense of insanity was abolished by statute, courts in the United States have reversed convictions on the ground that withdrawing the issue of "guilt" from the jury in a criminal case is unconstitutional.[7] No constitutional objections have been raised to changes in the contents of the "guilt" concept, such as changes in definitions of "insanity" or in the structure of intent, although, where such changes occur, that which the jury is passing upon is not identical with that it was passing on before.[8] This example shows that seeking to establish what people—in the case of law, particularly legislators and judges—mean when using terms such as "responsibility," "guilt" or "insanity" serves not only the purpose of satisfying an intellectual curiosity but also the purpose of practical law administration.

A social function such as that of determining the meaning of *responsibility, guilt, insanity,* should be geared to the aim which it pursues. If the determination of such meaning is to serve the purpose of scientific and legal communication, of bringing to the consciousness of lawmakers what is actually at stake in terms of practical solutions when the issue denoted by such terms is raised, and of facilitating legislative drafting, it cannot be limited to a mere "finding" of social usage. An additional, creative activity is necessary.

Social meanings are not always rational. Unless it is precisely our purpose to inquire into the phenomena of men's thinking

---

[7] State v. Strasburg, 60 Wash. 106, 110 Pac. 1020 (1910). Compare also State v. Lange, 168 La. 958, 123 So. 639 (1929); Sinclair v. State, 161 Miss. 142, 132 So. 581 (1931). Sanity is considered a requisite of "guilt."

[8] Strictly speaking, every new crime type introduced into the law and every extension of an old crime concept enlarge the concept of "guilt." Notice in this connection the enormous extension of the notion of attempt; significantly, this extension is a product of judicial interpretation, following doctrinal changes. There is room for doubt whether even the principle of *nulla poena* has been adequately considered in such situations.

and believing, we must try to make sense of what people attempt to say. We must apply to words of current usage a critical philosophical analysis, seeking to derive from them a core of rationally understandable thought. We must aim at finding that which can be "meaningfully said" among those matters which people attempt to convey by means of common or "legal language,"[9] and, if necessary, reformulate versions of such language, in order to express the thought behind it in a logically correct form.

However, it should be noted that, as indicated before, meaning in law is always sui generis. Much that cannot be otherwise "meaningfully said" in social life can very well be meaningfully said in legal life. Language in law purports to convey commands rather than merely descriptive propositions.[10] Legal sentences always ultimately "purport" to convey imperatives. Often a meaningful imperative may be conveyed by a sentence the terminology of which would be meaningless were it contained in a descriptive sentence. When the addressee of a command understands what action he is to take in response to such command, the latter has meaning even if apparently significant component parts of the commanding sentence are otherwise meaningless. For example, though there are no dragons or witches in actual existence, a law may define qualities allegedly

---

[9]On this see the writings of Wittgenstein and Stevenson. In a letter to Cynthia Schuster, dated May 5, 1952, Charles Stevenson said (see Schuster, *Peter Glassen on the Cognitivity of Moral Judgments*, in XXX MIND 277, at 95-96 [1961]: "So what I was really attempting to do . . . was not to give just what people meant, but only to 'salvage' from their meaning all that I, viewing the situation from an empirical viewpoint, could find intelligible."

[10]Apparently descriptive propositions in law may be interpreted to import commands or constituent parts of commands. Such an apparently descriptive proposition, for example a definition, may be valid in law even if it would be questionable in another context. I am using this interpretation derived from Kelsenian doctrine provisionally, this is, merely in order to indicate the distinctiveness of law as a frame of reference. But use of Kelsenian terminology, such as "rules," "validity," is not to be taken to exclude the possibility of philosophical-legal reduction of legal sentences to "is" propositions or to imply a necessarily normative interpretation of "rules," "validity," etc. See on this Silving, *The Lasting Value of Kelsenism*, in LAW, STATE AND INTERNATIONAL LEGAL ORDER, ESSAYS IN HONOR OF HANS KELSEN, 297-308 (Engel & Metall ed. 1964).

constituting dragonhood or witchcraft and delegate to certain persons authority to find from the presence of such qualities the givenness of such creatures. If then such person makes a finding to that effect, the dragon or witch has a legal operational reality, meaning that it gives rise to legal consequences, anything science may say to the contrary notwithstanding. It is most important at this point to insert a caveat. The difference between "descriptive" and "normative" sentences is a relative one. Reduction of one to the other category is not excluded. But neither is discourse in terms of this distinction socially meaningless.[11]

Since terms in law are always ultimately commands, any ontological meaning assigned to them is in the course of law application translated into operational terms. Phenomenologically each term then stands for that which it "does" in legal life, that is, the observable conditions and consequences which are attached to it. The translating process often follows the pattern of social usage. In a sense, all men are philosophers. When they use a term, they implicitly attribute to it a place in the totality of their image of the universe (*Weltbild*);[12] thereby they ascribe to its meaning certain operational qualities, in the sense of expected responses in emotion and in action on their own part and on the part of their fellowmen. Thus, for example, when "guilt" is understood to convey the idea of "sin," there obtains a social expectation that certain conditions must be met and certain sanctions must or ought to follow, whereas when "guilt" is taken to represent social harm, certain other conditions and consequences are contemplated. When an ontological conception of "guilt" appears in a legal context, it conveys given expectations, which are in turn translatable into legal rules. It is signifi-

---

[11]By "imperative" I merely mean to indicate distinctiveness of the legal frame of reference. Notice that, according to Wittgenstein, the meaningfulness of descriptive language may be always tested by expressing it in terms of command and response to such command. This, I suppose, does not exclude the practical distinction between descriptive and imperative language, as commonly used.

[12]On this see ENGISCH, VOM WELTBILD DES JURISTEN, Abhandlungen der Heidelberger Akademie der Wissenschaften, Philosophisch-historische Klasse, Jahrgang 1950. 2. Abhandlung (Carl Winter, Universitätsverlag 1950), at 17-18 and literature cited there.

cant to note that though the ontological meaning of a term used in a command may be irrational, the command operationally expressed through its medium may be rational in the light of a chosen policy objective.[13]

The common philosophy of a concept is not necessarily uniform or static. It may very well vary geographically or change in the course of time.[14] In the light of the dynamic nature of social meaning, a problem of crucial significance is that of the identity or continuity of the topic of discussion. What is it—we may ask—that has changed? What is the justification for applying to a variety of meanings a single term? Why, for example, do we speak of "guilt," although this term may mean different things to different people? Why, above all, is it necessary or desirable to find a common denominator for such variety of meanings? Of course unless we find such a common denominator, the controversy over the meaning of "guilt" will turn out to be but a semantic dispute. Mainly, however, our concern is with finding such common denominator due to our expectation that it will help us to clarify and to formulate in proper operational terms the meaning which we decide to attribute to "guilt."[15] Only if we can formulate a "general theory of guilt" will we be able to express in descriptively meaningful terms a particular concept of "guilt."

There are two potential sources of assuming an identity or continuity of meaning of a term to which various meanings have been socially attributed. One consists in the fact that there may be found a minimum meaning common to such varying meanings. The other lies in a community belief in the identity or akinness of the several meanings.

While any ontological doctrine of "guilt" may be fitted into

---

[13]Compare *supra*, in regard to "insanity."

[14]But judges are not justified in simply substituting a new rational meaning for an outmoded one intended by the legislators. For in attributing the latter meaning to the term in issue, the legislators impliedly conveyed a legal rule, which may be quite rational. See Silving, *Analogies Extending and Restricting Federal Jurisdiction; Erie R. R. Co. v. Tompkins and the Law of Conflict*, 31 Iowa Law Review 330 (1946).

[15]The same is true of such notions of "responsibility" and "insanity."

the general theory of guilt, provided that operational terms can be substituted for ontological ones, this form of expression, implying a basic critical philosophical approach, may not be acceptable to those who postulate the essential uniqueness and exclusiveness of their particular metaphysics of "guilt." Except within such extreme metaphysical approach, there is no incompatibility between formulation of a general theory of guilt and choice of a particular guilt doctrine. The former is a scientific task, the latter is a political choice, which may, of course, as any political choice, be determined by a preferred general philosophy.

It is thus our task in searching for the "meaning" of notions such as "responsibility" or "guilt" first to develop a general theory of the pertinent notion and thereafter, by applying a preferred standard, to invest this notion with more specific meaning. This methodological approach is equally proper as regards "responsibility" and as regards "guilt." However, historically, these notions have received distinctive orientations. The concept of "guilt" has been so strongly affected by theology that its political aspects and the potential impact of scientific considerations were obscured. Many modern psychiatrists reject the concept of "guilt" as meaningless. By contrast, the notion of "responsibility" has not been outright rejected as a priori senseless, and it is within the framework of discussions regarding choice of the type of "responsibility" that the conflicts between the "scientific" and the legal approach have been waged.

"RESPONSIBILITY"

In common usage "responsibility" is often taken to denote a personal quality of certain individuals. This may be found in colloquial expressions, such as "X is a responsible person" or "Y is an irresponsible person." The assumption made in such cases is that one can by examination or observation of the conduct of a person determine whether he is or is not a "responsible person." Of course, being a "responsible person" is taken to be a virtue of such individual, so that there is implied in statements of this type a normative evaluation, mostly incorporating community standards as to what is expected from an individual in terms of compliance with community norms. A somewhat similar type of inarticulate evaluation is implied in the frequent statements of lawyers and psychiatrists that an "insane person" *is not* or *cannot be* "responsible." However, when made in legal context such statement may also have the clearly normative meaning that such person *cannot* be made responsible constitutionally.

The indicated type of usage is thus "incorrect" only in the sense of suggesting as though "responsibility" were a quality of a purely descriptive nature. A "correct" usage, in the above-described sense, of the term "responsibility" is a normative one. "Responsibility" in the broadest sense is a moral or legal rather than a scientific concept.[16] It is best defined as the connection adopted in ethics or in law between certain conditions, such as certain mental and external factual data (e.g., intent or negligence and death causation), and certain consequences, such as social censure, imprisonment, fine, compensation. Decision makers shape these conditions and consequences for legal purposes with a view to achieving their preferred goals, the so-called "ends of criminal law." As stated by Dr. Paul K. Ryu, responsibility is a "relational concept."[17] This means that there is no absolute concept, state or quality of "responsibility." The conditions and consequences constituting "responsibility" are not each a separate phenomenon or occurrence suspended in the air or a quality inherent in the individual. Rather, to each type of condition or conditions complex there is assigned by law a particular type of consequence or a group of consequence types. In a rational system of law this assignment is based on rational considerations, so that the conditions and consequences are geared to each other in a sound manner. Such rationality is judged from the standpoint of the goals which operation of the responsibility concept is expected to reach. The choice of "ends," as well as of the conditions and

---

[16]Of course, by convention one could give this word any chosen meaning. The problem would then arise whether such convention would be functional.

[17]RYU, KOREAN CULTURE AND CRIMINAL RESPONSIBILITY (Yale Thesis 1958, on file in the Library of Yale Law School).

consequences which are to serve the chosen ends, is in large measure limited in democratic society by constitutional restrictions aimed at preservation of fundamental rights of men.

This definition of "responsibility" suggests not only the sphere of potential contribution of science to the shaping of a legal concept of responsibility but also the limitations imposed upon such a contribution. Scientific insight may be brought to bear on the elements of rational teleology implied in a sound system of responsibility. But it cannot resolve the normative problems of choice, the choice of goals or of their proper hierarchy, except perhaps indirectly by bringing to the attention of decision-makers the manner in which pursuit of a given goal would operate. Finally, as the goals themselves, considerations of scientific teleology also must yield to constitutional limitations, so that a method which is most appropriate scientifically may often have to be sacrificed to fundamental liberties.

Problems of "responsibility," though closely connected with each other, may be divided for purposes of presentation, into three topics: (a) the goals or "ends of criminal law"; (b) the consequences of responsibility or "sanctions"; and (c) the personal conditions of responsibility or "imputation."[18] In this section I shall deal solely with the two topics enumerated first. The last one will be discussed under the heading "guilt."

The misunderstanding between lawyers and psychiatrists, abundantly discussed in the literatures of both law and psychiatry, begins at the stage of "ends" to be pursued. It is thus important to clarify further the methodological problem in issue.

The "ends of criminal law" are ethical, political and social ideals, that is, they are normative and not scientific conceptions. The choice of normative ends—provided that they do not involve dedication to an abstract purpose at any cost—to be "rational" should take account of pertinent facts, particularly those bearing on the questions of whether a given end can be reached and, if so, what is the cost of reaching it. But a normative

---

[18]To be accurate, the objective parts of definitions of crime and the tests of ascertaining the presence of objective crime elements also form part of the "responsibility" concept.

choice, adoption or rejection of an "end" as a "value," cannot be made by a simple application of reason to facts, for values neither flow rationally from facts nor are automatically invalidated by facts. The function of science in the process of choice lies in its use as a tool, a fact-finding instrument, where facts have been normatively decided to be pertinent. Thus, in considering adoption of an end, decision-makers may take account, for example, of the fact-finding of psychoanalytic psychology that conscious pursuit of that end may be impeded by unconscious judicial and public motivations at variance with those consciously professed. The decision-makers may or may not decide that the mere fact of a goal being psychologically rooted in or impeded by a motive deemed objectionable does not nullify its value. This is itself a matter of normative decision. If they decide that the value is not thus *ipso facto* nullified, they should further consider, in the light of science, whether it is possible by judicial and public education to eliminate or modify the operation of the impeding unconscious forces. The decision-makers may make the final decision regarding adoption or rejection of the goal dependent on the answer to this question. But the ultimate decision upon adoption or rejection of an "end" must be theirs, for it is a normative decision.

It is thus fallacious to assume that the "ends of criminal law" can simply be logically derived from scientific findings of, e.g., psychoanalytic psychology regarding the motives which prompt man's actions and reactions. But this is precisely the method which has often been used in the numerous law reform proposals advanced in recent decades. As stated before, frequently, what appears to be a conflict between the legal and the "scientific" approach is in fact a conflict between legal and medical ethics. Confusion may be avoided by clarity regarding the exact line of demarcation between scientific finding and ethical choice. An example may illustrate the manner in which separation of the "scientific" from the "ethical" aspects of choice should be maintained.

The first issue before decision-makers entrusted with formulation of criminal law policy is choice of a basic ethical approach. That choice may or may not be made without regard to

any factual or scientific information. The problem of whether
the dominant ethics should be absolute or utilitarian ethics is
implied in all discussions concerning "ends"; however, this problem is never verbalized in this country,[19] utilitarianism being
tacitly assumed to be a self-evident approach even by those pro-
fessing adherence to various religious views.[20] The psychoanalytic
information that may or may not be regarded as pertinent to
the choice between absolute and utilitarian ethics concerns the
roots of ethical principles. Psychoanalysis has traced the preferred symbols of absolute ethics to psychological origins in
motives traditionally identified with vices. Self-sacrifice, altru-
ism, generosity, absolute truthfulness have been shown often to
originate in unconscious wishes that are diametrically opposed
to the noble sentiments apparent to the bearer himself as well
as to others. However, psychoanalysis, where it functions as
a science, does not avow any particular ethical preference. While
the Benthamite "pleasure-pain" principle may have served as
a prototype for the Freudian "pleasure-unpleasure" principle,
the latter has developed autonomously as a distinctly biological-
psychological and not as an ethical-political notion. The fact is
that whether or not one can judge ethical principles by their
origins is itself a normative ethical rather than a scientific problem. Within this context, it may be pertinent to note that absolute ethical ideals, by definition, defy "proof" or "disproof" by
reference to origins.

---

[19]Contrast with this approach the elaborate discussion of the type of prevailing
ethics by the Bundesgerichtshof of the German Federal Republic. Decision of the
Bundesgerichtshof (Great Senate in Criminal Matters), Feb. 17, 1954, 6 BGHSt.
46 (1954), holding that the question of whether sexual intercourse between
fiancés constitutes "lewd conduct" within the meaning of §§ 180, 181, PENAL
CODE (pandering), must be determined by objective ethical norms and not by
either community standards or community mores. For criticism of this decision
see Bockelmann, *Zur Strafbarkeit der Kuppelei,* JURISTISCHE RUNDSCHAU 361-364
(1954); Jescheck, *Zur Frage der Kuppelei gegenüber Verlobten,* MONATSSCHRIFT
FÜR DEUTSCHES RECHT 645-649 (1954).

[20]Another problem which decision-makers may have to face is whether it is
proper for them, in a democratic country adhering to the principle of separation
of state and church, to apply their religious preferences to law. Such separation,
of course, does not necessarily imply adoption of utilitarian ethics.

To arrive at a "rational" system of ends, it is necessary to view the pertinent facts and factors in context with each other rather than treat each as an isolated phenomenon. When this method is applied, it will appear that in law utilization of, for example, psychoanalytic knowledge presents a distinctive problem not to be equated with that of its use in other fields. An example may illustrate the point. While, as suggested above, e.g., retribution[21] is not necessarily eliminated as an "end of criminal law" on the sole ground that—as has been shown by psycho-analytic writers[22]—it is psychologically rooted in vengeance, awareness of such motivation may be most pertinent to its choice as an "end." Psychoanalytic insight into such motivation constitutes an important contribution to law. But in legal context the inquiry must be extended to other pertinent factors. For instance, one might inquire to what extent a defendant who is the victim of judicial "vengeance" disguised as "retribution" may obtain legal relief. The law possesses various tools of control aimed at prevention of mob justice and judicial error. Appellate judges who may never face the accused perhaps do not identify themselves with him to the same degree as a trial judge. It may be worth exploring whether the psychological relationship of appellate judges to the trial judge may not have a stronger impact on their decision than their relationship to the accused. It is important to remember that, historically, the trial judge was the "accused" on appeal, for judicial review grew out of a "trial" of trial judges. Legal "justice" cannot be fully equated with individual or family justice.

The choice of both ends and means in a democratic society must always remain subject to limitations imposed by the de-

---

[21]Modern "retribution," though rooted in "vengeance," cannot be simply identified with vengeance. Its meaning and function in modern law is discussed in SILVING, CONSTITUENT ELEMENTS OF CRIME, op. cit., supra, note 1, at 9-15; "Rule of Law" in Criminal Justice, in Mueller, ed., ESSAYS IN CRIMINAL SCIENCE 75, at 84-89 (1961).

[22]On this, see Reik, Geständniszwang und Strafbedürfnis, in PROBLEME DER PSYCHOANALYSE UND DER KRIMINOLOGIE 146 (1925); ALEXANDER & STAUB, THE CRIMINAL, THE JUDGE AND THE PUBLIC 218 (rev. ed. 1956); REIWALD, SOCIETY AND ITS CRIMINALS 202 (James transl. 1950).

mands for preservation of fundamental political and ethical principles. In evaluating an "end of criminal law," it is thus essential to visualize the effect of its realization upon individual liberties. For instance, while one might not dispute the desirability of a policy of reformation and treatment, advocated by many psychiatrists, account should be taken, in drafting new laws, of the political effects of an extreme treatment-oriented policy. A by-product of such policy has been extension of the notion of the state as *parens patriae* into the criminal law for adults. Psychiatrists often equate the state with a "parent" — a just, unjust, loving or hating parent.[23] Of course, such equation presumably purports to describe particular reactions of neurotic offenders to the state. No objection can be raised against the equation so long as it is confined to such description of neurotic reactions. But it is dangerous to extend it further by creating a general, presumably ideal, image of the state as a "good parent" or of a judge as a "just father." When carried over into political or legal ideology, the equation tends to support a distorted, "paternalistic," totalitarian ideal of state in the minds of men. Mature, freedom-loving men neither deify nor personify the state. They look upon it critically as a utilitarian device, an instrument serving accomplishment of certain limited and well-defined community ends. But it may be difficult to maintain this democratic impersonal concept of state when an altogether different anthropomorphic picture of state is used in "treatment" context. Though the psychiatrists' demand for treatment of offenders is meritorious, policy-makers must never lose sight of the fact that treatment imposed upon lawbreakers under state authority cannot be equated with a medical task, as generally conceived.

As we reach the problem of appropriate means toward the chosen goals, the potential contribution of psychological and

---

[23]See, e.g., Watson, *A Critique of the Legal Approach to Crime and Correction*, 23 LAW AND CONTEMPORARY PROBLEMS 611, 627 (1958). See also Guttmacher, *The Psychiatric Approach to Crime and Correction*, 23 LAW AND CONTEMPORARY PROBLEMS 633, 647 (1958), opposing preemption of the judicial function by psychiatrists on the ground that the judge as a "father figure" is "worthy of preservation by society."

psychiatric knowledge to law gains ground. But in this area there is greater disagreement among psychiatrists than in the area of goal determination. Some psychiatrists would like to see punishment entirely abolished and offenders classified by psychiatrists, not by judges, into two groups—those who should be treated and those who should be confined indefinitely.[24] Others would admit application of punishment to special groups of offenders for reformative or deterrent purposes.[25] The wisdom of granting psychiatrists a broad discretion in exercising judgment as regards confinement of a nonpsychotic offender for the remainder of his life, regardless of the crime for which he has been convicted, has been questioned.[26] But our law itself is making increasing concessions to the spokesmen of the law's "sister sciences" for a greater measure of control over disposition and treatment of offenders. Within the scope of the relatively indeterminate sentence device, there is appearing upon the legal scene the board of experts, replacing the court as sentencing authority and endowed with discretion in manipulating treatment methods and with power of extending at any time (within the maximum set by law) the term of sentence.[27] The new trend raises considerable doubts in the minds of those who believe that man's freedom—not completely forfeited by conviction—is better safeguarded where the sentencing power is more narrowly limited by law and wielded by independent judges who are used to thinking in terms of legal categories of jurisdiction, limitation of power and due process, than where such power is broadly defined and exercised by an administra-

---

[24]See, e.g., MENNINGER, THE HUMAN MIND 448-449 (3d ed. 1945); ZILBOORG, THE PSYCHOLOGY OF THE CRIMINAL ACT AND PUNISHMENT (1954).

[25]Waelder, *Psychiatry and the Problem of Criminal Responsibility*, 101 UNIVERSITY OF PENNSYLVANIA LAW REVIEW 378 (1952); ALEXANDER & STAUB, *op. cit. supra* note 22, at 210-211.

[26]See Wertham, *Book Review* (of ZILBOORG, *op. cit. supra* note 24), 22 UNIVERSITY OF CHICAGO LAW REVIEW 569 (1955); also *Psychoauthoritarianism and the Law, id.* at 336 (1955). Compare also a sociologist's critique, Hakeem, *A Critique of the Psychiatric Approach to Crime and Correction*, 23 LAW AND CONTEMPORARY PROBLEMS 650 (1958).

[27]See particularly the California Adult Authority, §§ 5075-5094, California Penal Code, West's Annotated California Codes (1956), as amended.

tive body composed of men who by training and profession are oriented to welfare rather than to social freedom. The sex psychopath laws, which deliver into the hands of experts for an indefinite time even minor sex offenders often not convicted of any crime, seem to frighten the experts themselves.

Bearing in mind a notion of "responsibility" thus circumscribed, we must now concern ourselves with the place of "guilt" within this notion.

"GUILT"

According to widely prevailing opinion, "guilt" is an independent notion, having a reality of its own, antecedent to "responsibility." One is "responsible" because he is "guilty." However, in Kelsenian jurisprudence, this relationship is reversed. One is guilty because he has been declared answerable or responsible. In fact, in the light of Kelsen's view of guilt, it is legitimate to say that "guilt" *is* personal answerability. Thus "guilt" is defined by its status within the notion of responsibility. Nor is "guilt" always required by law to constitute responsibility. But whenever it is so required, it functions as a particular type of condition of responsibility, namely, as a condition of imputation of an act or of answerability for an act to a given person. The definition of "guilt" as conditions of imputation to a person or as outright answerability affords a formal minimum concept of "guilt" which is common to all historical concepts of guilt.[28] Our present task is to find the general principle of variation in substantive notions of personal answerability. The object of our search is to determine wherein the several concepts of "guilt" vary from each other. The resulting definition of guilt will be a substantive one, in the sense of indicating the nature of the substantive discrepancies between these concepts.

Upon closer scrutiny, the same methodological process may be applied to "responsibility." However, this has not been done here because "guilt" affords a more convenient object of analysis,

---

[28]Community beliefs that there is a common denominator in the various concepts of guilt also afford the unity of this concept of varying connotations.

and, once the method becomes clear, it can be applied with relative ease to other notions.

A critique of historical and contemporary notions of "guilt" will serve as a background for introduction of what I believe to be a "correct substantive notion of 'guilt' in a free society."

Tracing the origins of the "guilt" concept would require engagement in anthropological studies, exceeding the scope of this volume. Psychological roots of the recently much discussed, often irrational, "sense of guilt" have been treated elaborately by psychological writers. Our present inquiry is not psychological. Our concern is rather with the historical idea of guilt that is directly reflected in certain modern legal guilt doctrines. I shall not go back further than to the Bible, which, via the Roman-canon law, has decisively influenced both the common and the civil law. Nor can I engage in an elaborate study of the biblical concept of guilt. I shall confine myself to a very brief reference to salient features of that concept.

Biblical guilt is predicated upon the presence of psychological factors, which seem to be intricately diversified. The minimum requirement of guilt is knowledge of wrongdoing,[29] and malice, evidenced by such acts as lying in wait or by previous hatred of the victim, is a mark of an especially blameworthy attitude, evoking particular Divine reprehension.

These features of the biblical concept of guilt have been introduced into law, giving rise to a psychological concept of guilt, on the one hand, and to a normative one, on the other hand. We thus encounter in modern law the "psychological doctrine of guilt," incorporating the biblical concept of guilt as a comprehensive psychological phenomenon (including consciousness of wrongdoing), and the "normative doctrine of guilt," incorporating the evaluational ingredients of the biblical concept. The former identifies guilt with intent or negligence; the latter defines it as blameworthiness. Neither of these doctrines affords a satisfactory formulation of "guilt" as that concept is commonly understood or as it actually operates in law.

---

[29]See Ryu and Silving, *Error Juris: A Comparative Study*, 24 UNIVERSITY OF CHICAGO LAW REVIEW 421, at 424-430 (1957), for discussion of the biblical, Talmudic, Roman and canon law exemption from responsibility for acts committed in error of the applicable law.

The "psychological doctrine's" equation of guilt with intent is questionable, if by intent we understand a descriptive category, namely, a state of mind of the actor. Certainly, in social usage the concept of guilt implies some element or qualification other than, or in addition to, intent. It has a normative connotation, invoking the idea that that of which one is said to be guilty is bad. In fact, traditional law refers to intent as malice, wicked will or vicious will or evil intent. These epithets suggest a censure of the intent. It is not sufficient if the actor possesses an "intent," it must be also bad or blameworthy to possess such intent. The combination of factual and normative elements is even more pronounced in the second type of "guilt" of conventional law, "negligence." The latter is often defined as a "disregard of care." In the case of inadvertent negligence, "disregard" seems to convey the notion of a total absence of any psychological element, unless psychoanalytical interpretations are admitted. But in conventional law there has been no conscious, systematic recognition of the unconscious. The "psychological theory of guilt," as conventionally formulated, is not a theory of guilt in a proper sense, but at best the expression of a particular rule derived from such theory. That rule provides that conduct must not be attributed to a person unless he intended it or its results or was negligent with regard to such results. This rule is one of limitation of responsibility, based upon a particular philosophy of criminal justice. It is a legitimate rule, but cannot be said to exhaust all the demands of the philosophy from which it is derived. Other normative implications must hence be considered. We are thus referred to the second doctrine of guilt, the "normative" one.

The development of the last mentioned doctrine in Germany may be traced to Reinhard Frank, who pointed out that though two acts may be committed with equal intent and be directed to the same legal interest, there might be a need for a differentiation in the degree of guilt involved in them, because one is committed under circumstances of greater freedom than the other.[30] If, then, variation is called for though the "intent" is

---

[30]Frank, *Ueber den Aufbau des Schuldbegriffs, in* FESTGABE, FÜR DIE JURISTISCHE FAKULTÄT DER UNIVERSITÄT GIESSEN (1907).

constant, it appears that "guilt" should not be deemed identical with "intent." The differentiation in the degree of guilt, according to Frank, is based on the fact that a criminal act committed while the actor enjoys greater freedom or is under less pressure is more blameworthy than one committed while the actor possesses lesser freedom. This Frankian interpretation gave the clue for elaboration of the concept of "blameworthiness" as an ingredient of guilt and for diversification of guilt depending on the degree of blameworthiness.[31]

Dohna finally introduced some methodological order into the confusion of normative and psychological factors in "guilt" by distinguishing between evaluation in terms of blameworthiness and the object of valuation, the conduct and intent to which the judgment of blame attaches,[32] a methodogical order it took a surprisingly long time to reach in the country of Kant. Dohna pointed out that "guilt" is a judgment of value which is passed upon "intent" as an "object" of evaluation. Finally, Welzel completely separated the element of blameworthiness from the object of blame, the external conduct and the intent, alleging that the intent that steers the conduct is inseparable from that conduct itself and that only jointly do these factors afford a *Tatbestand* (conduct as described by statute), so that there remains as "guilt" factor solely the element of "blameworthiness."[33] The resulting definition of "guilt" is simply "blameworthiness." Nor is this definition of the so-called "normative doctrine" a mere jurisprudential nicety. It is rather taken as a basis for advancement of significant legal rules. Prominent among these rules is that on the treatment of legal error. Whereas the "psychological doctrine," assuming knowledge of law to be an essential of "intent," excludes punishment for intentional crime of a person engaged in legal error, the "normative doctrine," contending that such error does not affect "intent," admits such punishment, advocating its reduction

---

[31]The normative approach was developed by other writers: BELING, UNSCHULD, SCHULD UND SCHULDSTUFEN (1910); GOLDSCHMIDT, DER NOTSTAND, EIN SCHULD-PROBLEM (1913); FREUDENTHAL, SCHULD UND VORWURF (1922).

[32]DOHNA, DER AUFBAU DER VERBRECHENSLEHRE 32 (2d ed. 1941).

[33]WELZEL, DAS DEUTSCHE STRAFRECHT 120-123 (7th ed. 1960).

depending on the degree of negligence in not securing the required legal knowledge and immunity only in the absence of negligence.

Welzel's argument is methodologically dubious. The fact that act and intent are inseparable in the reality of life does not import inadmissibility of their conceptual separation.[34] Equally dubious is Welzel's inference from the elimination of intent from guilt and its assignment to the *Tatbestand* that knowledge of law is not part of intent but pertains to illegality—an inference from which Welzel in turn derives the stated legal rules on error of law, as though these rules followed from that inference as a matter of logical necessity.[35] But, however dubious may be the method of Welzel's argumentation,[36] his arguments and conclusions have been adopted by German courts. The Great Senate in Criminal Matters of the German Bundesgerichtshof incorporated into the German law Welzel's definition of guilt: "Guilt is blameworthiness"—"*Schuld ist Vorwerfbarkeit.*"[37] From this proposition it in turn derived a rule on the treatment of error of law, as set forth by Welzel. The rule thus adopted by the Bundesgerichtshof is valid German law, even though the argument whereby it was reached was fallacious. To the extent that the definition of "guilt" as "blameworthiness" is thus translated by German courts into a specific functional rule on legal error, that definition is itself functional. Phenomenologically, that definition *means* that specific rule.

However, should the issue arise, what other legal rules may be derived from this concept of "guilt," a new methodological problem will be posed: can a direct analogy be drawn from the rule on legal error, on the basis of a similarity in the light of

[34]Welzel's argument is comparable to an allegation that since a color never exists in reality apart from an object bearing it, it cannot be conceptually separated from objects. Actually it would be impossible to express the observation that an object bears a certain color unless, conceptually, object and color were separable.

[35]Ryu and Silving, *Toward a Rational System of Criminal Law,* 32 REVISTA JURÍDICA DE LA UNIVERSIDAD DE PUERTO RICO 119 (1963).

[36]For further criticism of this method, characteristic of civil law doctrine, *id.*
[37]2 BGHSt. 194 (1952).

legal policy between the facts underlying that rule and the facts present in the new situation to be disposed of? Or should courts rather again proceed from the philosophical definition of "guilt as blameworthiness" as a starting point? The first mentioned method is mostly applied in courts of common law countries. Civil law countries rather apply the second mentioned method. Should German courts again be faced with the problem of the inferences to be drawn from the professed definition of "guilt" in terms of legal rules, it would seem desirable that they reach a more definite notion of what is "blameworthiness." What, according to the Bundesgerichtshof, is "blameworthiness"? On this may depend the choice of a legal "insanity" test.

As understood by Welzel and following him by the Bundesgerichtshof, blameworthiness lies in man's choice to conduct himself contrary to law when he could have conducted himself in accordance with law.[38] The system of ethics whereby man's failure to conform is judged is an "ethics of responsibility" rather than an "ethics of attitude." This implies that man is bound not only to conduct himself ethically, in accordance with his under-standing of ethics, but also to search for a correct decision. In other words, man must not only choose the "right" instead of the "wrong." He must also choose between what is "right" and what is "wrong." He must "search" for justice and not merely abide by it. "Guilt" or "blameworthiness" thus consists not only in doing wrong but also in choosing wrongly.

Welzel contends that this notion of blameworthiness founded upon freedom of choice is rooted in modern "scientific" insight. He points out[39] that the determinism of Lombroso, Garofalo and Ferri was to a large extent based on their belief in Darwin's conception of man as the most perfect product of evolution from biologically inferior animals. Since man appeared to these scholars as a specimen biologically better adapted than other creatures, his achievements were believed to be simply referable to the fact that he presents a higher stage in the natural phe-

---

[38]*Id.* at 200-201; for pertinent passages of the decision see Ryu and Silving, *supra* note 29, at 451; see also *id.* at 449, for discussion of the philosophical basis of Welzel's notion of guilt.

[39]WELZEL, *op. cit. supra* note 33, at 125-131.

nomenon of development. But recent research conducted by zoologists and animal psychologists has demonstrated that, far from being biologically better adapted than animals, man shows a regression in adaptation instincts, as a result of which he is more exposed to danger than they are.[40]

According to these researchers, man compensates for this shortcoming by intellectual achievements. Indeed, this shortcoming is the source of such achievements. Welzel interprets this capacity of man to overcome inherent defects by intellectual resources as his "existential freedom and liberation from organic ties," in the sense of Scheler's philosophy. Since he is oriented to the criteria of truth, meaning and value and can free himself of causal determinism, man is a "responsible" being. Crime— says Welzel[41]—is the product of causation; it is thus a proper subject of "criminology." But man can liberate himself of causal necessity by an act of will, and this is what makes him the subject of "criminal law," a "responsible" person. He is "guilty" when acting contrary to law, because he could have acted in accordance with law. This is the source of his blameworthiness.

While the source of man's blameworthiness is his free choice of crime, the justification of the state's right to punish, according to Welzel's view, lies in "assertion of the statal legal order."[42] Thus, apparently, punishment is linked to guilt in an orderly system of natural law rationality.

Welzel's philosophical foundation of blameworthiness and guilt obviously combines Kantian and Hegelian ideas. The notion of "free will" set up in opposition to "causation" is typically Kantian. This notion is not substantially advanced by the alleged scientific refutation of Darwinian findings, since disproving causation does not *ipso facto* import free will. Nor does the phenomenon of man's "overcoming causation" disprove causation. In any event, freedom of will is not a foundation of responsibility but at best a condition of the latter. From the fact that a man could act otherwise than he acted it does not

---

[40]Welzel cites particularly Storch and Lorenz.

[41]*Id.* at 131.

[42]*Id.* at 208-209.

follow that he may be punished if he acts as he does. The Hegelian view of punishment as assertion of the legal order, on the other hand, may be very well maintained without any reference to free will, except perhaps for the intervening Kantian notion that man must not be used as a mere means for statal ends. Welzel's philosophy does not actually connect the two elements of justification of punishment in statal needs and in individual "guilt."

Whatever may be the merits of referring blameworthiness to free will on a philosophical level, free will certainly cannot afford a practical test of blameworthiness, since it is not provable in a court of law. Significantly, the notion of "free determination of will" (*freie Willensbestimmung*) was eliminated from the definition of mental incapacity of the German Penal Code (§51 StGB) upon recommendation of prominent psychiatrists who asserted that they were unable to make scientifically valid assertions on such an essentially theological issue.[43]

Even if blameworthiness could be defined meaningfully as derived from freedom of choice, the problem of the source of the moral judgment implicit in a determination that a conduct or intent is blameworthy would still remain open. For surely guilt or blameworthiness does not consist exclusively in free choice. Whatever may be the nature of blameworthiness, the latter is undoubtedly conceived of as implying a moral value judgment, and perhaps the most crucial issue in defining guilt is what type of morality it is that gives it substance. Even in a single culture we may find a variety of moral standards, not to speak of the fact that there is often a discrepancy between prevailing verbal moral standards, that is, the standards which people profess to believe in, and the standards by which they actually abide. But even before the issue of conflict of moral conduct and moral judgment is reached, the question must be answered whether the proper standard is a popular cultural one or a supra-cultural and supra-individual standard of absolute ethics, or, indeed, a "constitutional" standard, whether or not of variable content.

---

[43]See on this Seelig, *Zum Problem der Neufassung des § 51,* in FESTSCHRIFT FÜR EDMUND MEZGER, 213, at 213-215 (1954).

In a much discussed decision, rejecting relativistic popular ethics as guides to moral legal judgment, the Great Senate of the German Bundesgerichtshof professed the German law's adherence to the ethics of Christianity as of the dominant religion, expressed in legal institutions such as that of monogamy.[44] It said that permitting popular standards or mores to prevail over the Christian morality of general law would be tantamount to allowing law to be overridden by factual community conduct, whereas it is the function of the law to guide such conduct. This decision was severely criticized by most German writers who claimed that disregard of popular standards of morality is itself unethical, since it results in imposition of the morality of one individual or group upon other individuals.[45] In England and in the United States the moral standards mostly prevailing in law are those of utilitarian ethics. But there are various versions of utilitarianism, so that diversity of standards is not precluded.

A most controversial issue recently debated in England concerns the proper scope of moral prohibition that may be enforced by law. One group argues that the state cannot prohibit an individual from engaging in any conduct of his choice unless that conduct is harmful to others.[46] The other group contends that the community, represented by the jury or by any group selected at random, may impose upon individuals its moral

---

[44]6 BGHSt. 46 (1954), holding sexual intercourse between fiancés to constitute "lewd conduct" (*Unzucht*) within the meaning of §§ 180, 181 of the GERMAN PENAL CODE (pandering), on the ground that by adopting the Christian conception of the institution of marriage, German law took the position that sex intercourse is admissable only in marriage, and that this position of absolute Christian ethics must prevail over community views or community mores.

[45]Bockelman, *Zur Strafbarkeit der Kuppelei,* JURISTISCHE RUNDSCHAU, 1954, pp. 361-364, at 363, states: ". . . [T]he moral norm which the individual recognizes as valid can be absolutely obligatory only as a standard and guide of his own conduct. However, it must not be simply taken as basis for the evaluation of acts of others. Whoever undertakes to do that raises his personal morality to the status of an objective legal norm. In the course of time the danger would arise of his becoming a witches' judge."

[46]See REPORT OF THE COMMITTEE ON HOMOSEXUAL OFFENSES AND PROSTITUTION, Cmnd. 247, H. M. Stationary Office 1957 (THE WOLFENDEN REPORT).

standards and enforce by law their obedience.[47] In the United
States a vigorous controversy has been waged as to whether
judges in rendering moral judgments should rely on their
own moral predilections or "hunches" or rather apply community views or community mores.[48] Some writers, indeed,
contend that enlightened decision-makers should assert their
own "overriding goals" in preference even to the "formal code."[49]
Jurisdiction to determine insanity exempting from guilt has
been debated widely both in England and in the United States,
some stressing the virtue of a lay jury's instinctual evaluation,
others advocating reliance on psychiatric expert opinion or
indeed delegation of decisive authority to psychiatrists.[50]

While thus the issues (of why certain psychological states
should be deemed to constitute guilt or what is blameworthiness
defining guilt) are widely open, scholars argue each his preferred notion of guilt as if it were a provable scientific proposition. Indeed, that which is common to the psychological and
the normative doctrines of guilt is their metaphysical orientation.
Adherents of both doctrines assume that "guilt" is inherent in a
given factor, either the mental attitude of the accused, according
to the "psychological doctrine," or the blameworthiness of his
conduct, according to the "normative doctrine." Each doctrine
assumes that "guilt" by its very nature emanates from the

---

[47]See particularly DEVLIN (Lord Justice Devlin), THE ENFORCEMENT OF
MORALS (Maccabean Lecture in Jurisprudence of the British Academy, Oxford
University Press, 1959); also Law, Democracy and Morality, 110 UNIVERSITY
OF PENNSYLVANIA LAW REVIEW 635 (1962).

[48]CAHN, who, in his SENSE OF INJUSTICE (1949), asserted that there is a
minimum sense of "justice," in the form of reaction to "injustice," in the heart
of every man everywhere at all times, has elsewhere expressed his choice of a
standard of adjudication to be the judge's own moral view and not the so-
called "community views" or "community mores." See Cahn, Authority and
Responsibility, in FREEDOM AND AUTHORITY IN OUR TIMES (Harpers 1953).

[49]Lasswell and Donnelly, The Continuing Debate Over Responsibility: An
Introduction to Isolating the Condemnation Sanction, 68 YALE LAW JOURNAL
869 (1959). The principal argument of this paper, that of isolating the con-
demnation sanction, has been known in Europe at least since 1893, when
Carl Stoos's PROJECT OF A SWISS PENAL CODE was published. See Exposé des
Motifs de l'Avant Project de 1893 (Basel-Geneva, 1893).

[50]For some aspects of this issue see Silving, Mental Incapacity in Criminal
Law, Infra, at 63-71, 89-92, 115-116, 131-133.

respective factor. This metaphysical, "natural law" view of guilt explains the violence of the controversy over the definition of guilt. Scholars of the various schools of thought act as if they were engaged in a theological dispute over Satan's qualities rather than in an argument over a legal issue. Thus, in the famous dispute over the defense of error of law waged by Mezger and Welzel the issue has been formulated in terms of what "guilt" is.[51] Mezger claimed that it *is* the psychological factor of intent, whereas Welzel contends that it *is* blameworthiness. From such metaphysical position scholars in turn derive a notion of the absolute logical necessity of certain legal rules. Each of them claims that the rule of his preference is or must be valid, since it is implicit in the only "true" conception of guilt—the conception he advances.

This approach is misleading. In law, in contrast to theology, there is no "true" conception of "guilt," though there may be a "valid" one, in the sense of conveying a legislatively assumed notion of guilt that is translated or translatable into enforceable rules of law. A "valid" concept of "guilt" is not necessarily a "correct" one, in the sense outlined above. Indeed, at the point of being introduced into law, a later "valid" concept of "guilt" may be descriptively senseless. If the arguments advanced by scholars merely purported to interpret the German Penal Code, these arguments would be methodologically proper to the extent that they actually attempted to convey the meaning of existing law. But these arguments are couched in ambiguous language, so that it appears as though they were reflecting eternal truths about the inherent nature of "guilt." This impression is strengthened when we read the assertion, which ultimately prevailed in the Draft of a German Penal Code of 1962, that a definition of guilt need not be included in the Penal Code, since this is a matter to be defined by "legal science."[52] Whence is "science" to derive the definition of guilt? As shown in a

---

[51]On this see Ryu and Silving, *supra* note 35, at 448-452.

[52]"Guilt," said Welzel, *op. cit. supra* note 33, at 53, "being a self-evident element of crime, is not especially mentioned in criminal law provisions." The Draft of a German Penal Code in its first reading (1958), nevertheless, contained the following provision: "Whoever acts without guilt shall not be

paper by Dr. Paul K. Ryu and the present writer,[53] that which civil law scholars call the "science of criminal law" is not a "science," and the method of deriving practical legal rules from the situs within the constructs of *Tatbestand*, illegality or guilt, of certain controversial substantive notions is sham; it consists in inferring from these constructs, under the guise of would-be "scientific" finding, matters which these scholars had previously put into them on the basis of a policy which has no bearing on the issues to be determined by such rules.

The weakness of such derivation of legal rules from doctrinal propositions on the "ontology of guilt," not geared to the ultimate operation of these rules in terms of their practical consequences becomes obvious as soon as we realize that in law that which is ultimately at stake is the legal rule. Only the latter is operationally and functionally expressed in law, for law is not a science but purports to be a system of guidance for conduct. Whatever may be the merits of a theoretical notion of "guilt," such notion is meaningless within the framework of law unless it is or can be translated into practical propositions, namely, rules of conduct. The rationality of law is predicated upon the rationality of the ends which legal rules purport to serve and the rationality of such rules as means to achieve these ends. Their soundness should be judged in the light of value considerations and teleology and not by quasi-theological

---

punished. Punishment must not exceed the measure of guilt." This provision was struck from the 1960 Draft. The elimination has been elaborately justified in the comments to the Draft. See ENTWURF EINES STRAFGESETZBUCHES (StGB) E 1960 MIT BEGRÜNDUNG, Bundesrat Drucksache 270/60 (Bonn, 1960), at p. 92. The draftsmen point out that "(t)here is no need for an express statement in the code of the provision contained in the first sentence. This provision evinces from numerous sections of the Draft. . . ." They further point to "the notion of guilt" being "alive among the people." Since the Draft uses the term "guilt" on various occasions in contexts in which its meaning is by no means clear (e.g., § 60: "The basis for the measure of punishment is the guilt of the actor"), it would seem that the rule of law requires its being defined. For the view that "guilt" must be defined by legal science rather than by legislation, see Welzel, *Wie würde sich die finale Handlungslehre auf das neue Strafgesetzbuch auswirken?* in MATERIALIEN ZUR STRAFRECHTSREFORM, Band 1, Gutachten der Strafrechtslehrer (1954).

[53]Ryu and Silving, *Toward a Rational System of Criminal Law, supra* note 36.

arguments regarding the "nature" of legal concepts. Value considerations may, of course, be based on ontological conceptions of "guilt." But if the legal ontology of "guilt" is to be itself rational, such conceptions ought not to be derived from purely formal constructs adopted for a definite purpose (as is the division of crime into *Tatbestand,* illegality and guilt) and which the legislator never visualized as potential determinants of "guilt" for any other purpose. Moreover, in considering adoption of a theoretical notion of guilt in law, decision-makers should take into account that notion's probable practical operation in the light of social purpose, for no theoretical notion is ever simply translatable into practical rules. The latter always imply either more or less than is conveyed by the theoretical notion. In a sense, rules of law have a meaning of their own that is independent of their theoretical basis, for their practical import can never strictly correspond to the theoretical propositions that support them. Unless the particular "guilt" concept advocated by a scholar is alleged to be that adopted by a positive law in issue, the method of inferring from the situs of a factor within one of the so-called crime constituents a particular legal rule, e.g., a given rule of legal error, in large measure leads to making legal decisions on the basis of sham issues. Whether or not a person who engages in criminal conduct in negligent error of law ought to be punishable for intentional crime should depend on the purpose of punishing such crime and the reasons for a grant of immunity in the light of the scope of applicability of such purpose, rather than on the question of whether or not knowledge of law *is* doctrinally part of intent or part of blameworthiness. Unless it can honestly be said that the German legislators included knowledge of law in the definition of intent as obtaining in positive German law or excluded such knowledge from intent, the issue of such inclusion or exclusion cannot be resolved "scientifically." Whether or not "intent" at law must also comprise knowledge of law, is not a question of "scientific finding" but one of legal determination. If an answer cannot be reached by use of other appropriate means of legal interpretation, then the principle of strict construction of criminal statutes requires the judiciary to decide in a sense most favorable to accused persons. Of course, one might argue that the so-called "science of criminal law," however dubious *per se,* has by long usage been incorporated into the civil law system of statutory interpretation. In any event, *de lege ferenda* an issue such as that of inclusion in, or exclusion from, "intent" of legal knowledge is ultimately one of policy choice, though policy may be influenced by considerations based on the policy-maker's ontological conception of "guilt." But it is essential that decision-makers be clearly aware of the ultimate operational meaning of their choice.

Legal concepts are tools making communication of legal rules possible. Viewed phenomenologically, they are but symbols of legal rules that are or may be conveyed by their means. In the last analysis for legal purposes they *are* these rules. This is also true of the concept of "guilt" as used in law. In this sense, any other interpretation of "guilt" as an ultimately legal concept is "incorrect," in that it reflects a fallacious view of legal operations. "Guilt" is a shorthand expression standing for those legal rules that relate to imputation of answerability to a person. According to the phenomenological theory of guilt, advanced by Felix Kaufmann[54] and developed on the basis of the Kelsenian formal notion of "guilt" as the result rather than the source of imputation, the content of "guilt" is the sum of certain *postulates* addressed to law, such as, that it ought to be so formulated as to make it possible to distinguish clearly guilt from nonguilt, that it should permit gradation, that it should be possible to differentiate within it intent and negligence as types of guilt, that it should allow for exemption for mental incapacity.

This phenomenological theory of guilt is heuristic in drawing attention to the ultimate issue that is posed in law whenever the "nature of guilt" is debated. Doctrinal notions of guilt are admittedly translated into the legal rules, whether in force or postulated, which these notions represent. This theory helps us realize that in law a descriptive proposition—notice that a statement formulated in terms of what guilt *is* purports

---

[54]KAUFMANN, DIE PHILOSOPHISCHEN GRUNDPROBLEME DER LEHRE VON DER STRAFRECHTSSCHULD (1929).

to be a descriptive proposition—is meaningful only to the extent that it conveys a legal rule, for the ultimate issue in law is not truth or falsehood but choice of values.

This should not be taken to mean that descriptive scientific propositions are not pertinent in law. The sciences, particularly the so-called "sciences of man," afford important items of consideration in formulating legal policies and in shaping rules functionally adapted to realization of such policies. But the so-called "science of criminal law" engaged in by civil law scholars under the name of "*Strafrechtswissenschaft*" or "*Strafrechtsdogmatik*" is not such rationally pertinent "science." Nor must any science ever be conceived of as a direct constituent of law; science as well as ethics can be part of law only in the form of their operational impact. The same is true of metaphysical doctrines to be encountered in law.

In formulating his phenomenological theory of guilt, Kaufmann made certain specific ethical and political assumptions. He thus assumed utilitarianism to be the proper philosophy of law, and the postulates of liberal democracy as prevailing in Austria at the time when he wrote to be generally valid postulates.[55] But, as is known, "guilt" is an ancient concept antedating the birth of utilitarian philosophy and political liberalism. Kaufmann's view of guilt hence reflects not a general concept of guilt but a specific historical one. However, his theory lends itself to enlargement into a general theory of guilt. Such enlargement requires but the realization that the postulates addressed to law which constitute "guilt" are not permanently fixed but rather vary with changing philosophies of law, its ontologies and epistemologies as well as its political philosophies. How "guilt" is to be defined in specific substantive terms depends on the type of postulates obtaining in a given legal system, postulates which, of course, may in turn be derived from ontological or ethical or political conceptions of "guilt." The definition of guilt in terms of the legal rules which "guilt" symbolizes affords, if these rules are rules of positive law, "guilt" *de lege lata*. One may, however, on par-

---

[55]*Op. cit. supra*, at 72-76.

ticular preferred policy grounds that may be derived from his general or political philosophy, formulate demands for introduction into the law of principles other than those in force, that is, for adoption of a different concept of "guilt," "guilt" *de lege ferenda*. Finally, a decision-maker or policy advocate may favor generally, or for special types of situations dispensing with any personal conditions of answerability. In such event one may speak of "crime without guilt."

The specific substantive content of the concept of guilt is always an expression of legal or policy demands, whatever the basis of their adoption. At the root of this concept there is always some political postulate, whether express or implied. There are thus various conceptions of guilt, an autocratic concept of guilt, a democratic concept of guilt, etc. There obtains between the prevailing form of government, in a broader sense of this term, and the concept of guilt a certain relationship, which may justify the assertion that there is a proper concept of guilt corresponding to a particular form of government. One might thus well say that in a theocracy or in a state in union with a church the proper concept of guilt is the theocratic one, meaning that the demands predicating imputation of "guilt" to a person are theocratic or theological and that the proper jurisprudence of guilt is ontological. Similarly, one might assert that in an autocracy consistency requires that the concept of guilt be autocratic and that in a democracy that concept ought to be democratic. However, the phenomenon of a mixed form of government may be noticed also in this field. Thus we may find in an otherwise autocratic state a democratic notion of guilt expressed in law and vice versa. A particularly frequent phenomenon is adoption of a theological concept of guilt despite prevalence of a system of separation of church and state. It should be noted that when I use the term "demands" I do not mean to suggest that particular notions of "guilt" or the rules into which such notions are translatable are always or even mostly formulated in terms of demands. I merely submit that notions of "guilt" in law always import such political demands, since in operational terms they realize them.

A most intricate problem is that of relationship between the

"law of guilt" and the "jurisprudence of guilt." The former consists of the legal rules relating to guilt, symbolized by a particular concept of guilt. The latter consists in the philosophy of guilt
adopted by scholars of a given legal system (metalegal jurisprudence) and/or by the law itself (legal jurisprudence or jurisprudence of the law). There is interdependence between these
two spheres. Thus, an ontological concept of guilt, when adopted
by legislators or judges may influence the law, as has been
shown to have been the case in Germany, where Welzel's jurisprudential doctrine of guilt was translated by the Bundesgerichtshof into particular rules on legal error. A critical, phenomenological doctrine of guilt may have a similar impact, although
that type of doctrine implies that the concept of guilt reflects
the law of guilt and not vice versa (except if reflection is taken
to indicate that the law of guilt originates in a concept of guilt).
It may also be significant to note that political philosophies
often have an impact on ontologies and may thus exercise, in
addition to their direct impact, an indirect influence upon the
law of guilt.

In summarizing it may be said that, assuming a minimum
definition of guilt common to all "guilt" notions, to be all conditions of imputation of answerability for an act or an event
to a person, the particular legal definitions of guilt vary from
each other in the contents of the political demands constituting
such conditions.

We are concerned especially with the meaning of "guilt" in
a "free society," namely, with the political demands which such
society posits as a requisite of holding a person "guilty." One
set of these demands belongs to the field conventionally classified as "criminal procedure." This is well recognized. Less recognized are the substantive law implications of the notion of "guilt"
within the indicated political framework. Two aspects of such
"guilt" ideology deserve special notice: those concerning the
psychological conditions of imputation and those relating to the
choice of standards from which the notion of guilt may be derived. Both have a bearing on the issue of "mental incapacity"
in criminal law.

In a free society any type of state intervention at criminal law into the life, liberty, property or other personality interest of an individual should be predicated upon a thorough comprehension of the human personality, of the operation of man's mind, the motivations that prompt his actions, his prospective reaction to projected interventions and their impact upon his future mental and social development. Such comprehension, of course, should be based upon insights of modern psychology and sociology, not upon obsolete scientific assumptions. A realistic psychology as the basis of imputation of guilt is of the essence of justice to the individual, for only such psychology can help decision-makers to realize why a man acted as he did and what punishment or other sanctions mean to him. Science in this sense is an indispensable tool of democratic law; law not based upon valid science is but a ritual.

Today, a proper evaluation of human action must proceed from an understanding of both the conscious motivations and intentions and the unconscious motivations that determine every expression of personality. To be sure, in democratic law "guilt" should not be imputed to a man on the basis of his unconscious attitudes.[56] Guilt gradations of limited scope, depending on degrees of objective probability of harm causation by the conduct charged, reflecting such attitudes, may be tolerated. But, wherever possible, unconscious factors bearing on evaluation of conscious action (e.g., unconscious inhibitions preventing consummation in cases of attempt) may and should be taken to limit or even to exclude imputation for punitive purposes; when there is a serious need for community protection, non-punitive intervention predicated not upon "guilt" but upon "danger" is warranted.

In regard to the choice of moral standards of determining guilt and the proper scope of legally enforceable morality, it is fashionable to point to the relativity and unverifiability of moral judgment. However, democracy, as a particular political, and hence moral, philosophy, makes such choice and thus disposes of

---

[56]"[F]or the practical need of adjudging man's character, the action and the attitude consciously expressed in it are mostly sufficient." FREUD, TRAUMDEUTUNG —UEBER DEN TRAUM, in GESAMMELTE WERKE (Imago Publishing Company, 1940), at 626.

the allegedly insoluble issues, such as those raised by the controversy between the German Bundesgerichtshof and its critics[57] or
by the debate between Lord Justice Devlin and the majority
members of the Wolfenden Committee.[58]

There is neither need nor occasion within the context of
formulating a system of ends of criminal law or a concept of
"guilt" — determined by such ends — for starting with first
principles. A penal code is but a part, though a distinctive one,
of a comprehensive order of life afforded by the total complex
of accepted standards and laws, including constitutions, of a
given country. In countries governed by constitutions, the aims of
all law are fixed by constitutional law. True, constitutional law
mostly consists of (a) rules of delegation of authority of "lawmaking" and of (b) rules of limitation of such authority. But
although these rules do not specifically determine the substantive
rules of penal law, they fix the scope of the criminal law ends
which legislators may adopt. Criminal law is distinct from
other branches of law in that it operates by means that are
highly deprivational. The normal sanction of criminal law is
liberty deprivation combined with a "defamation," the criminal
record. It follows from the principle of individual freedom,
which is implied in the very existence of a "constitution," that,
whatever ends may be pursued by legal branches other than
criminal, only very strictly limited ends may be pursued by
criminal law. To justify enforcement of an interest by the
methods of criminal law, it must be positively shown (a) that
such interest represents a basic need of society and not but a
proper social goal or the community's wish to impose its moral
views or mores on non-conformists; (b) that the respective
provisions can be effectively enforced by criminal law means,
so that they be neither a dead letter nor a pretext for enforcement of a policy extraneous to the avowed one; and (c) that the
policy pursued cannot be reached by means other than those
of the criminal law.

What, within such concept of the "ends of criminal law," is

---

[57]See text at notes 44 and 45.

[58]See text at notes 46 and 47.

"guilt"—"guilt" in the sense of the personal basis for application of punitive sanctions? It is "blameworthiness," of course. But it is not reprehensibleness in any broadly moral sense but rather a judgment of disapproval of nonconformance in a social-political, narrowly legal, sense. A person who breaches the law in a democratic society is "antisocial," not necessarily "immoral." To use biblical language, he breaches the "covenant," or to use Rousseau's variation upon the same theme, he breaches the "social contract." In this sense, he is "guilty," and in this sense only does political society have any right at all to punish him. Such society is not in any other sense a custodian of his morality.

In such political conception of "guilt in a free society" there are implicit significant demands in regard to the formulation of a comprehensive law of mental incapacity. In this sense, the exemption for incapacity is constitutionally imposed. Furthermore, the type of mental incapacity test which a law imposes is not constitutionally irrelevant. Nor are the procedures of establishing such exempting incapacity or the consequences of establishing it constitutionally indifferent.

Whether the problem of constitutionality will arise where the defendant has, against his will, been held "sane" and punished or "insane" and subjected to security measures, should his fate be permitted to depend on an intangible and misleading guide as is afforded, for example, in Durham?[59] The Durham "product" formula is clearly "misleading" and not only vague. Is it constitutionally proper to continue using it? An answer to be expected in our law is that whatever constitutional rights a defendant might have to a "proper test of insanity," he waives them when he pleads "insanity." But can he constitutionally waive application of a "meaningful" rather than a "meaningless" test?

Our courts have barely begun to inquire into the constitutionality of substantive criminal law notions. But the beginning that has been made[60] permits prediction of further developments. Will

---

[59] 94 U. S. App. D. C. 228, 214 F.2d 862, 45 A. L. R.2d 1430 (1954), holding that a defendant is not punishable if his criminal conduct was the "product of mental disease."

[60] Robinson v. California, 370 U. S. 660 (1962); Griswold v. Connecticut, 381 U.S. 479 (1965).

Leland v. *Oregon*[61] stand the acid test of constitutional reexamination? One may doubt this, especially in light of the powerful dissent.[62] Will *Durham* stand constitutional challenge on the ground that, admittedly, it does not mean what it says.[63]

Constitutional light will have to be shed also on the problem of interdisciplinary communication in the area of "mental incapacity," including addiction and inebriety accompanying criminal conduct. There is an imperative need for taking into account the fact that psychology, psychiatry, sociology, cultural anthropology, etc., use operational concepts oriented to the needs of the pertinent sciences and that such concepts may or may not be pertinent to the object of our search. "A rose is a rose is a rose" is a valid statement provided that the term "rose" is used each time in the same or in a specifically interrelated sense. Perhaps also psychiatrists might well say that "a schizophrenia is a schizophrenia" and this, indeed, might convey a functional meaning—namely, that there are implicit in a diagnosis of schizophrenia some "longitudinal" impressions which psychiatry has not yet verbalized, but which are communicable among psychiatrists, assuming them to have been exposed to presumably "similar" impressions. But should a psychiatrist testifying in court, assert as sole theoretical basis of his diagnosis, that he recognizes a schizophrenia when he sees it, a judgment relying on such diagnosis might be challenged as denying the accused due process.

In a legal system based on principles of due process the exemption for "mental incapacity" ("insanity") must be defined by law, preferably by statutory law; it must be geared to a defined concept of "guilt" within a clear concept of "responsibility." However, defining these concepts is not in ultimate analysis a pure process of "discovery"; it also requires "invention" of the best ways of coping with psychological, social and legal

---

[61]343 U. S. 790 (1952), upholding Oregon's requirement that the defendant prove insanity beyond a reasonable doubt.

[62]*Supra*, 802.

[63]See Carter v. United States, 252 F.2d 608 (D. C. Cir., 1957); cf. also McDonald v. United States, 114 U. S. App. D. C. 120, 312 F.2d 847, 851 (1962).

realities. Why does due process require that the exemption for "mental incapacity" be maintained and that this exemption be defined by law?

Several writers since Garofalo until the present have suggested jettisoning the notion of "insanity" and introducing a system of "scientific" adjusting of sanctions to the personality of the offender. The modern protagonists of this position in this country, whether lawyers or psychiatrists, however, have mostly insisted that, to be amenable to such "scientific" evaluation and treatment, the defendant must be held to have committed a "crime," whatever that may be. Happily, abandoning the "defense of insanity" to a charge of "guilt" is barred by our constitutions.

Of course, the assumption is made on the basis of historical experience that "insanity" is a "defense" which, whenever, raised, "benefits" the defendant. Actually, since it constitutes an "exemption" from, rather than a constituent element of, "responsibility," a broad conception and construction of "insanity" would seem always to benefit the defendant; nor would he seem to have a valid basis for challenging a court's raising the "insanity" issue. However, while modern definitions of "insanity" are broader than the historical ones, introduction of new systems of restraint for those held to be "insane" poses the question of whether such broadening may still be deemed an unqualified boon for them, especially where the commitment is not subject to a maximum term.

Systematic legislative disposition of the intricate constitutional conflicts inherent in this situation is urgent. No longer can such issues be resolved on a case-to-case basis, which is necessarily inadequate and inegalitarian. We must fully reevaluate the question whether there is any basis left in our times for insisting that "insanity" remain exclusively a "defense" which only the accused can raise. Since this rule often results in convicting defendants who would have a perfectly valid "defense of insanity" if they chose to use it, are we not convicting where there is no "guilt"? Is "guilt" also waivable? What does "guilt" mean in this context?

Nor is jettisoning the exemption for "insanity" with attendant "scientific" disposition a rational solution, since it fails to explain or to justify the great human cost in conducting an investigation and a trial, subject to all rules of due process, when the ultimate disposition is reached on grounds not significantly determined by the outcome of such efforts. It would also probably lead to extension of "psychoauthoritarianism" not supported by either significant disposition of the basic "responsibility" issue or by psychiatrists' actual preparation at this time to cope with crime or with offenders.

Even should the exemption for "insanity" be defined by law, delegating the authority to decide whether in a concrete situation a defendant is or is not "insane" to a board of psychiatrists, as suggested by some writers, would be objectionable. For in a determination of "insanity" for legal purposes, there is implicit not merely a medical but also a social finding which should not be entrusted to psychiatrists alone. Nor should the unity and continuity of the state's dealing with the defendant in criminal proceedings be disrupted by such division of powers. Rather, the court should combine the medical, psychiatric, sociological and legal approach by integration of psychiatrists and sociologists alongside with jurists, as "judges" over the total antisocial event and not as compartamentally separated agents. This is also consistent with new trends in psychiatry interpreting every human act as expression of his total unitary personality rather than a phenomenon detached from the remainder of his life and being.

"DANGEROUSNESS"

In the absence of "guilt" or where, as is sometimes said, "guilt has been extinguished by punishment," there may nevertheless obtain an urgent social need for appropriate preventive and protective measures against the "dangerousness" of the "guiltless" offender. The problem of such "innocent offender" is at present in the limelight of interest, in large measure as a result of a tendency in this country to interpret "guilt" as a magical force which not only calls for certain rituals of administration but also, negatively, by its mere absence, leaves the path open for indiscriminate handling of the individual. The tacit assumption is that this is not a matter of "criminal law" administration but one of "welfare" disposition, a "paternalistic" image of the state replacing the "adversary" notion of the state dealing at arm's length with the accused and convict.

In civil law countries in which focus on "guilt" has been even more marked than in some, but by no means all, of our recent pronouncements, and in which, by contrast to stress on procedure in our law of "guilt," the emphasis has been on the substantive "guilt" notion, there has developed as a distinct concept relevant in criminal law the notion of "dangerousness."[64] Though the separation of "guilt" and "dangerousness" has not been neat even in these countries, there obtains a clear aware- ness of the need for differential treatment of these phenomena and particularly for an over-all systematic application of dis- tinctive, yet strict, "legality principles" to administration of the law on "dangerousness." While in our law there is still notice- able a groping for detached solutions of demands of "due process" for persons acquitted by reason of insanity or found insane pending execution and termination of a punitive sen- tence, in civil law countries the "measure of security and cure," as a sanction distinct from punishment and appropriate in cases of "criminal dangerousness without guilt," has developed into a well-defined, well-organized "penal law" institution governed by principles of "rule of law." Indeed, the new judicial office of the "judge of sentence execution"—*giudice di sorveglianza, juge de l'application des peines*—was primarily created for the purpose of supervising the process of execution of "security measures" and of making judicial decisions as need arises for new determinations in the course of such execution.[65]

The laws of these countries reflect the need for a systematic differentiation not only between "punishment" and "nonpunitive sanctions," but also between "nonpunitive sanctions within the context of criminal law" and "measures of prevention and pro- tection" called for outside of such context. A line of demarcation

---

[64]On this see Silving, *"Rule of Law" In Criminal Justice, supra* note 21, at 115-121, 140-142, 145-147.

[65]*Supra,* at 130-138.

is being drawn between "civil measures" which are used to cope with an individual's "dangerousness" where he has not engaged in any criminal conduct and "penal law measures" which are administered by criminal courts where a defendant has manifested his dangerousness by engaging in such conduct but without attendant "guilt."

In *Baxstrom v. Herold*[66] the United States Supreme Court held that discrimination as regards requisites and type of commitment to a mental institution between a person who terminated a penal sentence and any other person is a denial of equal protection. It rejected the argument that differentiating the "civilly insane" from the "criminally insane" was a reasonable classification where the basis of petitioner's treatment as "criminally insane" was solely his having completed a penal sentence. There was no doubt that while serving his penal sentence Baxstrom, being mentally ill, was properly assigned to a mental hospital within the jurisdiction of the Department of Correction rather than to an institution under the control of the Department of Mental Hygiene.

Had Baxstrom been acquitted solely by reason of insanity or otherwise held not subject to punitive sanctions though found to have engaged in the criminal conduct charged, it would seem that the fact of his engagement in criminal conduct should be deemed a sufficient ground for inquiry into his "criminal dangerousness." This distinguishes such a person from one who has either not engaged in criminal conduct or has terminated a penal or protective sentence.

Between "civil commitment" and "punishment" there ought to be a third category, the "measure of security and cure at penal law," subject to systematic sui generis "legality" limitations, not identical with, but comparable to, those applied to punishment rather than to due process in civil commitment cases. The fact that a person in a case at bar has engaged in a "criminal conduct," even though without "guilt," is not an incidental but a crucial point, provided of course that we purge the special part of penal codes of "crimes" that should

---

[66]383 U. S. 107 (1966).

not have been made criminal in a free society.[67]

"RULE BY LABELS" AND TERMINOLOGY

The issue is to what extent it is possible in law to eliminate "rule by labels" and introduce exclusive "rule by meaning." The complaint addressed particularly to the *Durham* "insanity test" has been that it has introduced the former type of rule.[68]

"Labels," of course, in such context is but a derogatory reference to words, and words in our times are an imprescindible tool of law. Verbalization, indeed, of both abstract rules and of grounds of decision is a demand of democracy. Even if it could be shown, for example, that psychiatrists are by virtue of the similarity of their clinical experiences so well attuned to each other that they are invariably able to reach "similar" diagnoses in "similar" cases[69] without resulting "inequality of protection," administration of justice based on such unverbalized evaluation would violate "due process." Legal decision-making in a democracy requires legitimization of any official action by reference to general abstract principles, and this is predicated upon their verbal formulation. In law the issue of "labels" reduces itself to the problem of "vagueness and uncertainty."[70] While the latter may decrease in the course of applying the "label" to concrete situations, there remains the danger of its

---

[67]When an infinite variety of socially indifferent acts and omissions is made criminal, the fact that a person has committed a "criminal act" is not necessarily an indication of his "dangerousness," except where general "law-abidingness" is socially expected. This does not seem to be the case in this country, although some laws such as those punishing prison-escapes even where the imprisonment is unlawful convey the impression that it is. But where a conduct has been legitimately made criminal, engagement in such conduct ought to give rise to an inquiry into "dangerousness."

[68]See Judge Burger's critique of the test in Blocker v. United States, 288 F.2d 853, 857 (App. D. C., 1961).

[69]The meaning of "similar" in such case would be precarious; it would require some standard of "similarity" which is precisely that which constitutes the issue.

[70]The critique addressed to rule by "labels" may also stand for censure of the ontological approach to legal or psychiatric issues. But this does not seem to be the point in Judge Burger's critique. It is one of Dr. Szasz's arguments against the "Myth of Mental Disease," which appeared simultaneously with my *Mental Incapacity in Criminal Law*, and express some similar ideas. SZASZ, THE MYTH OF MENTAL ILLNESS (1961).

being interpreted in abstract terms that are descriptively meaningless which increases the confusion rather than eliminating or reducing it. This has been the case when the *Durham* "product of mental disease" test of "insanity" was interpreted in terms of "lack of free will."[71]

The term "insanity," which is used mostly in countries of common law tradition to indicate the general mental abnormality that affords an exemption from punitive responsibility, is so laden with the impact of its varied history that it cannot be redeemed for contemporary purposes. I have suggested as its substitute the term "mental incapacity."

True, this term is not free from ambiguity. It conveys the connotation of an "incapacity to commit the act charged" or "to form the required intent," whereas by hypothesis the defendant in a case where the issue of such exemption arises not only was "capable" of committing that act but, indeed, actually committed it, and in all likelihood wanted to do so. But it has been impossible to find in the common language vocabulary an appropriate unambiguous term.

It is important to note, however, that I am using the term "mental incapacity" in the sense of a general mental inadequacy rather than an "incapacity" for specific achievement. This is in accordance with my belief that there is hardly any such thing as an "insanity" limited to the "specific act" or to "the time of the act." But this should not be taken to imply advocacy of dispensing with the requisite of direction of criminal intent to the act charged—intent as a constituent element in punitive law, the "law of guilt" (*Schuldstrafrecht*). This direction remains essential, though the so-called "union of act and intent" in the sense of a simultaneity is not required.

In any case, in exemptions which, in contrast to constituent elements, are construed broadly, there is no need for a specific relationship between the mental state—herein, the "insanity"—and the external event—the act charged. "Insanity with regard to the act charged" suggests the discarded notion of "monomania."

---

[71]Carter v. United States, 252 F.2d 608 (D.C. Cir., 1957).

In a sense, the term used in civil law countries to denote what I have chosen to call "mental incapacity" would seem at first blush to be more felicitous than the latter. "Nonimputability," *Unzurechnungsfähigkeit*," "*inimputabilidad*," suggests that the law does not "impute" or "ascribe" the act committed or penal responsibility for its commission to persons within the given class. However, this usage is also dubious, since it denotes that which is not being imputed rather than the person to whom it is not being imputed. The term leads us back to the idea, apparently also implicit in the historical conception of "mental incapacity" in countries of the civil law, that the exemption is based on a quality of the act charged or absence of the required intent rather than on the total image of the actor and his act.

MENTAL INCAPACITY IN CRIMINAL LAW*

NOT TOO long ago the belief prevailed that insanity was a divine punishment for more or less identifiable sin.[1] Such a belief clearly did not justify exemption from punishment for crimes committed by mentally ill persons. With the progress of science, this belief was replaced by recognition of the fact that insanity is a scientifically cognizable phenomenon, mental disease. But the metaphysics of insanity was not simultaneously overcome. Mental disease, while no longer theologically or magically tainted, was still conceived of as an absolute ontological entity, only now possessing the immanent quality of exempting from state authority and legal punishment. In this view, mental disease must exempt from responsibility as if by force of its very nature. Legal rules do not possess the power to affect this natural law exemption.

The modern revolution in science, marked by Einsteinian physics, the economics of marginal utility, Freudian psychology and Kelsenian jurisprudence, originated a new philosophy of science. This philosophy sheds doubt on the old ontology of mental disease and of the mental incapacity exemption. The world of fixed things and exclusively conscious static psychological realities collapsed. The universe was desubstantialized. Physical things were shown to be constructs formed from phenomena observed from various physical standpoints; economic value was recognized to be the constructive result of various market valuations; mental life was shown to be a dy-

---

*This is an enlarged text of a lecture delivered in the Criminal Law Week of the Law Faculty of the University of Puerto Rico on Friday, June 23, 1961. It was first printed in II CURRENT LAW AND SOCIAL PROBLEMS (Macdonald ed., University of Toronto Press, Copyright, Canada, 1961). It is reprinted here by special permission of the University of Toronto Press.

[1]For remnants of this view see State v. Harrison 36 W. Va. 729, 15 S.E. 982, 18 L. R. A. 224 (1892), on origins of melancholia.

namic process, integrating immediately experienced phenomena of the conscious and indirectly experienced or reflected phenomena of the constructive unconscious. Similarly, Kelsenian thought questioned the metaphysics of traditional legal concepts. Kelsen taught that the key concepts in law do not denote preexisting realities of nature but rather symbolize functional constructs, which are creatures of law. Thus, crime and responsibility, guilt and innocence, ceased to be given "natural" theological realities and became constructive results of legal imputation or its negation. Guilt in this new light is imputed to man, ascribed to him by law; it is not inherent in him or in his conduct. Guiltlessness or exemption does not mean natural innocence or virtue but is denial of imputation. Obviously the question arose: Why in certain situations do we impute guilt to a man and why do we in other situations deny guilt or exempt? Thus there was reached the Copernican turn in criminal law thought: that ascription or non-ascription of guilt, constituting the concepts of crime and responsibility, and of denial of crime and exemption from responsibility, is not derived from immanent ontological states of preexisting natural crime and immanent responsibility or their absence, but from policy considerations, on the basis of which law does or does not ascribe guilt.

A change parallel to that which occurred in the sciences, from an ontological to a functional constructive approach, is noticeable in the philosophy of language. Originally, name-giving was the discovery of the nature of things. There comes to mind the biblical statement that God brought all things to Adam "to see what he would call them; and whatsoever Adam called every . . . creature, that *was* the name thereof."[2] The name *was* the thing; it reflected its nature and reality and lived in it. Naming or defining was an act of cognitive and logical necessity. In this truly biblical sense, the name "mental disease" was, until quite recently, considered to represent an ontologically given state of mind, to be discovered simply by medical observation. Is dipsomania a mental disease? Whether it is or

---

[2]Genesis 2:19.

not was thought to be quite independent of medical judgment recognizing it as such. There was thought to be no element of arbitrariness in including it in, or excluding it from, the definition of mental disease. Doctors could "discover," as one discovers an oil well, by observing the phenomenon dipsomania, whether it is or is not a mental disease. The law, of course, had no part in such inclusion or exclusion.

In the light of the modern philosophy of language, names or definitions are not immanent qualities of things but conventions. We agree to give to certain phenomena certain names, and we do so for a purpose, namely, that of communicating conveniently. We may very well call certain phenomena by a certain name for one purpose but not for another purpose. In the sciences we give names to phenomena for the special purpose of communication among men of a particular science. There is, of course, a policy in combining a number of phenomena under one name within a science: to enable men of that science to exchange meaningful information and instruction—meaningful in the sense of denoting features that are relevant from the standpoint of that science and enabling the dispensation of relevant professional judgments. Thus in psychiatry a doctor may tell another doctor that a patient is a schizophrenic, and by this means he tells his colleague that this patient is classifiable within a given psychiatric category and should be treated in a certain way. Doctors do not as a rule use the term "mental disease," but in the rare instances in which they do, they merely mean to tell each other that persons described by that term are in need of psychiatric treatment or hospitalization. What significance does a medical communication of this type have in the area of criminal law? Prima facie, none whatever. Lawyers are not parties to the communication convention of doctors. To us this communicative scheme of doctors is as Chinese is to people who do not speak Chinese. Our policy is distinctive; our frames of reference and standards of relevance are different; and it is to legal policy, legal frames of reference and legal standards of relevance that our means of communication, our language, and our names and definitions are geared.

Of course, law is a more "social" discipline than is medicine.

It must communicate meaning not only within the circle of lawyers but also to laymen. Moreover, it must consider knowledge afforded by the sciences, particularly by psychology and psychiatry. To be able to address itself meaningfully to men, law must take into account the ways in which the human mind operates. To pierce the veil of psychological and psychiatric knowledge, it is imperative for lawyers to establish some means of communicating with psychiatrists and psychologists. This can be done in one of two ways: either by creating a special language of forensic psychology and psychiatry, based upon conventions between lawyers and psychiatrists, or by law's adopting psychological and psychiatric terminology of widest and least controversial use, provided that that which such terminology stands for is found to be legally relevant. However, it is important to stress—since this has often been misunderstood—that the difficulty of communicating between law and psychiatry lies not in the fact that psychiatrists disagree with each other or frequently reverse themselves—lawyers do that also—but in the fact that they do so on legally irrelevant grounds[3] or on grounds whose relevance to law has not been demonstrated.[4]

---

[3]See, e.g., Judge Burger's opinion (concurring in result only) in Blocker v. United States, 288 F.2d 853, 857, at pp. 860-861 (D.C. Cir., 1961).

[4]ROCHE, THE CRIMINAL MIND (Isaac Ray Award Book, 1958) at 15, suggests: "If lawyers and psychiatrists will agree to regard 'mental illness' and 'insanity' less as they are verbally defined and more as what we do to people to whom we attach such terms, we will be nearer the sharing of behavioral reality not only that of others but of ourselves." For this Dr. Roche cites Bridgman's statement, "The true meaning of a term is to be found by observing what a man *does* with it, not by what he *says* about it." There are two difficulties which render this suggestion impracticable in the field of law–psychiatry intercommunication. Observations of psychiatrists' "doing" can be useful in law only if such observations can be conceptualized and verbalized, for law must generalize and must express its generalizations. Bridgman's suggestion admits verbalization of observations regarding what is done. If what the psychiatrists are doing is susceptible of verbalization, there should be no problem, for it would hardly matter whether the verbalization is done by psychiatrists or by lawyers. But the fact is that psychiatrists claim that such verbalization is often impossible. Secondly, psychiatrists' "doing" presents a distinctive problem. In contrast to physicists, psychiatrists operate predominantly verbally; they communicate with patients linguistically, but the language of this communication is distinctive and not communicable to persons not possessing an intricate knowledge of psychiatry.

The ontological approach to language is being overcome successfully in the area of legal language generally. Thus, we have witnessed the failure of the one-time belief that the nature of an issue as being one of law or fact is an immanent quality of such issue, so that the question of whether an issue X presents a question of fact or a question of law may be resolved simply by observation of X and itself answered as a question of fact. The distinction between law and fact has now been shown to be relative and functional, and the question whether issue X presents a question of fact or a question of law is today known to be a question of law and not a question of fact. Yet the old metaphysical view of fact or question of fact is maintained tenaciously in the area of exemption for mental incapacity. The inconsistency of this view with the now generally prevailing jurisprudence of law and fact calls for a closer examination of certain assertions, such as whether psychopathy is a "mental disease" is a "question of fact," which the jury must answer.

If we want to build a rational structure of criminal law we must start with fundamentals. In order to formulate a sound exemption for mental incapacity we must view the task before us as posing this basic question: What is the purpose of the exemption? An exemption is assumed to be an exception from responsibility for the commission of crime which normally takes the form of punishment. An inquiry into the purpose of the exemption must hence proceed from a notion of the nature and function of that from which the exemption is to be granted, namely, punishment. We must ascertain the purpose of punishment and then seek the conditions in which that purpose is inapplicable. The quality or condition that is incompatible with the policy objective of punishment should afford a definition of the exemption. The problem of exemption ought to be cast in terms of the questions: What is the meaning and function of that from which we exempt? and What quality is it that does not respond to this meaning and function? rather than in terms of an a priori notion that mental disease possesses an inherently exempting power, the sole problem being to discover the exact meaning of such disease.

Today, the meaning and function of punishment ought to be considered in conjuction with another type of state intervention in criminal law, namely, the measure. The division into punishment, on the one hand, and "measures of security and cure," on the other, corresponds to the duality of purpose pursued by criminal law: the punitive or retributive end and the protective and curative end. An exemption from punishment, accordingly, does not mean exemption from all state intervention; a person who, because of his mental state, is found to be exempt from punishment, may very well be subject to the second type of sanction, the measure. However, in this paper I shall deal only with exemption from the punitive scheme. The discussion of measures to be applied within the protective scheme to persons exempt from punishment by reason of mental incapacity I shall take up in another publication. In this paper I shall: discuss the purpose of punishment and the area to which it is inapplicable; critically review the available tests of exemption; and present a new test of the mental incapacity exemption.

THE PURPOSE OF PUNISHMENT AND THE AREA TO WHICH IT IS INAPPLICABLE

It would far exceed the scope of this paper were I to undertake an exhaustive study of the various views on the policy or function of punishment expressed throughout history. Moses, Mordecai, Christ and Mohammed, Confucius and Buddha, Plato, Aristotle, Draco, Solon, Cicero, St. Augustine and St. Thomas, Pufendorf and Spinoza, Bentham, Beccaria, Montesquieu and Rousseau, Kant, Hegel and Fichte, Hobbes and Feuerbach, to mention but a few of those whose thought has shaped notions of legal morality, would have to be consulted. I shall select four views that seem to me to be particularly pertinent to a contemporary discussion, since they fit into the schemes of ideas expressed in laws which are now in force, and in drafts and reform projects of civil and common law countries. The first view is that punishment is a response to guilt or culpability; the second is that it is a functional means of deterrence; the third is that it is a reformation device; and the fourth is that it is a social-political means of asserting and maintaining legal prohibitions of relative gravity.[5] If we assume the first view

<hr/>

[5]For a more elaborate treatment of this position of the writer, see Silving,

to be correct—this, in fact, is the view most frequently en- countered in our decisional law—we ought to conclude that a person must not be punished if he is not guilty; if we accept the second view, we should decide that a person must not be punished unless he is deterrable or unless other persons can be deterred by his being punished; if we assume the third view to be correct, it follows that a person who is not re- formable ought not to be punished; and if the fourth view is taken to apply, the inference is that a person must not be punished if this does not serve law's assertion. In this scheme the definition of incapacity appears to be determined by the policy of punishment. Assumption of a converse relationship also implies a policy disposition, but the true policy considera- tions motivating such disposition may not be conscious.

As the above-mentioned meanings and purposes of punish- ment often overlap, so do the views on incapacity. Nor are these purposes necessarily exclusive of each other; rather, they may be combined in various schemes. Indeed, it is possible to derive partial solutions to the problem of incapacity from each of these purposes, provided that we assume them to be valid at least in certain areas. When punishment is assumed to serve more than one purpose, caution should be exercised to avoid confusion of the several purposes and particularly indiscriminate or unconscious substitution of one purpose for another. For this reason each potential purpose should be viewed in isolation. This method of analysis also helps clear elaboration of the distinctive significance of each such purpose for the formulation of exemption on the ground of incapacity.

A. Guilt as Directive in Punishment: Mental Incapacity Exemption Conceived as a Quality Excluding Guilt

Guilt is one of the most elusive concepts in ethics, religion and law. In Anglo-American law, there has recently been little concern with the meaning of guilt or culpability. As may be seen from the manner in which the term culpability has been

---

'Rule of Law' in Criminal Justice, in Mueller, ed., Essays in Criminal Science (1961) 77, at 85-89.

used in the American Law Institute's Model Penal Code,[6] it is taken to mean interchangeably two things: (a) the mental element in crime: intent, recklessness or negligence; (b) a type of blameworthiness, at times identified with the attribution of responsibility for failing to observe a proper standard of conduct,[7] at other times taken to refer to social censure generally. By contrast, in civil law countries the meaning and function of guilt have been the subject of vigorous controversy and voluminous legal literature.[8] But the theory that may provide the most valuable contribution to clarification of the issue is of prewar vintage: the phenomenological theory of guilt. In the following paragraphs I shall discuss: 1. guilt as identified with intent; 2. guilt conceived of as blameworthiness; 3. guilt in the light of phenomenological thought; 4. guilt as interpreted by the present writer.

1. Guilt as Intent

If we proceed from the concept of guilt or culpability in its widest sense, as accepted by usage, its simple equation with, for example, intent is questionable, provided that by "intent" we mean a descriptive category and not, as is often implied, a sort of objective culpability, such as the attribution of intent notwithstanding the absence of knowledge of what one ought

---

[6]AMERICAN LAW INSTITUTE MODEL PENAL CODE, Tentative Draft No. 4 (1955), § 2.02, entitled "General Requirements of Culpability," deals with the mental element, labelling it as "minimum requirements of culpability" (§ 2.02(1)). In subdiv. (2)(c) of the same section, the risk which it is "reckless" to take is qualified as one of such nature and degree that "its disregard involves culpability of high degree. In subdiv. (2)(d), "negligently" is circumscribed in terms of "substantial culpability."

Since this essay was written there has become available a Proposed Official Draft of the Model Penal Code (1962). The latter will be cited hereinafter only where it has introduced innovations.

[7]Alternatives to "culpability" qualifications in the definitions of "recklessness" and "negligence" (see ibid.) are: "its disregard involves a gross deviation from proper standards of conduct" (2.02 (2)(c)); "substantial deviation from the standard of care that would be exercised by a reasonable man in [the actor's] situation" (2.02 (2)(d)).

[8]On some aspects of this controversy see Ryu and Silving, Error Juris: A Comparative Study (1957), 24 UNIVERSITY OF CHICAGO LAW REVIEW 421, at 440-458.

to know, on the basis of other men's knowledge. For guilt is a normative concept, invoking the idea that the conduct of which one is said to be guilty is bad. Even if we prefer to discourse in the descriptive psychologizing fashion of the philosophical positivistic method, in which values are considered in terms of factual reactions to concepts viewed as values, that is, in terms of the beliefs or feelings which people entertain that things are good or bad, we must still concede the good or bad to be distinctive reaction contents, namely, normative contents. Hence, guilt cannot be simply defined as intent or negligence *per se.* Some link is missing that would indicate that to have a certain type of intent is or is felt to be bad. Thus guilt must be assumed to imply at least some element or qualification other than intent.

When we apply the doctrine which equiparates guilt with intent to the area of exemption, the need for a qualification becomes obvious. A person suffering from melancholia or from paranoia undoubtedly intends to commit the acts he in fact commits.[9] As Roche points out, "mental illness does not abolish intent but *releases it.*"[10] Indeed, the intent of a mentally ill person is usually more intensive than that of a healthy one. Yet, according to the overwhelming weight of opinion, a person suffering from melancholia or from paranoia ought to be exempt from punishment. Scholars in common and civil law countries alike have suggested that to intend must mean to intend rationally or to intend with rational motivation, and that to know must mean to know with feeling or to know profoundly and not merely on a verbal level.[11] But, strangely enough, neither rational motivation nor profound knowledge is required in cases where mental incapacity is not in issue. This means that if we are to follow these suggestions, we must assume that a normal individual may very well be guilty

---

[9]See Royal Commission on Capital Punishment, 1949-53, REPORT 1953 (Cmd. 8932), p. 110 (hereinafter cited as ROYAL COMM. REPORT).

[10]*Supra* note 4, at 88.

[11]See Hall, *Psychiatry and Criminal Responsibility,* 65 YALE LAW JOURNAL 761, 774-775 (1956); Ernst Seelig, *Zum Problem der Neufassung des § 51,* in FESTSCHRIFT FÜR EDMUND MEZGER (1954), 213, 223-226.

if he intends irrationally or knows superficially, but that an individual suffering from mental incapacity is exempted when his knowledge or intention is so characterized. This brings us back to the initial question of what constitutes the mental incapacity that produces this effect.[12]

Although no one today believes that mental illness necessarily excludes intent, the pertinent exemption is often referred to as mental incapacity to commit crime, as though the disease necessarily removed the mental element of crime. Nor is this but an anachronistic manner of speech. Mr. Justice Frankfurter, for example, has expressed the view that, since proof of the accused's insanity is equivalent to proof that "he had not the mind capable of commiting murder," to impose upon him the burden of proving insanity beyond a reasonable doubt is inconsistent with the constitutional requirement that the prosecution must prove the mental element of intent, premeditation and deliberation as part of guilt.[13] In what sense is a mentally ill person incapable of committing a crime? Since he is often capable of forming an actual psychological intent as well as of deliberating and premeditating, obviously "incapacity to form an intent" implies something other than actual inability to form the psychological state of mind which is usually assumed to constitute the mental element in crime. That qualifying factor, which renders the conduct and the mental state of the mentally ill person, as distinguished from similar conduct and mental state of a healthy one, not guilty, is the object of our search.

Since the notion of the mental element, as understood today, cannot provide the answer to our query for the proper test of the so-called mental incapacity exemption, we must look to

---

[12]If we prefer to put the issue in terms of "intent," then the question is: At what degree of loss of "ego control" is a person to be deemed no longer free enough to have a *relevant* intent"? One might *call* this an issue of "free will." Of course, "relevant" is a normative concept.

[13]See Mr. Justice Frankfurter's dissent in Leland v. Oregon, 343 U.S. 790 (1952) (holding Oregon's requirement that the accused prove insanity beyond a reasonable doubt constitutional, the Supreme Court majority finding that the prosecution's burden of proving all elements of crime, including wherever pertinent "purpose and malice, premeditation and deliberation," satisfies the requirement that the prosecution prove "guilt"), at 802.

other potential solutions. We may recall that traditional law refers to intent as malice, wicked will or vicious will, or evil intent. This implies a type of qualification such as has been suggested already, namely, a normative one. The quality that precludes guilt is one which renders the conduct of the person concerned not blameworthy. Thus the doctrine which defines guilt as the psychological factor in crime—a doctrine that might be expected to yield an answer to the question of what psychological qualities should exempt from punishment—does not afford a solution. We must still inquire wherein exactly lies the element of blameworthiness in guilt.

2. *Guilt as Blameworthiness*

Assuming guilt to include or, indeed, to be blameworthiness, the problem is to determine the standard of the judgment of blame. It may be religious, ethical or social-political. In a legal system which adopts the principle of separation of church and state, a religious standard is excluded except where it assumes the guise of a general cultural or community standard. As a rule, the same is thought to be true of a secular ethical standard. In common law countries the relevant standard is usually assumed to be a social one, since even those who insist that it must be moral actually think of morality as a system of moral norms that are culturally accepted.[14] Blameworthiness is thus predominantly believed to be rooted in a community judgment. It reduces itself to those qualities of conduct or of being which the community considers to be bad. One might expect exemption from blameworthiness to be definable in terms of the factors that eliminate these qualities. But the fact is that the exempting qualities are not deemed to be fully inferable in this negative manner from the guilt-constituent factors; they are rather derived from an independent community judgment. Indeed, leading German jurists have taken the converse position, namely, that the meaning of guilt must be inferred from the principal exemption from guilt, the exemption of legal

---

[14]See, e.g., DEVLIN (Lord Justice Devlin), THE ENFORCEMENT OF MORALS (Maccabaean Lecture in Jurisprudence of the British Academy, 1959).

error, and that there ought to be no other definition of guilt in a code.[15]

From the standpoint of a system of rule of law, everything which is considered to be legally blameworthy is contained in the patterns of conduct and of mental state described by statutes. By the same token, if any element of blameworthiness as thus required is missing, there is, within a system of *nullum crimen sine lege*, no need for an exemption. Were the assertion that insanity excludes intent taken seriously, no plea of insanity would be necessary. Yet it is required in our law.

Whatever the essence of blameworthiness in the judgment of the community, it may not afford a basis for defining what is not blameworthy, for community judgment does not necessarily operate in terms of simple logic. Exemption from guilt in the judgment of communities need not be equated with absence of that which constitutes guilt, but may well be rooted in an independent consideration. I shall not dwell upon the scope of admissibility of such inconsistent approach. For this is but a partial issue of a comprehensive problem which cannot be discussed in this paper—that of the limitations which the idea of democratic law imposes upon rule by community judgment. But two questions require special treatment in any contemporary discussion of mental incapacity, because their resolutions implied in recent leading decisions and policy suggestions are based on inadequate jurisprudential analyses. These questions are to the extent that community judgment affords an admissible standard: a. What is its proper form of manifestation? and b. What is the proper basis of its formation?

A. MANIFESTATION OF COMMUNITY JUDGMENT

The community, as a body of individuals, must act through an agent. The question is: What community organ should be authorized to express community judgment on blameworthiness or on exemption from it? Is it the legislature, the courts

---

[15]MAYER, DER ALLGEMEINE TEIL DES DEUTSCHEN STRAFRECHTS (1923), 316, states: "The doctrine of error is . . . not but a consequence to be derived from the doctrine of guilt; it is the doctrine of guilt itself. . . ."

or the juries? That the decisive role in defining blameworthiness, whether it be expressed in descriptions of crime or in personal qualifications of offenders, must be attributed to legislatures is treated as a truism in civil law countries. In the United States, *per contra*, the view has been advanced that a determination of blameworthiness is a judgment upon a moral issue which must be rendered by the jury, since this issue is one of fact. One might wonder how this fits the definition of the term "fact" as conceived in the ancient rule, *ad quaestionem facti non respondent judices, ad quaestionem juris non respondent juratores.* Traditionally, judges were required to be just, whereas jurors have been described as men good and true, although of course in the very early days of legal development truth and justice were not clearly separated. In our times, to be sure, juries have been expected to manipulate justice, even *contra legem.* That they must answer senseless questions, however, is an innovation introduced by Judge Thurman Arnold, who advocated treatment of such questions as "moral issues."[16] Judge Arnold justified assignment of moral issues to juries not on the assumption that a moral question is one of fact,[17] but rather on his anthropological approach to social ideals. In the light of the latter, scientific truth, morality, justice to the accused, rule of law, are all symbols of irrelevant content which have no direct impact upon legal reality, since law develops, "as language develops, in spite of, and not because of, the grammarians."[18] The function of these symbols is to dramatize legal processes, which are rituals that impress the public and thus enhance the prestige of law. Trial by jury is such a ritual, and hence to uphold a jury's authority in passing judgment on blameworthiness is more significant than either consideration of scientific truth or meting out justice to the accused. Thus, in the much cited *Holloway case,*[19] the District of Columbia

---

[16]Holloway v. United States, 148 F.2d 662 at 666-667 (D.C. Cir., 1945).

[17]He stated that "the issue of the criminal responsibility of a defendant suffering from mental disease is not an issue of fact in the same sense as the commission of the offense." *Ibid.*, at 666.

[18]ARNOLD, THE SYMBOLS OF GOVERNMENT (1935), at 34.

[19]*Supra* note 16, at 667, where Judge Arnold said that "to command respect

Court of Appeals approved submission to the jury of "scientific" evidence which the court itself stated to be false, even though it considered such evidence decisive of the issue of exemption on the grounds of mental incapacity. The policy ideal incorporated in this case is government by illusion, indeed, by deception of the public, serving an imaginary public good, to which the man Holloway may just as well be sacrificed. The psychiatrist, Dr. Roche, in turn, apparently believing Judge Arnold's views to reflect prevailing legal ideas, declared that since the question raised by the ruling in the *Durham case*,[20] whether an act is "the product of mental disease or defect," is not scientifically answerable—being scientifically senseless—it is a moral question which the jury must answer.[21] Judge Bazelon in the *Durham case*[22] managed to escape the jurisprudential nihilism of Judge Arnold by declaring that the issue of mental incapacity must be answered by the jury since it raises a moral problem and thus an issue of fact. Because of the great importance which the *Durham case* has assumed in recent legal disputes, it is necessary to discuss the methodological basis of its assignment to the jury of the questions of

---

criminal law must not offend against the common belief that men who talk rationally are in most cases morally responsible for what they do." At the same time, he pointed out that this common belief is scientifically wrong, for it is based on the incorrect assumption that "there is a faculty called reason which is separate and apart from instinct, emotion, and impulse, that enables an individual to distinguish between right and wrong and endows him with moral responsibility for his acts" (at 666). Compare with this position the enlightened statement of Mr. Chief Justice Warren in Blackburn v. Alabama, 361 U.S. 199, at 209 (1960): "Nor have we overlooked the testimony of the Chief Deputy that Blackburn 'talked sensible,' was clear-eyed, and did not appear nervous. But without any evidence in the record indicating that these observed facts bore any relation to Blackburn's disease or were symptoms of a remission of his illness, we are quite unable to conclude that such an inference can be drawn." Modern psychiatry teaches that composure and calmness after the commission of a crime does not indicate mental health. In a Puerto Rican case, evidence of calmness and reasoning ability after commission of the crime was given almost decisive weight as against overwhelming proof of schizophrenia. Pueblo v. Sánchez Maldonado, 79 D.P.R. 116, at 121-122 (1956).

   [20]Durham v. United States, 94 U.S. App. D.C. 228, 214 F.2d 862 (1954).
   [21]ROCHE, *supra* note 4, at 259-268.
   [22]*Supra* note 20, at 875-876.

defining the general terms "mental disease" and "product of mental disease" on the ground that these are "questions of fact."

When stating that definition of key concepts in the mental incapacity exemption is a question of fact, Judge Bazelon merely repeated a theme elaborated by the New Hampshire judges in 1869–71.[23] In doing so, he seems to have overlooked the fact that words are means of communicating ideas and that identical words may communicate entirely different ideas in 1870 and in 1954—indeed, may be meaningful in 1870 but meaningless in 1954.[24] Actually, both the phrase "issue of fact" and the phrase "mental disease" have an entirely different meaning today from that attributed to them in 1870, and the phrase "product of mental disease" was believed to be meaningful in 1870 but is deemed without meaning today.

When the New Hampshire judges, in formulating their famous mental incapacity test, expressed the view that what constitutes mental disease and what is a product of such disease are questions of fact to be answered by juries, they proceeded from the assumption prevailing at the time that the quality of a question, as one of fact or law, is an inherent ontological attribute.[25] In recent decades, however, as suggested above, the one-time belief in the absoluteness of the distinction between law and fact has been abandoned. Today it is general law-school knowledge that "law" and "fact" in the statements "this is a question of fact" or "this is a question of law" indicate normative determinations reached by decision-makers on policy grounds rather than immanent attributes of the given ques-

---

[23]State v. Pike, 49 N.H. 399 (1870); State v. Jones, 50 N.H. 369 (1871). The New Hampshire judges, however, did not describe this issue as a moral one. They rather thought the questions of whether a man posssses a mental disase and whether his act is a product of such disease are questions of the same nature as the question of whether he has fever. So is the question of what a mental disease is.

[24]Notice the developments in the philosophy of language, marked by names such as Rudolph Carnap, Ludwig Wittgenstein and John Wisdom.

[25]On Judge Doe's insistence upon the immanent quality of a question, as one of "fact" see Reid, *Understanding the New Hampshire Doctrine of Criminal Insanity*, 69 YALE LAW JOURNAL 367 (1960).

tions.[26] Whether a question is one of law or one of fact is a question of law and not a question of fact. When it is thought desirable on policy grounds to assign a question to the jury, it is characterized as a question of fact; the reverse procedure of characterizing a question as one of fact by merely observing its nature is no longer deemed valid. However, the policy of assigning a question to the jury as one of fact is not entirely unrelated to certain features of the question that is in issue— features that must be evaluated in the context in which that question appears. One of the relevant features is the degree of generality of the potential answer to the question.

As suggested by Mezger,[27] the distinction between law and fact is one between the general and the particular. The problem is: At what level of generality should we assume a question to be general enough to be deemed a question of law? Levels of generality of questions of diverse content can be compared, and it is thus possible to decide whether a question is one of such generality as is usually—meaning, so far as issues other than the one being discussed are concerned—thought to qualify a question as one of law. But, of course, as a matter of sound policy, the analogies ought to be drawn from identical fields of law, for a determination of a question as one of law or of fact implies a jurisdictional disposition; and one may very well wish to declare a question of identical level of generality to be one of fact in civil cases but not in criminal cases. In drawing analogies of this nature it is also important to consider whether the jury possesses the necessary relative qualifications for determining the questions which are being compared.

In the *Durham case* Judge Bazelon drew an analogy, such as has been suggested, when he said that the questions of fact under the test laid down in the case, namely, whether the

---

[26]See Silving, *Law and Fact in the Light of the Pure Theory of Law*, in SAYRE (ed.), INTERPRETATIONS OF MODERN LEGAL PHILOSOPHIES (1947), at 642-667.

[27]"The decisive demarcation line runs not between the 'factual' and the 'legal' but between the 'individual circumstance' and the illegality of the 'total act.'" Mezger, in *Strafgesetzbuch nach dem neuesten Stand der Gesetzgebung*, LEIP-ZIGER KOMMENTAR (founded by Ebermayer, Lobe, Rosenberger) (1953) at 449.

accused suffered from a mental disease and whether his act was the product of the disease, "are as capable of determination by the jury as, for example, the questions juries must determine upon a claim of total disability under a policy of insurance where the state of medical knowledge concerning the disease involved and its effects, is obscure or in conflict."[28] Even if the analogy applied in this instance could be said to be methodologically unobjectionable, it would be improper to invoke such a private law analogy in criminal law, since the requirements of legality are much more stringent in the latter branch of law than in the former. Apart from this, is the level of abstraction or generality similar in the two situations? Clearly, "total disability" is a more determinate concept than "mental disease": that for which a person must be disabled is known, whereas responsibility, of which the mentally diseased is supposed to be incapable, is precisely that which we are expected to determine by the term "mental disease." Disability in insurance is an earning disability that can be expressed in dollars and cents by comparing pre-injury average wages and post-injury earning potential or actual earnings.[29] Also, in regard to a lay jury's qualifications for answering the questions, expecting a jury to decide whether a claimant has lost his earning ability is obviously more rational than requiring it to determine whether an accused was responsible. What is the source of this peculiar equiparation of the issue of "disability" and that of "irresponsibility"?

Any student of the New Hampshire cases who notices their persistent concern with whether a legal test is or is not necessary, is bound to ask: a test of what? In some passages the judges speak of a test without indicating what is being tested; in

---

[28]*Supra* note 20, at 875.

[29]"Total disability" is not "absolute helplessness" but "total earning unfitness." VANCE, HANDBOOK ON THE LAW OF INSURANCE [3d ed. 1951], at 1050. In workmen's compensation statutes "total disability" imports payments of certain percentages of total wages, whereas "partial disability" imports payments of percentages of the difference between prior pay and post-injury earning capacity or actual wages. See SCHNEIDER's WORKMAN's COMPENSATION (Permanent Edition 1940), vol. IV, for the respective provisions.

others, of insanity as object of the test; in still others, they seem to use the term "lack of responsibility" as equivalent to insanity. One gains the impression that they are using the concept of insanity or mental disease or irresponsibility as if that concept itself were an existentially given entity. To define such concept, in the opinion of the New Hampshire judges, requires discovery of the inherent attributes of such an entity rather than agreement or convention over a functional use of a term. While insanity is a subject of medical study and hence a medical matter, it is a reality which medical men may discover but whose scope they cannot determine for any purpose. Thus, whether dipsomania is a kind of insanity is not a matter of medical conventional definition but a question of fact. One doctor may make the correct discovery about this question, while another doctor may err. But there has since occurred a total desubstantialization of scientific concepts. Scientific definitions are reached by convention aimed at facilitating communication. Medical men may properly agree to define mental disease in such a manner as to include psychopathy or neuroses; they may equally properly agree to define the term so as to exclude these states. The agreement to choose the former or the latter alternative is guided by considerations of medical intercommunication with a view to medical dispositions. The assumption that the definition implies a "discovery" of any attributes that are inherent in the notion of mental disease or, indeed, of any attributes that are also relevant in law, is not warranted. In fact, Judge Bazelon now asserts that the medical label given to a subject's condition is not decisive and that "(1)egal consequences depend rather upon the jury's determination, from all the facts, as to the individual's mental health or illness."[30] This complicates the issue, adding the problem of finding the discipline to which mental disease, as used in the Durham test, belongs. For, obviously, within that test, in order

---

[30]See Judge Bazelon's dissenting opinion in Lyles v. United States, 254 F.2d 725, 734, at 735-736 (D.C. Cir., 1957), *cert. denied,* 356, U.S. 961, 78 S. Ct. 997 (1958). "Testimony that the individual suffers from a named condition," Judge Bazelon said, is of aid to the jury "only to the extent that the jury is otherwise informed of the nature of the condition."

to ascertain whether, for example, a psychopath is exempt, the jury must establish whether at the time of the act he suffered from a "mental disease" or "illness."

In its famous "moral judgment" conclusion, the *Durham case* states that whether a person is to be classified as suffering from a mental disease depends on the moral judgment of the jury.[31] This is a peculiar and misleading usage of language, reducible to the assertion that mental disease is a moral quality. The nature of this moral quality is not disclosed except to the extent of implying that it is predicated upon "all the facts." This, then, is apparently the meaning of the phrase that mental disease is a question of fact. Analytically it amounts to delegating to juries the function of determining general issues, such as whether kleptomaniacs, pyromaniacs, psychopaths, as classes, ought to be exempt from punishment. Determining whether such broad classes should or should not be exempt is as much a legislative task as is the question of whether persons engaged in error regarding an essential fact ought to be exempt. The dubiousness of this delegation of power to juries is magnified by the fact that juries are at the same time misled by being told that they must find whether the person concerned suffered from a mental disease,[32] which term, within modern linguistic usage, conveys the idea of a psychiatric category. The Durham position is indefensible within a system governed by the rule of law, both on the ground that it delegates essentially legislative power to juries and on the ground that it misleads the jury, the accused and the public. It is by no means coincidental that this position has been reached by methods which defy the contemporary philosophy of language, new insights into psychological reality and the modern jurisprudential conception of law and fact.

The legality principle, of course, has a narrower rationale in the area of the mental incapacity exemption than in that of specific legal prohibitions. In the latter area, the principle requires that man know or be able to know what he must not

---

[31]For text of the passage see *infra* note 156.

[32]See Judge Burger's opinion in Blocker v. United States, *supra*, note 3, at 869.

do to avoid punishment and that this knowledge or knowability be present in advance of the commission of crime. But it is not important that he know in advance of crime under what terms he will be held to have possessed or not to have possessed mental capacity, for that knowledge does not and should not affect his decision to act or to forego acting. However, legality in the sense of protection against arbitrariness and inequality of law administration also applies to the mental incapacity exemption. On this ground, to use another example, it is as improper to leave the scope of the term "mental disease" (as a test of exemption) to the jury's definition as it would be to give the jury authority to determine what constitutes self-defense under a rule providing exemption for anyone acting in self-defense, without further specification.

B. FORMATION OF COMMUNITY JUDGMENT

On what basis should community judgment be reached? The principal question is: What role should the psychiatric expert play in arriving at such judgment? At the legislative level, in order to formulate a sound mental incapacity exemption, legislators ought to know how the human mind operates, for today this is much less a matter of common knowledge than it was once assumed to be. Psychiatrists and psychologists must tell them what generalizations can be made. If no functional generalizations can be made, the implication is that the exemption cannot be cast or cannot be fully defined in terms of psychiatric categories; in this event legislators must derive its operational categories from disciplines other than psychology, for example, from sociology. In no event should they leave the matter of determining mental incapacity on a case-to-case basis to the jury under psychiatric guidance, without specification of the nature or scope of such guidance. In assessing the usefulness to law of different kinds of scientific insight, a distinction should be observed between those that can be put in general categories and those that cannot. One might even doubt that a discipline that cannot generalize meaningfully may be classified as a science, as normally understood.

At the trial level, psychiatric experts are needed as witnesses testifying to observations of operations of the mind of the accused. Whether or not the psychiatrist should be permitted to testify in terms of conclusions, such as whether or not the accused comes within the exemption as defined, depends on whether or not the psychiatrist can support opinions he expresses on rational grounds. If such grounds cannot be verbalized, his opinions should not be admissible. An accused may be rational or irrational, but the administration of justice—of which expert testimony forms a part—must be rational. No expert opinion should be allowed to stand if it is based merely on feeling and intuition.

3. Guilt in the Light of Phenomenological Thought

According to the phenomenological theory of guilt developed by Felix Kaufmann on the basis of the Kelsenian notion of imputation, guilt does not exist *per se,* but rather consists in ascription of guilt by virtue of certain postulates addressed to law; indeed, guilt is these postulates. It is a symbol summarizing certain social-political policies; it means the totality of functions which that concept is supposed to perform.[33] Applying this approach to our own policies, guilt would mean or

---

[33]KAUFMANN, DIE PHILOSOPHISCHEN GRUNDPROBLEME DER LEHRE VON DER STRAFRECHTSSCHULD (1929). The author states, at 72-76:

"The concept of guilt is closely connected with that of the purpose of punishment. As a rule, one assumes the presence of guilt when he regards punishment to be proper and one assumes the presence of grave guilt when he regards severe punishment to be proper. . . .

". . . [L]et us consider what are in general the aims of a theoretical analysis of the concept of guilt. The aim is often expressed by proclaiming what 'function' the concept of guilt is to 'perform'. Thereby, the following ends are postulated: Firstly, it should be defined in such manner as to make it possible to distinguish with precision guilt from non-guilt; secondly, it should permit gradation that might make it possible to speak of a greater or lesser 'graveness' of guilt; thirdly, it should be possible to deduct from it the logical relation of the 'types of guilt', intent and negligence, to it [guilt] as overall concept; fourthly, it should be clear that the grounds which exclude guilt, in a narrower sense (state of necessity, duress, substantial error), actually obliterate the guilt element; and fifthly, there should appear the relation of guilt to mental capacity or incapacity.

"Actually, the task involved [in formulating the guilt concept] is to carry out an *abstraction* of a certain type. One is conscious of the fact that each of the five mentioned relationships contains the same element and the task is to *isolate* it."

represent the demands, among others: that no one must be deemed guilty unless he possessed the required intent or recklessness; that no one should be punished severely if he committed a minor act, meaning an act of small social harmfulness; that no one should be punished unless all elements of crime have been proven properly; and so forth. We could equally well say that unless all the demands we thus address to law are fulfilled, it would be unjust to punish a man or to hold him responsible or to blame him, blame meaning social censure rather than a particular moral, religious or ethical blame. Though Kaufmann believed in a utilitarian notion of guilt, his theory, in its philosophical implications, lends itself to enlargement into a general theory of guilt. Guilt as a general sociological concept may assume various contents, depending on the preferred approach, whether it be theological, metaphysical, utilitarian, existential, and so on.

4. Guilt as Interpreted by the Writer

Guilt in law is always an expression of legal or policy demands. In a theocracy or in a state in union with a church, these demands are theological; in a state governed by some other philosophy, they are the demands of that philosophy. In a democratic state—I believe democracy to be a sui generis philosophy—these demands are democratic.[34] Subject to certain limitations implied in the concept of democracy—for example, those imposed by civil liberties—the community determines the contents of legal rules; but just as the community does not define the meaning of democracy, its philosophical judgment on the nature of guilt, as contrasted with its social judgment on legal contents, cannot afford a proper basis for defining guilt. Rather, adoption of a "democratic concept of guilt" may be demanded of legislators just as adoption of a democratic law of election may be demanded of them.[34a]

---

[34]On the sui generis nature of the philosophy of democracy see Silving, *The Conflict of Liberty and Equality*, 35 IOWA LAW REVIEW 357 (1950). To what extent the tenets of such philosophy permit incorporation by law of particular theological or secularly philosophical views, is an intricate problem which cannot be discussed in this paper.

[34a]Since this essay was published I have given further thought to the problem

Wherein does the democratic concept of guilt consist? In a democracy, obedience to demands of the community, formalized in duly enacted law, is a duty of citizenship. Guilt consists in violating the basic political postulate of substantial conformity to community rules. Dr. Paul K. Ryu and the writer expressed this idea in the following terms: "We believe that in a free society the sanction of the community is imposed neither for 'rebellion' nor for 'disobedience' but simply for violation of a duty toward the community—the actor's duty, as a member of the community, to abide by its rules."[35] This definition led us to postulate admission of error of law as a general defense open to any man without requirement that the error be based on a mental incapacity. The mental incapacity exemption is distinguishable from the error of law exemption in that it is concerned with the general fitness of the individual as a law-participant, representative of the community, rather than with the single issue, "Did he know the law? Did he know that the specific act he was committing was legally 'wrong'?" However, there should be a certain correlation between the rule on legal error and the definition of the mental incapacity exemption. The assumption is made that an important part of the process whereby a group becomes a legal community is that its members share in the making and maintenance of law, whether in the form of enforcement or obedience. Such sharing of law presupposes a certain standard of normality in cultural patterns and personality makeup, a standard that may vary from one community to another. Application of punitive law presupposes awareness of the law; it also presupposes subjects who are normal, average members of the community to whom laws are addressed. A person who does not meet the minimum standard

---

of the role to be accorded to community judgment in formulating crime concepts. I reached the persuasion that since every "crime" carries sanctions that limit civil liberties, the community or a popular majority has no discretion in a democracy to create crimes. Constitutions define the type and scope of the interests that may and should be protected by criminal law. Legislative authority is limited to casting in specific terms the prohibitions and sanctions purported to protect these interests. Compare Silving, *Philosophy of the Source and Scope of Criminal Law Prohibition*, in Slovenko, ed., CRIME, LAW AND CORRECTIONS (Thomas, 1966), 232.

[35]Ryu and Silving, *supra* note 8, at 468.

of balance in personality organization that qualifies him as "representative of his community" ought not to be held guilty of crime against that community. Since he is not an average law participant, law cannot be meaningfully asserted against him.

This norm is based on a political and not on a scientific principle. Guilt in a democratic society is a social-political concept.

B. Punishment as a Functional Means of Deterrence: Mental Incapacity as "Nondeterrability" or Unfitness to Serve as Means of Deterring Others

As stated above, if punishment is assigned the function of deterring the actor, then we must assume that persons whose state of mind is such that they are not susceptible to deterrence by punishment ought not to be punished. If, on the other hand, punishment is expected to function as a deterrent to others, then those whose punishment would not deter others ought not to be punished. One might, of course, generally define mental incapacity for legal purposes as "nondeterrability," and leave it to psychiatrists to advise in each case whether or not the accused is deterrable. But that non-deterrability cannot be assumed as the exclusive standard of exemption from punishment follows from the fact that such assumption would lead to exclusion in the first place of the most controversial group, namely, psychopaths. Moreover, non-deterrability by punishment is not the most outstanding characteristic of psychotics—the group which undoubtedly should be exempt from punishment;[36] nor is deterrability by legal punishment a special feature of the average individual. The Danish Penal Code, which adopts the non-deterrability test, formulates it as a merely supplementary category.[37]

Michael and Wechsler expressed the view that punishment's

---

[36]See MacNiven, *Psychoses and Criminal Responsibility*, in RADZINOWICZ & TURNER (eds.), ENGLISH STUDIES IN CRIMINAL SCIENCE (1949), vol. II (entitled MENTAL ABNORMALITY AND CRIME), 8, at 52-53; Davidson, *Criminal Responsibility: The Quest for a Formula*, in HOCH & ZUBIN (eds.) PSYCHIATRY AND THE LAW (1955), 61, at 63-64.

[37]DANISH CRIMINAL CODE OF 1930, as amended (transl. by Giersing and Grünhut, trans., G.E.C. Gad—Publishers, Copenhagen, 1958), §§ 16, 17.

failure to deter a mentally ill person applies to others also; normal persons are not deterred by the sight of an insane person's being punished because they do not identify themselves with him and do not expect to share his fate.[38] For this the authors cite no psychological authority. That identification with the accused works on such rational level may well be doubted in the light of the studies made by representatives of dynamic psychology.[39] In any event, the doctrine of deterrence, formulated classically in the high days of belief in man's rationality and in his ability always to calculate in business-like fashion the balance of pleasure and pain, has lost its scientific foundation: We have acquired some knowledge of the unconscious, which follows its own scheme of pleasure. But we have not yet acquired sufficient insight into the impact of punishment upon the unconscious to be able to say generally whether or not punishment of a mentally ill person deters others. Even proceeding from a conventional view of deterrence, one might well doubt that so-called normal persons do not identify themselves with those mentally ill persons who do not manifest outward signs of madness and who, nevertheless, ought to be exempt from punishment, according to a consensus of opinion. In sum, we do not have sufficient knowledge of the operation of deterrence generally to be able to accept it as a principal basis of punishment; by the same token, no foundation has been laid for defining the mental incapacity exemption simply in terms of non-deterrability. One might suggest non-deterrability as a separate, supplementary ground of exemption, but this is unnecessary, given a comprehensive test, as will be recommended below.

However, in the law of measures, the doctrine of deterrence may serve a useful function. In the case of the so-called psychopaths or sociopaths, whose most characteristic feature is their individual non-deterrability, there is good reason for adopting

---

[38]Michael and Wechsler, *A Rationale of the Law of Homicide*, 37 COLUMBIA LAW REVIEW 701, at 752-757 (1937).

[39]The "scapegoat ideology," described by Reik, Wittels, Alexander and Staub, Reiwald, and others and believed to be based on "identification with the accused," is not predicated upon mental health of the latter. Notice that the prototype of all scapegoats was an animal.

special devices, as are suggested by Danish experiences with special treatment centers for such persons.[40]

C. Punishment as a Means of Reformation: Mental Incapacity as an Inability to Be Reformed

Constitutions, statutes and judicial decisions often proclaim reformation to be the principal, indeed, even the sole, aim of criminal law state intervention. I have submitted in another context[41] that though reformation may be a proper aim of state intervention by methods other than those of the criminal law, the latter is not a fit province for reforming the offender. Certainly, punishment by the state is hardly an appropriate means of achieving reformation. As a direct reformative device, punishment is expected to function via its deterrent effect; but, as has been shown, the effectiveness of deterrence is doubtful. At best one could assert that punitive intervention provides an opportunity for reformative treatment. The primary obstacle to a consistent use of treatment during the course of punishment is that the latter must ultimately be limited by the scope of the crime committed, whereas the extent of intervention required by the need for treatment is not proportionate to the graveness of the precipitating crime.

However, assuming reformation to be a proper end of punishment, exemption should be accorded to the unreformable. In a dual system this result is less absurd than in a monistic one, for acquittal of a person found to be unreformable on the ground of insanity would automatically open the possibility of applying protective measures. Nor would it be necessary to cast the test in terms of absolute unreformability. It would suffice to formulate the mental incapacity exemption as "incapacity to be reformed by punitive means or in the course of punishment." This, however, would place within the exemption's scope a large number of persons whom the public would hardly con-

---

[40]Compare *supra* note 37. The pertinent measures will be discussed in a separate paper.

[41]On this see Silving, *'Rule of Law' in Criminal Justice, supra* note 5, at 138-140.

sider fit grantees of exemptions from "blame." Psychiatrists, many of whom oppose punishment in principle, are likely to extend the classification "unreformable" to an unduly large group of offenders. Also to be considered is the difficulty of diagnosis.[42] Again, as in the case of deterrence, the reformative potential of an individual may be an important consideration within the law of measures.

Of greatest practical significance is the positive harm which punishment may cause certain subjects. There are persons who, far from being deterrable or reformable by punishment, are likely to deteriorate as a result of punitive intervention. Could the likelihood of deterioration be accepted as a workable basis for exemption? The Danish test makes allowance for it. But the usefulness of the harm feature as a special ground for exemption is dubious. If the general test of mental incapacity is wide enough, it will embrace individuals with this feature. In the event that such an individual does not come within the exemption, he might in appropriate cases be accorded probation, provided that he is not dangerous.

D. Punishment as Law Assertion: Mental Incapacity Exemption Where Punishment Is Not Law Assertive

When assumed to have the function of manifesting law's prohibition of socially undesirable conduct, punishment is necessary

---

[42]Andanaes, Review of v. Eyben, Strafudmaling (1955-1956), 6 BRITISH JOURNAL OF DELINQUENCY 152, at 155, notes how little we understand "about reformation of the individual offender. We know little of what positive or negative significance punishment has for the criminal; still less ground do we have for judging the probable influence of a penalty of 30 days for example, instead of 3 to 6 months."

It may be interesting to note that the Supreme Court of Poland held the notion of the "unreformable" (art. 84 POLISH PENAL CODE OF 1932) to be "contrary to the principles of socialist legality and to the paramount tenet that, under the conditions of a popular State, there can be no question of unreformable crimes, for a popular State affords full opportunity of integrating every criminal—after completion of his punishment—in the creative effort of the nation, contributing to the education of the criminal." Decision rendered on April 8, 1952 (IV, K. 19/51), COLLECTION OF SUPREME COURT DECISIONS 1952, item 67, at 228. This decision obviously proceeds from the assumption that the exclusive sources of crime or of unreformability of the offender are economic conditions. Dynamic psychology

to document the prohibition rather than as a means of inflicting suffering upon the actor. Inflicting suffering should never be the purpose of legal operation, though it may be an unavoidable incident of another proper aim, as is that of law documentation. Punishment is necessary simply because no other device has yet been invented to serve such documentation. Treatment cannot function as its substitute, since it must be geared to the offender and not to his crime and is thus inapt to reflect the relative gravity of the prohibition that has been violated; even in the law of measures, which is focussed on the offender, the relative gravity of the criminal act should be a highly relevant consideration.

An important implication of interpreting punishment as a means of law assertion is the insistence on equality of treatment. Nondiscriminatory punishment of those who commit the same category of act in similar circumstances is a condition of the state's right to punish as a means of asserting its prohibitions.

Implicit in the concept of similarity of circumstances is that of an average personality makeup. It follows that a "nonaverage" individual should not be subject to the punitive treatment devised for average community members. Measures are the appropriate devices applicable to the "nonaverage." Measures, of course, must also be administered on an egalitarian basis, but equality in measures is judged from the standpoint of their distinctive aim: protection of the community. As the protective need varies, so do the types of indicated measures, due consideration being given even in the context of measures to the seriousness of the criminal act that has been committed.

Summary

Assertion of legal prohibition is the proper end of punishment. Such assertion, however, is not admissible except as a reaction to "guilt." Mental incapacity is that mental makeup which renders

---

refutes this assumption by pointing to the deeper psychological roots of criminality. However, within the political ideology and constitutional doctrine of the western world, the notion of the "unreformable offender" is repugnant to the basic postulate of "man's dignity."

these postulates inappropriate for certain types of persons. As guilt is violation of the basic political demand of abiding by the law addressed to the average community member, nonaverage personality makeup, which makes it extraordinarily difficult for an individual to conform to the community's norms, excludes guilt. Law assertion applied to the "nonaverage" person, who is not properly representative of the group mind, is socially inadequate. This view of the policy of punishment will guide the writer's formulation of the mental incapacity exemption. Before suggesting a new definition of mental incapacity, however, it is necessary to outline the definitions that are now available in laws and reform drafts and projects.

AVAILABLE MENTAL INCAPACITY TESTS

The available mental incapacity tests must be presented in historical perspective because in many of them ancient policy reasons and scientific or philosophical background have become obscured; the principle of legal inertia helps to maintain atavistic legal rules by beclouding their true historical rationales. As so often happens in law, the original reason for a rule is long forgotten though the rule itself lingers on by the sheer weight of its age, while desperate attempts are made to find a new rationale for it.

This part of the paper is divided into two sections, the first dealing with total and the second with partial exemption tests. The tests will be considered according to principles of similarity rather than chronologically. Anglo-American law will be discussed first, and civil law tests will be presented for purposes of comparison. In the former, the prevailing total exemption rules are the *M'Naghten* rules, either alone or as supplemented by the Irresistible Impulse test, on the one hand, and the *New Hampshire-Durham* rule, on the other hand. Revised versions of the combination of *M'Naghten* and Irresistible Impulse are the tests of the Model Penal Code. Comparable tests in civil law countries are those of the German and Swiss federal law, whereas the Spanish test resembles *Durham*. I shall discuss *M'Naghten's*, the Model Code's and the German test in one subsection, and the New Hampshire, *Durham* and Spanish test in another.

Total Exemption Tests: A. M'Naghten's Case, Irresistible Impulse, Model Code Tests, German Test

1. M'Naghten

M'Naghten's case[43] furnishes a background that is allegedly inconsistent with the rules that bear the accused's name. M'Naghten was a paranoiac who believed himself to be persecuted by Tories and to have been compelled by them to commit the murder for which he was indicted.[44] Even in the very act of diseased killing he committed a truly Freudian slip: he wanted to kill Sir Robert Peel, but mistook Peel's secretary, Drummond, for him and killed Drummond. M'Naghten was acquitted on the ground of insanity, although he undoubtedly knew that he was doing something "he ought not to do" according to the law of the land. Since the crime was political, a debate ensued in the House of Lords, and the Lords addressed to the judges of England an inquiry about the proper tests for acquittal on the basis of mental incapacity. The judges' answers constitute the famous M'Naghten rules, formulated in an advisory opinion of uncertain scope: It is possible that the judges only purported to define the mental incapacity exemption applicable to persons suffering from delusions.[45] The fact that

---

[43] (1843) 10 C. & F. 200 (H.L.)

[44] M'Naghten said: "The Tories in my native city have compelled me to do this. They follow and persecute me wherever I go, and have entirely destroyed my peace of mind. . . . They have accused me of crimes of which I am not guilty; they do everything in their power to harass and persecute me; in fact they wish to murder me. It can be proved by evidence." Ellison and Haas, *A Recent Judicial Interpretation of the M'Naghten Rule* (1953), 4 BRITISH JOURNAL OF DELINQUENCY 129.

[45] This interpretation is obviously suggested by one of the questions to which the so-called right-wrong rule is the answer: "What are the proper questions to be submitted to the jury, where a person alleged to be afflicted with insane delusion respecting one or more particular subjects or persons is charged with the commission of a crime (murder, for example), and insanity is set up as a defense?" If the answer given by the judges is responsive to this question, then it is clearly limited to a situation where delusion is present.

rules of this nature are persistently followed in many parts of the common law world should make us pause to reflect on the true historical meaning of these rules and the nature of their impact on contemporary thought.

The judges' answer that has played the most significant role in Anglo-American law is known as the right-wrong test, reading thus: ". . . to establish a defence on the ground of insanity, it must be clearly proved that, at the time of the committing of the act, the party accused was labouring under such a defect of reason, from disease of the mind, as not to know the nature and quality of the act he was doing; or, if he did know it, that he did not know he was doing what was wrong." Our first task is to establish the historical rationale of the test. Undoubtedly, the decisive part of the test—the part which has provided the basic incapacity definition throughout the common law world for over a century—is the "knowledge" portion, knowledge of the nature and quality of the act and knowledge that it was wrong. Lack of knowledge apparently was that which in the judges' opinion absolved the defendant from responsibility. For certainly no firm opinion had yet developed that mental disease *per se* justifies impunity. Let us not forget Ferri's remark that "(l)ess than one hundred years" before his time "the insane were punished as guilty and were objects of public execration, because the effect of a diseased organism was imputed to their malevolent will."[46]

Professor Ryu and I have found two clues to the historical meaning of the *M'Naghten* test.[47] We traced the test to two remote sources—sources which so often supply the historical solution for contemporary legal rules—the Bible and Roman law. The right-wrong test goes back to the good and evil test,[48] and the latter constitutes both the rationality standard of the Bible[49]

---

[46]FERRI, CRIMINAL SOCIOLOGY, in MODERN CRIMINAL SCIENCE SERIES (1917), at 356-357.

[47]Ryu and Silving, *supra* note 8, at 430.

[48]Arnold's case (1724), 16 St. Tr. 695, at 765; cf. prosecution's contention in Earl Ferrers case (1760), 19 St. Tr. 866, at 947. For discussion of these cases see Turner, ed., RUSSELL ON CRIME (10th ed. 1950), vol. I, 48-49.

[49]Genesis 2:9, 17; 3:22.

and the biblical condition and origin of sin.[50] Sin began with acquisition of knowledge of good and evil, and remained predicated upon such knowledge. The Bible exempts from punishment persons acting in ignorance of the prohibition. Both the Talmud and the canon law consider guilt to be predicated upon the actor's knowledge of the law that is being violated because, according to these sources, guilt is defiance of the law, disrespect for the laws of God or disobedience to the Lord.[51] In early foreign legal sources we also find the mental incapacity exemption based on a doctrine of legal error which is undoubtedly referable to the Bible via canon law. Thus, the Siete Partidas[52] declare that the *"loco o desmemoriado"* (lunatic or person without memory) is not subject to punishment because "he neither knows nor understands the error he makes."

Surely the stated features of biblical law could hardly have failed to influence decisions at a time when judges believed that the knowledge precluded by insanity was awareness that a crime was a violation of "the laws of God and nature,"[53] of which the phrase "the laws both of God and man," appearing in the *M'Naghten* instructions,[54] is but a slight variation. The law of error dominates not only the right-wrong portion of the judges' answers but all the other answers as well. The answer to the first question submitted by the Lords asserts that a person who knew that "he was acting contrary to law" is responsible, even though he suffered from a delusion that he was "redressing or revenging some supposed grievance or injury, or producing some public benefit." This answer perfectly reflects the historical and contemporary rule of the "law of error of

---

[50]The knowledge acquired by original sin, the knowledge of "good and evil," was knowledge of sex taboos, which was apparently deemed the prototype of knowledge of prohibition generally (Genesis 2:25; 3:7, 10, 11, 22).

[51]On this see Ryu and Silving, *supra* note 8, at 424-425, 427-429.

[52]VII, lib. III, titulo 8°, quoted in QUINTANO RIPOLLES, COMENTARIOS AL CÓDIGO PENAL (1946), vol. I, at 64: *"Otrosi decimos, que si algun home que fuese loco o desmemoriado, matase a otro, que no cae por ende en pena alguna, porque no sabe ni entiende el yerro que face."*

[53]Bellingham's case (1812), COLLINSON, LUNACY, vol. I, 673 n., cited in RUSSELL, *supra* note 48, at p. 50.

[54]Lord Chief Justice Tindal's charge to the jury in the *M'Naghten case, supra,* quoted in Russell, *supra,* at 115-116.

law."[55] The answer to the fourth question states that if "a person, under an insane delusion as to existing facts, commits an offence in consequence thereof . . . he must be considered in the same situation as to responsibility as if the facts with respect to which the delusion exists were real." This is precisely the rule obtaining in the law of error of fact.[56] The duality of "error of fact" and "error of law" is considered in the crucial knowledge test, contained in the answer to the second and third question, which deals with knowledge of the nature and quality of the act (knowledge of fact) and knowledge of wrong (knowledge of law). The phrase "nature and quality of the act" is likewise derived from the law of error, namely, the Roman-canon law notion that, to be relevant, an error cannot be simply an *error qualitatis* but must affect the "nature" of the thing, its "substance"; it must be an error as to its *materia* and *qualitas*.[57]

One might argue, of course, that the crucial *M'Naghten* rule appears to test rationality rather than error, the relevant passage reading: "labouring under such a defect of reason, from disease of the mind, as not to know. . . ." But remarkably little concern has been shown throughout the century about the *M'Naghten* stress on disease of the mind or defect of reason.[58] What matters in *M'Naghten*, as in the Bible, is lack of knowledge and not insanity, which in the Bible—far from constituting an excuse—was believed to be a source of divine inspiration.[59]

There is one feature of the right-wrong rule which does not appear in the other *M'Naghten* answers and which deserves special consideration: the phrase that the defendant, to be

[55]On this see Ryu and Silving, *supra* note 8, at pp. 455-456. A person who knows the legal provision but disagrees with it will not be excused.

[56]As stated by Perkins, in PERKINS ON CRIMINAL LAW (1957), 826, an error of fact will excuse only if it is "of such a nature that the conduct would have been lawful had the facts been as they were mistakenly supposed to be."

[57]Digest 18. 1. 9. 2; *ibid.* 18. 1. 14.

[58]See on this MORRIS, *The Defences of Insanity in Australia,* in Mueller, ed., ESSAYS IN CRIMINAL SCIENCE, *op. cit., supra* note 5, 273 at 278.

[59]For citations see Silving, *Psychoanalysis and the Criminal Law* (1960), 51 JOURNAL OF CRIMINAL LAW, CRIMINOLOGY AND POLICE SCIENCE. Notice also Saul's change from prophetic inspiration (I Samuel 10:6, 10-12) to mental disease (I Samuel 16:14, 15-23; 18:10-12).

exempt, must not have known that he was doing what was "wrong." In contrast to this formulation, the answer to the first question states that the defendant acting under a delusion is responsible if he knew that he was acting "contrary to law," meaning thereby "the law of the land." The meaning of the term "wrong" in the right-wrong test has been a most controversial subject, and it would seem that its use, in contrast to the immediately preceding use of the term "contrary to the law of the land," suggests that the purported meaning is moral rather than legal wrong. Yet in England, as well as in many other jurisdictions, including Puerto Rico, it has been held that wrong means contrary to the law of the land.[60] Much has been said about this subject, but the law of error alone can afford the proper solution as intended by the *M'Naghten* judges. In the situation obtaining in the first answer the defendant has admitted that he knew the law of the land; with this the issue of error of law is foreclosed. In the situation obtaining in the right-wrong answer, the defendant puts his error of law in issue. But how can he do that? The judges' obvious answer is that "the law is administered upon the principle that every one must be taken conclusively to know it, without proof that he does know it." Yet the judges seem to be in a dilemma, there apparently being some relevance in the defendant's contention that he did not know that what he was doing was wrong. One might hence expect that such wrong in the judges' view must be either, not the wrongfulness of the particular act, but a general abstract wrong or a moral wrong. But the first alternative was specifically rejected by the judges, who insisted that the knowledge in issue must be "the party's knowledge of right and wrong in respect to the very act with which he is charged." In regard to the second alternative, England, the country closest to the rule, interprets wrong as legal and not a moral wrong.

The judges' answer seems to suggest that the decisive concept is an intermediate one. They apparently encountered the basic difficulty facing all those who insist on legal knowledge as a

---

[60]On the state of the rule in England see Morris, *supra* note 58 at pp. 284-285; in Puerto Rico see Pueblo v. Alsina, 79 D.P.R. 46, at 66-68 (1956).

condition of responsibility: Can laymen be expected to know the law of the land? And they seem to have solved this problem in exactly the same manner it was solved by modern advocates of the defense of *error iuris*. To be responsible, a layman cannot be expected to know the words of the law or the pertinent legal rule itself; but he must have made an "evaluation in the lay sphere, parallel" to the evaluation expressed in the law.[61] He need not have actual knowledge of the law of the land, but he must know "that the act was one which he ought not to do," and the norm contained in his understanding of that which he ought not to do must correspond to that expressed in the legal prohibition.[62] There must be a parallelism, not an identity, between that which the law prohibits and that which in the actor's view is a legal wrong. The actor's knowledge must be a knowledge of law, but not a technical knowledge of the precise wording or meaning of the legal rule. It is rather a knowledge of the norm expressed in the legal prohibition. For example, concerning the law of homicide, he must know that killing is a crime. The question remains of how this interpretation can be reconciled with the conclusive presumption of legal knowledge expressly mentioned by the judges. That presumption apparently applies only to knowledge of the law of the land, but not to knowledge of the norm expressed in law. Only if the actor knows, in his lay fashion, that what he is doing is legally wrong, and not otherwise, is he conclusively presumed to know the full scope of the law of the land. Except as thus interpreted, the words of the *M'Naghten* opinion seem to make no sense.

Thus, all the *M'Naghten* answers are ultimately reducible to rules on "error."[63] Their rationale is derived from the law of error. In no event do these rules attempt to define insanity or to set forth an exemption deriving its justification from an immunizing quality of insanity. They do not aim at exempting the

---

[61]On this see Ryu and Silving, *supra* note 8, at p. 463.

[62]The actor must have a layman's understanding of the law—an understanding that reflects the essence of the legal prohibition without amounting to the technical comprehension expected of lawyers.

[63]The history and justifications of the law of legal error are discussed in Ryu and Silving, *supra* note 8, at 423-439.

mentally ill, but purport to exempt a defendant engaged in error, whether of law or fact. In the *M'Naghten* era apparently the law was in a stage of transition regarding both the defense of legal error and the place of mental disease in criminal responsibility. Thus these two puzzling legal notions came to be confused in one answer that has since confused generations of lawyers.

In evaluating the *M'Naghten* right-wrong rule, we must keep in mind that historically it is a rule closely connected with the defense of error of law and of fact. It is part of a comprehensive system of law based upon a philosophy that conceives of punishment as a sanction imposed upon disobedience to law, contempt of the law or of the authority which issues it. Disobedience, of course, is predicated upon knowledge of the prohibition. In a sense, this rule is a corollary of the legality principle which makes it a condition of punishment that the law upon the violation of which it is imposed be knowable to the offender. The latter principle is a postulate focussing on the objective quality of the law's being knowable in advance of the offense, whereas the mental capacity rule focusses on the subjective factor of personal capacity to know or actual knowledge of the pertinent law. Accessibility of law is stressed in the Bible.[64]

M'Naghten's root in the law of error affords a clue to its persistent appeal to lawyers. Rejection of the defense of legal error is a solution based on convenience, not on requirements of justice. One of the several instances in which a tendency to revert to the ancient defense of error is noticeable is the defense of insanity.

The challenges of the *M'Naghten* right-wrong test may be divided into several conceptual phases: (a) the phase concerned with the propriety of the moral discernment test; (b) the phase in which doubt was cast on irrationality being a proof of mental illness; and (c) the phase in which the contention was advanced that the mental incapacity definition should not be couched in terms of any particular symptom.

In the first phase much criticism was based on the alleged

---

[64]Deuteronomy 30:11-14.

inability of psychiatrists to testify regarding moral values. Zilboorg particularly, but others as well, have asserted that psychiatrists cannot honestly testify to an accused's knowledge of right and wrong, since the latter concepts present no scientifically cognizable categories.[65] This criticism is based on a methodological fallacy. There is an essential difference between approving of or accepting social or legal postulates as valid or as values in a normative sense, that is, recognizing their obligatory force, and admitting their existence as contents of thought or of the conscience of the community. The latter existence *is* a scientifically provable reality. The sciences which deal with this reality are anthropology, sociology and social psychology. Dynamic psychology, of which Zilboorg purports to be a spokesman, itself describes man's "modifying his wishful thinking to conform to the realities of existence," a change "from thinking on the basis of the *pleasure principle* to thinking on the basis of the *reality principle*,"[66] as a phenomenon of normal human development. As he grows, the infant learns to sacrifice or postpone gratification in order to earn parental love; the mature person must do so to earn social approval or at least to incur no social disapproval, of which the community censure expressed in legal punishment is but a particular form. An average conscience, a normal superego, is essential to mental health.[67] Perhaps the

---

[65]"The psychiatrist [in court] is asked whether a given person knew the difference between right and wrong; this is not a psychiatric question." ZILBOORG, THE PSYCHOLOGY OF THE CRIMINAL ACT AND PUNISHMENT (Isaac Ray Award Book, 1954), 112. See also ROCHE, *supra* note 4, at 107.

[66]MENNINGER, THE HUMAN MIND (3d ed. 1955), 323.

[67]Said Zilboorg, the foremost critic of the law's alleged demand that psychiatrists recognize the reality of social "right and wrong":

"It so happens that psychoanalysts consider criminals anti-social people, and also psychologically sick people. We do not consider *criminality* but the *criminal*, and while we call his criminal acts anti-social we do not consider them psychopathological because they are anti-social, but because psychologically they are not normal regardless of whether the acts are anti-social or not. When a man rapes and kills a woman, or when a woman kills her child, we consider them psychologically abnormal not because the law calls them criminals, but because the capacity to love in such individuals is perverted: it is associated with death instead of life; it is not genital but anal-sadistic, primitive, archaic, infantile." Zilboorg, *Social Responsibility*, in Eissler, ed., SEARCHLIGHTS ON DELIN-

psychiatrists' complaints over testifying on a matter alien to their science when answering the question of whether the accused knew that he was doing what was wrong could be avoided if the term "knew" were replaced by "believed."

As the alleged metaphysics of the right-wrong notion, so has also the "transcendental meaning" of the "nature and the quality of the act" been subjected to vigorous criticism.[68] This criticism is entirely unwarranted in the light of the historical meaning of the phrase "nature and quality." As shown above, in the Roman-canon law, which profoundly influenced the development of English criminal law, that phrase denotes those qualities of the act which constitute its very nature, that is, those of its attributes which give it its distinctive relevance in the given context. Translated into contemporary language, "nature and quality" means that quality which corresponds to the legal or statutory description of the crime charged, or putting it differently, that quality which makes the act criminal.

In the second phase of the critique of M'Naghten the attack focussed on its taking rationality to be a test of capacity when dynamic psychology had shown that unconscious, irrational motivations influence actions of all normal individuals. Of course, there is a difference between an irrational conduct of an

---

QUENCY (1949), 329, at 335). Since the social aspects of rape and child-killing are apparently irrelevant to this psychiatrist, one might expect him to answer the obvious question of how he reaches the conclusion that it is undesirable to have a sexuality that is "not genital but anal-sadistic, primitive, archaic, infantile." Is this undesirability evinced in science? In THE PSYCHOLOGY OF THE CRIMINAL ACT AND PUNISHMENT, supra note 65, at 122, Zilboorg concedes that the demands of psychiatrists that their views be admitted into open court are, "be it underscored again and again, . . . of a moral nature." In Social Responsibility, ibid., Zilboorg also admits (at 337) that psychoanalysis "is based primarily on humanistic individualism," which is a moral position. One might then wonder why the same author rejects the imputation that psychoanalysis should help to fight such obviously anti-individualistic political movements as fascism on the ground that this would imply abandonment of the "scientific" stand. Confusion of the scientific and the therapeutic functions of the psychiatrist is often combined with a lack of appreciation of the distinctiveness of the social responsibility of the psychiatric profession. For a rational approach to the problem of values in psychiatry see HARTMANN, PSYCHOANALYSIS AND MORAL VALUES (1960).

[68]ZILBOORG, supra note 65, at 3-26.

otherwise normal person and such conduct of a mentally ill person. Perhaps the difference may be found to lie in the amenability of the former to be persuaded by rational reasoning that his own conduct was irrational or, generally, to be rationally motivated. But acting upon irrational beliefs—even failure to be persuaded by rational arguments—alone cannot be taken as a test of mental incapacity, for this would place all those holding peculiar religious beliefs within the category of the mentally incapacitated.

The third phase of the challenge of *M'Naghten* is marked by its critique in the *Durham* case. There Judge Bazelon said: "The fundamental objection to the right-wrong test . . . is not that criminal irresponsibility is made to rest upon an inadequate, invalid or indeterminable symptom or manifestation, but that it is made to rest upon *any* particular symptom. In attempting to define insanity in terms of a symptom, the courts have assumed an impossible role, not merely one for which they have no special competence."[69]

Of course, psychiatrists judge whether a person is mentally ill or in need of treatment on the basis of observable symptoms, whether these be physical or behavioral. How else can we reach other men's minds?[70] In fact, in the light of contemporary critical philosophy, reality consists only in symptoms, in the sense of the observable and meaningfully expressible by language; use of language that seems to suggest reference to a reality behind symptoms is only an abbreviated manner of connecting a plurality or selectivity of symptoms for purposes of convenience. Descriptions of so-called psychological realities are always denotations of symptom groups. Etiological explanations are likewise expressions of symptoms of etiology. To be meaningful, any psychological concept must be reducible to symptoms. Indeed, symptoms are not representatives of something; they are the thing itself. The mind, the conscious, the unconscious and so

---

[69]Durham v. United States, *supra* note 20, at 872.

[70]Of course, one might well doubt that we can ever know other men's minds, but if we can do so, there is no doubt that the vehicle of such cognition is symptomatic behavior. See WISDOM, OTHER MINDS (1952).

on are constructs ultimately expressive of groups of symptoms,[71] just as the object of modern physics is a construct built from data (symptoms) obtained from different physical points of observation. None of these concepts represents a separate ontological entity.

However, Judge Bazelon's rejection of symptoms seems to refer to a specific "symptomatology." It reflects psychoanalytical stress on etiological factors rather than on symptoms in terms of presently observable deviations of behavior or failures of functioning. To explain why this essentially correct psychoanalytical position cannot be incorporated in law adequately, it is necessary to explain the difference between psychoanalytical and conventional symbolism.

When a psychoanalytical patient communicates with his psychiatrist, the contents of his speech assume a meaning which does not correspond to the conventional social understanding of terms such as are used. The words are set within a new frame of reference established by analytical science and relating present experience to one long past. Identity or disparity of meaning is not the same in conventional symbolism and in analytical symbolism. What has been said of words is also true of other personality expressions. The total behavior complex of the patient means something different in psychoanalysis from what it means in general social life. Also, the relevance and significance of behavior are judged by its relation to past experience, its etiology, rather than by its present social import. Mental illness as a pattern of behavior is thus evaluated in terms of etiology rather than in terms of a present significance. For example, failure to distinguish right from wrong, in the light of psychoanalytical interpretation, may have several meanings, depending on the etiology of such failure, while it has a constant meaning in other social contexts.

---

[71]Freud "discovered" the unconscious by listening to what patients said and by observing what they did. All these statements and conduct patterns were to him symptoms of the unconscious. In realistic terms, these "symptoms" *are* the unconscious, for certainly no one has experienced it directly. When the "unconscious" becomes conscious, the now conscious is again a "symptom" of the formerly unconscious.

But there is a significant difference between the social import of this psychoanalytical insight in psychiatry and in law. Psychiatry does not require a final discrete definition of those mental phenomena which are to be relevant for its purpose. It may proceed tentatively and experimentally. But the law must operate on the basis of discrete definitions that might serve as standards of final determinations. Psychoanalysis does not provide the law with workable tools of such determinations. It can supply only a very broad definitional frame for the mental incapacity test, as, for example, ego impairment. Resort to symptoms is thus imperative, though the symptoms need not consist of such narrow and inflexible features of specific faculty failure as the M'Naghten knowledge defect.

Inability to testify in terms of symptoms has been also a favorite argument of psychiatrists opposed to the M'Naghten test. They indeed assert that their diagnoses are made longitudinally,[72] and that how they are reached cannot be verbalized wholly.[73] I assume that those methods that cannot be verbalized are intuitive. This means that such diagnoses are referable to symptoms in the mind of the psychiatrist that cannot in turn be related or unequivocally related to symptoms exhibited by the subject of observation. What these psychiatrists, then, assert is that they ought to be permitted to testify not to their opinions supported by rational evidence but to their own intuitive reactions to unspecifiable experiences. It is submitted that if the law is to accept the psychiatrists' intuitive judgments of mental incapacity as bases of exemption, much more would have to be done than reformulating the incapacity test, as has been done in the Durham case. Intuitive judgment, charismatic dispensation of justice, has been alleged in civil law countries to be a peculiar function of the lay jury. Where the limits of reason are crossed, a juror is expected to feel what the true facts are. Because feeling is the source of their ultimate judgment, jurors are not expected to state any reasons for their findings. But to permit a

[72]OVERHOLSER, THE PSYCHIATRIST AND THE LAW (Isaac Ray Award Book 1953), at 25.

[73]Whitehorn, Report to the Governor's Commission on Legal Psychiatry, Maryland, quoted in MACDONALD, PSYCHIATRY AND THE CRIMINAL (1958), at 65.

witness—the expert is in the last analysis one—to testify to his feelings, as contrasted with his rational observations and opinions, would constitute such departure from established rules of proof of the common law as to call perhaps for a constitutional amendment. Whatever the shortcomings of *M'Naghten*, its inadequacy does not lie in forcing psychiatrists to state the bases of their opinions.

The most significant criticism of *M'Naghten* is addressed to the narrowness of the test. The latter does not exempt all those who, in the light of sound policy, merit exemption. In trying to fit *M'Naghten* into a broader exemption policy, the adherents of the test claim that it stands for more than it verbally expresses. Invoking the unitary conception of the human personality, prevailing in modern psychology, Jerome Hall, for instance, alleges that since such a conception implies a necessary affecting of reasoning by mental illness, an impairment of reasoning may be taken as a test of such illness.[74] The opponents of *M'Naghten* rejoin that "the various functions of mentation are disparately affected in various diseases and different individuals,"[75] so that it is possible for a person suffering from a serious disease not or not yet to show any signs of defective reasoning or knowledge capacity. There are states of mind which, in the light of sound policy, ought to be included in the exemption, but in which there is a marked failure in feeling or volition though no apparent cognitive failure. The M'Naghtenites, in turn, advance the proposition that knowledge means more than mere knowledge or verbal knowledge. According to them, it means profound or sound knowledge, the knowledge of a rational individual, in which feeling and volition participate.[76] This is sheer semantics. The opponents might as well accept the challenge and merely ask that the meaning of knowledge as interpreted by the modern M'Naghtenites be verbalized or specified in the statutory or other legal definition of the in-

---

[74]Hall, *supra* note 11, at 774–775.

[75]GUTTMACHER, *Principal Difficulties with the Present Criteria of Responsibility and Possible Alternatives*, Appendix B, §4.01, MODEL PENAL CODE, Tent. Draft No. 4 (1956), 170, at 175.

[76]Hall, *supra* note 11, at 780, 784.

capacity test. For this would obviously require introduction into the test of both volition and feeling.

However, the defect of the knowledge test is not only that it is too narrow but also that it is at times too wide, from the standpoint of sound policy. Not only is a failure of cognition not the sole test of mental incapacity, but flagrant, absurd cognitive failures do not necessarily point to such incapacity.[77] Some other or additional test is thus essential. The adherents of *M'Naghten* might say that such additional test is afforded by use of the term "disease of the mind." But since the meaning of this term is by no means fixed, it can hardly supply the needed interpretative aid in important borderline cases.

2. Irresistible Impulse

The *M'Naghten* test has been supplemented in many jurisdictions by the so-called irresistible impulse test, which exempts from punishment those who, while aware of the wrongfulness of their conduct, acted under an impulse which they were unable to resist. Criticism of the test has focussed on the term "impulse." It has been said that there are situations of grave mental illness, such as melancholia, characterized by brooding and meditation, where the ultimate criminal act is by no means spontaneous but was prepared and premeditated.[78] To meet this criticism, some tests modify the irresistible impulse test to read "inability to conform one's conduct to the appreciation of criminality." But the inadequacy of the irresistible impulse test lies not only in the use of the term "impulse" but also in the concept of the irresistible. When is a person unable to resist an urge of a temptation? Critics have called attention to the fact that many of those allegedly unable to resist do resist temptation when a "policeman is at the elbow."[79] Although the fact that

[77]CLECKLEY, THE MASK OF SANITY (3d ed. 1955), at 21–22, points out that "one finds throughout the nation, and probably over the world, a horde of citizens who stoutly maintain beliefs regarded as absurd and contrary to fact by society as a whole. Often these people indulge in conduct that to others seems unquestionably irrational." Some of their practices are "no less fanciful than the delusions of patients confined in psychiatric hospitals."

[78]See ROYAL COMM. REPORT, *supra* note 9, at 110.

[79]MODEL PENAL CODE, Tent. Draft No. 4, comments of §4.01, at 158. See also Davidson, *supra* note 36.

such persons can restrain themselves under such, but not under other, circumstances does not indicate that they ought to be held responsible, it does indicate that incapacity to resist cannot serve as the proper standard of exemption or, at least, that it cannot serve as such standard without inclusion of additional circumstances. Thus, we are again referred to the question of what the decisive circumstances are for purposes of the exemption.

3. The Model Penal Code Tests

The American Law Institute's Model Penal Code submits in a tentative draft one principal test and two alternative tests.[80] The principal test provides that a person is not responsible for criminal conduct if at the time of such conduct "as a result of mental disease or defect he lacks substantial capacity either to appreciate the criminality of his conduct or to conform his conduct to the requirements of law." In alternative (a) the capacity part is formulated differently: "his capacity either to appreciate the criminality of his conduct or to conform his conduct to the requirements of law is so substantially impaired that he cannot justly be held responsible." In alternative (b) that part reads: "he lacks substantial capacity to appreciate the criminality of his conduct or is in such state that the prospect of conviction and punishment cannot constitute a significant restraining influence upon him." Paragraph (2) reads uniformly: "The terms 'mental disease or defect' do not include an abnormality manifested only by repeated criminal or otherwise anti-social conduct."

Some features are common to all these tests: (a) Each comprises two items—description of a disability and indication of the source of disability; (b) in each test one disability variant is cognitive; this disability is uniformly described as lack of "capacity to appreciate the criminality of his [the actor's] conduct"; (c) the disability in each test is related to the specific act charged; (d) the source of disability is described in all tests as "mental

---

[80]Tent. Draft No. 4 (1955), §4.01, at 27. The Proposed Official Draft (1962) adopted the principal test.

disease or defect"; (e) in each test the disability must be "a result of mental disease or defect"; (f) the term "substantial" recurs in all versions. I shall deal first with the common features and then discuss those aspects in which the tests vary from each other.

In *State v. Jones*,[81] Judge Ladd criticized the first *M'Naghten* answer by pointing out the inconsistency of denying an exemption to an actor if he "knew . . . that he was acting contrary to law, by which is meant the law of the land," while proceeding on the assumption that "[t]he law is administered upon the principle that *every one* must be taken conclusively to know the law of the land, without proof that he does know it." Judge Ladd was concerned with the problem of how the required knowledge of law was to be proven when such proof was barred by the conclusive presumption. The Model Code test, to be sure, requires not knowledge but capacity to appreciate, which is a distinct improvement. Still, one manner—perhaps the best— of proving defendant's capacity to appreciate the criminality of his conduct is proving that he did appreciate it. If the test is adopted, we will continue to witness the strange spectacle of evidence being adduced that a person alleging that he was mentally diseased or defective knew that what he was doing was a crime, when such knowledge is not required of a mentally healthy person.

Indeed, the strongest argument against use of any test requiring legal knowledge or capacity to know criminality is contained in this policy question: If knowledge of criminality is not a general requisite of responsibility, why should its absence or a lack of capacity to acquire it constitute an exemption ground? Surely, no serious contention is being advanced that the conclusive presumption of legal knowledge is based on a realistic belief that mentally healthy persons actually know the law or, indeed, appreciate it. A similar question is posed by the use of the term "appreciation" rather than "knowledge." Apparently, appreciation, as distinguished from knowledge, is intended to convey the notion of healthy knowledge, knowledge with attend-

---

[81] 50 N.H. 369, at 386 (1871).

ant feeling or meaningful knowledge, which some M'Naghtenites have read into the term *knowledge*. But why should capacity of such profound knowledge be required of the person whose mental incapacity is alleged when no profound knowledge is necessary in the case of a mentally healthy person?

Both capacity to appreciate and capacity to conform (or in alternative (*b*) deterrability by the prospect of punishment) are related to the specific crime that has been charged. Such relation is meaningful in *M'Naghten,* since relevant error of law is error regarding the specific prohibition which has been violated. But what meaning does this specificity have in the Model Code? As shown, knowledge is not in issue. Hence, capacity to know could be significant only as bearing on the nature or degree of the mental disease or defect. Assuming, then, that the crucial factor is mental disease or defect and that incapacity is but its symptom or a modifying factor, it is pertinent to inquire whether such incapacity actually has any bearing on the mental state of the actor. The answer is that this depends on the type of prohibition that happens to be in issue. If a person does not appreciate the criminality of killing a perfectly innocent neighbor,[82] such lack of appreciation has a clear bearing on his mental capacity within the mores of our society. But if the accused does not know that killing six hundred persons in order to save the lives of thousands is a crime, the German Bundesgerichtshof held that such error may be excusable, since the prohibition of killing under such circumstances is by no means evident to most people and, indeed, constitutes a highly controversial ethical and legal issue.[83] A person who either

---

[82]See Pueblo v. Alsina, 79 D.P.R. 46 (1956). Alsina's killing of a neighbor, Aida Acosta, was completely unexpected. About a month before the act he purchased a revolver, and about two weeks before killing Aida he is supposed to have said that she was interfering with his matrimonial matters (*ibid.* at 49). The Court noticed that there was no evidence whatever of such interference on Aida's part. After diagnosing the accused's condition as "schizophrenia of the paranoid type," the psychiatric expert, Dr. Fernandez Marina, stated (at 51): "Such person, for instance, when asked whether it is bad to kill, says that it is bad to kill, but when asked whether it is bad to kill in self-defense, says that it is not bad, for he believes himself to be persecuted and thinks that when he kills the persons concerned he does so in self-defense and thus believes that it is not bad to kill at that moment."

[83]Decision rendered Nov. 28, 1952 (IV Strafsenat), reported [1953] NEUE

does not or cannot appreciate the criminality of such killing or cannot conform to such prohibition need not be mentally ill. There are many provisions in the Penal Code of Puerto Rico as well as in other codes which I cannot appreciate.

While the requirement of "capacity to appreciate and to conform" (or to be motivated by the prospect of punishment) undoubtedly limits the class of those suffering from a mental disease or defect, use of the phrase "as a result of" rather suggests that the incapacity clause does not describe or define mental disease or defect for legal purposes, so that the latter is a subject of independent proof. Thus, we are referred back to the term "mental disease" that has been so vigorously criticized as vague and uncertain by opponents of the *Durham* test. In the Model Code psychopaths are specifically excluded from the exemption.[84] But what about neurotics? Are persons suffering from kleptomania or pyromania or the types of persons described in Alexander and Healy's ROOTS OF CRIME[85] mentally diseased persons? The Model Code does not answer these questions, since it does not, even to the extent that this is done in *Durham*,[86] define mental disease.

The phrase "as a result of" is but an equivalent of "product,"[87] so that the criticism of the product notion of *Durham*, to be dis-

---

JURISTISCHE WOCHENSCHRIFT 513. For discussion see Silving, *Euthanasia: A Study in Comparative Criminal Law* (1954), 103 UNIVERSITY OF PENNSYLVANIA LAW REVIEW 350, at 356–359.

[84]See par. (2) of §4.01, *supra* text at note 80.

[85]ALEXANDER and HEALY, ROOTS OF CRIME (1935).

[86]In the Durham case, *supra* note 20, at 875, "disease" is defined as "a condition which is considered capable of either improving or deteriorating," whereas "defect" is said to be "a condition which is not considered capable of either improving or deteriorating. . . ."

[87]The dictionary meaning of "to result" is "to proceed, spring, or arise, as a consequence, effect. . . ." WEBSTER'S NEW INTERNATIONAL DICTIONARY (2d ed. 1953). After criticizing the Durham "product" notion, the draftsmen of the Model Code state: "While we agree . . . that mental disease or defect involves gradations of degree that should be recognized, we think the legal standard ought to focus on the *consequences* of disease or defect that have a bearing on the justice of conviction and of punishment" (comments to §4.01, at 159–160). The dictionary meaning of "consequence" is "1. That which follows something on which it depends; that which is produced by a cause or ensues from any form of necessary connection; . . . 3. *a*. Chain of causes and effects; . . . *b*. Act of following something else as a result; relation of an effect to its cause."

cussed when analyzing that case, is partially applicable to the phrase "as a result of" in the Model Code tests. True, there is a difference between the functions performed by the causation concept in *Durham* and in the Model Code tests. In *Durham* the disease is supposed to cause the commission of crime,[88] whereas in the Model Code it must cause the incapacity to appreciate or to conform. The latter statement might be taken to mean that the incapacity is an expression or a symptom of the disease, and in this sense is less objectionable than the statement that the disease produces criminal conduct. But the question remains whether it is possible to say that the defendant "would have been capable of conforming had he not suffered from the disease,"[89] which is implied in choice of the term "as a result of." Nor is this a "logician's nicety,"[90] but a matter involving the very usefulness of a test which affords no standard that is applicable in practice, the issue it raises not being answerable.

Since the Model Code definitions do not seem to render independent proof of mental disease dispensable and since "result of" plainly means "product of," it is submitted that the draftsmen's purposes might be better served if the phrase "as a result of" were replaced by the copula "and." But if this is done, it would become even more obvious that something is required as a test of responsibility where mental capacity is in issue that is not required in cases in which the issue does not arise.

There is no general objection to using the term "substantial" in law. It is often impossible to avoid the term, and while "substantial" does not make the meaning of a sentence quite determinate, it may make it less indeterminate than it would otherwise be. But the extent to which it adds to the determinateness of a sentence depends on the total framework within which it is used. "Substantial," of course, implies that the subject which it qualifies is graded and indicates a relative degree, as compared with some standard. But the Model Code does not mention any

---

[88]On this particularly Carter v. United States, 252 F.2d 608 (D.C. Cir., reh. den., 1957), at 615-617.

[89]*Ibid.*

[90]*Ibid.* For the pertinent passages see *infra* text at note 154.

standard of comparison. We learn from the comments[91] that "substantial incapacity" means that the incapacity need not be complete, as required in *M'Naghten*. The Code's draftsmen admit that there is in the reality of life no such thing as a complete impairment. While realizing the precariousness of the term "substantial" impairment when no principle is suggested "that measures how substantial it must be," they eventually dismiss the problem saying, "if capacity is greatly impaired, that presumably should be sufficient."[92] But the standard does not appear to be sufficient to the Reporter and a Council minority who suggest that it is necessary to state how substantial the impairment must be. With this, our attention is directed to alternative solutions suggested by Council minorities. Alternative (*a*) merely submits a less deceptive version, for it recommends no greater specificity but rather refers determination of the degree of incapacity that is necessary in order to exempt a defendant to the jury, which presumably is to decide on a case-to-case basis. This is implied in the version, "was so substantially impaired that he can not justly be held responsible," advocated by the Reporter. Other Council members rejoin that "it is unwise to present questions of justice to the jury."[93] The degree of jury discretion can be reduced by indication of the policy of the exemption, for in such event the impairment must be judged as "incapacity" with regard to the factor that is relevant in the light of such policy. Alternative (*b*) expresses such policy in the incapacity definition, "is in such state that the prospect of conviction and punishment cannot constitute a significant restraining influence." This phrase is more determinate than the phrase "lacks substantial capacity to conform." Without indication of a standard of comparison or of the policy of the test, lack of "capacity to conform . . . to the requirements of law" remains vague and uncertain, notwithstanding addition of the qualification "substantial." Nor could this test be much improved were the actual standard of comparison, "complete incapacity,"

---

[91]Comments to § 4.01, Tent. Draft No. 4, at 158.

[92]*Ibid.* at 159.

[93]*Ibid.*

expressly incorporated in its wording. For since, admittedly, there is no such group as the totally incapacitated, it is virtually impossible to determine what constitutes a substantially greater impairment than that assumed to be present in such group. The capacity of average community members might afford a more realistic standard of comparison.

The concept of lack of "capacity to conform . . . to the requirements of law," which appears both in the principal test and in alternative (a), is most precarious. In discussing the German test, I shall deal at greater length with the objections raised against use of this concept. But to the extent that its shortcomings are evident from a critical reading of the Model Code and its comments, it is proper to indicate them in the present context. The Code commentators tell us that when using the phrase, "lacks substantial capacity to conform," they actually mean to convey the standard suggested by alternative (b). They inform us that "the question that is most precisely relevant for legal purposes" is "non-deterrability" and that the latter "is the determination that is sought," but that its assessment, meaning, an estimate of the subject's responsiveness to "a single influence, the threat of punishment," is "too difficult for psychiatric judgment," and that, for this reason, "non-deterrability . . . must be reached by probing general capacity to conform to the requirements of law."[94] In other words, incapacity to conform to the requirements of law is but a substitute for nonsusceptibility to being influenced by the threat of punishment imposed by law upon violation of the prohibition. Is it then the draftsmen's contention that incapacity to conform to a given law can be psychiatrically proven whereas nonresponsiveness to the threat which this law imposes cannot be proven? It would seem that the line between such incapacity to conform to a specific, given law and nonresponsiveness to the threat which it imposes is rather tenuous. Indeed, it would seem that whether a person is capable of conforming is less answerable than whether he can be motivated by a threat. This, of course, should not be taken to imply approval of the test of alternative (b), for that test is based upon a doctrine of deterrence, so that

---

[94]*Ibid.*

the critique of that doctrine submitted above is applicable to (b).

The main inadequacy of the majority test and alternative (a) lies in the limitation of incapacity to the spheres of knowledge and will. Is it really true that a person who in a state of melancholia kills his children because he believes that he is thus sparing them future suffering lacks either capacity to appreciate the legal prohibition against killing or capacity to conform his conduct to this requirement of law? Such person knows that killing is a crime and has sufficient self-control to resist a temptation to kill. His incapacity lies in a loss of a sense of reality, in a general collapse of total personality organization rather than in a specific failure of either knowledge or will power.

A significant objection addressed to all the versions is that their policy, as expressly stated in alternative (b) and as admittedly followed in the other versions, is not consistent. If this policy is to exempt persons who cannot be affected by punitive-correctional methods, that is, those who are not susceptible to deterrence, one might well ask why the Code specifically exempts in paragraph (2) those who are clearly "non-deterrable," namely, psychopaths.

Finally, none of these tests includes in the mental incapacity exemption apparently temporary mental disturbances, such as the disturbance of consciousness in Germany or the temporary mental disturbance in Spain. Persons acting in such mental states merit inclusion, provided that, contrary to the rules obtaining in civil law countries, when acquitted on the ground of mental incapacity, such persons ought to be subject to measures.

4. German Tests

The present German provision on mental incapacity reads thus: "Where the actor, at the time of the act, because of a disturbance of consciousness, because of a pathological disturbance of mental functioning or because of mental debility, is incapable of appreciating the impermissibility of the act or of acting in conformity to this appreciation, the act is not criminal [literally, there is no criminal act]." §51[1], German Penal Code.

Of the numerous tests, whether formerly in force or recommended by reform drafts and projects, I shall directly discuss only four: the one now in force; the tests of the Reform Drafts of 1956 and 1960; and the test recommended by Seelig. Common to the first-mentioned test, the tests of the Reform Drafts and the Model Code tests are: (a) a dualistic approach expressed in the requirement that there be a defined incapacity and a defined source of such incapacity, at least in regard to the principal exemption category; (b) specificity of incapacity, in the sense of its limitation to the specific act that has been committed; (c) division of incapacity into cognitive and conative incapacity. I shall first discuss the policy basis of the incapacity concept, since a uniform policy, reflected in a consistent treatment of the law of error and of that of mental incapacity, is one of the great merits of the German approach. It contrasts favorably with the lack of a consistent philosophy in the Model Code.

A. The Philosophy of the "Incapacity" Concept

The fact that "incapacity to appreciate" and "incapacity to conform" are related to the specific act that has been committed has a different import within the framework of German law from that which the same phenomenon has within the context of the Model Code. The German requirement that mental incapacity be one disabling the actor with regard to the specific act charged and the German stress on incapacity to know the law reflect a consistent policy oriented to an elaborate philosophy of guilt and punishment. The notion of guilt is principally expressed in German law in the rule on "error of law." The defense of such error has been admitted in Germany judicially, on the ground that it is implicit in the requirement of guilt. If an accused did not know the prohibition that he violated, he is excused, unless he acted negligently in not ascertaining the prohibition.[95] Hence there is a rational basis for inquiring whether he did or did not have capacity to know that prohibition or to conform to such knowledge, whereas raising the

---

[95] 2 BGHSt. 194 (1952), a landmark decision rendered by the Great Senate in Criminal Matters of the Supreme Court in Civil and Criminal Matters.

same questions within the Model Code is not consistent with its general adherence to the principle *error juris nocet*. It may be interesting to note that the 1956 and the 1960 drafts of a new German Penal Code attempt to consolidate the law of mental incapacity with the law of error of law by gearing the "incapacity to appreciate" and "to conform to such appreciation" to illegality (*Unrecht*) of the act rather than—as is the case in present German law—to its being not permissible (*das Unerlaubte*),[96] which commonly means prohibited by either law or morality. While "*Unrecht*" is also ambiguous, it is the same term that is used in the drafts' provisions on legal error.[97]

B. So-called "Mixed System"

The approach reflected in the German tests is mixed or, as is usually said, "biologicopsychological," "biological" indicating the source of incapacity and "psychological" denoting the specific state of mind at the time of the act. Reference in legal literature to the source of incapacity as "biological" is based on the view that mental disease originates exclusively in biological factors.[98] But in judicial interpretation the term "biological" is taken to include psychic determinants of mental incapacity, such as a blinding rage.[99] The phrase "mixed biologicopsychological" is interpreted to indicate that there must be a definite basis or source of "incapacity to appreciate or conform," so that the latter alone does not afford an exemption ground. The doctrinal stress that such a source must produce a specific

---

[96]ENTWURF DES ALLGEMEINEN TEILS EINES STRAFGESETZBUCHS 1956 (Bonn 1958) (hereinafter cited as GERMAN DRAFT 1956), comment to § 23, at 30; ENTWURF EINES STRAFGESETZBUCHS (StGB) E 1960, Bundesrat Drucksache 270/60 (hereinafter cited as GERMAN DRAFT 1960), comment to § 24, at 132; the latest Draft [published after the appearance of this essay], E 1962, Bundestag Drucksache IV/650 [see supplements to footnotes where its position deserves notice; cited as German Draft 1962], comment to § 24, at 140.

[97]Compare in the 1956 Draft §§ 23 and 20, in 1960 Draft §§ 24 and 21, and in the 1962 Draft §§ 24 and 21.

[98]Compare Judge Doe's view that mental disease is a physical state, *infra*, 115.

[99]On this see German Draft 1960, comment to § 24, at 129. The 1962 Draft (comment at 139) assumes that the source of incapacity need not be a "disease" but may be a "normal" condition.

incapacity to commit the act charged, while consistent with the dominant philosophy of guilt, is open to criticism on other grounds; it reflects a survival of obsolete psychiatric notions, akin to the persistence of the monomania notion in our law. Both the 1956 and the 1960 drafts explain direction of disease and incapacity to the specific act by the relativity of incapacity to incur guilt.[100] The draftsmen point out that a man may at the time of the act be incapacitated with respect to some acts but not to others.[101] This is, of course, inconsistent with the view of modern psychology that a mental disability affects man's total personality and hence anything he may do. The newer insight is also obscured by the unrealistic specification of the faculties of appreciation and conformity. Relativity of capacity in German law is also inconsistent with formulation of incapacity itself in absolute terms, "is incapable" being the key word. The Model Code's "substantial impairment" of capacity is certainly more in accord with psychological reality.

C. CRITIQUE OF THE INCAPACITY FORMULA

The criterion, "capacity to appreciate and to conform," has been introduced into the law in 1933 by the Law on Dangerous Habitual Criminals,[102] to replace the original version formulated in terms of exclusion of "free determination of the will." The substitution followed the advice of prominent psychiatrists, Aschaffenburg in Germany and Wagner v. Jauregg in Austria.[103] The psychiatrists' objection to the original version was that it unnecessarily involved the issue of free will. But the same objection now appears to be applicable to the substitute.

In 1948 the present version became the target of a vigorous critique by a leading psychiatrist, Dr. Kurt Schneider, who

---

[100]On this ground they reject a purely "biological" test, such as is, e.g., the test of the FRENCH PENAL CODE, art. 64, which defines the exemption ground simply as *démence*. The 1962 Draft similarly requires the incapacity to be directed to the act charged; it assumes that such division of man's mental functioning is possible. Comment, at 140.

[101]GERMAN DRAFT 1960 comment to § 24, at 130.

[102]Law of Nov. 24, 1933 [1933], Reichsgesetzblatt Part I, at 995.

[103]On this see Seelig, *supra* note 11, at 214–216.

asserted that no man can answer the question of whether the accused possessed capacity of appreciation and conformance, adding that when psychiatrists answer such questions they actually rely solely on their finding the so-called biological basis either present or absent.[104] Schneider stated that Section 51 "is based on a psychology of action that is not realistic and cannot be reconciled with contemporary psychological opinion." The jurist Seelig pointed out that this critique does not apply to capacity to appreciate but does apply to capacity to conform. The latter, as formulated by Mezger and others, is reducible to capacity, at the time of the criminal conduct, "to act or not to act." To find whether the actor possessed capacity to conform, the observer must be able to ascertain whether the actor could have acted otherwise than he did act. This may be said to reopen the problem of free will, but, above all, when raised retrospectively, presents a most precarious, if not insoluble, issue. Mezger accordingly suggested that the ultimate problem of capacity to conform must be reduced to the question of "whether the actor can be justly held criminally responsible for his act."[105] This formula, of course, is precisely that advanced by Professor Wechsler. Seelig pointed out that it leaves the judge without any legal criterion, though supplying him with one was undoubtedly the purpose of qualifying the biological portion of the test. One might well inquire whether as thus conceived, the notion of capacity to conform serves any useful purpose.

Actually, the conformity test is but a disguised version of the older concept of "free determination of the will."[106] To demonstrate that it often misses the relevant issue, Seelig uses an example which resembles that presented by the Royal Commission on Capital Punishment in support of its critique of the irresistible impulse test. A schizophrenic teacher, Wagner of

104*Ibid.* at 213-214.

105*Ibid.* at 224-225.

106This, of course, is also a biblical idea. In the Bible, it is forcefully expressed in the Lord's words to Cain (Genesis 4:7): ". . . [S]in lies in wait at the door, and his desire is directed toward you, but you shall rule over him" [author's translation from the Hebrew].

Degerloh, killed his wife and children, whom he believed to suffer from an inheritable disease, set fire to buildings and fired from two pistols at all men in the community, allegedly in order to take revenge on his detractors.[107] Seelig correctly noted that the question of whether Wagner could have acted otherwise is not meaningful.

There is no objection, of course, to a basic free will policy, as reflected in, for example, the error of law defense.[108] But an attempt to integrate that policy in a legal text, such as the statutory test of mental incapacity, must fail, since a test of that type cannot operate functionally, being ultimately reducible to the issue "could the subject have acted otherwise than he did act?"

As will be shown, the source of incapacity in German law is not conceived as narrowly limited to cognitive and voluntaristic categories. But this neither eliminates nor modifies the shortcomings of the incapacity concept itself, although in decisions of law the incapacity test is often disregarded, as it is disregarded by psychiatric experts.

Seelig's submission that the present test of capacity to conform be replaced by a test of capacity to act in accordance with rational motivations deserves attention. It has the great advantage of emphasizing precisely that which a psychiatrist will take into consideration when inquiring into the mental state of a defendant, namely, his motivations,[109] whereas psychiatrists hardly ever examine whether the defendant could have acted otherwise than he acted.

My doubts regarding the usefulness of Seelig's test are mainly based on the observation that there are many queer people who believe and act upon notions that to others may seem absurd, for example, members of all types of quasi-religious sects, and who might therefore qualify for Seelig's exemption, though this is hardly what Seelig intended. "Incapacity to act in accordance with rational motivations" is a significant notion, when it operates within a broader test of mental incapacity, that takes ac-

---

[107]Reported in Seelig, *supra* note 103 at 220–221.

[108]See decision cited *supra* note 95.

[109]Seelig, *supra* note 103, n. 2, at 224.

count of the combined sociological-psychiatric aspect of the mental incapacity exemption, by stressing the impairment of a personality, as compared with the mental state of the average community member.

D. THE SO-CALLED BIOLOGICAL BASIS

The biological source of incapacity in German law is broadly conceived. To be sure, merely atypical personality features, such as excessive suggestibility, sexual dependence, character weakness, afford no basis of exemption.[110] But the exempting quality need not be a pathological one. A "disturbance of consciousness" within the meaning of Section 51 may have its source in normal phenomena, such as drowsiness, exhaustion, a strong emotion, for a considerable reduction or a dimming of consciousness is sufficient. Thus, acts committed in a state of extreme anger or anxiety have been excused.[111] To exempt, drunkenness need not be such as to exclude consciousness; impairment is sufficient, for example, a heavy drowsiness produced by alcohol consumption. Nor does mere capacity to remember the incident or proof of goal-directed conduct exclude the possibility of a disturbance of consciousness at the time of the act.[112] It is believed that the liberal treatment of so-called nonpathological states in German law is commendable, whereas the handling of pathological states is systematically less felicitous. I shall hence discuss the "disturbance of consciousness" and the "pathological states" in separate subdivisions, stressing the decisional aspects of the former.

i. *Disturbance of Consciousness.* The accused, a quiet, warmhearted, good-natured person of conciliatory, peaceful disposition—but for years exposed to the nagging of both his domineering wife and a domineering mother-in-law—in the course of a violent controversy, accompanied by a struggle, cut his

---

[110]MAURACH, DEUTSCHES STRAFRECHT, ALLGEMEINER TEIL (2d ed., 1958), at 341–342.

[111]SCHÖNKE-SCHRÖDER, STRAFGESETZBUCH, KOMMENTAR (7th rev. ed., 1954), at 222-223 (hereinafter cited SCHÖNKE-SCHRÖDER). See also 12th ed., 1965, at 364.

[112]Decision of the Bundesgerichtshof, in GOTDAMMERS ARCHIV FUR STRAFRECHT UND STRAFPROZESS (1955), at 269, cited in MAURACH, *supra* note 110, at 342.

wife's throat with a potato-paring knife accidentally on hand. The Bundegerichtshof held[113] that he had acted in a state of "disturbed consciousness" qualifying him for total exemption, even though he was declared by psychiatric experts to be perfectly normal. The trial court had found that he administered the cuts "'in an excessive affect,' without at the time having regained control of himself." On the basis of expert opinion, it reached the conclusion that "due to the high-grade affect, the accused's capacity of cognition as well as his inhibitive capacity were possibly excluded." But the prosecution contended on appeal that a disturbance of consciousness within Section 51 requires that there be present certain specific circumstances such as sleep, drowsiness, hypnosis, brain damage, fever or poisoning, and that a normal person, in the absence of "other defects in the mental and moral sphere," "even at the peak of excitement . . . remains capable 'to realize his own emotional excitement and motives of action focused on the object'." The Bundesgerichtshof rejected this view, supported by psychiatric literature and expert opinions in the case, relying on other psychiatric authorities and on a prior decision holding that "high-grade affects of anger and anxiety may exclude responsibility." "The loss of self-control," said the court, "may be based on a complete lack of self-consciousness in the sense of the actor's intellectual awareness of his own self and of his relation to the environment. But such loss can be also rooted in a profound disturbance of the emotional life and the drives, hence of the emotional sphere of the human personality." In answer to the prosecution's warning of the danger implicit in admitting exemption in cases such as that at bar where the alleged dimming of consciousness can only be inferred from the accused's self-serving assertion, since neither the victim nor third persons are available as witnesses, the court wisely pointed out that "as the instant case itself confirms and as life experience shows . . . sudden outbursts of affect do not accidentally arise in man, as a lightning coming from a clear sky, but . . . as a rule, such outburst is preceded

---

[113]Decision of Oct. 10, 1957 (IV, Strafsenat), reported in (1958) 11 Neue Juristische Wochenschrift 266.

by a long development and history. The latter are usually accessible to proof by witnesses even after the act."[114] The history of the accused's marriage, the constant tension to which he was exposed, the court said, are provable and have been proved in the case at bar; they abundantly show that at the moment of acting he may well have reached a breaking point.

On similar grounds, the First Senate of the Bundesgerichtshof had held in 1952,[115] where the defendant had killed his brother with a hammer in the presence of two men, in alleged self-defense against an unarmed attack by the brother, that the provision on total exemption may have been applicable. The court below had found that there was present in the case "a sudden acting out of the bitterness which accumulated throughout the years against the degenerate brother," a violent habitual drunkard.

ii. *Pathological States.* As pointed out before, this part of the German provision is not felicitously formulated, although on the whole decisional law has interpreted it in a commendable manner. There are two notions of pathological states, "pathological disturbance of mental functioning" and "mental debility." They will be discussed separately.

"Pathological disturbance of mental functioning." The Reichsgericht gradually enlarged the class of states within this category. Included are undoubtedly all the psychoses, whether inherited or acquired, whether somatogenic—those which are based on organic or physiological phenomena—or psychogenic—those in which, as the commentators of the 1960 draft put it,[116] "the

---

[114]The court was profoundly moved by the fact that after killing his wife, the accused had lifted her body and kissed her, saying; "Do it well, Irmgard." The history of the marriage was indeed pathetic. He was completely dependent on his wife sexually. She constantly threatened to divorce him. Before the crime she had come to his apartment to ask for the family book in order to initiate divorce proceedings. They nevertheless had sexual intercourse. Thereafter she repeated her insistence on divorce, asking for the family book. The struggle that followed began when he tried to prevent her from leaving and it then developed into a violent battle when she wanted to open the window so that neighbors might hear their quarrel.

[115]3 BGHSt. 195 (I. Strafsenat), decided July 1, 1952, g.M., at 198-199.

[116]Comments to § 24 at 130; *cf.* also Draft 1962, at 138.

organic bases . . . , referability to bodily causes, have not yet been clarified." An attempt is made to follow the development of psychiatric knowledge. Thus, the so-called *lucida intervalla,* that is, periods which in manic-depressive psychosis, for example, fall outside the stages of acute illness, and in which pursuant to older doctrine the accused was held responsible, are now believed not to disrupt the continuity of the process of disease; accordingly, in law, prevailing opinion demands exemption.[117] But beyond the psychoses, there is a measure of uncertainty which is reminiscent of our own experience with use of the term "mental disease." The disturbance must be diseased (*krankhaft*), pathological. But neuroses and psychopathies are not a priori excluded. In cases of the latter, characterized by "incapacity of conceiving moral notions," it has been held that an exemption will lie if the incapacity is based either on "a pathological cause or a defect of mental organization."[118] Doctrinally, a distinction is being drawn between instances in which the psychopathy is constitutionally acquired and cases in which it is due to environmental influences. The latter are without any clear reason believed not to fall within the exemption.[119] The same criterion is applied to kleptomanias, pyromanias, etc.[120] In sex offenses, the test of exemption is said to be whether or not the deviation is of pathological origin.[121] "Pathological disturbance of mental functioning" also includes mental defect.

As may be readily seen, the same objections which have been advanced against use of the term "mental disease" in our law are also applicable to the notion of pathological disturbance of mental functioning.

"Mental debility." There is considerable uncertainty regarding the meaning and scope of the final category, that of "mental debility," literally "mental weakness" (*Geistesschwäche*). The legislative purpose in adding this category was "to include, in

---

[117]MAURACH, *supra* note 110, at 344.

[118]RG DR 1939, cited SCHÖNKE-SCHRÖDER, *supra* note 111, p. 223.

[119]MAURACH, *supra* note 110, at 344.

[120]*Ibid.* at 345.

[121]E.g., senility; *ibid.* at 345.

an expression accessible to the layman, borderline cases."[122] The difference between this and the pathological disturbance category is said to be one of degree rather than of kind.[123] Mental debility, as well as pathological disturbance, may consist in a disturbance in the sphere of thought or in "the spheres of the will, feeling or drives."[124] Psychopathy is sometimes labelled "mental debility."

Recent Reform Drafts. The Reform Drafts of 1956 and 1960 commendably attempted to avoid the prevailing uncertainty regarding inclusion or exclusion of psychopaths and neurotics. The 1956 draft included them, the 1960 draft excluded them. The test of the former reads thus:

> Section 23. *Incapacity to Incur Guilt Because of Mental Disturbances*
>
> A person acts without guilt where, at the time of the act, he is incapable, because of mental disturbance, which is pathological or based on congenital or acquired deviation, or because of a temporary [transitory] disturbance of consciousness, to appreciate the illegality of the act or to act in conformity to this appreciation.

The comments to Section 23[125] state that a "disturbance" caused by a "congenital or acquired deviation," as contrasted with a "pathological disturbance," includes "the neuroses, the causes of which may be found in situations of mental conflict; furthermore, disturbances in the drives, above all the psychopathies, which are conceived of as 'personality variants'. . . ." But the deviation from the norm of mental state must be considerable.

The test of the 1960 draft reads thus:

> Section 24. *Incapacity to Incur Guilt Because of Mental Disturbances*
>
> A person acts without guilt where, at the time of the act, he is incapable, because of a pathological mental disturbance, because of an equivalent disturbance of consciousness or because

---

[122]*Ibid.*

[123]KOHLRAUSCH-LANGE, STRAFGESETZBUCH (42d rev. ed. 1959), comment to § 51 VI, at 197.

[124]*Ibid.*

[125]GERMAN DRAFT 1956, at 29.

of mental deficiency, to appreciate the illegality of the act or to act in conformity to this appreciation.

In contrast to the prevailing law and the 1956 draft, that of 1960 formulates the biological basis of incapacity differently in the provision on total exemption and in that on diminished responsibility.[126] The total exemption provision does not apply to neuroses or to psychopathies.[127] The differentiation between psychoses and neuroses and psychopathies proceeds from a distinction between disturbances which affect "the core of personality" and those which have no such impact on personality,[128] a distinction which is hardly clear. The departure from present law is particularly regrettable since the latter has been elaborated in the course of years of judicial interpretation, which undoubtedly reflects a social need for enlargement of the group of those exempted. The draft expressly purports to narrow down the judicial constructions of "disturbance of mental functioning" and "mental debility" contained in leading decisions of the Bundesgerichtshof and the Reichsgericht. According to the former court, "disturbance of mental functioning" "comprises, beyond the circle of mental diseases within the meaning of medical science, all disturbances which impair the conceptions [ideas, perceptions, *Vorstellungen*] and feelings that are present in a normal and mentally mature man making him capable of forming a will, whereby it is irrelevant whether the impairments in issue are those of the reasoning activity or those of the life of the will, of feelings or of the urges."[129] As stated before, the Reichsgericht had held "mental debility" to further extend the scope of the exemption.[130] It may be mentioned parenthetically that the phrase "an equivalent disturbance of consciousness" is most precarious and if adopted can be predicted to become the source of grave problems in practice.[131]

---

[126]GERMAN DRAFT 1960, § 25.

[127]*Ibid.*, comment to § 24, at 130.

[128]*Ibid.*, at 130-131.

[129]B.G.H., reported in 1955 NEUE JURISTISCHE WOCHENSCHRIFT 1726, No. 19, cited in 1960 Draft comment to § 24, at 131.

[130]73 RGSt. 121.

[131]The term "equivalent" mental abnormality is used in the SWEDISH PENAL

Total Exemption Tests: B. The New Hampshire Test, The Durham Rule, The Spanish Test

1. The New Hampshire Test

The New Hampshire cases follow a distinctive policy and a consistent method, as did the *M'Naghten case*. Their reasoning proceeded from the assumption that crime, as well as a contract or a last will, must be the product of intent (or will); when anything that would be otherwise a contract, a will or a crime is produced by something other than intent, the requirements of law are not fulfilled; the otherwise criminal act is not punishable, the contract is void, the testament null. Said Judge Doe in *State* v. *Pike*: "[A] product of mental disease is not a contract, a will, or a crime."[132] This separation of conduct produced by mental disease from conduct produced by intent followed the general doctrine that "if the alleged act of a defendant, was the act of his mental disease, it was not, in law, his act, and he is no more responsible for it than he would be if it had been the act of his involuntary intoxication, or of another person using the defendant's hand against his utmost resistence."[133]

The problem of incapacity exemption arising from this conception was quite simple: One had to establish that which produced the act; if this was not intent, the act was that of an extraneous force alien to the actor and he could not be held responsible for it. The question, "who or what produced the act?" could be answered either "John Doe did it" (John Doe's intent did it) or

---

CODE incapacity test, chap. 5, § 5. It has been preserved in chap. 32, § 2 of the latest Code of 1965 (Transl. Sellin, Ministry of Justice, Stockholm 1965). For summary of the various mental incapacity laws see Heldmann, *Zurechnungsfähigkeit, Zurechnungsunfähigkeit und verminderte Zurechnungsfähigkeit*, in Institut für ausländisches und internationales Strafrecht in Freiburg i. Br., MATERIALIEN ZUR STRAFRECHTSREFORM, RECHTSVERGLEICHENDE ARBEITEN I ALLGEMEINER TEIL (Lang-Hinrichsen ed., Bonn 1954), vol. II, at 345.

The German Draft of 1962 preserved the 1960 test. But the Committee on "Penal Law" of the German House of Representatives substituted for "equivalent" the term "profound." Report of the Committee, Bonn, 1965.

[132]49 N.H. 399, at 438 (1870).

[133]*Ibid.* at 441.

"The mental disease did it." This idea was by no means new in 1870. "Erskine said in *Hadfield's* case, that delusion is the test when it appears to have produced the act, but not when it does not appear to have produced the act."[134] The distinctive feature of the New Hampshire cases was that an attempt was made to reach a more general concept of that which may produce the act to the exclusion of intent, and this concept was found in mental disease. But "mental disease" or "insanity" in the New Hampshire cases, just as "delusion" in *Hadfield,* was conceived of rather as an ontological entity that entered the human being as an extraneous agent and that acted and produced effects independently of him, as though he had no part in this. It was apparently thought that the existence of this entity called insanity or mental disease and the activities and products of that entity were realities that had nothing to do with law: Mental disease and its production of acts were phenomena which only science could observe, find and attest to. Judge Ladd said that they were matters to be determined by the jury, "upon the question whether the act was the offspring of insanity; if it was, a criminal intent did not produce it; if it was not, a criminal intent did produce it, and it was crime."[135]

Judge Doe[136] exalted the achievements of modern science which had overcome the superstitious biblical belief that insanity was "demoniacal possession," disencumbered investigation of the subject of mental disease "of all theological complications," and thus found that "insanity is a disease." But his own notion of mental disease and its causal operations was still deeply ingrained in the demonic conception carried over from the Bible. In the Old Testament, insanity entered and left Saul as an "evil spirit."[137] Christ healed those "possessed with devils" by casting out "the spirits,"[138] sometimes by finding, at their request, a new home for them in swine.[139] Judge Doe emphatically disbelieved

---

[134]State v. Jones, 50 N.H. 369, at 394 (1871).
[135]*Ibid.* at 398-399.
[136]State v. Pike, *supra* note 23 at 436-437.
[137]Compare the citations from I Samuel, *supra* note 59.
[138]Matthew 8:16.
[139]Matthew 8:28-32.

this. But he believed that insanity is a "physical disease or the result of physical disease" that had the power to cause acts independently of the actor, so that such acts were not "his acts," so to speak, not his "possessions" or "emanations" but the "possessions" or "emanations of mental disease."[140] As his notion that mental disease is an entity alien to its bearer, so was Judge Doe's notion of causation ontological. A century after Hume's critique of causation, Judge Doe apparently believed in the pre-Humean idea "that there exists an objective connection between cause and effect, a connection inherent in the things themselves— an inner bond such that the cause somehow brings about the effect. Hence, the cause is conceived of as an agent, a substance emitting force."[141] Professor Kelsen found a corresponding view supporting such notion of causality in "the experience of the operation of the will of man, who considered his ego or his 'soul' (a concept similar to that of force) as the 'cause' of his actions." In Judge Doe's and Judge Ladd's opinions the parallelism of such notion of causality operating by natural forces, on the one hand, and causality emanating from the will or intent of man, on the other hand, is strikingly reflected. In the opinion of the New Hampshire judges, either disease or intent is the moving force that causes the act, each of these forces functioning as an ontological entity endowed with an independent existence, as a substance emitting force.

When mental disease is thus conceived of as an existentially given entity, law is hardly the proper discipline to determine its necessary incidents, attributes or the correct test or tests of

---

[140]A case cited in both State v. Pike, *supra* note 23, at 429, and State v. Jones, *supra* note 134, at 397, decided shortly before these cases, Boardman v. Woodman, 47 N.H. 120, held that a person possessed by a delusion could make a valid will unless the latter was the "offspring of the delusion." Judge Ladd pointed out in the Jones case (at 397-398) that accordingly one might say that a man "who labors under a delusion that his legs are made of glass, or that he is charged with controlling the motions of the planetary system, but is in other respects sane," need not be deemed incapable of making a valid will. But he refused to express either assent to or dissent from the manner in which the subject had been treated, since in criminal law delusion as cause of an act has been used as a criterion only in Hadfield's case.

[141]KELSEN, SOCIETY AND NATURE (1943), at 249.

proving it. Nor is law the proper authority to find whether an act was "caused by disease." If there are any pertinent laws that govern these matters, they are laws of nature, not legal laws. Law's attempts to determine by its own resources the proper test of mental disease or of its causal operations is hence absurd. Thus, there evolved the sentence which constitutes the core of the New Hampshire rule, that "the only general, universal element of law involved in the inquiry" into the exemption of mental incapacity is that the accused is not responsible if his act "was the offspring or product of mental disease."[142] All other issues—whether there is such a mental disease as dipsomania, what is the proper test of mental disease, indeed, whether there is a single test or several tests of such disease, when is an act a product of such disease—are by nature and logic issues of fact and not of law. Said Judge Ladd: "Whether the defendant had a mental disease . . . seems to be as much a question of fact as whether he had a bodily disease; and whether the killing of his wife was the product of that disease, was also as clearly a matter of fact as whether thirst and a quickened pulse are the product of fever."[143]

It is indeed interesting to note that doubts concerning the validity of these naïvely realistic philosophical and "scientific" assumptions were raised not by a lawyer but by a medical man, Dr. Isaac Ray. In a letter to Judge Doe, dated May 3, 1868, he pointed out that since the law recognized only a certain kind or degree of insanity as having any legal consequences, the courts could not very well avoid the duty of defining by tests and rules what that kind or degree is. "If, then," Dr. Ray said, "insanity may or may not disqualify, must not this fact be recognized, in some way, by the statute?"[144]

2. The Durham Test

The ontological concept of an intent or a disease producing the

---

[142]State v. Jones, *supra* note 134, at 398.

[143]*Ibid.*

[144]Quoted in Reik, *The Doe-Ray Correspondence: A Pioneer Collaboration in the Jurisprudence of Mental Disease*, 63 YALE LAW JOURNAL 183, at 188-189 (1953).

act has no longer any place in our age of desubstantialization of the universe. Not a trace is left of the notion of causation of the preHumean era—of causation as a connection that is inherent in the things themselves. Mental disease has ceased to be, as Judge Doe believed it to be, "only physical disease, or the result of physical disease."[145] The human mind is no longer thought of as divided into compartments, in which the will or intent occupies a separate place, that may be literally taken over or occupied by disease. Nor do we believe that disease is an alien intruder into man's mental life. We view it as distinguishable from health in degree rather than in kind. Indeed, there is no discrete concept of mental disease at all, which might be found to exist in any given case as a pure matter of fact. Our notions of logic, semantics, as well as of legal doctrine, particularly regarding the law-fact dichotomy, have undergone a thorough change. And yet, in the year 1954, Judge Bazelon enunciated in the District of Columbia the very same rule—except for one addition—that was proclaimed in New Hampshire in 1869–70 on the basis of conceptions of an act-producing metaphysical will and an act-producing ontologic entity, mental disease, which even in 1869–70 reflected obsolete ideas. The *Durham* test reads thus:

> The rule . . . is simply that an accused is not criminally responsible if his unlawful act was the product of mental disease or mental defect.
> We use "disease" in the sense of a condition which is considered capable of either improving or deteriorating. We use "defect" in the sense of a condition which is not considered capable of either improving or deteriorating and which may be either congenital, or the result of injury, or the residual effect of a physical or mental disease.[146]

Very little needs to be added to what has already been said about *Durham*. What was simple error in the New Hampshire cases turns into absurdity in *Durham*, the meaning of the very words used having undergone a revolutionary change. When the

---

[145]Letter of Judge Doe to Tyler of Sept. 5, 1866, *ibid.*, at 187.

[146]Durham v. United States, *supra* note 20, at 874-875.

New Hampshire judges proclaimed mental disease that produces the act to constitute a logically necessary, a natural, exemption ground, and the questions of what are mental disease and its products to be pure matters of fact, they did so because they believed that when an act is the product of mental disease it is not the product of intent or indeed an act of the accused, and because they believed that the concepts of disease and product, and that of law and of fact are existentially given. Their reasoning, though proceeding from scientifically and jurisprudentially false premises, was methodologically correct. By contrast, today, the statement that an act is the product of mental disease is a presentation of psychological reality known to be fallacious, and the statement that what is mental disease and what are its products are matters of fact is misleading, since it appears to suggest a "givenness" of these notions which, in the light of contemporary knowledge, they do not possess. This raises the significant issue of the logics of *Durham*.

As pointed out by Dr. Roche,[147] the notions of "mental disease,"of its relation to the act, of "intent," and so on, convey an entirely different meaning today from that they once possessed:

> The term "mental disease" merely designates behavior which, in a given society, is regarded as maladapted; it designates an altered internal status of the individual vis-à-vis his external world as interpreted by others.[148]

> [C]riminality and mental illness cease to be a demoniacal possession which has the self-contained faculty of turning itself on and off and "causes" one to do wrong; they become more meaningful processes reflecting the breakdown of psychic controls and the release of latent antisocial drives common to all.[149]

> Mental illness does not cause one to commit a crime nor does mental illness produce a crime. Behavior and mental illness are inseparable—one and the same thing.[150]

---

[147]ROCHE, *supra* note 4, at 88-89; also Roche, *Insanity and the Criminal Law* 22 UNIVERSITY OF CHICAGO LAW REVIEW 320 (1955).

[148]ROCHE, *supra* note 4, at 15.

[149]*Insanity and the Criminal Law, supra* note 147, at 323.

[150]*Ibid.*, at 322. Neither "disease" nor "production" are simple observable "facts."

[M]ental illness does not abolish intent but *releases* it.[151]

Since we no longer believe in any of the notions from which the New Hampshire cases proceeded—any more than we believe in an ether permeating the universe—to repeat the rule which these cases enunciated as though, by the same type of logical deduction, we could arrive at it in our times, is methodologically erroneous. *Durham* is not only wrong law. It is senseless. The defense of the *Durham* rule in *Carter* v. *United States*[152] affords a flagrant demonstration of its untenability. There the Court said: "When we say the defense of insanity requires that the act be a 'product of' a disease, we mean that the facts on the record are such that the trier of the facts is enabled to draw a reasonable inference that the accused would not have committed the act he did commit if he had not been diseased as he was."[153] The footnote to this passage is indeed illuminating.[154] After stating that the Government must prove "beyond a reasonable doubt" that there is a relationship between the disease and the act that is "critical in its effect in respect to the act," the Court explains the term "critical" thus:

> By "critical" we mean decisive, determinative, causal; we mean to convey the idea inherent in the phrases "because of", "except for", "without which", "but for", "effect of", "result of", "causative factor"; the disease made the effective or decisive difference between doing and not doing the act. The short phrases "product of" and "causal connection" are not intended to be precise, as though they were chemical formulae. They mean that the facts concerning the disease and the facts concerning the act are such as to justify reasonably the conclusion that "But for this disease the act would not have been committed."

Should anyone puzzle how anything that is "not intended to be precise" can be proven "beyond a reasonable doubt," the answer apparently may be found in the following statement:

> To the precise logician, deduction of the foregoing inference

---

[151]ROCHE, *supra* note 4, at 88.
[152]252 F.2d 608 (D.C. Cir., 1956, *reh. den.* 1957).
[153]*Ibid. at* 617.
[154]*Supra* m. 16.

involves a tacit assumption that if the disease had not existed
the person would have been a law-abiding citizen. This latter
is not necessarily factually true and can rarely, if ever, be
proved, but in the ordinary conduct of these cases we make
that tacit assumption. For ordinary purposes we make no mention of this logician's nicety.

Disregarding this confession of "logical failure" of the test—a
failure which is hardly excusable by being labelled a "logician's
nicety"—there remains the truly critical admission that the product feature of the test "can rarely, if ever, be proved." I submit
with great respect that a test the essential elements of which
are not provable is utterly meaningless and not merely wrong.

3. The Spanish Test

As shown, in the view of the New Hampshire judges, insanity
excludes intent and thus must of logical necessity constitute a
ground for exemption. It would be possible to argue that if the
prosecution could establish the presence of intent (producing the
act) notwithstanding insanity, the defense could be rebutted.
This, however, is not the law, but no explanation is offered why
it is not. Possibly, a reason may be found in the fact that intent
or malice was not at common law an ultimately psychological
phenomenon but a product of a peculiar mixture or indeed
identification of primitive psychology, morality, religion and law
and that it retained this character even after insanity ceased to
be regarded as a moral quality and was recognized as a medical-
psychological phenomenon. It would require a special study in
the history of legal concepts to ascertain how exactly the notion
developed that "[t]he legal idea of malice includes the idea of
sanity."[155] Perhaps a similar study would be necessary in order
to explain the process of reasoning which leads from the *Durham*
rule to the ultimate paragraph of the *Durham* opinion stating

---

[155]State v. Pike, *supra* note 23, at 431. The passage continues: "and the legal
presumption of malice threw the burden of proving insanity on the defendant."
Compare also *ibid.* at 442: "Sanity being an essential element of malice, must be
proved by the state beyond all reasonable doubt."

that the rule but reflects the settled doctrine of free will and intent.[156]

The role played by intent in the doctrine of the mental incapacity exemption in common law development is paralleled in civil law countries by the significance attributed to the notion of will. But in some penal codes the connection between the exemption and the concept of *dolus*, as consisting of knowledge and will, is made explicit, whereas in other penal codes this is not the case; upon closer scrutiny, it becomes clear that only rarely has the law actually reached an independent notion of the exempting quality or of the policy of the exemption. The idea persists that the mentally ill are exempt because they actually lack either knowledge or will.

In the Italian Penal Code the relationship of the incapacity exemption to *dolus* is clearly verbalized. *"Dolus"* is defined as "cognition (foresight) and will."[157] A person is responsible (*imputabile*) only if he possesses "capacity to understand and to will" (*capacità d'intendere e di volere*),[158] and is not responsible if at the time of action "he was, by reason of disease, in such state of mind as to exclude capacity of understanding or

---

[156]Said Judge Bazelon in conclusion: "The legal and moral traditions of the western world require that those who, of their own free will and with evil intent (sometimes called *mens rea*), commit acts which violate the law, shall be criminally responsible for those acts. Our traditions also require that where such acts stem from and are the product of a mental disease or defect as those terms are used herein, moral blame shall not attach and hence there will not be criminal responsibility. The rule we state in this opinion is designed to meet these requirements" (*supra* note 20, at 876). This passage reflects the view expressed in the Holloway case (*supra* note 16). But since Durham insists on the psychiatrists' freedom to give the jury all relevant and no irrelevant information—a position rejected in Holloway—it is pertinent to inquire whether the cited passage does or does not imply an ultimate concession to the Holloway philosophy of deceit as regards the role of intent in mental incapacity cases. Not only "free will," but indeed, the very concept of "will" plays little systematic role in recent psychologies. See, e.g., Rapaport, Kurt Lewin, in Rapaport (ed.), ORGANIZATION AND PATHOLOGY OF THOUGHT 144-152, 507 n. 49 (Columbia Univ. Press, 1951).

[157]Article 43 of the ITALIAN PENAL CODE (1930) defines crime as "dolose or pursuant to intent" (*doloso, o secondo l'intenzione*) when the result of action is "foreseen and willed [desired]" (*preveduto e voluto*).

[158]*Ibid.* art. 85. Notice that not only "incapacity" but "capacity" also is defined.

willing."[159] The terms "understanding" and "willing" are read literally. Clearly, no profound knowledge or will with feeling is taken to be required to render a person responsible. The Corte di Cassazione explicitly declined to extend the exemption to a psychopath on the ground that a person of that type possesses "both cognitive and conative capacity and is incapacitated solely in the sphere of feeling," which is not enumerated in the statute defining the exemption.[160]

The history and wording of the Spanish test would appear to suggest a total departure from the obsolescent knowledge and will test. In fact, both in history and wording, this test is reminiscent of *Durham*. It was devised with expert psychiatric assistance to meet the demands of modern psychiatric insight. While defining felonies and misdemeanors as "voluntary acts and omissions,"[161] the Spanish Penal Code (1944) submits a distinctive definition of the mental incapacity exemption. This definition simply exempts "the alienated" (*el enajenado*), adding to this group that of the temporarily mentally disturbed.[162] As

---

[159]*Ibid.* art. 88.

[160]Decision of the Corte di Cassazione (Sezione I) of April 15, 1955, reported in 61 GIUSTIZIA PENALE II, 183 (1956). There the court said:

"La Hara, though possessing the capacity of distinguishing right from wrong and lawful from unlawful and though capable of determining his conduct in accordance with his own ideas, is nevertheless drawn to do wrong or to commit crime, because he does not feel any aversion against wrong and crime and is not disposed to obey the laws and to abide within the range of ordered social life, preferring to satisfy his low and egoistic instincts by *short-cut and illegal methods*. And, since of the mental faculties, that is, the feeling, the intelligence and the will, which subjectively characterize the opinion, the code in force, for purposes of responsibility, takes into consideration only the last two and not the first, the decision [below] which affirms the principle of the responsibility of constitutionally immoral persons is legally correct and not objectionable in the light of the prevailing rules.

"The expert had . . . found that La Hara did not suffer from any relevant defect in the field of 'ideation or critical faculties' or in that of 'volition,' but that he showed 'characterological features of abnormal affectivity' and 'preponderant instinctivity.' This does not fall within article 89, Penal Code [diminished responsibility]. The accused is responsible."

[161]SPANISH PENAL CODE OF 1944, art. 1.

[162]*Ibid.* art. 8, al. 1°. These provisions have been preserved in the Revised Text of the Penal Code 1963.

the American *Durham* rule had been, so the Spanish clause was hailed as a mark of great progress.[163] Yet, a look at doctrinal interpretation and decisional law shows that introduction of the new test has produced no revolutionary change in practice and that absence of knowledge and/or will continues to be used as the true criterion.[164] Thus, for example, Quintano Ripolles[165] believes it to be self-evident that the function of psychiatrists in the administration of this test is strictly confined to submitting to the court a simple clinical diagnosis, a finding of the presence or absence of the reality of mental change, whereupon the court must decide whether "such change was or was not a determining factor in the commission of the act charged and *whether or not it affected the volitional and intellectual capacity of the actor*" (emphasis added). Compared with the test of the Spanish Code of 1870, which exempted "the imbecile and the lunatic, unless he acted in a lucid interval" (*el imbécil y el loco a no ser que éste haya obrado en un intervalo de razón*),[166] the present test has been held to enlarge the exemption in conformity to changes in psychiatric opinion. Thus, under the new test, the Supreme Court, in a decision rendered on October 5, 1944,[167] abandoned the previous view that the relevant disease of the mind must have a physiological basis and held a person whose disease was diagnosed as rooted in psychic factors not to have been responsible. But although allegedly based on the new scientific formula, the decision rationalized its results by use of the ancient knowledge test.[168] Throughout, the court's pronouncements express continued adherence to the knowledge and will test.[169]

---

[163]QUINTANO RIPOLLES, *supra* note 52, at 66.

[164]For this criterion in Spain is a venerable one: it goes back to the Siete Partidas. Cf. *supra* note 52.

[165]*Ibid.*

[166]*Ibid.*

[167](Sala II), cited *ibid.* at p. 76.

[168]A woman who drowned her child and attempted to commit suicide was found by the court to have committed these acts in a "moment of despair," "*without being aware of the acts*" which she committed, and solely remembering that she had another disappointment with her husband" [emphasis added].

[169]In a single volume of a digest of decisions of the Supreme Court of Spain in criminal matters, the 1948-49 Appendix of Manuel Rodriguez Navarro, Doc-

Thus, notwithstanding adoption of an allegedly scientific test, the criterion in Spain, as in other civil law countries, has remained the ancient one—that of knowledge and will. The knowledge portion is clearly derived in civil law countries, as in common law jurisdictions, from the one-time law of legal error. Carrara, an author cited as much in as outside his native Italy, defined insanity (*pazzia*) as "a morbid state which, depriving man of the capacity of knowing the true relations of his acts to the law, has impelled him to violate it, without his being aware of such violation."[170]

Since, in Spain, knowledge and will rather than mental disease (*enajenación*) are the real issue, and since *enajenado* (the alienated), implying a non-temporary condition, does not cover all situations in which a person may be deprived of his cognitive and/or conative faculties, another supplementary test has been added. That test is called temporary mental disturbance (*trastorno mental transitorio*), which corresponds to our notion of temporary insanity. The test is considerably narrower than the German test of disturbance of consciousness. Since decisional

---

TRINA PENAL DEL TRIBUNAL SUPREMO, Appendice II, see pp. 35-36 for pertinent cases (1960), there are several statements expressing continued adherence to the knowledge and will test. The court required proof that the accused "acted in a state of complete annulment of his will, which put him in a state of unconsciousness or, at least reduced consciousness" (*ibid.*, sentencia 29-5-948; Rep. Jurisp. ARANZADI, p. 870). In another case the court held a finding of the court below of "a normal and perfect functioning of the accused's faculties of knowledge and action at the time of committing the offenses" to be "equivalent to a declaration of a perfect mental equilibrium on that occasion" (sentencia 24-1-949; Rep. Jurisp. ARANZADI, p. 46). In a third case the court found the accused's "lucidity of judgment manifested during trial" to be inconsistent with an even transitory mental disturbance at the time of the act (sentencia 9-5-949; Rep. Jurisp. ARANZADI, p. 662.

Though the Spanish test does not in terms require the act to be the "product" of the mental disease, such requirement is being read into it. Thus, QUINTANO RIPOLLES *supra* note 52, at 69, states that whether or not a kleptomaniac or pyromaniac will be held responsible for a crime depends on whether that crime "falls within the radius of his disease." Thus, the former will be held responsible if he commits arson but not if he commits larceny, and the latter will be punished if he commits larceny but not if he commits arson.

[170]CARRARA, PROGRAMMA DEL CORSO DI DIRITTO CRIMINALE), vol. I. (Spanish transl.; Madrid 1922), cap. II, par. 248.

law often requires total unconsciousness, meaning, "not a mere obfuscation of understanding but a total absence of the latter,"[171] there is reason to doubt that the test adds anything to the voluntary act requirement. The Supreme Court's insistence that the disturbance must be a "pathological one producing an (absolute or limited) annulment . . . of the capacity to know or to evaluate one's own acts or, which is the same, loss or limitation of will or of free self-determination,"[172] reduces this test to but a variant of the principal one. Moreover, in contrast to German courts, the Spanish Supreme Court has shown no understanding whatever of mental realities such as were already known in Dr. Ray's days, for example, that a person may act with "goal-direction" and apparent rationality and yet be in such mental condition as to make these factors but parts of a total, confused scheme of disease.[173]

Partial Exemption Tests

I understand by partial exemption: 1. the so-called partial responsibility, which is an exemption from responsibility not within all criminal law rules but within certain rules only; for example, a person thus exempt may be found incapable of premeditation, which means that he cannot be convicted of any crime which requires that state of mind; 2. the so-called diminished responsibility, which creates an intermediate notion between full mental capacity and full mental incapacity, leading

---

[171]See decisions cited in QUINTANO RIPOLLES, supra note 52, at 76.

[172]Sentencia 2-4-949; Rep. Jurisp. ARANZADI, p. 645, in Rodriguez Navarro, supra note 169, at 37.

[173]Thus, where "a chronic alcoholic, with psychopathic reactions, being in the afternoon of the act in a state of such extreme drunkenness as to suffer from vomiting spells," went to the house of a long-time friend whom she often visited and taking advantage of the latter's momentary absence (in the kitchen of the same apartment), entered an alcove, opened a safe with her own (the accused's) key and took 800 pesos, which she then kept until the police seized them," the Supreme Court reversed the acquittal based on an expert's opinion that the accused was in a state of temporary mental disturbance. The Supreme Court based this reversal on the alleged inconsistency of such temporary insanity with the "rationality" of her acts (Sentencia 15-4-948; Rep. Jurisp. ARANZADI, at p. 572, in Rodriguez Navarro, ibid., 37-38).

to reduction of punishment without affecting the crime type or degree.

1. Partial Responsibility

The principal case in the United States dealing with this concept is *Fisher* v. *United States*.[174] The petitioner, convicted of first-degree murder under the District of Columbia Code,[175] defining such murder as killing with "deliberate and premeditated malice," contended that though he was of sufficiently "sound memory and discretion" to commit murder in the second degree—defined as killing "with malice aforethought"[176]—he was not "capable" of "deliberation and premeditation," having been found to be a person of "psychopathic aggressive tendencies, low emotional response and borderline mental deficiency." Whether or not the Supreme Court's affirming of the conviction and death sentence was correct depends on what is meant by "deliberation and premeditation" and whether or not the described qualities of the petitioner exclude or tend to exclude such deliberation and premeditation. "Malice aforethought" is not more than "intent," though the "intent" in murder need not always be directed at producing death.[177] "Malice aforethought" may be less than "intent" to kill but is never more than that.[178] "Premeditation and deliberation" at most add to the "intent" an element of "second thought" or an "appreciable time"[179] for thinking the matter over. In *Fisher* the time available for deliberation and premeditation was extremely short. Is it then contended that a person may be incapable of deliberating and premeditating for

---

[174]328 U.S. 463, 90 L. Ed. 1382, 66 Sup. Ct. 1318 (1945).

[175]1940 ed., title 22, § 2401.

[176]*Ibid.*, title 22, § 2403.

[177]See PERKINS *supra* note 56, at 38-40, for the various types of "intent" which qualify as "malice aforethought" or "man-endangering-state-of-mind."

[178]See Turner v. Commonwealth, 167 Ky. 365, 180 S.W. 768, L. R. A. 1918 A. 329 (1915), for review of authorities. "Intent" as used in the text includes mere negligence as regards death.

[179]Bullock v. United States, 122 F.2d 213-14 (D.C. Cir., 1941); Bostic v. United States, 94 F.2d 636, 639 (D.C. Cir., 1937). In some of the states "premeditation and deliberation may be simultaneous with the formation of the intent to kill." United States v. Wilson, 178 F.S. 881, 885 (Dist. Ct., D.C., 1950).

as much as half an hour and yet be mentally fit to be guilty of a serious crime? Can mental disease be dissected into such neat parts or discrete degrees? It is submitted that if *Fisher* proves anything, it proves the total inadequacy of our notions of intent and premeditation and of defining mental incapacity in terms of these notions.

The definition of partial responsibility submitted above also comprises what is known as diminished responsibility in Scottish law and in the English Homicide Act, 1957.[180] For the pertinent rules of the common law of Scotland and the new English rule[181] provide that in cases where the accused is found to fall within a mental category lesser than that of the M'Naghten rules, he is to be convicted not for murder but for a lesser crime, "manslaughter" in England and "culpable homicide" in Scotland.

The English test of such diminished responsibility provides that when a person kills another, he shall not be convicted of murder if "he was suffering from such abnormality of mind (whether arising from a condition of arrested or retarded development of mind or any inherent causes or induced by disease or injury) as substantially impaired his mental responsibility for his acts and omissions in doing or being a party to the killing." This test is vaguely reminiscent of that recommended by the majority of the Royal Commission on Capital Punishment, "to leave to the jury to determine whether at the time of the act the accused was suffering from disease of the mind (or mental deficiency) to such a degree that he ought not to be held responsible."[182]

That the diminished responsibility test of the Homicide Act 1957 hardly affords any guidance to judges may be seen from the fact that the English Bench is turning, for illumination on instructions to juries, on the meaning and scope of such re-

---

[180]5 & 6 Eliz. II, c. II. The pertinent provision is contained in § 2(1).

[181]On these provisions see Edwards, *Diminished Responsibility*, in Mueller, ed., ESSAYS IN CRIMINAL SCIENCE, *op. cit.*, *supra* note 5, at 301; Hughes, *The English Homicide Act of 1957* 49 JOURNAL OF CRIMINAL LAW, CRIMINOLOGY AND POLICE SCIENCE 521 (1959); Prevezer, *The English Homicide Act: Attempts to Revise the Law of Murder*, 57 COLUMBIA LAW REVIEW 624 (1957).

[182]ROYAL COMM. REP., p. 116.

sponsibility, to the practice of Scottish courts.[183] Such vagueness of a statutory test is hardly compatible with standards of "legality."

The criticism of partial responsibility as advocated in the *Fisher case* is also applicable to the English and Scottish notion of so-called diminished responsibility. Is it realistic to assume that a person may not be sufficiently sane to be guilty of murder in the first degree—in England, of murder—but "sane enough" to be guilty of murder in the second degree—in England, of manslaughter, in Scotland, of culpable homicide? Implicit in such assumption is an unrealistic view of the mental element in crime. This is combined with a failure to realize that guilt in modern law should be conceived of functionally, as a policy-oriented social notion, rather than metaphysically. This failure accounts for the fact that no provisions were made at the outset for meeting the need for protection against the dangerousness of persons of diminished responsibility, though it is now expected that the necessary public protection will be afforded by provisions of the recently enacted Mental Health Act, 1959.[184] Similarly, the Model Penal Code, while specifically providing for admissibility of proof of mental disease or defect for the purpose of showing that the accused was not capable of the particular state of mind that is charged,[185] makes no provision for assigning such a person to a mental hospital or for any other measure of cure or care that might protect the community. We ought to face the fact that Fisher was dangerous.

2. Diminished Responsibility

In instances where the accused is found to be partially responsible, a Scottish judge may, in addition, consider the reduced mental capacity in mitigation of punishment.[186] This implies that Scotland also admits diminished responsibilty in the narrower sense in which this term is used in this paper. But the point is incidental and requires no elaboration.

---

[183]Edwards, *supra* note 181, at 319.

[184]7 & 8 Eliz. II, c. 72.

[185]§ 4.02, Tent. Draft No. 4 (1955).

[186]For authorities see Edwards, *supra* note 181, at 306.

The laws of many civil law countries have provisions on diminished responsibility. These provisions vary from country to country: in some, reduction is mandatory, in others, discretionary; some follow fixed reduction principles, for example, the German rule incorporates the reduction scheme established for cases of attempt;[187] others leave the matter entirely to judicial discretion, for example, the Swiss Federal Penal Code adopts such rule.[188] Of greatest importance are the provisions subjecting persons of diminished responsibility to measures. Since such persons are also amenable to punishment, though a reduced one, the problem of conflict between punishment and measures calls for resolution. There is a general tendency to permit punishment to yield to a measure, so that in an increasing number of cases such persons incur no punishment at all and are subjected only to a measure. But this result, generally believed to be desirable, may be reached directly by including persons of diminished responsibility in the group of those exempt from punishment and subject to measures, rather than by deviation from an initial principle of combining punishment and measures.[189]

In the scheme advocated by this writer the length and extensiveness of permissible measures depends very decisively on the type of criminal act that has been committed, so that there

---

[187]Sections 51 and 44, GERMAN PENAL CODE.

[188]Article 11, SWISS FEDERAL PENAL CODE of 1937.

[189]On this see Silving, *"Rule of Law" in Criminal Justice, supra* note 5, at 117-119 and 142-163.

There are two approaches to formulation of "diminished responsibility" tests: (a) repetition or incorporation by reference of the total incapacity test, with indication that the mental states and/or resulting faculties are present in smaller degree; (b) adoption of sui generis standards of diminished capacity. The German rule on diminished responsibility (§ 51(2), GERMAN PENAL CODE) adopts the former technique. A similar technique is advocated by the 1956 DRAFT, art. 24. But the Swiss Federal "diminished capacity" test is distinctive (art. 11, SWISS FEDERAL PENAL CODE), and the German DRAFT 1960 adds to the sources of incapacity of appreciation or conformity, enumerated in the total incapacity rule, another special "diminished responsibility" clause: "because of another severe mental deviation" (§ 25). This clause is intended to apply the benefit of "diminished responsibility" to "psychopathies, neuroses and disturbances in the drives" (see comment, at p. 133). But, of course, both the SWISS FEDERAL PENAL CODE (arts. 14-16) and the GERMAN DRAFT 1960 (§ 82) provide for application of measures to persons of "diminished capacity." Cf. also the 1962 Draft §§ 25 and 82.

is a certain concordance between punishment maxima and maxima in measures. But, subject to certain limitations, a measure may—indeed, when its basis ceases to exist, must—be terminated at any time, so that on the whole a measure is realistically preferable to punishment. This should militate against adoption of a sweeping all or nothing, total mental incapacity rule, placing minor disabilities on the same level with major diseases when the prospect of early release in the former is extremely high, whereas in the latter it is practically nonexistent, so that a person in the former category receives a perhaps unjustifiable advantage over the fully responsible one. However, since the concept of diminished responsibility is highly questionable, and since in criminal law there obtains a general *favor libertatis*, borderline situations should be included in any definition which affords an advantage. Hence, the submission is that the category which would otherwise qualify for partial or diminished responsibility ought to be included in the class of those enjoying full punitive exemption.

Summary

In contrast to the older rules, neither their modern adaptations nor the newer rules are oriented to a consciously conceived and consistently followed criminal law policy. *M'Naghten's* rules are the product of a policy of protecting those engaged in error of fact or of law, for such error was once deemed to exclude an essential of crime, disobedience to law. The New Hampshire test purported to interpret intent and causation by intent, as understood by those who formulated the rule. Within the knowledge of the New Hampshire judges, the test was meaningful, for these judges thought that mental disease actually excludes a constituent element of crime, intent.

The modern rules which resemble *M'Naghten*, that is, the Model Penal Code rules and the mixed system civil law rules, such as the German one, are structured in terms of certain incapacities and sources of such incapacities. In none of these rules is it made clear whether the ground that justifies the exemption is the source, that is, the mental disease or defect, the incapacity indicating merely the degree of disease required for exemption, or the incapacity *per se*. This in itself makes it difficult to determine what policy these rules follow. The incapacity may affect the faculty of knowledge or that of conformity. Incapacity to appreciate or to know is but a modification of the *M'Naghten* knowledge test. Knowledge capacity must be related to the particular crime that is in issue. In our law this results in the paradoxical situation that when a person claims to have been insane, the law insists that he is not punishable if he had no capacity to know the law which he need not know if he is sane. Capacity to conform is particularly vulnerable, since it is ultimately reducible to capacity to have acted otherwise. Psychiatrists have asserted that it is impossible to answer the question: "Could John Doe have acted otherwise than he acted?" It is idle—perhaps, indeed, senseless to debate whether such a question is or is not absolutely unanswerable; for surely an answer could be given, if at all, only after a very long study of the person concerned that would acquaint the observer with all the motivations to which such person was subject and such a study cannot be made within the confines of criminal procedure. In fact, those who advocate this test often concede that it ultimately reduces itself to a problem of justice to be disposed of on a case-to-case basis. An alternative suggested by Seelig, that the issue be put in terms of capacity to be motivated by rational considerations, though preferable to the test of capacity for conformity to the legal rule, is particularly questionable in communities where there are large groups of persons who are not generally thus motivated.

The *Durham* test was adopted in order to accommodate psychiatric experts who themselves profess not to be able to supply the law with functional definitions or, indeed, to verbalize the grounds of individual diagnoses. Precisely because psychiatry is unsettled regarding such questions as whether comprehensive classes of mental states, psychopathies and neuroses are included in the term "mental disease"—a term, *nota bene,* that does not appear in many psychiatric textbooks—Durham has chosen that term as the key concept of its definition of the mental incapacity exemption. This is actually intended to permit one psychiatric expert to testify that these categories are included while another expert testifies that they are not included. No objection could be raised against such allowance were it shown that such inclusion or exclusion is based on divergence of psychiatric insight into the nature of the pertinent mental states and that the points of divergence are relevant to a legal policy issue. But the fact is that the source of disagreement (or reversal) among psychiatrists is a variance in classification which, whatever meaning it may have in medical "communication," is for legal purposes purely verbal. Nor is the real ground of such classificatory testimony free from a normative moral taint that is rooted in the psychiatrist's desire to inculpate or exculpate. While juries are expected not to feel bound by psychiatric interpretations but to form an independent opinion, based on factual scientific data supplied by psychiatrists, the question whether an exemption is justified is put to them in terms of whether the accused suffered from a "mental disease," although it is not even known to what discipline this concept belongs, since it is now declared not to be a psychiatric category. Moreover, the whole issue is obscured by interchangeable designation of the jury's task as consisting in finding presence or absence of mental disease, in a moral judgment, and in determination of a question of fact.

It is submitted that whether broad classes such as psychopathies or neuroses should afford a ground for exemption is a question of sufficiently general scope to be properly determinable by legislatures and not juries. This in a democracy is clearly a legislative task, much as it is a legislative task to define crime or any exemption from criminal responsibility. To be sure, it would be utopian to believe that legislatures can define either crime or a mental incapacity exemption with absolute certainty, that is, with such certainty as would make adjudication but a syllogistic operation. But questions of such degree of abstraction as whether psychopaths or neurotics should be exempt are certainly not of a type to admit no general answer that would afford a fair measure of equality in treatment. To this extent, legal certainty barring arbitrariness and inequality is of the essence of justice. Of course, legislative formulation of a sound exemption is predicated upon acquaintance with scientific data on how the human mind operates. These data should be supplied by psychologists and psychiatrists.

The most absurd feature of the attempt in the *Durham* test to be scientific is the use of sham scientific terminology. The phrase "product of mental disease or defect" has been shown by psychiatrists to be meaningless. Psychiatrists are truly unable to answer the question whether an act is or is not "the product of mental disease," whereas their assertion that they are unable to testify whether an accused "knew that what he was doing was wrong" is based on a fallacy in methodology. Nor is the former inability based on a "logician's nicety"; it is rather rooted in legally relevant psychiatric insight into the realities of mental life. In the light of this fact bearing on the practical aspects of psychiatric expert testimony, it is unnecessary to dwell on the jurisprudential question whether or not law can operate without logic.

In each and every respect, the reasoning behind the *Durham* test is methodologically fallacious, whereas the New Hampshire cases, being based on mistaken psychiatric, scientific and philosophical "knowledge"—a wrong, but bona fide, "knowledge"—were disposed of by a correct methodology. There is as much difference between *Durham* and the New Hampshire cases as there would be between the trial of a witch today and such trial during the Middle Ages, when the belief prevailed that witchcraft was an actual craft that produced social harm, that might kill, injure or render insane. Witches' trials were not immoral then, but they would be immoral today. In the same sense, the New Hampshire cases administered justice, whereas the same is not true of *Durham.* It may be interesting to note that *Durham* relies heavily on the *Holloway Case,* in which Judge Arnold turned into law his jurisprudential view that justice is not important, law being governed by the rule not of law but of popular illusion created by legal ritual.

Should there be a need for a practical demonstration of the fact that definition of the mental incapacity exemption simply as "mental disease" is not a functional policy disposition, such confirmation is afforded by the history of the administration of the Spanish test which defines the exemption by one word, *"enajenado."* The Spanish Supreme Court applies this test as if it did not exist. It simply continues to adjudicate cases on the basis of the old criterion of knowledge and will.

The notions of partial and diminished responsibility proceed from erroneous fundamental conceptions of the mental element in crime, premeditation and deliberation, malice aforethought and so on. Moreover, the concept of such responsibility has the awkward practical result of calling for administration of criminal law on an assumption which defies recognition of a unitary notion of the human personality, namely, on the assumption that an individual may be partly sane and partly insane; this, in fact, is the implication of subjecting him to both punishment and measures administered successively, as is done in some civil law countries.

It would thus seem that we are left in a vacuum, all available tests and definitions having failed. To formulate a new test, we must return to fundamentals.

RECOMMENDED TEST

As pointed out in the first part of this paper, an exemption test ought to be based on the policy that is being pursued by the criminal law. In a punitive context, the policy of exempting from punishment should be derived negatively from the purpose of punishment; those persons whose punishment would not serve such purpose ought to be exempt. The purpose of punishment, as shown, is to document the relative social reprehensibleness of the offense that has been committed. The individual who is to be punished is selected as an object of such demonstration on the basis of his "guilt." Guilt in the criminal law of a democracy is not a theological or a metaphysical-philosophical notion. Nor is it a moral notion in the narrower sense of the term. It is a social-political concept to the effect that an individual, as a member of a community, is called to account for violating a social norm; in a sense, for having put in question the validity of the norm.

Such being the policy of punishment, its target is obviously the normal, average member of the community. A person who is not normal or average need not be punished; provided that, if he is dangerous, another purpose of law, namely, community protection giving rise to measures, may come into play. Normality thus postulated is not divisible into distinctive faculties. In many situations, of course, it may be possible to find specific, conspicuous symptoms of abnormality. Thus, a person is not normal if he has a conception of reality which is consistently divergent from that accepted by group consensus,[190] or has less power of self-control than average community members, [191] or shows emotional reactions that differ widely from those of the rest of the community. But it is not suggested that such specific symptoms be used to define mental incapacity.

The policy implicit in the mental incapacity exemption formulated in terms of the socially "nonaverage" is also expressed in other types of exemptions, for example, in the general defense of so-called "inexigibility of lawabidance" or "inexigibility of a different conduct," recognized in some civil law countries. The philosophy of this defense is that no one should be punished for a violation of law if he acted in circumstances in which most community members would have acted as he did. Just as heroism should not be expected by criminal law, so law that is devised for the average citizen should not be enforced indiscriminately against a person who has exceptional difficulties in meeting legal requirements. The correlation of non-exigibility and mental incapacity consists in the fact that the former applies when conduct otherwise illegal is average or normal, whereas

---

[190]Whitehorn, *Psychodynamic Approach to the Study of Psychoses*, in ALEXANDER and Ross, ed., DYNAMIC PSYCHIATRY (1952), 255 at 281, says: "In attempts to define psychosis, the point has often been made, descriptively, that psychotic thinking is unrealistic. Since reality is itself a concept difficult to define and to use with precision, the descriptive value of this statement is dubious. The discriminative value of the statement is also diminished by the observation that nonpsychotic persons also foster many illusions and carry on a large part of their mental operations with the use of prejudiced attitudes and folk beliefs which could scarcely be called realistic or even logical. A more useful criterion than reality is the consensus of the group."

[191]Average self-control depends much on expectation and habit within a given community. A Sicilian is not expected to possess as much self-control as an inhabitant of a Nordic community.

the mental incapacity exemption is accorded to the "nonaverage" individual, with the proviso that if he is also dangerous, society must take steps to protect itself by measures.

The "nonaverage" must be understood as a mixed sociological and psychiatric category. For in a democracy we cannot assume a priori that nonconformity is itself evidence of abnormality. There must be a serious failure in the individual's psychic organization, a grave impairment of his ego functioning. Since no one can be said to possess a perfectly balanced personality, abnormality must be assumed to begin at some discernible degree of imbalance. But since no mathematically precise variations in degree can be fixed, we must be satisfied with indications that the degree of imbalance is very great, as compared with the relative balance of average community members. There being no such thing as a universal normality, the particular community to which the individual belongs must be always assumed to afford the proper standard of comparison.

Normality is a precarious standard even if applied to a single community.[192] To make the mental incapacity test as definite and certain as the subject permits, it is proposed to be formulated in terms of comparison with the relative mental fitness of the majority of community members rather than with a group average and of a very considerable deviation from the mental fitness of such majority. Specification of the area of unfitness as that of social adjustment is also expected to facilitate application of the test.

Except in cases of habitual criminals who engage in crime as a matter of routine, crime is not an average occurrence in the life of any individual, and so it may be assumed that at the time of its commission a normal individual acts in a state of impairment of ego functioning. It thus seems improper to limit the test either to the time of the act's commission or to a relation to that act. There is hardly any psychological realism in the usual limitation of mental incapacity to the state of mind obtaining

---

[192]On this see, e.g., NOYES and KOLB, MODERN CLINICAL PSYCHIATRY (5th ed. 1958), p. 130.

"at the time of the act."[193] Nor could mental incapacity be established retrospectively with such precision. It is hence submitted that the formula use the words, "at the time of the act and for some time prior thereto." However, this should not be taken to exclude states of allegedly temporary mental disturbance from the exemption. As correctly pointed out by the German Bundesgerichtshof, "sudden outbursts of affect do not accidentally arise in man, as a lightning coming from a clear sky, but . . . as a rule, such outburst is preceded by a long development and history."[194]

As regards the relation of the mental state to social norms of conduct, reference to the criminality of the specific act charged implies recognition of "monomania," which has been discarded as a psychiatric category. Thus the test should be formulated in broader terms, namely, to relate to the actor's general capacity regarding social norms and rules.

In a previous publication I referred with approval to a test suggested by Bromberg and Cleckley, which poses the question of mental incapacity in the following terms: Was the functioning of the accused's "ego so impaired that he could not, because of genuine disability, act within the limits of social demands and rules?"[195] However, I had reservations about using the terms "could not" and "genuine disability." Both appear to be vague, and the former lends itself to being nullified by deterministically oriented psychiatrists. I hence suggested the following modified version: "Was the accused's ego so impaired that he was very considerably less than the majority of the people within the community capable of conforming to social demands and rules?"

---

[193]As pointed out by ROCHE, *supra* note 4, at 84-85, "to the psychiatrist intent has the meaning of a behavioral event, the precursors of which operate within the accused in a structured manner having an instinctual source and having a flow into final pathways of action." The so-called union of act and intent doctrine is psychologically unrealistic as well as legally questionable. Jackson v. Commonwealth (1896), 100 Ky. 239, 38 S.W. 422, 66 Am. St. Rep. 336. For cases in which insistence on such "union" leads to absurd results see HARNO, CASES AND MATERIALS ON CRIMINAL LAW AND PROCEDURE (4th ed. 1957), p. 46, n. 2.

[194]Compare *supra* text at note 114.

[195]Silving, *supra* note 59, at 29.

Having given further thought to this test, I became concerned with the use of the words "capable of conforming." In the context of mental incapacity, these words undoubtedly mean "being able to act otherwise." As pointed out above, such words, even when put in comparative terms, require an answer to a question which may be read as raising the issue of free will, and which either is not answerable by psychiatrists at all or would present practically insuperable difficulties. Because of the ambiguity of the term "ego," it appeared unwise to introduce the concept of "ego functioning" in the law. Hence I am now suggesting the following formulation of the exemption: "No punishment shall be imposed upon a person if at the time of engaging in criminal conduct and for some time prior thereto his integrative functioning was so impaired that he had a very considerably greater difficulty in complying with social demands and rules than does the majority of the members of the community."[196]

For purposes of defining the incapacity exemption the community should be that community which issues the norm that has been violated, in other words, the state. But there are many people whose life is so confined to narrower communities that it would be neither realistic nor just to apply to them such broad standards, as, for example, the state of mental health of the people of Puerto Rico. Hence the community should be understood to mean a narrower group, such as the population of the district from which, in the event of jury trial, a jury is drawn. But a community of persons living in a given geographical district is not necessarily homogeneous. There are varieties of social and cultural subgroups, some of which may be closer to similar subgroups of other communities than they are to other subgroups within their own community. Of particular importance is belonging to a group in which criminal habits are not distinctive, since the group generally practices such habits. When a person raised in a generally law-abiding group persistently follows criminal patterns, this in itself might in extreme cases point to mental deviation. But in a criminal group he may be

___

[196]The term "integrative functioning" was suggested by Dr. Angel Miranda.

a normal criminal, that is, a person "whose psychic organization is similar to that of the normal individual, except that he identified himself with criminal prototypes (sociological etiology)."[197] Hence, in determining whether the accused's integrative functioning was so impaired as to justify exemption, the court must assume as the standard of comparison not only the functioning of the broader community but also that of the particular group to which the accused belongs, whether social, educational, professional and so on.

Summary

The recommended test exempts from punishment persons to whom the preferred philosophy of punishment does not apply: the psychologically-sociologically clearly and distinctively "non-average." This test defines as exempt persons whose integrative functioning is so impaired that they have considerably greater difficulty conforming to social demands and rules than the majority of community members. The community is the population of the district from which, in the event of jury trial, a jury would be drawn and the narrower community to which the accused belongs, whether it be educational, professional or social. The disability is of general scope, affecting the subject's relationship to social demands and rules rather than merely his relationship to the specific conduct with which he is charged. The relevant time of impairment is broadened; the impairment must have existed at the time of conduct and for some time prior thereto.

This test is expected to eliminate the false assumption implicit in other mental incapacity tests as though we were concerned with a specifically psychiatric issue. Law is a social discipline and is concerned with social and antisocial conduct. The psychiatric aspects such conduct presents are of merely indirect significance. The social nature of law ought to be emphasized in every legal rule, including that on mental incapacity. Forensic psychiatry should be clearly understood to be a distinctive discipline, a sui generis social science.

---

[197]ALEXANDER and STAUB, THE CRIMINAL, THE JUDGE AND THE PUBLIC (rev. ed. 1956), p. 45, at 210-211.

Sound law, that is, law based upon a rational social policy and operating on the basis of a rational view of psychological and social reality, must take into account the social purpose of a mental incapacity exemption, the operational meaning of a given exemption formula, its impact on the individual concerned and the community, and the teleological aspects of its prospective functioning. Psychology and psychiatry may throw light on many issues involved in choosing an appropriate mental incapacity test. These sciences can tell us how men's minds operate. Our social philosophy must guide our judgment on the policy issue of how much we ought to demand of men.

CONCLUSION

In those rare situations in which a mental disability is of such nature as to actually negate "intent" or "premeditation," there is no need for a mental incapacity exemption. Exemption from punishment accorded to certain persons on the ground of mental disability is generally the result of policy considerations. But these are often disguised under a claim of inherent disability, constituting an exemption that is not conferred by decision makers but imposed upon them. A rational mental incapacity exemption should be based on a conscious policy guided by a clear notion of the ends of punishment and the conditions under which those ends are not applicable. In a democracy law addresses itself to the people and commands their obedience. In doing so, it must carefully consider both what is exigible and of whom it is exigible.

THE CRIMINAL LAW OF MENTAL INCAPACITY*

Redefining the mental incapacity exemption is but a partial problem of a much broader task, that of revising the total area of the criminal law of so-called "insanity." In the fields of procedure and of the measures to be applied to persons "acquitted by reason of insanity" conservatism, on the one hand, and lack of realism and consistency, on the other hand, have been as marked as in the field of the exemption criterion. The same is true of the law of "unfitness to proceed." All these segments of the "law of insanity" require systematic treatment. Such treatment ought to consist of a rational evaluation of our present disparate rules pertaining to the phenomenon of mental incapacity in all its criminal law phases and aspects, formulation of new realistic rules, and their concordance and consolidation into a consistent scheme oriented to a sound policy. It is the purpose of this paper to present such scheme of a "criminal law of mental incapacity."

In previous publications the writer has submitted a test of exemption from punitive responsibility by reason of mental incapacity at the time of, and for some time prior to, engagement in the criminal conduct charged.[1] That test reads thus:

"No punishment shall be imposed upon a person if at the time of engaging in criminal conduct and for some time prior thereto his integrative functioning was so impaired that he had a very considerably greater difficulty in complying with social demands

*Reprinted by special permission of the JOURNAL OF CRIMINAL LAW, CRIMINOLOGY AND POLICE SCIENCE, Copyright © 1962 by the Northwestern University School of Law, Vol. 53, No. 2.

[1]Silving, *Psychoanalysis and the Criminal Law*, JOURNAL OF CRIMINAL LAW, CRIMINOLOGY AND POLICE SCIENCE 19, 29 (1960); on the revised version, quoted here in the text, see *Mental Incapacity in Criminal Law*, *supra*, at 135-139.

and rules than does the majority of the members of the community." [2]

The writer believes that this test presents several advantages. It is not simply a remnant of an ancient policy geared to the defense of error of law rather than to that of mental deviation, as is *M'Naghten's* test, nor a reflection of a preconceived naively realistic notion of an immanent exempting quality of "mental disease" that "produces" crime, as is the *Durham* test.[3] Nor does it incorporate, as do the Model Penal Code tests,[4] a "free will" formula, which—however meritorious its metaphysical corollary may be—is not operational in practical context.[5] The quoted test proceeds from fundamentals of criminal law, the doctrine of punishment. The assumption is made that exemption from punishment ought to be conceded in situations to which the policy of punishment is inapplicable. The general purpose of punishment, in the opinion of the writer, is documentation of community prohibitions of relative gravity.[6] Application of punishment is justified by the actor's "guilt," which in a democratic society consists in imputation of responsibility for violation

---

[2] By "community" is meant the population of the district from which, in the event of jury trial, a jury is drawn, provided that in determining whether the actor's integrative functioning was impaired special attention ought to be given to the comparative functioning of members of particular groups to which the actor belongs, such as his social, educational, professional, religious or other group.

[3] M'Naghten's Case (1843), 10 Clark & F. 200, 8 Eng. Rep. 718; Durham v. United States, 84 U. S. App. D.C. 228, 214 F.2d 862 (1954). For a critique of these tests, see *Mental Incapacity in Criminal Law, supra,* at 86-93, 116-120.

[4] MODEL PENAL CODE § 4.01, for text and critique of this and former alternative tests see *Mental Incapacity in Criminal Law, supra* at 94-101.

[5] Lack of "substantial capacity to conform [one's] conduct to the requirements of law" means in the last analysis "could not, substantially, have acted otherwise than he did act." This posits the issue of "free will." Of course, it is one thing to assume a philosophical position of "free will" as justifying punitive state intervention in principle and an entirely different thing to attempt "proving" by legal methods that a given individual did or did not possess "free will." Such proof is as impossible as was proof that Ballard did not shake hands with Christ or take dictation from Him in United States v. Ballard, 322 U.S. 78 (1944). See Silving, *The Unknown and the Unknowable in Law,* 35 CALIFORNIA LAW REVIEW 352 (1947).

[6] See Silving, *"Rule of Law" in Criminal Justice,* in Mueller, ed., ESSAYS IN CRIMINAL SCIENCE 77, 84-89 (1961).

of the citizenship duty of abidance by community rules.[7] Such imputation is not warranted unless the actor is an average community member, with a view to whom laws are made. Accordingly, an exemption ought to be granted to the nonaverage, that is, a person whose psychic organization deviates considerably from that of the majority of community members. This test is relative in a dual sense. It takes account of the fact that mental deviation is not an absolute category, but is a departure from the socially normal in mental life, making the individual concerned appear "insane" to others, so that he is "insane in relation to others."[8] It also reflects the notion that mental incapacity is susceptible of gradation. Hence, the exemption criterion is formulated in comparative terms and indicates the degree of departure from the "normal" that qualifies for exemption. In this test psychiatry plays not a primary but only a derivative role. Its function within the operation of the test is appropriate to the needs of the described criminal law policy. But the psychiatric reference terms used in the test have been chosen with a view to conveying meaning to psychiatrists. While disagreement over the scope of these terms is not excluded, the test reflects the chosen policy, which may help to specify its meaning.

Of course, the mental incapacity exemption as conceived in the recommended test is very broad, meaning that a large group of persons may be expected to qualify within it for exemption from punitive responsibility. This feature of the test may raise doubts in the minds of many criminal law students. Such doubts, however, ought to be evaluated not in isolation but rather in the light of the total criminal law scheme of which such exemption is a functional part. Whether an exemption from punitive responsibility ought to be formulated in broad or narrow terms should depend on the operational meaning of the exemption, the results which such exemption entails in a given legal system. For an exemption from responsibility cast in terms of a "defini-

---

[7] See *Mental Incapaicty in Criminal Law, supra* at 73-74.

[8] "Mental disease" indicates alteration of an individual's internal status "vis-à-vis his external world as interpreted by others." ROCHE, THE CRIMINAL MIND 15 (1958). Robinson Crusoe could not conceivably be insane.

tion" of mental incapacity is not merely a cognitive statement; it is, as any meaningful part of a statute or code, a dispositive and not merely a descriptive category, a norm rather than a scientific proposition, although the choice of such norm ought to be made in the light of scientific insight. A definition of mental incapacity is analytically reducible to a rule for the guidance of law enforcement agencies, a legal provision instructing courts what group of persons shall be selected by them for distinctive treatment. Obviously, such selection ought to be rationally determined by the nature of such treatment. Thus, how broadly a mental incapacity exemption or a definition of mental incapacity should be formulated ought to depend in a sound policy scheme on the nature and scope of the treatment of the mentally incapacitated. A narrow definition of mental incapacity carries the serious policy disadvantage of compelling legislators to deal punitively with the large group of persons falling within a border area of sanity, so-called "abnormal" persons, who are not comprised by the definition of the "insane" or "mentally diseased or defective." Thus, for example, the Model Penal Code imposes an "extended term," that is, aggravated punishment, on "abnormal" offenders.[9] No explanation is offered why it has been found appropriate to deal with such persons punitively—indeed with increased punitive severity, implying a judgment of greater blameworthiness—rather than curatively.

The suggested test of mental incapacity, however, as any test of exemption, calls for implementing institutions and rules of evidence and procedure adapted to the requirements of that particular test. As a realistic criterion of the mental incapacity exemption, it ought to be set within a general framework of rational rules in regard to its allegation and proof. An important part of the law governing mental incapacity as related to the engagement in criminal conduct, i.e., the so-called "incapacity to commit a crime" or "incapacity at the time of the act," is the allegedly "procedural" notion of "unfitness to proceed," since, paradoxical as this may seem, effective assertion of the "mental

---

[9]MODEL PENAL CODE § 7.03 (3) (Tentative Draft No. 2, 1954; Tentative Draft No. 4, 1955; Proposed Final Draft No. 1, 1961). The Proposed Official Draft of the Model Code (1962) was published after the appearance of the present essay. The sections hereinafter cited have remained unchanged.

incapacity exemption" is predicated upon actual, realistic "mental fitness" of the accused to assert and maintain against the prosecution's attacks his own former incapacity. Finally, perhaps the most significant aspect of the mental incapacity exemption from punishment in modern times is the scheme of "measures of security" to be applied to persons acquitted by reason of "mental incapacity." Similarly, a finding of "unfitness to proceed" calls for application of rational discriminatory "measures."

Before discussing the several enumerated topics it is necessary to emphasize certain basic assumptions made in this paper in accordance with policy demands submitted by the writer in previous publications.

A dual approach dividing criminal law state intervention into "punishment," on the one hand, and "measures," on the other hand, is advocated for the purpose of avoiding confusion of the ends pursued by law, with resulting injustice to the individual. It is wrong to punish a person or to extend his punishment beyond the degree proportionate to his "guilt" on the ground that he is "dangerous"; likewise, it is irresponsible on the part of the state to let a "dangerous" person continue endangering the community. To guarantee individual freedom to the utmost possible extent, state reaction to "guilt" and state reaction to "danger" must be kept clearly distinct and separate, so that any state organ, whether legislative or judicial, may be able at any time to answer the broad habeas corpus query, fundamental in a democracy: "Why do you restrain this man's freedom?"[10]

The "law of measures," as the "law of punishment," should be subject to principles of the "rule of law." Measures ought to be governed by general legal rules and administered by courts throughout the period of state intervention. They should not be excessive, meaning, restrictive beyond proportion to the type or degree of the "danger," just as punishment ought not to exceed in gravity the degree of "guilt." There ought to be uniformity and

---

[10]"The great writ" has been often interpreted somewhat narrowly. McNally v. Hill, 293 U.S. 131 (1934); Eagles v. Samuels, 329 U.S. 394, 307 (1946); Parker v. Ellis, 362 U.S. 574 (1960); in Puerto Rico, Dìaz v. Campos, 81 D.P.R. 1009 (1960). It is nevertheless susceptible of a broader interpretation, expressing a philosophy of government that confers powers strictly limited to precisely such intervention as is clearly called for in the type of situation involved.

continuity of policy in criminal law administration from the initial step taken with regard to an individual until the ultimate termination of all criminal law state intervention into his life. Trial and sentence ought to constitute a continuous process governed by a clear and uniform policy. However, there ought to be inserted between the trial stage, concerned with the determination of "responsibility" in principle, whether punitive or in measures, and the sentencing stage, devoted to deciding upon the exact terms of punishment or measures, as the case may be, an investigative procedure purported to provide the court with the necessary scientific personality evaluation of the person concerned. Such a scientific evaluation should be made in a special psychiatric and sociological examinations center, should be based on verifiable data rather than the gossip-type information often supplied in probation reports and should be subject to legal scrutiny by the defense in an adversary "sentencing trial." It thus should afford a proper foundation for a just sentence in a democratic society.[11] But such evaluation must not be taken as the sole determinant of disposition. Objective criteria are essential safeguards of personal liberty.

This paper is divided into two parts. The first deals with problems arising prior to the sentencing stage. One section thereof is devoted to discussion of the rules of procedure and evidence applicable in the process of determining mental incapacity relating to engagement in the criminal conduct charged; the second section is dedicated to evaluation of the law of so-called "unfitness to proceed" in its definitional and sanctioning aspects. The second main part deals with the scheme of "measures" to be applied to persons "acquitted by reason of mental incapacity."

I. PROBLEMS PERTAINING TO THE "TRIAL STAGE"

A. Procedure to Determine Mental Incapacity Related to Engagement in the Criminal Conduct

1. Who May Raise the Mental Incapacity Issue?

The draftsmen of the Model Penal Code of the American Law

---

[11]For a critique of Williams v. New York, 337 U.S. 241 (1949), see Silving, "Rule of Law" in Criminal Justice, supra note 6, at 78-89.

Institute considered allowing the trial judge to raise the defense of incapacity, but rejected it on insufficient grounds. Section 4.03 declares "mental disease or defect excluding responsibility" to be "an affirmative defense." In a comment to this provision[12] the draftsmen explain that while giving the trial judge authority to raise the issue of incapacity at the time of crime was "considered desirable," "such provision was finally omitted as being too great an interference with the conduct of the defense." But a defendant's refusal to allow such issue to be raised might, in the draftsmen's opinion, be weighed as a factor in deciding whether he is mentally fit to proceed. Of course, no weight whatever can be attributed to such refusal in those, by no means rare, cases in which raising the issue of mental incapacity is undesirable in the objective self-interest of the defendant, though desirable from the standpoint of the community.[13]

---

[12]MODEL PENAL CODE § 4.03, comment at 194 (Tent. Draft No. 4, 1955).

[13]In Overholser v. Lynch, 288 F.2d 388, 392 (1961), the Court of Appeals for the District of Columbia, relied on the rule in Davis v. United States, 160 U.S. 469 (1895), and held that "insanity is not strictly an affirmative defense and can be raised by either the court or the prosecution." The majority also inferred this rule from "almost a positive duty on the part of the trial judge not to impose a criminal sentence on a mentally ill person." *Id.* at 393. In answer to the appellee's contention that he had carefully considered entering a plea of guilty, with the advise of counsel, the majority pointed out that "this decision was one which appellee and his counsel did not have an absolute right to make," in the light of the above cited duty of the court. Judge Fahy, dissenting, *id.* 394, at 395, noticed that the case presented "a serious question . . . involving the right of a person accused of a misdemeanor who is competent to plead guilty and is represented by counsel, not to be compelled by the court to enter a plea of not guilty." But he found it unnecessary to resolve "this most difficult question," since he considered "the commitment which eventuated from the trial . . . invalid for other reasons." It is instructive to read the decision of the majority in the light of the fact that for the purpose of a commitment in the District of Columbia after acquittal solely on the ground of insanity, D.C. CODE ANN. § 24-301 (Supp. 8 1960), dangerousness of the defendant need not be proved, and according to the dominant opinion, the purpose of the commitment is treatment and not protection of the community from danger. One might query whether in a free society it is not better to impose punishment upon a person not "guilty" because of insanity at the time of the act, than to impose psychiatric treatment against his will and without positive showing of mental illness, where the charges against him were misdemeanors involving two checks of $50 each cashed on a single day. [For discussion of the impact of the automatic detention provision on the burden of proof, see United States v. Naples, 192 F. Supp. 23, 39-40 (D.D.C. 1961)].

In Lynch v. Overholser, 269 U.S. 705 (1962), the Supreme Court of the United

It is an assumption based solely on historical grounds that the trial judge's authority to raise the issue of mental incapacity constitutes a greater "interference with the conduct of the defense" than does his power to inquire into the question of crime commission or intent under a general denial of guilt. The mental incapacity exemption is by no means coextensive with the absence of intent, since mental illness often releases rather than inhibits intent; nevertheless there may be sound policy reasons for treating mental incapacity and absence of intent in a similar manner procedurally. At law no factor can be said to possess an immanent "defense" status, as such status is conferred by law upon certain factors, often on policy grounds. Whether any given matter ought to be treated as an affirmative defense

---

States in effect held that a person could not be assigned to a mental institution on the basis of an acquittal by reason of insanity, predicated merely upon reasonable doubt as to his sanity, unless he had pleaded insanity. Clearly, such automatic assignment supported solely by doubt regarding defendant's sanity was unconstitutional where the crimes charged were minor misdemeanors against property. I submit that had the conduct charged and proved been homicide, the assignment would have been proper.

In civil law countries courts have the authority and the duty to raise the mental incapacity issue in appropriate cases. Among the countries of English legal tradition, Israel has introduced a rule permitting the court to raise such issue. Section 6 (b) of the Law Concerning the Mentally Ill 1955, SEFER CHUKIM 187 (of 6.7. 1955), P. 121, provides as follows: "When a person is charged with crime and the court finds that the accused committed the criminal act with which he is charged but finds, either upon evidence adduced by one of the parties or upon evidence brought before it upon its own motion, that the accused is not subject to punishment because he was [mentally] ill at the time of the act and that he still is [mentally] ill, the court shall order that he be confined in a mental hospital."

Other pertinent provisions of the same law read thus:

"(c) An order of the court under subdivision (a) [order for confinement in a hospital of a defendant unfit to plead] or under subdivision (b) is for the purpose of appeal deemed a judgment of conviction.

"(d) In order to make it possible for the court to decide whether an order under this section is called for, the court may order, upon motion of one of the parties or upon its own motion, that the accused be medically examined and, if necessary for the purpose of examination, that he be confined in a hospital.

"(e) The order under this section shall be executed by the District Psychiatrist . . . ." [author's translation].

Section 17(a) authorizes the Psychiatric Board to release a person confined by virtue of § 6.

or as part of the crime elements should be determined functionally, in terms of the results of alternative solutions.

Where mental incapacity is treated as an affirmative defense, the accused alone decides whether the measures provided for those acquitted by reason of insanity can be applied to him, even though these measures presumably are primarily means of community protection. The crucial problem is hence to determine whether it is sound criminal law policy to confer such power of decision upon the accused. It may, of course, be proper in some stiuations but not in others. In such cases there is a conflict between the public interest in community protection and the individual interest in freedom to choose limited imprisonment in preference to a potentially longer detention in a mental hospital; a democratic solution is predicated upon comparison of the weight of the pertinent interests in differential situations.

Whether the court and prosecution should have the authority to raise the issue of mental incapacity should be viewed not in isolation but rather in the light of the scope of the definition of "mental incapacity," the bearing of such definition on the issue of "dangerousness," and the relation of the nature and gravity of the crime charged to that issue. The public interest in protection rises with increasing scope of the mental incapacity exemption, but not necessarily proportionately, since the added incapacity situations involve less serious mental deviations. The definitions of "mental incapacity" are geared to the actor's "guilt" and bear only indirectly on his "dangerousness." The strongest indicia of the latter are the nature and gravity of the act charged. The type of crime in issue affords both an objective and a general standard of dangerousness and, for the purpose of determining the scope of court authority with a fair degree of precision, these features of objectivity and generality are significant enough to override the consideration that the gravity of the precipitating crime is not the only test of dangerousness.

It may not be desirable to expose a person who engaged in conduct which, given the required state of mind, would at most constitute a misdemeanor and thus presumably does not present a grave social danger to the involved operation of the scheme of mental incapacity measures unless he himself chooses this alternative in preference to punishment. Moreover, the treatment of mental incapacity is usually lengthy and might be disproportionate to the seriousness of either the disease or the criminal act committed. The imposition of time limitations upon criminal law measures where the precipitating crime is minor might render effective functioning of the system of mental incapacity measures illusory. Thus, in cases involving misdemeanors, "mental incapacity" should remain an "affirmative defense" which only the accused can raise. But in felony cases, in which by hypothesis a serious harm has been caused, so that there is some indication of danger of similar harm in the future, the state has the duty to take steps for the protection of the community. In felony cases the public interest in protection overrides the pertinent individual interest. Hence, in such cases courts and the prosecution should have the power to raise the issue of "mental incapacity."

An intricate problem may arise in a trial of a misdemeanor case when the evidence abundantly shows that the defendant suffered from a mental incapacity when he committed the act charged, but he refuses to raise the issue of such incapacity. To resolve this problem, it is necessary to consider the significance or purpose of requiring that an issue be "raised" by the accused in a criminal trial. The core of our philosophy of criminal procedure, the adversary nature of our criminal trial, would seem to be at stake. Yet, it is possible to argue even within this philosophy that barring others than the defendant from "raising an issue" — except where another offense is involved — is but a means of limiting the process of evidence and of guaranteeing that the defendant have an opportunity to controvert adverse evidence. Taking judicial notice of an obvious fact is hardly "inquisitorial." When evidence, indeed overwhelming proof, of insanity, becomes available incidentally, it would be a distortion of justice and prejudicial to public faith in its administration were the court forced to render a judgment which it knows to be clearly inappropriate, in the sense of violating the avowed policy of the law. Of course, the defendant's civil liberties must be safeguarded; he must have an opportunity to controvert the evidence of mental incapacity, and the measure to be imposed in the case of acquittal by reason of mental incapacity must be limited to the same maximum as is imposed upon the punishment for the criminal conduct in which he engaged.

Where the court and the prosecution are authorized to raise both the issue of "mental incapacity related to the criminal act" and that of "fitness to proceed"—they may raise the latter under conventional law—, the question is posed: How does the court or the prosecutor come to suspect that the defendant may not be "fit to proceed" or may have committed the criminal act in a state of incapacity? This brings us to the second point of importance: At what stage and by whom should the mental state of a defendant be examined?

2. Bases of Doubt Regarding Mental Capacity or Fitness to Proceed

The view that lay persons are as qualified as psychiatrists to testify to "mental incapacity" is no longer supported by anyone except certain of our legal authorities.[14] Courts in foreign countries have emphatically rejected it.[15] The behavior patterns from which laymen commonly infer absence of mental incapacity, particularly calmness after crime commission and rationality, have been shown not to constitute proof of mental health. The first mentioned phenomenon has been pointed out by psychiatrists to suggest an exactly opposite inference.[16] In fact, not even

---

[14]On this see OVERHOLSER, THE PSYCHIATRIST AND THE LAW 111-112 (1953).

[15]In Germany, the Bundesgerichtshof (Supreme Court of the Federal Republic of Germany in Civil and Criminal Matters), implying that on any question of psychological evaluation experts are better qualified than laymen, reversed a conviction of a sex offense because the trial court found it unnecessary to hear experts concerning the trustworthiness of the testimony of a child seven years old (7 BGHSt. 82 (V. Strafsenat), Dec. 14, 1954). The court said, at 83-85: "There is general agreement concerning the fact that there are means of arriving at the truth that are available to the medical expert and, according to some authorities also to the psychological expert, but are not available to the court, at any event during trial . . . ." The court did not refer to any special tests, such as narco-analysis or lie-detectors, which are prohibited in Germany. It referred simply to psychiatric and psychological knowledge and experience, as contrasted with the crude psychology of lay interrogators.

[16]Guttmacher, *Criminal Responsibility in Certain Homicide Cases Involving Family Members*, in PSYCHIATRY AND THE LAW 73, 91 (Hoch & Zubin ed. 1955), observed that of the thirty-six cases examined by him personally in the Medical

a psychiatrist is qualified to testify to the mental state of a person unless he has examined him adequately.[17] Only in certain situations is mental disease so obvious as to arouse immediate suspicion even in the mind of a layman. Since the court's superficial observations are not sufficient to insure the spotting of all defendants who may not be fit to proceed or who may have

---

Office of the Supreme Bench of Baltimore, Md., "Most of the psychotic individuals showed little affective reaction to the homicides." But courts take no notice of such scientific findings.

Pueblo v. Sánchez, 79 D.P.R. 116 (1956), is an instructive case. The accused, when told that his cows which were illegally grazing on the campus of the University of Puerto Rico were seized by the guards, in a fit of blind rage purposely ran over with his jeep one of the guards and killed another by hitting him over the head with a tube. A few minutes later he was found by a policeman when, tube in hand, he tried to stop passing cars. When asked to explain his conduct, Sánchez immediately answered: "I killed two persons and wish to surrender." He then asked the policeman to take him to the police station at Hato Rey and not to that of Rio Piedras, because—he said—in Rio Piedras the police would kill him. On the way to the police station he said: "I killed these impudent fellows; they will no longer abuse me, abusing me is finished." The evidence submitted in support of the defense of insanity consisted of proof of (a) heredity factors; (b) specific conduct pointing to insanity; (c) expert testimony; and (d) the manner in which the crime occurred. Proof was adduced that three brothers of the accused were confined in a mental institution, two of them suffering from schizophrenia and the third from oligophrenia; that three paternal uncles had committed suicide and that the accused's father had attempted a suicide. It was shown that both before and after commission of the crime the accused on various occasions engaged in soliloquy, cried without motive, unexpectedly left his work, bit the muzzle of a cow because she hit him with her tail, suddenly started running without reason, attacked his friends in the course of debates, and attempted suicide. Notwithstanding all this evidence, the Supreme Court held that the jury was justified in finding the accused sane, since his own wife had testified that he was well for periods of months; since his request that he be taken to the Hato Rey station for fear that they might kill him in Rio Piedras showed that he could reason rationally; and since the prosecutor who questioned him testified that he was calm and serene at the Hato Rey station, answered questions correctly, and showed no sign of incoherence, so that the prosecutor never doubted his sanity.

The writer and a group of law students spoke to Sánchez at the penitentiary where he is serving his life sentence. He was placed in the psychiatric wing of the institution. He answered a student's question as to the motive of his action saying that he was not responsible for his action; rather, it was all his brother's fault, since his brother was responsible for everything bad that ever happened in the world.

[17]This has been recognized by the MODEL PENAL CODE § 4.07 (3) (Tent. Draft No. 4, 1955; Proposed Official Draft 1962.

committed the felonious act charged in a state of incapacity, some other method must be adopted to assure that no injustice is done due to inadequate safeguards.

The Model Penal Code provides for psychiatric examination in advance of trial only in cases where either "the defendant has filed a notice of intention to rely on the defense of mental disease or defect excluding responsibility" or "there is reason to doubt his fitness to proceed, or reason to believe that mental disease or defect of the defendant will otherwise become an issue in the cause."[18] In those situations in which the issue of "mental illness" may or, indeed, must be raised by the court,[19] it is obviously pertinent to inquire: Whence comes the doubt that the defendant does not now or did not at the crucial time possess the required capacity? If doubt must arise before an examination is ordered, the principal source of protection of both the defendant and the community is unreliable lay hunches. Hence, there is a clear need for a procedure of advance examination of a defendant, at least in all felony cases, a procedure in the nature of that conducted under the Briggs Law of Massachusetts.[20]

The Briggs Law provides for a preliminary examination of persons "indicted by a grand jury for a capital offense or . . . known to have been indicted for any other offense more than once or to have been previously convicted of a felony." The clerk of the court or the trial justice gives notice to the Department of Mental Health, and the Commissioner of Mental Health thereupon appoints two impartial experts to examine the person concerned. The practice is to appoint only diplomates of the American Board of Psychiatry and Neurology for such examinations.[21] A report is filed and made available to the court, the prosecution and the defense. The report itself is not admissible

---

[18]*Id.* § 4.05 (1).

[19]People v. Burson, 11 Ill. 2d 360, 143 N.E.2d 239 (1957); State v. Lucas, 30 N.J. 37, 152 A.2d 50, 69 (1959). For discussion of the virtually unlimited manner in which the present mental condition of the defendant may be introduced into a criminal trial, see Note, *Amnesia: A Case Study in the Limits of Particular Justice*, 71 YALE LAW JOURNAL 109, 123 & nn. 76 & 77 (1961).

[20]MASS. ANN. LAWS c. 123 § 100 A (Supp. 1955).

[21]See Flower, *The Psychiatric Examination of Offenders in Massachusetts*, in PSYCHIATRY AND THE LAW, 97, 102 (Hoch & Zubin ed. 1955).

in evidence, but the psychiatrists who prepared it may be called as witnesses.[22]

It is submitted that a preliminary examination should be limited to situations in which the precipitating crime is a felony. In misdemeanor cases it should be ordered only if the defendant requests such examination. The practice of bringing to the attention of the court the presence of an issue of recidivism in advance of determination of the defendant's guilt of the precipitating crime is highly prejudicial to him. Treatment of a "repeated offense" as a procedural unit interferes with independent evaluation of the evidence regarding the precipitating crime, for there is a general tendency, not only of the jury but of the court as well, to assume guilt when it becomes known that the defendant has committed a crime before. It may not be possible to prevent knowledge of the court from being conveyed to the jury by various methods of unconscious communication in a trial. Still, there is an undoubted interest that the defendant be given an opportunity to defend himself against the charge of recidivism; moreover, in recidivism cases there is a great likelihood of a mental incapacity background, so that it is most desirable that the defendant in such cases be psychiatrically examined. These conflicting interests can be reconciled. Recidivism should not be permitted to be mentioned at all until after conviction for the crime that gives rise to the proceedings. Only after conviction should the court be given information regarding prior convictions. Recidivism then becomes an issue for the purpose of sentencing, which, as suggested, should be the subject of a separate adversary hearing before court and jury. Prior to that hearing there ought to be a mandatory examination in the psychiatric and sociologic examinations center to determine whether the crime repetition has a mental disease background.[23]

---

[22]See OVERHOLSER, *op. cit. supra* note 14, at 120-125.

[23]Compare Silving, *"Rule of Law" in Criminal Justice, supra* note 6, at 142, 150.

In our law there is at present a conflict of views in different jurisdictions on the question whether the interest in alleging prior convictions in indictments and informations, such allegations being a condition of the certainty of charges or dictated by treatment of recidivism as an independent crime type, overrides the need for protection of the defendant against the prejudicial effect of knowledge

If it does, the conviction based on the assumption that the accused was not mentally incapacitated at the time of crime commission should be revoked and an acquittal by reason of mental incapacity entered, so that measures rather than punishment become applicable.

As is well known, examination may often require confinement in a mental hospital. Such detention of a person presumed innocent may raise constitutional questions,[24] and it should certainly

---

of prior convictions on the part of fact finders. On this conflict and the various methods of reconciling both interests see 42 C.J.S., *Indictments and Informations* § 145, at 1057-1062 (1944 and Supp. 1961).

[24]The issue of constitutionality of a court order for a psychiatric examination of the defendant has been argued for a long time, but the dominant view today is that such an officially imposed examination is constitutional. Jessner v. State, 22 Wis. 184, 231 N.W. 634 (1930); State v. Myers, 220 S.C. 309, 67 S.E.2d 506, 507, 32 A.L.R.2d 430 (1951), and cases cited by the court; State v. Livingston, 105 S.E.2d 73, 79 (S.C. Sup. Ct. 1958); State v. Swinburne, 324 S.W.2d 746, 750-51 (Mo. Sup. Ct. 1959). See also MODEL PENAL CODE § 4.05, comment, at 195-196 (Tent. Draft No. 4, 1955) (list of statutes providing for pretrial examination of a defendant's mental capacity). For a recent case holding constitutional prearraignment mental examinations by the People without equal opportunity of the accused, not represented by counsel, see Early v. Tinsley, 265 F.2d 1 (10h Cir. 1960), *cert. denied* 364 U.S. 847 (1960).

Certain justifications and reservations advanced by courts in this context are clearly rationalizations. Thus, for example, waiver of the privilege against self-incrimination is inferred from a prospective plea of insanity. State v. Myers, *supra,* 67 S.E.2d, at 507-508; State v. Swinburne, *supra,* at 750-751; Early v. Tinsley, *supra.* There is a touch of Münchhausen argumentation in the court's contention in the last cited case, at 2-3, that a defendant whose mental incapacity is in issue can waive his privilege against self-incrimination by voluntarily and knowingly submitting to the examination, as well as in the contention that as regards such person the examination was not deceitful. If the defendant turns out to be mentally ill, he cannot validly waive any privilege and the examination as regards such person is necessarily "deceitful." The realistic ground on which such examination may be ordered is the necessity of determining whether the person concerned is fit to proceed and the great public interest in ascertaining impartially whether he should be subject to punishment or to measures, if it be found that he committed the act charged.

As will later be seen, the defendant should be given an opportunity from the very outset to be examined by a psychiatrist or psychiatrists of his choice. Other safeguards must be afforded, so that a device of necessity might not be extended beyond an unavoidable minimum intervention into human freedom.

As pointed out in Jessner v. State, *supra,* 231 N.W., at 636, if any violation of the constitutional rights of an accused is authorized by a statute providing for a pretrial examination, "It must be ascribed to the provision which authorizes his

not be prolonged beyond necessity. Hence, every effort should be made to avoid it unless clearly shown to be necessary, and where it is necessary, to reduce the time of detention to a minimum. In some cases there is no need for a protracted process of examination. And the period of examination should be extended only for reasons involving persons engaged in legal proceedings. It is hence suggested that a psychiatric clinic be made available in which criminal cases are given preference. Confinement in a mental hospital should be imposed only if the clinic psychiatrists find that ambulatory examination appears insufficient. Where confinement is necessary, the maximum period should be fixed at a low point, for example, ten days, with the proviso that the court may extend it for additional ten-day periods, but not beyond a maximum of, e.g., sixty days.

The court should have discretionary power to appoint two qualified psychiatrists to examine the defendant and report the results of such examination as a substitute for referral to the clinic or hospital. Such an appointment should be made particularly in a misdemeanor case where the defendant asks for a preliminary examination.

Whether the official examination is made by clinic, hospital or specially appointed psychiatrists, the defendant should have the right to be examined by one or two psychiatrists of his own choice, as well. Furthermore, he should have the right to request that a consultation be held between the official psychiatrists and the psychiatrist or psychiatrists of his choice. This is to avoid so far as feasible any differences in the reports that are not truly meaningful, such as mere diversity of terminology, which might confuse the trial participants. If, as a result of such consultation, an agreement can be reached upon a diagnosis, a joint report ought to be filed. In such case there is no need to expose the defendant to a cumbersome hearing on the issue of incapacity, unless he insists upon it. Hence, on the basis of a joint report,

---

commitment to a hospital of the insane for the purposes of observation. . . ." But, in the light of the intricacy of the issue of incapacity in certain cases, such commitment may be an indispensable condition of effective performance of the diagnostic task. Yet such commitment, being a necessity device, should not be prolonged beyond the limits imposed by necessity.

the court should have the power to find the defendant: (a) either fit or unfit to proceed; or (b) not guilty by reason of insanity, provided in this instance that commission of the criminal act is admitted. If no agreement is reached, separate reports ought to be filed with the court. If the disagreement concerns fitness to proceed, a hearing must be held, for which either party and/or the court may require any or all of the psychiatrists who filed reports to appear and submit to cross-examination. The court ought to have authority to call additional psychiatrists. If the disagreement concerns capacity at the crucial time, or if commission of the criminal act is not admitted, a trial must be held. At such trial any or all of the psychiatrists who submitted reports should be available to testify and to submit to cross-examination. Either party and/or the court should be able to call additional experts, subject to the court's power to limit their number. Clearly, all reports filed must be made available to both the prosecution and the defense.

3. Evidence of Mental Incapacity Relative to the Act Charged

The recommended test of "mental incapacity" related to engagement in the criminal conduct charged is complex and may call for presentation of a combination of evidentiary material. It is "culture-oriented," meaning that the mental state of the accused must be evaluated in relation to that which is normal in a given community. A double proof must be adduced: that of the mental state of the accused, and that of the mental state of his environment, i.e., of the "community" to which he belongs, including the group or groups within the district in which he lives, of which he is a member. Thus, psychiatrists alone may be unable to supply the necessary evidence. Other persons acquainted with the beliefs, customs, reactions and expectations of the relevant "community" may be called upon to supply the necessary information. As to such sociological matters, sociologists may qualify as experts. Also, any persons belonging to the community may be permitted to testify as regards its beliefs, customs and notions of expected conduct.

As suggested before, however, laymen are not equipped to express opinions on the mental state of the accused. They should not be permitted to testify, for example, that the accused appeared to them to be of sound or of unsound mind, for they do not as a general rule possess the scientific knowledge necessary to evaluate or interpret conduct in terms of psychiatric categories. They should be permitted to testify in descriptive terms as to the manner in which the accused behaved before, during or after the act, provided that a psychiatrist supplies information regarding the relevance and psychiatric import of such behavior under the circumstances. Should a layman testify to conduct or other matters the relevance of which has not been proved, the jury should be instructed to ignore such testimony in reaching a decision as to the mental state in issue.[25]

In regard to the mental state of the accused, psychiatric and, in some types of cases, psychological testimony is of the essence. But a psychiatrist or psychologist should be permitted to give his opinion regarding the accused's state of mind only if he has examined the accused. A psychiatrist or a psychologist may also

---

[25]In United States v. Naples, 192 F. Supp. 23, 40-41 (Dist Ct., D.C. 1961), Judge Holtzoff cited cases in which the United States Supreme Court held that a layman may express an opinion based on his own observations as to whether a person is of sound or unsound mind, and cited the observation of the Judicial Committee of the Privy Council in Attorney-General for the State of South Australia v. Brown [1960], A.C. 432, 452, that "The previous and contemporaneous acts of the accused may often be preferred to medical theory"; Judge Holtzhoff then concluded that "lay testimony on the issue of insanity may be of two kinds: opinions of lay witnesses based on their own observations; and evidence of the previous and contemporaneous acts of the accused." The latter is adopted as acceptable in the text; however the authoritative views cited by Judge Holtzoff as well as his subsequent reliance on the rationality of the accused's conduct as evidence of his sanity are submitted to be open to doubt.

In sum, my submission is that a layman may testify as to (a) what are the beliefs, customs and expectations prevailing in the community to which he belongs; (b) what he saw or heard the accused do or say prior to, during or after the act. In testifying to beliefs, customs and expectations prevailing in the community, of course, a layman is interpreting the states of mind of community members. However, such interpretations differ from interpretation of the state of mind of an individual, in that they actually but reflect matters of common knowledge within the community. It is also true that every description of conduct implies an interpretation, and to this extent a lay testimony regarding the accused's conduct may include elements of psychiatric evaluation. However, certain limitations on the descriptiveness of testimony are implied in the nature of language as the medium of testimonial evidence.

testify on general propositions of psychiatric or psychological science, and on the issue of the validity of the procedure followed, or the general scientific propositions stated or assumed, by another witness.[26]

An expert should be allowed to testify freely, and so far as possible without interruption. He should be permitted to present, in the form of his choice, a comprehensive picture of the accused's mental life and include psychologically or psychiatrically pertinent observations though they may not appear to a layman to bear on the state of mind relative to the act charged.[27] The expert should be interrupted only if he testifies in an inadmissible manner or if it appears that he is about to reveal inadmissible matters, such as those bearing on commission of the act (if the act is not admitted) or prior criminal conduct of the accused.[28]

---

[26]On the last point see MODEL PENAL CODE § 4.07 (3), end of last sentence (Proposed Official Draft 1962).

[27]The Socratic method of elucidation of truth by a process of question and answer directed to specific points is not suitable as an initial method of inquiry where the "truth" consists of a comprehensive existential reality rather than of a composite of mosaic-like pieces. Questioning in such cases need not be dispensed with as a method of testing and checking upon the psychiatrist's testimony, although one might consider the possibility of calling upon another psychiatrist rather than upon a lawyer to function as interrogator. My submission is that the court should include an associate judge who is a trained psychiatrist, and such judge would be particularly qualified to pose any questions which a court might normally address to the expert. The presence of a psychiatrist member of the court ought to afford a safeguard against the kind of double-talk now frequently encountered when law and psychiatry clash on the forensic scene. On composition of courts see Silving, *"Rule of Law" in Criminal Justice, supra* note 6, at 149.

Chief Judge Biggs, in United States v. Currens, 290 F.2d 751, 771-73 (3d Cir. 1961), rejected the *Durham* formula, but expressed approval of its permitting the psychiatrist to "give a picture of the whole man to the court and jury" rather than restricting him to answer specific questions. *Id.* at 771. But since Judge Biggs did not question the present method of interrogating the expert in our law, his remarks must be taken to refer solely to the type of specific questions that may be posed to the expert; thus, he was approving interrogation directed not only to the "knowledge test" (*M'Naghten*), but to consideration of other mental factors as well.

[28]While in many jurisdictions by statute information acquired by a physician in attending a patient in a professional capacity is privileged, see, for example, Taylor v. United States, 222 F.2d 398, 401 (D.C. Cir. 1955), doubt remains as to extension of a similar privilege to the event where the physician has been appointed by the court to examine the defendant. See GUTTMACHER & WEIHOFFEN,

Before testifying, he should be instructed by the court in regard to the type of evidence that is inadmissible and admonished that he must not, under sanction of contempt, disclose any in-

PSYCHIATRY AND THE LAW 275-276 (1952). In England, according to these authors, it seems to be considered unethical for the examiner even to discuss the circumstances surrounding the crime with the suspect, let alone to reveal his statements to the authorities. It may be difficult to visualize a full psychiatric examination in which a particular topic is carefully avoided. But a rule barring disclosure of any knowledge regarding commission of the crime has been mentioned by the Supreme Court of South Carolina in State v. Myers, 220 S.C. 309, 67 S.E. 2d 506, 508 (1951). In the District of Columbia, for example the doctor-patient privilege bars disclosure of matters regarding *commission of the act* in question, but has been made specifically inapplicable "to evidence relating to the *mental competency or sanity* of the accused in criminal trials where the accused raises the defense of insanity" [Emphasis supplied]. D.C. CODE ANN. § 14-308 (Supp. 8 1960). Under this provision, can the prosecution or court comment upon a defendant's refusal to cooperate in a court-ordered examination? Doubts have been expressed regarding the propriety of such comments in light of the privilege against self-incrimination where the issue is the defendant's sanity, which at common law is an essential component of *mens rea*. Krash, *The Durham Rule and Judicial Administration of the Insanity Defense in the District of Columbia,* 70 YALE LAW JOURNAL 905, 920 (1961).

The fact that sanity is a condition of *mens rea* for purposes of conviction does not necessarily mean that it must be treated in all respects in the same manner as intent, negligence or other components of *mens rea*. Certainly, sanity has not been so treated for purposes of the burden of proof at common law, under the rule in the M'Naghten Case, or under the law of several American jurisdictions. Nor need it, as a matter of logical necessity, be treated as is intent for the purpose of the privilege against self-incrimination. There is a difference between compelling a person to admit that he intended to kill and requiring him to submit to a psychiatric examination that might reveal that he was sane at the time of the alleged killing, especially when he cannot be compelled to utter words in the course of the examination. But, viewed from a practical standpoint, either the privilege or the full value of the expert testimony as to mental capacity must be jeopardized, for it is very difficult effectively to evaluate the accused's mental state without revealing or hinting at commission of an act that may have played an important role in his life.

The realistic justification for admission of disclosure of information regarding an accused's mental state by the physician appointed by the court to examine him lies in the overriding interest in the ascertainment of such mental state by experts at a time when lay observations on the subject have been discredited. Expert testimony on the issue of sanity is necessary, for without it there could be no evidence sufficient to support a verdict, either of conviction or of acquittal by reason of mental incapacity. It is important to bear in mind that in our times either course leads to state intervention, so that the operational meaning of many of our traditional legal principles, such as the presumption of innocence and the presumption of sanity, has changed.

formation he may possess that is protected by the rules on inadmissibility. After making a comprehensive statement, the expert may be questioned as to particular points and cross-examined.

4. Disposition and Remedies in Cases of Mental Incapacity

Where a court or jury has rendered a verdict of "not guilty by reason of mental incapacity," the court should assign the defendant to the special examinations center for a further examination and report to assist the court in determining whether any measure ought to be imposed and, if so, what type or types of measures may be appropriate to the case. As suggested before, such assignment should also be required in cases of conviction where, upon a mandatory inquiry by the court, it is shown that the accused has been convicted before.

Another adversary hearing ought to be held on the issue of sentencing. A judgment of "not guilty by reason of mental incapacity" and a sentence imposing measures should be appealable, as are judgment of conviction and sentences imposing punishment.

B. Determination of Fitness to Proceed; Measures Imposed Upon the Unfit; Remedies

1. Selecting the Proper Test

The test of "fitness to proceed" is generally thought to be different from that of "mental capacity relative to the commission of crime." The Model Penal Code follows the dominant view in providing that "no person who as a result of mental disease or defect lacks capacity to understand the proceedings against him or to assist in his own defense shall be tried, convicted or sentenced for the commission of an offense so long as such incapacity endures."[29] In the comment the draftsmen criticize the practice in some jurisdictions of declaring persons unfit to proceed on a mere showing that they are psychotic, with the result that such persons are committed; they cite with approval the practice followed in England, where "the inquiry appears to be

---

[29] § 4.04 (Tent. Draft No. 4, 1955).

genuinely focussed on the defendant's capacity to understand and to defend."[30] The desire to keep the test within narrow limits is motivated by consideration of the disadvantages attaching to a finding of unfitness. Such disadvantages, in the opinion of the Model Code draftsmen, are (a) that the defendant "is committed for custody and treatment under the shadow of a trial if he recovers, possibly on a capital charge," which is "hardly an aid to therapy"; (b) that many such persons have a sense of grievance that they had no trial; and (c) that there always remains the possibility of such person being innocent and deprived of the opportunity to clear himself.[31]

In our law the trial of a person unfit to proceed is absolutely void, even when he is represented by counsel.[32] If constitutional

---

[30]*Id.*, comment at 195.

[31]*Ibid.*

[32]Overholser v. Lynch, *supra*, note 13 at 391; Ashley v. Pescor, 147 F.2d 318 (8th Cir. 1945). See also Silving, *Testing of the Unconscious in Criminal Cases*, in SILVING, ESSAYS ON CRIMINAL PROCEDURE 189, at 208-212 (Dennis, Buffalo, 1964).

Of course, a person cannot be deemed "present" at the trial if he is but bodily there; rather, he must be aware of the "meaning" of the things said and done in the course of procedure, and he must certainly be aware and in control of his own communications and dispositive actions. As will be later shown, he must be able to "conduct his defense." At this point, however, I should like to deal only with the accused's knowledge and control of his own communications and actions. There should be no need in our constitutional system to stress that an accused in a criminal case must be aware and in control of what he himself is "saying." "Saying" means communicating an intended meaning, and not some exceptional meaning not commonly attributed to such types of communication. If he is in fact "communicating" something other than what he thinks he is communicating or intends to communicate, it is as if he were speaking a language he did not understand. His "presence" is merely formal and there should be no doubt that a trial under such conditions fails to meet constitutional requirements.

Such is the situation, for example, when lie-dector tests are allowed to be used in criminal proceedings. The constitutional doubts regarding application of such tests are magnified where the subject, though "fit to proceed," belongs to a borderline class of those deemed "fit." For this reason it seems proper to warn again against use of such fascist methods of investigation in our criminal proceedings.

Professor Skolnik, *Scientific Theory and Scientific Evidence: An Analysis of Lie-Detection*, 70 YALE LAW JOURNAL 694, 724-725 (1961), has misunderstood the nature of the legal, constitutional, and psychological "issue" when criticizing my argument against admission of lie-detector tests in criminal proceedings. He apparently believes to have met my contention that the lie-detector tests the "unconscious" by stating that "lie detection does not bring out *repressed* materials in the individual's life history," since "[w]hat the polygraph actually tests is 'conscious' conflict between the answer given to the interrogator and the facts as believed by the accused," and since the physiological responses recorded by the polygraph and thus serving as media of apprising the investigator that the subject is lying "arise out of emotions felt by the individual while lying," which emotions are consciously felt. "It is important to emphasize," says Mr. Skolnik, "that such feelings are always *consciously* felt. Freud makes this emphatically clear: 'It is surely of the essence of an emotion that we should feel it, i.e., that it should enter consciousness. So for emotions, feelings, and affects to be unconscious would be quite out of the question.' There is, thus, no interference by lie detection with 'freedom of the will' in the sense of unconscious probing. Of course, the subject's answers may be unconsciously motivated, but this is true of any testimony. In that sense, there is never any 'freedom of mind and will.'" For the stated reasons, Mr. Skolnik also denies the propriety of my joining the polygraph with so-called "'truth serums' under the heading 'objective tests.'"

Before dealing with probing the "unconscious," in the psychoanalytical sense, by means of a lie-detector (of course, I hope that the "probing" itself is not "unconscious" as is suggested by Mr. Skolnik's use of language), it may be useful to inquire into the matter of probing the contents of the accused's mind by use of his own verbal utterances in such a manner as to make them potentially convey a social meaning different from their normal meaning. Verbally the accused communicates "I did not do it," but his autonomic responses "communicate" for him that he does not believe his verbal statement to be true; thus he actually "communicates" that he knows he did it. It is irrelevant that this unusual meaning of the verbal utterance is conveyed by use of a by-product of that utterance, rather than by attributing to the utterance an exceptional "code" meaning. The fact remains that such unusual meaning is not intended to be conveyed by the speaker, and that he may be unaware that he is conveying it. This method of probing is not comparable to compelling a person to speak so that he might be identified by the sound of his voice, for the lie-detector method actually probes the contents of the human mind. It compels him to reveal what he thinks, to admit when he does not wish to admit. It is an "objective" method of inquiry, in that the subject is "used as a medium of proof" (*Beweismittel*) against his will and thus in violation of his right to "conduct" his defense.

Even more significant is the fact that the autonomic response which serves as a medium of "communication" of the contents of the accused's mind is elicited by the emotion or feeling of "anxiety." "Anxiety" is an affective response to a danger which may well be representative of irrational unconscious ideation. FREUD, *Inhibitions, Symptoms and Anxiety*, in XX COMPLETE PSYCHOLOGICAL WORKS OF SIGMUND FREUD (Strachey transl. 1959), 164-168. ". . . [I]t is also meaningful"—said FENICHEL, THE PSYCHOANALYTICAL THEORY OF NEUROSIS (1955), at 17—"to talk about unconscious sensations, feelings, or emotions." Freud said in the very paper cited by Professor Skolnik, *On the Unconscious*, in 4 COLLECTED PAPERS 89, 112 (The International Psycho-Analytical Library 1948): "It is possible for affective

provisions are to be meaningful, they must be interpreted in the light of their spirit rather than by their mere letter. To be meaningful, the requirement of fitness to proceed cannot be deemed satisfied where the accused has but a superficial "understanding" of the proceedings or a verbal ability "to assist in his own defense." The mere fact that an accused talks rationally and is able to "tell his attorney of the events as he recalls them" has been held by the United States Supreme Court insufficient to qualify

---

development to proceed directly from the system Ucs [unconscious]; in this case it always has the character of anxiety, the substitute for all "repressed' affects." Even in the cited paper Freud's theory of the affects was by no means as simple as Professor Skolnik seems to assume on the basis of two sentences taken out of context. Moreover, this paper was first published in 1915. Since that time the psychoanalytic theory of the affects has undergone many changes; today it constitutes one of the most controversial topics of psychoanalysis. See E. Jacobson, *The Affects and their Pleasure-Unpleasure Qualities in Relation to the Psychic Discharge Processes*, in DRIVES, AFFECTS, AND BEHAVIOR 38 (Lowenstein ed. 1953).

For legal purposes it is most significant that the lie-detector response is produced by fear, for this is a typical means of inquisitorial questioning. Professor Skolnik says that it is irrelevant how a response is "motivated," since any testimony may be "unconsciously motivated." He forgets that there is a decisive difference between eliciting an answer that may incidentally be "unconsciously motivated"—although even incidental motivation by fear may cast doubt on the propriety of using such answer as evidence—and utilizing such motivation, particularly the motivation of fear, as a specific means of eliciting an answer, apart from the fact that the answer itself in lie-detection is not an "answer" in the sense of purposeful communication.

As seen, lie-detection is an "objective" method of testing. It is thus properly joined with "truth sera" under the heading "objective tests." The fact that there are also distinctions between these tests, of course, is not a bar against their being grouped together for purposes to which their similarity is relevant. In one respect the lie-detector test may be said to be more objectionable than the "truth serum" test: It utilizes anxiety as a medium of investigation. Mueller expressed this metaphorically by saying that "the polygraph chair . . . does not look unlike the electric chair!" See Mueller, *The Law Relating to Police Interrogation Privileges and Limitations*, 52 JOURNAL OF CRIMINAL LAW, CRIMINOLOGY AND POLICE SCIENCE 1, 11 (1961). Quite clearly, when subjected to any of the "objective tests," the person concerned is "not fit to proceed." Compare Silving, *Manipulation of Unconscious Reactions in Criminal Cases*, in ESSAYS ON CRIMINAL PROCEDURE, *op. cit., supra* 223, at 225-231.

It may be pertinent to note that the accused's unfitness to proceed renders his trial invalid also in civil law countries. See, for instance, the German STRAFPROZESSORDNUNG (Code of Criminal Procedure), §§ 205, 338 (5); on this see SCHWARZ, STRAFPROZESSORDNUNG, comment to § 205 (22d rev. ed. 1961).

him as capable to stand trial.[33] Clearly, he must be able to interpret the events meaningfully and not merely to relate them, particularly where a significant element of the offense charged is his mental relation to the events. But there is no precise notion in our law of the function which the accused must be mentally equipped to perform in order to qualify as "fit to proceed." The term generally used to describe this function is "assistance," the accused being expected to "assist" his attorney in the defense. Yet, this term does not properly reflect the otherwise prevailing notion of the attorney-client relationship, according to which the accused is the *dominus litis* and his attorney is but an agent. Crucial decisions are thus made by the accused and not by his attorney. Nor can an attorney commit the accused in any significant matters against his will; indeed, in some jurisdictions it is insufficient if the attorney makes such a commitment in the presence of the accused when the latter preserves silence.[34] Accordingly, "fitness to proceed" should be cast in terms of the defendant's "capacity to conduct the criminal proceedings against him in a meaningful manner" rather than in terms of "capacity to assist in the defense." This calls for a high degree of performance capacity.

One may well doubt the realism, in the light of present scientific insight, or the rationality, in the light of present conceptions of philosophy, of the disparate treatment of "mental capacity to commit crime" and "fitness to proceed." We have learned that the human mind does not lend itself to fragmentation into topographically distinctive compartments. But we continue to divide that mind historically, that is, to conceive of mental phenomena

---

[33]In Dusky v. United States, 362 U.S. 402 (1960), the Supreme Court stated the test of a defendant's capacity to stand trial to be "whether he has sufficient present ability to consult with his lawyer with a reasonable degree of rational understanding—and whether he has a rational as well as factual understanding of the proceedings against him."

[34]Thus, in Puerto Rico, for example, by virtue of a statutory provision — CODE OF CRIMINAL PROCEDURE, art. 164; 34 L.P.R.A. § 403, a guilty plea was valid only if made by the accused "personally." A plea of guilty to a felony made in the presence of the accused by his attorney is null and void, and a sentence based on such allegation is subject to review by habeas corpus. Jiménez v. Jones, 74 D.P.R. 260, 263-64 (1953). Cf. Rule 69, Puerto Rico Rules of Criminal Procedure, 1963.

as distinctive and separable episodes, treating them as independent, fixed and immutable entities. Not only is this treatment based on a lack of insight into the continuity of mental life—a continuity present even where it may appear disrupted—but also it proceeds from a questionable philosophical assumption of a distinctive fixed past mental reality that "existed" apart from its present symptoms or its present reflection in the mind of a person. It is unnecessary to delve into intricate problems of the philosophical struggle between realism and idealism or of the possibility of giving either of these positions a meaningful linguistic expression; for surely in law a past event is meaningful only when it is or can be proved. Leaving aside perjury, distortion and bars imposed by the limitations of linguistic expression, for legal purposes a past event is but its present mental reflection—either a direct reflection in a recollection or an indirect one, built upon some other symptom. The same is true of past psychological states. They exist to the extent that they are remembered. Since a person's mental experience is never truly conveyable to another, the subject who has a mental experience, for example, "intends" to commit a crime, would seem to be the approximately best qualified witness to that experience. While this may appear doubtful in the light of psychoanalytic insight, in law the testimony of the accused as to his "intent" to commit the crime charged—if he chooses to testify—is a significant, if not the most significant, item of evidence. Since such "intent" exists today only as a recollection, it is hardly possible to separate the intent from the recollection. That "intent," phenomenologically, *is* a recollection. Obviously, permitting, e.g., a psychotic person to testify to his past "intent" cuts deeply into the very substance of such intent.

Since a trial culminates in a disposition—and in a rational legal system is emphatically not a ritual but a social institution which derives meaning from the fact that it thus results in a socially adequate disposition—every procedural aspect of trial should be viewed in the light of the dispositive portion of law. One might query whether a sanction for a past conduct can be meaningfully applied to a defendant regardless of his present mental state relative to that conduct and its accompanying mental state.

It seems unjust to punish a man who has no present insight into the conduct for which he is being punished or into the full meaning of such conduct. There is at stake the total doctrine of "guilt" as present imputability of a past event.[35]

Perhaps the law of the future will succeed in integrating the test of mental incapacity and that of unfitness to proceed. But such integration is predicated upon a complete reevaluation of our basic legal conceptions of the mental element, a total review of the notions of "intent," "recklessness," even "motive," as historically fixed phenomena. Until such reevaluation is made, we must tentatively accept a distinctive notion of "fitness to proceed." Yet, even today we must not forget that such fitness is an integral part of essential elements of crime. In a sense, it is itself an element of crime. Legality requires adoption of a broad notion of "unfitness to proceed."

However, methods are available to reduce and to modify the disadvantages incident to a finding of unfitness. One such method may help to put an end to the criminal proceedings in

---

[35]For an interesting treatment of the problem of amnesia and its bearing on fitness to proceed see Note, Amnesia: A Case Study in the Limits of Particular Justice, supra note 19. The problem of any man's capacity to defend himself in a criminal trial is always open to some doubt, for hardly any individual can preserve a proper balance of mind in the face of his own criminal trial. Should a mere neurotic wish for conviction constitute unfitness? As remarked by Judge Holtzoff in United States v. Naples, 192 F. Supp. 23, 41 (D.D.C. 1961): "The fact is that all criminals commit mistakes and it is generally their own errors that lead to their apprehension and conviction. A perfect crime is unknown." A long time ago, Mittermaier and Hans Gross puzzled about "the very extraordinary psychological problem" of confessions which are of no conceivable benefit to the person concerned. See GROSS, CRIMINAL PSYCHOLOGY 31-33 (Kallen transl., Modern Criminal Science Series 1918). Psychoanalytical writers explained this "extraordinary problem" when they discovered that an offender often unconsciously desires to be punished (Freud, Der Verbrecher aus Schuldewusstsein, in X GESAMMELTE SCHRIFTEN, Internationaler Psychoanalytischer Verlag 312). The traces of crime left by the offender that lead to his capture are hardly attributable to accident. Should an accused be held "unfit to proceed" merely because he left such traces?

It would seem that, as in the case of mental incapacity relative to the act charged, so in the case of fitness to proceed, the test should be interpreted on a comparative basis, that is, taking into consideration the normal degree of fitness possessed by defendants in criminal cases.

appropriate cases; another one pertains to the consequences attaching to a finding of unfitness.

2. Objective Trial

The gravest injustice is inflicted upon a person by criminal law commitment upon a finding of unfitness to proceed when it later turns out that he had not committed any criminal act. Moreover, the psychiatric opinion regarding a defendant's capacity to stand trial may often turn on the question whether he in fact committed the act with which he is charged.[36] On this question may also depend desirability of commitment even of the civil type, when the person concerned is otherwise found to be mentally ill,[37] for legal "insanity" is not *per se* an indication of danger, whereas commission of serious criminal violence may be such an indication.

The Royal Medico-Psychological Association of Great Britain and Ireland (1924) suggested the following solution of this important problem.[38]

> When a person is found unfit to plead, we would suggest that a plea of not guilty should be recorded by the Court, and the trial on the facts allowed to proceed in his absence if he cannot properly be present in Court, arrangements being made for him to be represented by counsel and solicitor.

Such procedure, of course, would be unconstitutional in the United States.[39] But a modified form of the same idea may not be unconstitutional. Where a defendant is found unfit to pro-

---

The precariousness of our concept of "fitness to proceed" is perhaps best reflected in a recent holding of the Supreme Court of the United States that such fitness does not imply capacity to waive the assistance of counsel. Westbrook v. Arizona, 384 U.S. 150 (1966).

[36]MacNiven, *Psychoses and Criminal Responsibility*, in MENTAL ABNORMALITY AND CRIME 8, 63 (Radzinowicz & Turner ed., II English Studies in Criminal Science 1949).

[37]Eaton, *Functions of the Psychiatrist in the Court and Prison*, in CRIME AND INSANITY 165, 170-171 (Nice, ed., 1958.)

[38]Quoted by MacNiven, *supra* note 36, at 63. See also MASS. JUDICIAL COUNCIL, THIRTY-SIXTH REPORT 22-24, 27-28 (1960), quoted in MODEL PENAL CODE § 4.06, comment (Proposed Final Draft No. 1, 1961).

[39]Compare *supra* note 32.

ceed and it is further found that such unfitness is not likely to be of short duration, a "tentative trial" might be held, in which a "public defender of the rights of the mentally ill" would appear in the defendant's behalf. On the basis of such trial, the defendant might be found not to have committed the act charged or otherwise acquitted, provided however that he could not be thus acquitted on the ground of insanity, for he must not on the basis of such trial be subjected to any type of state intervention. Nor could he be found in such trial to have committed the criminal act or prejudiced in any other manner. A denial of a declaration that the defendant did not commit the act charged or a refusal to acquit in a tentative trial should not be admissible in evidence in any later trial of the defendant.

3. Measures Imposed Upon Persons Unfit to Proceed

When the court finds that a person lacks fitness to proceed, the Model Penal Code provides that "the Court shall commit him to the custody of the Commissioner of Correction to be placed in an appropriate institution of the Department of Correction for so long as such unfitness shall endure."[40] This disposition seems harsh, especially since at this stage the defendant is presumed innocent; in functional terms this presumption means that he should not be subjected to any normal consequences of guilt. Nor is such commitment necessary in all cases for preventive or protective purposes. Though mentally ill, the defendant may be neither dangerous nor in need of treatment; he may be treatable as an outpatient; or the crime charged may be minor, indicating no particular danger to society even if it should be repeated. Where the crime charged is not minor, the danger of its repetition and the social loss such repetition would entail ought to be weighed against the restriction of a man's liberty when he has not been convicted of any crime and may well be innocent. The "objective trial" that has been recommended would afford some safeguard against abuse of detention in instances of this type. However, where such trial fails to result in a finding that the defendant did not commit the act charged, refusal of such find-

---

[40]MODEL PENAL CODE § 4.06 (2), *supra* note 4. The Proposed Official Draft prefers entrusting custody to the Commissioner of Mental Hygiene.

ing must not be deemed even a prima facie showing of crime commission. The principle of *favor libertatis* requires limitation of automatic assignment to a mental institution to situations of grave social danger. The danger, at this stage, must be measured by the graveness of the act charged. Assignment to an appropriate institution should be ordered in all cases where the act charged falls within the category of crimes against life, bodily integrity or health of a person or persons. In cases other than these, such assignment should be predicated upon a showing by the prosecution of danger of irremediable serious harm to the community.[41]

Of course, in instances where the trial is suspended due to the defendant's unfitness to proceed there obtains a social interest in the advancement of the trial. For this reason, the court ought to have power to order that the defendant be treated, if such treatment is psychiatrically indicated, even where he is not confined in a mental institution, and provided that he consents to such treatment. The court should also have power to order appropriate protective measures, such as to place the defendant under supervision of a social work agency and to prohibit him from frequenting taverns or driving a car, as the circumstances may suggest. The court should order a periodic examination of the defendant, whether or not detained in a mental hospital, with a view to ascertaining whether he has recovered fitness to proceed.

---

[41]In the District of Columbia, United States v. Pound, Crim. No. 76028, D.D.C., Nov. 26, 1945, raised the issue whether a defendant unfit to stand trial can be detained indefinitely, when the probability of his recovery is very minute. But the issue within due process would seem to be whether such person may be detained at all unless he is shown to be dangerous. Krash, *supra* note 28, at 917, suggested that due process may be said to require that a defendant be released even though he may be dangerous if it appears that he will never recover sufficiently to stand trial. It would seem, however, that orderly procedure in such cases requires dismissal of the charge, rather than a discharge notwithstanding dangerousness, when the person concerned was detained in the first place on no rational basis other than the prospect of a future trial. It is submitted that a rational rather than doctrinaire approach requires that the court be given power in all cases of manifest and serious danger to order a temporary emergency measure of continued detention until civil commitment proceedings are instituted and terminated.

For the purpose of appeal, any court order declaring a defendant unfit to proceed or assigning him to a mental hospital or imposing upon him any other measure should be deemed a conviction.[42]

When the defendant recovers fitness to proceed after a long time has elapsed since suspension of proceedings, the court should have power to dismiss the charge unless prosecution and trial appear to be clearly in the public interest. The court should weigh the length of time that has elapsed against the seriousness of the charge in considering the advisability of dismissal.

II. THE SCHEME OF MEASURES APPLICABLE IN CASES OF ACQUITTAL BY REASON OF MENTAL INCAPACITY

As stated in the introduction, punishment ought to be confined to the distinctive purpose pursued by its means. It should never be imposed on the assumption that it might serve any one of a number of mutually interchangeable purposes, such as retribution, deterrence, reformation or community protection. The prevailing uncertainty and flexibility of the so-called ends of punishment violate the dignity of man, who—if necessity dictates that he be used as a means to an end other than himself—should never be used as a means to some indefinite end. It is unjust to punish a man or to increase his punishment without some basis in his guilt, on the ground that he is dangerous. The proper reaction to "danger" is a "security measure."

A planned, systematic diversification of punishment and measures is not merely a jurisprudential nicety, a requirement of legal aesthetics or of *elegantiae juris*, but is a significant safeguard against encroachment upon civil liberties. Lack of systematization in measures has resulted in this country, on the one hand, in a relative failure to appreciate that in measures, just as in punishment, a "legality" issue is posed, and on the other hand, in a haphazard assertion of civil liberties. Thus, according to the Model Penal Code, a person accused of committing a minor crime—for example, of stealing property of small value—when found unfit to proceed would be assigned to the Department of

---

[42]Compare § 6(c) of the Israeli law cited *supra* note 13.

Correction without possibility of trial or release until he recovered, although he may not have committed the act at all and, even if he had, may not require such detention on the basis of the nature of the disease from which he suffers. In contrast, the methods obtaining, for instance, in the District of Columbia for unconditional or conditional release from a mental hospital[43] to which a person "acquitted solely on the ground that he was insane at the time of . . . commission" is assigned, have become notorious.[44] When the problem of such release is in issue, we find psychiatrists pleading for "civil liberties" of the person thus detained after an extremely brief period although that person has admittedly killed another human being and although no contention is made that the detainee has recovered from his disease.[45] This contrasts strangely with the lack of any evidence of humanitarian concern for the "civil liberties" of the petty thief confined for an indeterminate period as unfit to proceed, although there is certainly no sufficient warrant in psychiatric authority for assuming that such thief is particularly likely to turn into a killer.[46]

---

[43]D.C. Code Ann. § 24-301 (Supp. 8 1960).

[44]See Hakeem, *A Critique of the Psychiatric Approach to Crime and Correction,* 23 Law and Contemporary Problems 650, 661-62 (1958); Goldstein & Katz, *Dangerousness and Mental Illness: Some Observations on the Decision to Release Persons Acquitted by Reason of Insanity,* 70 Yale Law Journal 225 (1960); Krash, *supra* note 28 at 944-946.

[45]Miss Hough, whose case aroused much attention, killed a visitor who came to express his sympathy to her over the recent death of her father (a psychiatrist), because, as she later said, the victim became "psychologically aggressive." She committed this homicide in May, 1957, but had been known to suffer from paranoid schizophrenia of the aggressive type at least as early as 1945. See Hough v. United States, 271 F.2d 458 (D.C. Cir. 1959); see particularly Judge Miller's dissenting opinion, *id.* 463, 468.

[46]Norval Morris in his brilliant monograph on The Habitual Criminal (1951) found "specificity of recidivism" to prevail in the "preventive detainees" whose cases he examined, *id.* 317-322, whereas in "confirmed recidivists" the same writer found 38% showing variation in crime types, *id.* 360-366. In Alexander & Healy's Roots of Crime (1935), the subjects of study showed no deviation from one crime pattern. The Wolfenden Report (Report of the Committee on Homosexual Offenses and Prostitution, Cmnd. 247, H.M. Stationary Office 1957) stated, par. 57, at 23: "We are authoritatively informed that a man who has homosexual relations with an adult partner seldom turns to boys, and *vice-versa,* though it is apparent from the police reports we

As in the punitive scheme, so in the scheme of "measures," the "legality principle" must determine the direction and scope of the pursuit of protection in a democratic society. This principle affords the standards of the systematization of protective measures. Space limitations bar discussion of general rules of "legality" as applied to "measures," but for the specific purpose of recommending "measures" to be applied in "mental incapacity" cases, it is necessary to point out certain guides based upon the "legality principle."

1. As there must be no punishment except where there is guilt (*nulla poena sine culpa*), so there must be "no measure except for protection against danger." Furthermore, as punishment ought not to be excessive, meaning, disproportionate to guilt, so measures ought not to exceed in scope and duration the danger which they are purported to avert. For this reason, except where a minimum period is prescribed by reason of a presumptive minimum duration of danger, a measure may be terminated at any time by the court either ex officio or on motion of the prosecution, the head of the institution in which the person concerned is detained, or that person himself. Where a measure is imposed for a time exceeding a certain minimum duration, mandatory review of continued dangerousness at stated intervals is of the essence of legality.

2. The conflict between the social interest in community protection against danger emanating from a human being and the individual interest in freedom ought to be resolved in conformity to the "legality principle." As in all areas of civil liberties, the aim must be to establish a proper balance between the social and the individual interest.

In this context it is important to note that a certain coordination is necessary between the punitive and the protective scheme. Since, to meet the presumption favoring freedom in the punitive field, the recommended definition of mental incapacity exempting from punitive responsibility has been formulated in broad terms, the notion of "dangerousness" against which protection

---

have seen and from other evidence submitted to us that such cases do happen." See also MACDONALD, PSYCHIATRY AND THE CRIMINAL 143 (1958).

by measures may be afforded should not be too narrow. For example, the recommended definition has been extended to include conditions which in many countries come within the notions of "partial" and "diminished responsibility."[47] Persons of such reduced responsibility, while enjoying full exemption within the recommended definition, may be as dangerous as those who suffer from grave mental illness. They ought to be treated by measures. However, there should be no undue discrepancy between maxima of intervention by way of measures and punitive maxima.

3. A significant "legality" safeguard is elimination of arbitrariness and inequality of treatment. Hence, the aim must be in measures, as in punishment, to afford whenever possible objective standards and tests.

4. It is important to stress that the "criminal conduct" engaged in by the defendant, in addition to being a significant indicium of the actor's "dangerousness," performs a crucial "political" function in the law of measures as well as in the punitive scheme.

No criminal law state intervention should be permissible unless the person concerned has "done something" cognizable at criminal law. When it is necessary for the protection of the public or of the individual himself to detain an individual or to restrain his freedom in any other way though he has not committed any "criminal act," civil commitment or other civil or administrative measures are the proper forms of intervention. One might argue that insistence on a distinction between a civil and a criminal law commitment is a superfluous formalism, since in either type of commitment the person concerned is deemed "not guilty." "Not guilty," according to this interpretation, is a metaphysical quality, whereas in the phenomenological view of "guilt" adopted by the writer, "not guilty" merely means that certain legal-political demands have not been fulfilled in regard to the particular individual in the specific case, with the result that he is not held punitively responsible.[48] Such individual may nevertheless be

---

[47]Compare Silving, *Mental Incapacity in Criminal Law, supra* at 125–130.

[48]On the "penal," though not "punitive," nature of measures see Silving, *"Rule of Law" in Criminal Justice, supra* note 6, at 145. On the meaning of "guilt" see Silving, *Mental Incapacity in Criminal Law, supra,* at 71–74; cf. also *Introduction, supra* at 45–48.

"responsible" in measures, provided that the proper demands of the protective province of criminal law are applicable in his case. One could express this by saying that there obtains within the protective scheme a distinctive concept of "guilt" possessing no moralistic connotations and not predicated upon the presence of technical *mens rea,* but presupposing the existence of "criminal conduct" as described by law.[49] Nor is absence of *mens rea* tantamount to a realistic lack of a mental element, be it intent or recklessness or consciousness of illegality,[50] although these mental factors are not punitively ascribable or imputable to the mentally incapacitated defendant. Still, one might query why it is necessary to differentiate between such nonmoralistic protective "guilt" at criminal law and the corresponding factor that gives rise to administrative or civil measures, and why "criminal conduct" should be made a condition of criminal law intervention.

The answer to the first question is that differentiation between criminal law and administrative intervention is necessary because the proper aims of criminal law are distinctive from those of administrative law, so that distinctive types of limitations are applicable in the two fields. The protective function of criminal law is limited in a democratic society to the necessary minimum called for in criminal law context. Thus, for example, care for the mentally ill, which constitutes an important reason for a civil law commitment, is not a proper ground for criminal law commitment, though once committed at criminal law the person concerned ought to receive the necessary care. Nor is treatment and cure a direct goal of criminal law commitment. Treatment

---

[49]Such concept of "guilt" referring solely to engagement in criminal conduct or to production of a criminal harm prevails in large segments of the population. The question most commonly raised when the issue of "guilt" is posed is "Has he done it?"

I am using the term "criminal conduct" in the sense of a conduct engaged in under such circumstances and entailing such results as to fulfill the requirements of a statutory description of a crime, but for the absence of the required intent or recklessness, knowledge of illegality, or mental capacity. The German DRAFT OF A PENAL CODE, 1960 (ENTWURF EINES STRAFGESETZBUCHES (StGB) E 1960 (Bundesrat Drucksache 270/60, 1960), § 11 (1) 2, adopts a similar concept called "illegal act" (*rechtswidrige Tat*). Cf. also Draft 1962.

[50]On the latter as part of *mens rea,* see Ryu & Silving, *Error Juris: A Comparative Study,* 24 UNIVERSITY OF CHICAGO LAW REVIEW 421, 430, 440-442 (1957).

is a proper criminal law "measure" solely as a means of eliminating or reducing dangerousness,[51] aimed at advancing release
of the defendant and at protection of the community.[52] The direct function of criminal law measures is the protection of others
against the dangerousness of an individual who has done something cognizable at criminal law, as a law concerned with socially harmful acts.

The second question, as to why criminal conduct must be a
condition of criminal law intervention, raises the highly controversial issue of "predelictual measures," that is, according to prevailing definition, measures applied preventively, in anticipation
of criminal conduct. There has been a great deal of confusion
regarding these measures, attributable in a large degree to a lack
of proper analysis in the light of principles of political philosophy
applicable to criminal law.

Adherents of predelictual measures claim that no objections
can be raised against them on legality grounds so long as these
measures are administered strictly in accordance with statutes
that describe each measure and the situations to which it may
be applied, and so long as these measures are imposed by courts
of ordinary criminal jurisdiction. Thus, the requirement that
criminal law intervention be limited to situations in which the
subject has done some definite antisocial "act," in the opinion
of these scholars, is a dispensable formaliy. But this argument
is based on misunderstanding of a most significant substantive
aspect of legality which bars any type of criminal law state intervention unless there is present an actual, definite, clear and identifiable harm to persons other than the person concerned. A man's
existential situation, his objectionable general life conduct, his
manner of being (*modo de ser*), his "being thus" (*So-Sein*), is
not a proper basis for either punishment or measures. The so-
called "criminal law of the actor," which purports to attach

---

[51]In the law of punishment it may be an imprisonment substitute or a means
of abbreviating detention. On this see Silving, *"Rule of Law" in Criminal Justice,*
supra note 6, at 139-140.

[52]Once the individual has been committed, treatment may be called for as part
of the care for the individual, which the state should afford to anyone in its
custody.

criminal sanctions to the type of personality which a man possesses rather than to a specific harmful act committed by him,
has been discredited in the postwar era, particularly as a consequence of its having been carried *ad absurdum* by the National
Socialist regime.[53]

True, in the province of measures there is a marked tendency
to stress qualities of the person concerned, his personality and
general life conduct. Indeed, the decisive factor in the law of
measures is dangerousness, which is to a large degree a personality feature. Hence, this law is a "law of the actor," and its
foremost function is precisely to relieve punitive law of its protective aspects and thus facilitate its functioning as a "law of
guilt," in the sense of responsibility for a definite crime. But, as
shown by the German experience with National Socialist criminal
law philosophy, which foussed on "what a man is" in disregard
of "what he does," there is a greater social danger in adopting
a criminal law, even of measures, which is wholly oriented to
personalities and requires no specific act to warrant state intervention, than there is in leaving potentially dangerous personalities at large. Emphatically, a "criminal act" is and must remain
an essential requirement of legality in measures, as well as in
punishment.

A caveat is necessary in regard to the scope of the "act-require-
ment." It is possible to manipulate this requirement by creating
special types of "criminal conduct" which have the misleading
appearance of valid statutory crime types, distinguishable from
other crime types solely by being sanctioned by measures and
not by punishment. Whether a provision creating a criminal conduct thus sanctioned is justifiable in a democratic society depends, as does the legality of any criminal law provision, on
whether the conduct thus proscribed is sufficiently harmful to
society, in the sense of violating essential legal interests of persons other than the offender, to warrant imposing upon such
conduct highly limitative criminal law sanctions.[54]

---

[53]On the history of the "law of the actor" see Silving, *"Rule of Law" in Criminal Justice, supra* note 6 at 98-104.

[54]There are two opposing principal views on what is and what is not a proper
subject of regulation and sanctioning by the criminal law. According to one of

To be subject to penal law "measures," an insane person must have engaged in a *"criminal* conduct." This is an important safeguard of the legality of any measures imposed upon him. We shall henceforth deal with such conduct solely as a potential indicium or symptom of such person's dangerousness. Our tasks in the following are to find the proper standards by which "dangerousness" and its degree might be judged; thereafter we must seek measures differing in stringency and scope depending on the degree of "danger" to be averted; and lastly, we must settle the proper procedure for the ascertainment of "dangerousness" and of its degree. The first mentioned tasks will be discussed in

these, the criminal law may or indeed ought to enforce either Divine or popular notions of morality. For a recent exposition of the latter version see DEVLIN (Lord Justice Devlin), THE ENFORCEMENT OF MORALS (Maccabaean Lecture in Jurisprudence of the British Academy 1959). According to the second view, the function of criminal law is confined to prohibiting and sanctioning conduct which is harmful to others, "harm" being understood to mean an injury other than a mere offensiveness to moral sensitivities. This view has been recently expressed in the WOLFENDEN REPORT, *supra* note 46, at 9-10. Some believe that the choice between these two positions is a matter of moral preference. It is submitted that such is not the case. The position adopted by the WOLFENDEN REPORT is a dictate of legality. A man's freedom from criminal law state intervention into his life is a civil liberty, immune against majority rule unless a clear and serious harm to the community or any member thereof exists or is obviously threatened. The mere fact that a popular majority or a representative group of the community, such as a jury or the famed "Clapham Bus" commuters, desires intervention into the life of a person because it is displeased with the general manner in which he conducts his life or with what he may be doing is not a sufficient ground in a democracy for prescribing or permitting state intervention, any more than such intervention into the affairs of a man's conscience, religion, or opinion is justifiable simply because the majority finds them nonconformist or obnoxious. This philosophy of government precludes enactment of any such legislation as the vagrants laws, common in both common and civil law countries. It may be noted parenthetically that there is no objection against creation of special "criminal conduct" types sanctioned solely by measures, such as is the Italian "agreement to commit a crime," ITALIAN PENAL CODE art. 115 (2) & arts. 215, 228. It may be argued that in cases of this nature there is "criminal law" state intervention without a "crime." But as in the case of measures applied to persons acquitted solely by reason of mental incapacity, there is present, while not a "crime," a "criminal conduct," as described by statute and sanctioned by measures in conformity to a statute. So long as such criminal conduct fulfills the requirement of creating a harm cognizable in criminal law, no objections can be raised. This requirement is not fulfilled in the Italian "putative crime," also sanctioned by measures. *Id.* art. 49 (1) & (4).

Section 1, and a separate section will be devoted to treatment of constitutional and procedural aspects.

A. Substantive Provisions

This section deals in separate subdivisions with: 1. the test of "dangerousness"; 2. the rule of proportionality of measures to danger; and 3. special categories of the mentally incapacitated, "habitual offenders" and "offenders not susceptible to punishment."

1. Test of "Dangerousness"

The question of the proper test of "dangerousness" is controversial. In doctrinal disputes waged in civil law countries views are divided between the "objectivists," who attribute a more or less decisive significance to the "act" committed by the defendant, and the "subjectivists," who believe the role of that act to be negligible.[55] As most doctrinal disputes among civil law scholars, this one is conducted on a metaphysical level. The contention is made that what *is* "dangerousness" must be determined independently from the protective need, since "dangerousness" is a condition and determinant of protection.[56] Within a functional view of "dangerousness," however, its definition is not merely the result of an objective finding of "danger," but also depends on the scope assigned to the protective goal, involving a policy decision on how much danger society must tolerate. That decision in turn depends upon the important constitutional issues of the extent to which the defendant's civil liberties may be permitted to yield to the protective interest of the community or of certain of its members, and of the proper methods of ascertaining dangerousness. The debates waged in civil law countries on whether "dangerousness" is a "quality of the actor" or a "quality of the act, are barren."[57] "Dangerousness" is simply a factor

[55]On the variety of views on this subject see OLESA MUÑIDO, LAS MEDIDAS DE SEGURIDAD 55-81, (Publicaciones del Seminario de Derecho Penal y Criminología de la Universidad de Barcelona 1951).

[56]*Id.* at 73.

[57]These debates are cast in terms suggesting that the issue is one involving the innate "nature" of dangerousness. The problem has been also raised in civil

or a combination of factors raising a justifiable protective need, meaning that protection of that need is authorized in a democratic society. There need not be a single indicium of "dangerousness." "Danger" may evince from a combination of indicia, some personal, others situational and, among the former, the "act" committed by the defendant may play a more or less decisive role, as compared with other factors. But "legality" requires that so far as possible the indicia of "dangerousness" and their relative weight under varying circumstances be formulated.[58]

Use of prediction tables in aid of determining dangerousness poses a constitutional problem. A minimum requisite of the constitutionality of admitting them in evidence is a specific showing of (1) the accuracy of the fact findings upon which they are based; (2) the scientific reliability of the method used in preparing them; and (3) their pertinency to the case at bar. Special doubts as to the propriety of relying on such tables obtain where inferences drawn from them are disfavorable to the defendant. If used at all, they should be given but supplementary, minimal weight. It may be desirable to have the issue of their admissibility first examined by the psychiatric and sociological examinations center, which may or may not recommend their use by the court. The court should have no discretion to admit them against the advise of the center, but should be free to exclude them notwithstanding their approval by the center.

A. THE CRIMINAL "ACT" AS INDICIUM OF "DANGEROUSNESS"

As seen, the criminal "act," or that which we have chosen to call "criminal conduct," performs a dual function in the law of measures; it is a condition of legality and an indicium of "dangerousness." An incident of its latter function is a third role, to which attention has been drawn by civil law scholars. They have

---

law countries whether the danger against which criminal law protection may be afforded must be one to the community at large or whether it is sufficient if only certain individuals are endangered. This distinction is equally barren.

[58]Article 133 of the ITALIAN PENAL CODE, though in terms a sentencing guide for punitive purposes, is considered to be a catalogue of indicia of dangerousness, which is an important factor in punishment as well as in measures.

distinguished between "objective danger" and "subjective danger or fear."[59] We may discard *a limine* as irrelevant at criminal law those fears that are wholly illusory. But a fear, perhaps a panic, aroused in the community by a serious crime, for example a homicide, though committed without punitively attributable *mens rea,* is a valid consideration in determining whether protection should be afforded, though this consideration may not be alone decisive.

The extent to which the nature and gravity of the act are symptomatic of the dangerousness of the actor is a most controversial subject. Does commission of a criminal act permit prediction of future criminality on the part of the actor? If so, is repetition of crime of the same nature and gravity to be expected, or is future variation from a previous pattern equally probable? In particular, is a petty or small offender likely to turn to serious crime? Is an offender against property likely to endanger the life and health of his fellow men?

Psychiatrists stress that we must treat "criminals instead of crimes,"[60] and that "criminals cannot be classified on the basis of the type of crime they commit."[61] This approach no doubt finds support in the psychoanalytic finding that crimes of apparently and legally widely differing patterns may stem from similar unconscious motivations.[62] But in the face of the psychological "pandeterminism" asserted by many psychiatrists, such "actor-orientation" can hardly be taken to imply that the type and gravity of the act committed by a defendant are not determined

---

[59]On this see OLESA MUÑIDO, *op cit. supra* note 55, at 57-59. Garofalo, who originated the doctrine of "dangerousness," spoke of *temibilità,* the quality of evoking fear. On this see *id.* at 64.

[60]KARL A. MENNINGER, THE HUMAN MIND 455 (3d enlarged ed. 1955).

[61]ZILBOORG, THE PSYCHOLOGY OF THE CRIMINAL ACT AND PUNISHMENT 128 (1954).

[62]Thus, for example, political crimes, in the light of psychoanalytical interpretation, may represent parricide. On this see the comprehensive treatment by JIMÉNEZ DE ASÚA, PSICOANÁLISIS CRIMINAL 97–104 (5th enlarged ed. 1958), and literature cited there. If, then, given different conditions, the stage is set for some other crime against authority, for example, a teacher, see MIRA Y LÓPEZ, MANUAL DE PSICOLOGÍA JURÍDICA 162–163, (4th ed. 1954) (describing the case of a boy stealing pencils from his teacher), it is conceivable that such crime will be committed.

by his unconscious psychological motivations. Dr. MacNiven states that a person's "nature, his education, and his ethical and social training" in many instances modify his conduct even in mental illness.[63] In the light of psychoanalytic insight there is mostly a sufficient likelihood of a causal connection between unconscious motivations of the actor and the type and gravity of the act committed by him to justify assumption that such features of the act have a bearing on his crime potential and thus afford an indicium of what may be expected of him. True, we are all potentially dangerous; Goethe allegedly said that he could well imagine having committed any conceivable crime.[64] But when a person has committed a crime, particularly a serious one, surely the probability of his committing one in the future is greater than in the case of a generally law-abiding citizen.

While unspecificity of recidivism has not been proved, there is sufficient indication in experience for fearing that in the case of reincidence the individual will repeat the same type of criminal act as the one he has committed before.[65] Certainly, a person who in a state of mental incapacity has killed another may be assumed more likely to commit another homicide than a person who in a similar mental state has committed merely petty larceny. This assumption justifies diversification in treatment of persons acquitted on the ground of insanity depending on the nature and gravity of the crime committed by them.[66]

In the process of determining the degree of a person's dangerousness and the scope of danger-adequate measures, the nature and gravity of the actor's conduct and hence of the anticipated harm ought to be the most significant items of consideration. Also, the required degree of probability that the harm will occur should be in inverse proportion to the seriousness of such

---

[63]MacNiven, *supra* note 36, at 52.

[64]2 H. GRIMM, GOETHE 245 (7th ed.), quoted in WELZEL, DAS DEUTSCHE STRAFRECHT 163 (6th ed. 1958).

[65]Compare *supra*, note 46.

[66]For diverse provisions as regards persons acquitted by reason of insanity depending on the nature of the criminal act they committed and diverse terms of confinement in a mental hospital depending on the same factor see ITALIAN PENAL CODE art. 222.

harm.[67] When combined with the element of fear aroused within the community by an act of killing, the symptomatic value of such an act in regard to the objective probability of repetition of the same pattern should suffice to warrant certain minimum measures of protection. No one who in a state of mental incapacity has killed another ought to be released before the lapse of a minimum period of, for example, two years, during which the subject should be observed and treated. This time may also be used to study the environmental conditions in which he has lived as well as those to which he must "return" upon release and to make adequate plans for his future adjustment under conditions most favorable to it.[68] It is not necessary that he remain throughout the period of detention in a mental hospital; in appropriate cases or at appropriate stages he may be assigned, for example, to a special colony or a training center.

True, a disposition for such minimum detention period would raise a serious constitutional problem. But the alternative is delegation of authority to psychiatrists or courts, acting under psychiatric advice, to determine whether the individual concerned continues to be dangerous. It is submitted that a psychiatrist's evaluation of the issue of continued dangerousness, though entitled to considerable weight, is not in the present state of knowledge sufficiently supportable by readily verifiable objective data to justify risking the danger to the community incident to an early release, when the precipitating act was a homicide. Also, the community's freedom from fear deserves such minimum protection.

The community fear and the prognostic situation obtaining in cases where a homicide has been committed in a state of mental incapacity are applicable both to situations of chronic mental disease and to those of temporary mental disturbance, though

---

[67]On this see HURWITZ, CRIMINOLOGÍA 427 (Spanish transl. Haro-García 1956).

[68]Mental illness, though "cured," leaves mental scars. Also, the impression it leaves in the community affects the subject's "acceptance" when he returns, rendering his adjustment more difficult by exposing him to unusual stress. Though there may be a therapeutic value in a return to normal life and the previous environment, see Hough v. United States, 271 F.2d 458, 462 (D.C. Cir. 1959), in some cases there might be considerations favoring choice of a new environment, less likely to contribute to the type of stress that precipitated the criminal act.

there may be some difference in degree. The killing of another human being in a state of "mental blackout" can hardly be assumed psychologically "accidental," meaning not rooted in the defendant's total personality. The community must be protected against recurrence of fatal "blackouts." Even those acting in so-called "states of automatism"—in whose case traditional doctrine assumes the absence of an "act," requires no plea of insanity for acquittal and excludes application of measures[69]—can hardly be deemed to produce death "accidentally."[70]

---

[69]"Automatism" is defined by HENDERSON & GILLESPIE, A TEXT-BOOK OF PSYCHIATRY 115 (8th ed. 1956), thus: *Automatic movements or automatisms occur ni a pathological sense, without the subject's being aware of their meaning, and even without his being aware of their happening at all.* Various states are referred to under this term, such as states resulting from a discharging cerebral focus, see Mulder, *Psychoses with Brain Tumors and Other Chronic Neurologic Disorders,* in 2 AMERICAN HANDBOOK OF PSYCHIATRY 1144, 1146-1147 (Arieti ed. 1959), and various psychogenic states of dissociation, such as somnambulism, automatic writing and fugue states, see NOYES & KOLB, MODERN CLINICAL PSYCHIATRY 62-63 (5th ed. 1958). In law harm committed in such state is deemed not to constitute "an act" or a "voluntary act," so that the issue of intent or sanity does not arise at all. Thus, for example, in R. v. Charlson [1955], I W.L.R. 317, the prisoner, without any apparent motive, called his ten-year-old son, telling him that there was a rat to be seen standing on a stone in the river adjoining the house. When the boy came, the prisoner picked up a wooden mallet from the floor and struck the boy twice on the head, causing blood to flow. He then picked up the boy and threw him out of the window into the river. The boy fell 25 feet into the river and suffered severe injuries. The prisoner could give no account of his motivation for acting as he did. He raised no plea of insanity, but medical evidence was given to the effect that his actions were consistent with his having a cerebral tumor, a condition in which a person is liable to an outburst of impulsive violence, "quite motiveless," and over which he has no control. He was acquitted even of the charge of inflicting grievous bodily harm, for which no specific intent needs to be proved. For further examples see GLANVILLE WILLIAMS, CRIMINAL LAW, THE GENERAL PART 11 (1953); see also MODEL PENAL CODE § 2.01, comment at 121-122 (Tent. Draft No. 4, 1955).

[70]Williams, *Automatism,* in Mueller, ed., ESSAYS IN CRIMINAL SCIENCE, *supra* note 6, at 345, notices that exclusion of the mental incapacity issue in such cases with consequent inability to assign the defendant to a mental hospital or otherwise to avert the danger which he represents is a wrong disposition from the standpoint of policy. The author says: "It seems that lawyers are prisoners of their own conceptual scheme." *Id.* at 346. The conceptual scheme itself is based on incorrect psychiatric assumptions. NOYES & KOLB, *op. cit. supra* note 69, at 62, explain dissociation thus: ". . . in a person in whom there is an active incompatibility between repressed elements in his mental life and the rest of his personality, the repressed components may escape from the forces that are repressing them, be-

Where the act committed by the accused is less than homicide but would, except for his mental incapacity, constitute a felony against the bodily integrity of a person, an automatic minimum measure should also be applied, although it should be correspondingly less stringent than in the case of a homicide. In neither situation should the minimum detention provisions exclude further extension of measures upon a finding of continued dangerousness. When such extension beyond the minimum period is sought, the nature and gravity of the act committed should still be an important item of consideration in determining the issue of dangerousness. In all cases other than those in which minimum measures are applicable, dangerousness should be an object of proof, rather than automatically inferable from the act. Again, however, the nature and gravity of the act should be an important item in determining dangerousness.

The significance of the criminal conduct as an indicium of dangerousness is gaining increasing recognition in the District of Columbia when release of a person acquitted solely by reason of insanity and automatically assigned to a mental institution[71] is in issue. In estimating "the safety of the community in case the defendant is released," courts realize that

---

come separated from the usual consciousness, organize a personality of their own, as it were, and thus dictate behavior. This new, or *secondary personality*, has its own consciousness which has no recollection of the usual or *primary personality* and carries out acts independent of it. . . . The disposition and character possessed by the secondary personality may be quite different from that shown by the primary personality. This contrast should naturally be expected since the secondary personality is made up of material that has been repressed, that is, has been rejected by the primary personality because it was not of a nature to be consciously entertained or satisfied." This explanation disproves the apparent assumption of the law that an act committed in a state of automatism is not attributable to the actor even in the sense in which acts committed by an insane person are attributable to him. There is no conceivable reason to differentiate the two situations. An act committed in a dissociation state is not psychologically "accidental"; it is rather motivated by the repressed material of which the secondary personality is made up.

[71]D.C. CODE ANN. § 24-301(3) (Supp. 8 1960). The terms of unconditional release are "recovery of sanity" and prognosis that the subject "will not in the reasonable future be dangerous to himself or others." For construction of this section see Overholser v. Leach, 103 U.S. App. D.C. 289, 257 F.2d 667 (D.C. Cir. 1958), *cert. denied,* 359 U.S. 1013 (1959); Isaac v. United States, 284 F.2d 168 (D.C. Cir. 1960).

the type of crime which [the subject] committed must be considered in that connection. For example, there is less danger to the community if an embezzler should be released and repeats the crime of embezzlement than if a murderer is released and possibly repeats a crime of that type.[72]

While thus in the recommended scheme the nature and gravity of the act committed by the defendant may justify certain minimum measures and also serve as an indicium of dangerousness whenever it must be proved, the same act should also, for constitutional reasons, afford a basis for the maximum of state intervention in measures, as well as in punishment. Since the punishment imposed upon a conduct presumably reflects its gravity, the maximum of such punishment may be taken to afford a proper standard for the maximum in the area of measures. As mentioned before, regardless of "danger," the maximum length of detention by way of measures ought to bear a certain relationship to the maximum period of punishment that might be imposed upon the precipitating criminal conduct, if it were a crime. In felony cases, it is believed that the maximum detention period should not exceed the maximum period of punishment. In instances of misdemeanors, a corresponding limitation would frustrate any treatment effort and thus the preventive purpose of detention. A relative increase of detention maxima may afford a solution, which might be constitutionally justified on the ground of the defendant's choice expressed in his plea of insanity, as required in misdemeanor cases,[73] although one may well argue that such justification is dispensable. In instances in which detention beyond the limits thus set is necessary, civil commitment proceedings should be instituted.

As seen, in the District of Columbia concern has been expressed about the problem of the potential bearing of the gravity

---

[72]Judge Holtzoff's opinion in Hough v. United States, quoted in Circuit Judge Miller's dissent in Hough v. United States, 271 F.2d 458, 463, 466 (D.C. Cir. 1959).

[73]If, as has been recommended earlier in the text, mental incapacity in misdemeanor cases remains an "affirmative defense," there is very little likelihood that it will be a frequent issue in crimes on which a small penalty is imposed.

of the act on the constitutionality of protracted detention.[74] But there has been no systematic consideration of either the scope of the relationship that must exist between crime gravity and the length of detention or, generally, between danger and detention.[75] The submission of the writer is that no man, however dangerous and whatever the gravity of his act, may be detained indefinitely at criminal law, and that crime gravity, as objective determinant, and as one of the indicia of dangerousness, should be taken as a standard of the scope of permissible detention or of any other measures.

B. THE MENTAL ELEMENT IN "MENTAL INCAPACITY" CASES

In our law the state of mind of a person acquitted on the ground of insanity "at the time of the act" is not further diversified for the purpose of imposing "measures." Once thus acquitted, he is treated uniformly, except that in some jurisdictions his "insanity" at the time of acquittal may be relevant to the issue whether a measure may be imposed at all. The assumptions underlying this position are not realistic and should be reexamined.

Acquittal on the ground of insanity is deemed in our law to imply that the accused acted without "intent."[76] As interpreted in *Carter v. United States*,[77] he lacked the "vicious mind" or "vicious will" which "motivates a criminal act" and which it is the "basic import of criminal law" to punish. This interpretation is further explained in the light of "accepted philosophy"—which, it is alleged, "has never changed" even in *Durham v. United States*—to mean that the ultimate reason for not punishing a person suffering from a "mental disease or defect" is that "in doing the act he is not a free agent, or not making a choice, or unknowing of the difference between right and wrong, or not choosing freely, or not acting freely."[78]

---

[74]See particularly the thoughtful opinion of Judge Fahy in Ragsdale v. Overholser, 281 F.2d 943, 949 (D.C. Cir. 1960).

[75]*Id.* at 950.

[76]This view, stressed in the New Hampshire cases, State v. Pike, 49 N. H. 399 (1870); State v. Jones, 50 N. H. 369 (1871), has also been accepted in Durham v. United States, 94 U.S. App. D.C. 228, 214 F.2d 862, 876 (1954).

[77]252 F.2d 608, 616 (D.C. Cir. 1957).

[78]*Ibid.*

However theoretically valid, the metaphysical "free will doctrine," thus proclaimed to translate the meaning of the mental
incapacity exemption, is functionally meaningless, since it does
not lend itself to being administered in any specific context. To
be legally meaningful, the "free will" thesis would have to be
operational, that is, useful in solving practical legal issues, specifically, by affording a test whereby it might be possible to
determine whether or not a person had acted "freely."[79] The
assumption that the wording of the *Durham* formula is the practical corollary of that thesis is entirely gratuitous.

On the other hand, if the phrase "vicious will" is taken to
convey the notion of conduct deviating grossly from certain ethical standards,[80] one might query why the conduct of a mentally
ill person ought not to be judged by these standards. Such person can act with as much intensity, brutality, and conscious disregard for the rights and feelings of others as a normal person.
The answer given to this query in our law seems to be that a
mentally ill person has no "mind" but is *"amens (id est) sine
mente,"*[81] "without a mind." Having no mind, he cannot possess

---

[79]Judge Burger, concurring in the result only in Blocker v. United States, 288
F.2d 853, 857, 869 (D.C. Cir. 1961), suggested that if the meaning of *Durham*
can be actually translated into "acting knowingly and freely," the latter criterion
should be placed "squarely before the jury" rather than hidden from it. Though
this criticism is logically valid, the fact is that neither the jury nor anyone else
could answer the question whether the defendant "acted freely," since this question means: "Could he have acted otherwise than he in fact acted?"

The "free will" test has also been recommended by Chief Judge Biggs in
United States v. Currens, 290 F.2d 751, 774-75 (3d Cir. 1961). Judge Hastie,
dissenting in part, *id.* at 776, aptly remarked that "psychiatrists may well reject
talk of destroying the will as unscientific imagery." For a critique of the test of
"capacity to conform" see Silving, *Mental Incapacity in Criminal Law, supra*
at 100–101.

[80]This, in fact, is the ancient meaning of *mens rea*, See 1 RUSSELL, CRIME 25
(10th ed. Turner 1950).

[81]See Carter v. United States, 252 F.2d 608, 616 (D.C. Cir. 1957). There
Judge Prettyman noticed, 252 F.2d, at 616 n.13 that exculpation is not "only for
the individual who is 'without mind,' like a wild beast." In the text, however,
he uses the term in the following connection: "If a man is *'amens (id est) sine
mente'* in respect to an act to such an extent that in doing the act he is not a
free agent. . . ." This seems to mean: (a) that the individual must be "without
a mind with regard to the particular act he is committing" (query: does "without
a mind" mean "without intent?"); (b) that this lack of intent or mind qualifies
him as "unfree." If the first proposition were sustainable, it should be sufficient.

a "vicious mind" or "vicious will," and for this reason he cannot be blamed for his conduct. The view of psychological reality expressed in this answer is obsolete, and the rationale of the mental incapacity exemption based upon this view is anachronistic.

Dynamic psychiatry has shown that, for example, schizophrenic patients "are by no means completely different from the rest of mankind. They share in the broad, basic psychodynamically important characteristics of human living—anticipatory striving at conscious and unconscious levels toward what is desired and against what is dreaded. . . ."[82] The thinking and acting of psychotic persons is not senseless but rather follows a logic which, however, operates within a frame of reference different from our own. Thus, even a psychotic person may possess an "intent" with regard to the precipitating act. The exemption from punitive responsibility of the mentally ill must be based on grounds other than absence of "intent,"[83] if by "intent" we mean a psychological reality. The ground of exemption must be not that such persons do not "reason" or "intend" or "feel" but rather that they "reason" or "intend" or 'feel" in contexts divergent from those of the mental operations of the majority of the community members, and that this divergence of contexts affords a social-political ethical ground for not applying to them the rules adopted with a view to the average community members. Only in this sense is the "intent" of the mentally ill person not imputable to him punitively. The problem arising within the law of measures is whether such "intent," found not to be determinative in the punitive scheme, should be deemed relevant so far as imposition and choice of measures are concerned.

The subject's state of mind with regard to the precipitating act may be relevant in the law of measures in two ways: as bearing on the character of the act and as a symptom of "dangerousness." The qualification of external conduct as a crime or

---

[82]Whitehorn, *Psychodynamic Approach to the Study of Psychoses,* in Alexander and Ross, ed., DYNAMIC PSYCHIATRY 255, 274 (1952).

[83]Nor should it be based on ignorance of law or lack of consciousness of illegality (criminality), as is implied in M'Naghten's Case, *supra,* note 3. There may be instances in which such ignorance is a feature of the mental impairment, but this is not always the case.

as a particular crime type mostly depends on the accompanying state of mind; apart from certain states of mind, such as intent or recklessness, a given outward behavior may not be criminal at all or may constitute but a minor misdemeanor. If the mental element were to be deemed wholly irrelevant for purposes of measures, it would be impossible to give within the law of measures any weight to the nature and gravity of the criminal behavior in issue. For example, crimes of specific intent would have to be eliminated from consideration, so that burglary and trespass would be considered as equivalent. Secondly, mental illness often releases rather than excludes "intent," and this factor has a clear bearing on the actor's "dangerousness."

According to a doctrine prevailing in German and Italian law, in contrast to ours, a person suffering from mental incapacity may possess a so-called "natural intent" or act with a so-called "*de facto*" negligence."[84] Such intent or negligence does not render him punitively responsible. But measures may be predicated upon its presence. Thus, assignment to a mental hospital of a person who committed a criminal act in a state of mental incapacity has been held to require presence of all crime elements, including the mental element of "natural intent"; that is, the actor must have known what he was doing, e.g., that he was killing a human being, lacking only an "inner relationship to the illegality content of the act."[85] But when such "intent to kill a human being" is present, for example, an erroneous assumption, produced by delusions, of a state of fact in the event of which the act would have been justified, for instance, by self-defense,

---

[84]The intent of a mentally incapacitated person is called in Germany "natural intent" (*natürlicher Vorsatz*), in Italy "abnormal will" (*volontà abnorme*); "*de facto* negligence*" is the author's free translation of the Italian term *negligenza semplice*. For the doctrine of "natural intent" see MAURACH, DEUTSCHES STRAFRECHT, ALLGEMEINER TEIL 206, 288, 338 (2nd ed. 1958). For the Italian doctrine of "*volontà abnorme*" and "*negligenza semplice*" see REPORT ON THE DRAFT OF A NEW ITALIAN PENAL CODE 1949/50 (*Relazione* I, pages 56-58). The draft itself uses the phrase "*azione diretta alla produzione dell'evento*" (action directed to production of the event), art. 75, dealing with criminal conduct in a state of intoxication.

[85]KOHLRAUSCH-LANGE, STRAFGESETZBUCH, comments to § 59, GERMAN PENAL CODE, A. II 2 c, at 218; comments to § 42 b, A I 2, at 123 (42d ed. 1959).

does not exclude application of measures.[86]

This civil law concept of "natural intent" reflects—perhaps unwittingly—the modern psychiatric view that a mental patient is not "completely different from the rest of mankind" but possesses a relevant "mental life," though a distinctive one. The "natural intent" or "recklessness" with which the subject acted is a proper item of judicial consideration in establishing the nature and seriousness of the act, as a symptom of its "dangerousness," as well as for the direct purpose of evaluating the actor's "dangerousness." What bearing such "intent" has on the actor's dangerousness may be shown by psychiatric evidence. But, contrary to the German rule, absence of a "natural intent" should not a priori disqualify an actor for subjection to measures, particularly assignment to a mental hospital. "Natural intent" and "de facto negligence" should be relevant items of consideration for the purpose of a finding of dangerousness but not a necessary condition of such finding.

C. PLURALITY OF CRIMINAL CONDUCT

Psychoanalytic writers, particularly Glover, have drawn attention to the high probability of mental disease evincing from the very fact of crime repetition.[87] Where the background of crime repetition is mental disease, the danger of further criminal activity is high. When the precipitating crime has been independently found to have been committed in a state of mental incapacity, former crime, though it led to conviction, is also likely to have been committed in a state of incapacity. A former acquittal by reason of mental incapacity substantiates the probability of a pathological background of crime repetition and thus of danger. But it is necessary to stress at the outset that danger of future criminal activity does not per se justify protective detention, for the crime likely to be repeated may be minor, and it may be found that treatment with a view to prevention can be promoted if the person concerned remains at liberty. A find-

---

[86]Decision of the Bundesgerichtshof (V. Strafsenat), July 9, 1957, reported in 10 NEUE JURISTISCHE WOCHENSCHRIFT 1484 (1957).

[87]GLOVER, THE ROOTS OF CRIME 327-338 (1960).

ing of "habitual criminality"[88] should not by itself be taken to indicate the necessity or the required length of detention. Whether detention is warranted and, if so, what its maximum should be depend on the nature and gravity of the anticipated criminal activity and on the effectiveness of detention to serve an ultimate protective purpose. In any event, repetition of criminal conduct as a symptom of dangerousness and as a basis for imposition and choice of measures constitutes a major issue in the law of measures.

Another significant problem in the symptomatology of dangerousness is "crimes concurrence," consisting in commission of several crimes by a single act.

Repetition of Criminal Conduct. In an address delivered at the Third International Congress on Criminology Professor Manuel López-Rey y Arrojo drew attention to the problem of whether in counting the number of crimes committed by an offender, those engaged in during minority should be included.[89] He pointed to the undesirability of preserving a criminal record of juvenile crimes, from the standpoint of the rehabilitation of the juvenile offender. Yet, crimes committed during minority have a special bearing on the actor's "dangerousness." Other problems arising in the treatment of crime repetition are: whether it is necessary to insist on previous conviction or, indeed, on execution of the previous sentence;[90] what importance is to be attributed to repetition of the same crime type (specificity) in evaluating the probability of future crime; what is the significance of the relative degree of gravity of the pertinent crimes; what number of previous criminal activities should be required to warrant qualification as a special crime type; and,

---

[88]I am using the term "habitual criminality" to designate repetition of criminal activity by a mentally ill person, to be treated by measures, as contrasted with "recidivism," which I am using in the sense of an exclusively punitive category. See Silving, *"Rule of Law" in Criminal Justice, supra* note 6, at 142. For further discussion of "habitual offenders" see *infra* text at note 97, *et seq.*

[89]See SUMMARY OF PROCEEDINGS (September 12-18, 1955) 36-37 (British Organizing Committee 1957).

[90]Art. 67, SWISS FEDERAL PENAL CODE, requires the previous sentence to have been executed.

what symptomatic import is to be assigned to previous acquittal on the ground of mental incapacity.

It is submitted that all these issues ought to be treated differently in punitive context, that is, as relevant to the punishment for "recidivism," and in the context of measures. No one should be subject to aggravation of punishment on account of a crime committed by him during minority or in a state of mental incapacity or by reason of a crime for which he was not formally convicted. But within the scheme of measures distinctive policy considerations require adoption of different rules. That an offender repeated a pattern of behavior which he adopted before reaching majority should not be deemed an item of "guilt" aggravation. But, as indicated above, the earlier an offender has begun a criminal career, the more likely he is to persist in it; juvenile crime, indeed offenses committed during childhood, bear importantly on the probability of future repetition. For the purpose of administering measures, juvenile crimes ought to be considered indicia of "dangerousness." Neither as regards such crimes nor as regards crimes committed in adult life should proof in the law of measures be required to consist of submission of a record or of a showing of conviction or of sentence execution. But, to avoid unfairness, there ought to be proof of previous criminal activity beyond a reasonable doubt. In this context, availability of a criminal record is significant. The argument favoring immediate destruction of records of juvenile crimes, though most persuasive in punitive context, does not apply within the protective scheme in which punitive "guilt" is not in issue. It may be desirable to render such records inadmissible at any time in punitive context but admissible in regard to measures.

In regard to "specificity" of the crime pattern, whatever may be the rule within the punitive scheme, in the scheme of measures repetition of the same crime pattern may be taken to bear importantly on "dangerousness." But the definition of "specificity" in this scheme must be cast in terms of similarity or relatedness of the ultimate "motives" that prompted the several acts, whereas similarity of outward conduct may be taken only to be evidence of such similarity or relatedness of motivation. Yet, even within the protective scheme, invoking a minor criminal activity in evidence of a particular dangerousness of a major crime is dubious. For there is at present no sufficient scientific evidence that a person who has committed a minor crime is generally likely to commit a major one in the future or that a person with a record of a minor and a major crime will in all probability repeat the latter; in the absence of such evidence, an inference to that effect would violate basic standards of "legality." Thus, where a person has successively committed a minor larceny and a homicide, it is unwarranted to infer from the mere presence of the larceny record an increased homicidal "dangerousness," in the sense of a greater probability that he will commit another homicide. But there would seem to be no objection on grounds of "legality" against assuming such person to present an increased danger of repeating the larceny, since crime repetition *per se* is a factor to be considered in evaluating dangerousness.

Prior acquittal solely on the ground of mental incapacity may also have a bearing on probability of future crime repetition. But in this instance again the probability of repetition inferred from such former acquittal alone should be taken to apply exclusively to equally grave or lesser crimes under consideration.

(Conceptual) Concurrence of Criminal Conduct. In addition to successive crime or "recurrence" of criminal conduct, wrongly designated as an instance of "crime concurrence," namely, as "factual (substantive or material) crimes concurrence" *(concorso materiale di reati, concurso real, concours matériel ou réel, Realkonkurrenz)*, there is another multiple crime figure called "conceptual crimes concurrence" *(concorso ideale, concurso ideal, concours formel ou idéal, Idealkonkurrenz)*. It is a most intricate construct, which for present purposes may be briefly and not quite precisely defined as commission of several crimes by a single act.[91] Where the precipitating act committed in a state of mental incapacity constitutes several crimes, e.g., consists in a single setting of a bomb which causes the death of several

---

[91]The concept of "a single act" is most precarious, the term "act" being ambiguous. Adoption of a different basic notion for purposes of definition of "conceptual crime concurrence" is hence desirable. I am using the phrase "a single act" for reasons of space economy.

persons or in a single movement of putting a match to property which causes the burning of a house and the death of a person therein, the question arises whether this multiplicity of criminal qualification ought to be taken to bear on the actor's dangerousness.

As stated before, the nature and gravity of the "criminal act" committed by the person concerned have an important bearing on his "dangerousness." These concern both the behavior proper and the ensuing consequences, even unintended ones. The consequences of a person's act are very seldom accidental, so that even in the absence of foresight or in the case of inadvertent negligence grave consequences may warrant application of security measures. Multiple consequences fall within the category of gravity increase, so that even in the absence of *mens rea,* multiplicity of harm may be taken as a symptom of increased dangerousness. Of course, a "natural intent" to produce several consequences may be highly relevant to the issue of dangerousness. It follows that in evaluating the actor's dangerousness the court ought to take into account the fact that by his criminal conduct he fulfilled the external requisites of one criminal statute several times or of several criminal statutes, and that the court may take into consideration the "natural intent" with which he acted.

D. Miscellaneous Indicia of "Dangerousness": Personality Evaluation

The described "indicia of dangerousness" should not be taken as "required conditions," in the sense of conditions which must be found to be cumulatively present to warrant a judgment of "dangerousness." The "act" requirement constitutes an exception, in the sense that a criminal "act" must be present in all cases in which a "measure" is imposed. But this requirement is a "legality safeguard," as are also the maxima imposed upon measures and expressed in terms of correspondence to maxima of punishment for the pertinent crime. To the extent that the above-discussed factors are symptoms of "dangerousness" proper, the requirement of the presence of any one of them is governed by rules of scientific rationality. The complex of rules which make it the duty of the court to consider some of these "symptoms" ("the court shall consider") and authorize it to consider others ("the court may consider") is in the nature of a "sentencing guide" which, though obligatory in the sense of a comprehensive scheme, is not obligatory in detail. The court "must consider" certain factors and must find the presence or absence in the case of each; but it may adjudge the person concerned "dangerous" though one or more of these factors are not present, provided that it must state the reason why, notwithstanding such absence, it reached its conclusion. The facultative factors should function only exceptionally as sole, and as a rule as supplementary, grounds of judgment, but failure even to consider them should not constitute reversible error. Much depends on the nature of the particular case. E.g., in a situation of a neurosis or psychopathy, "natural intent" may have a different bearing on dangerousness than it has in cases of schizophrenia or mental deficiency.

In the light of the unavoidable flexibility of any guides that may be adopted, expert opinion on "dangerousness" assumes a decisive importance. Such opinion should present an overall "personality evaluation" of the subject, setting forth the nature and etiology of the mental incapacity from which he suffers as well as a "prognosis" and a "recommendation" of appropriate measures. The "prognosis" ought to state the nature and degree of the "danger" which the case presents, if possible in terms of the type or types of crime which the subject is likely to commit. Alternative measures and their relative fitness to accomplish the aim of averting the danger of such crime ought to be suggested, so as to enable the court to weigh the degree of freedom deprivation incident to each alternative against its effectiveness.

2. Principle of Proportionality of Measure to Danger

It is of the essence of democratic policy-making to weigh considerations of individual liberty against those of the efficiency of harm-preventive measures. This implies diversification of "danger," depending on the nature of the anticipated harm and the degree of probability of its occurrence, and diversification of measures in accordance with the degree of their relative interference with individual freedom. The measure to be imposed, though perhaps not the most effective means of averting the particular danger, should be appropriate, in the light of the balance of the interests in protection and in freedom, to the nature and probable degree of the harm that is being anticipated. Clearly, protracted confinement of a person for fear that he may pass checks without adequate funds may not be justified, whereas such confinement of a person likely to kill another may be fully warranted. The required degree of probability of harm ought to be in inverse proportion to the degree of the gravity of harm.

Where the precipitating act is homicide or a felony against the bodily integrity of a person, a danger of further homicide or serious bodily harm may be taken to be implied in the nature of the precipitating act. A minimum measure of confinement ought to be ordered automatically upon proof of such act, the order stating a finding of dangerousness to be based on an irrebuttable presumption.[92] Confinement beyond such minimum period ought to be predicated upon a specific finding, after an adversary hearing, of a certain degree of probability that the subject will commit further acts of the type he committed. However, the protective need in such cases is so great that the required degree of probability should not be high and that the burden of proof should be shifted to the person concerned. While absolute certainty that such person will never again commit acts of the type in which he engaged can never be achieved,[93] it would seem proper to insist on convincing evidence that he is not substantially more likely to kill

---

[92]Such finding stating the facts of the "criminal conduct" and setting forth the presence of dangerousness is necessary as a protection of the subject against arbitrary disposition. There may be most exceptional grounds for dispensing with confinement even where dangerousness would be otherwise irrebuttably presumed, for example, if it can be shown that the person concerned is at the time of the order permanently incapacitated, so that he cannot conceivably repeat a crime of violence, e.g., that he is paralyzed. For further reasons for requiring a hearing, if requested, and an express finding of "dangerousness" even in cases where the latter is otherwise irrebuttably presumed see *infra* text, at note 134.

[93]In Rosenfield v. Overholser, 262 F.2d 34, 35 n.1 (D.C. Cir. 1958), it was held that the medical witness is not required to "give an absolute guarantee that the patient will never again be mentally ill or dangerous. Reasonable foreseeability, based on careful diagnosis and prognosis by competent persons, is the test."

in the foreseeable future than are average community members.[94] Conditional release in such instances should be subject to a similar test, except where the terms of such release, e.g., strict supervision, are expressly found to afford an adequate substitute safeguard against harm. A therapeutic need must not be permitted to offset the interest in protecting human life.[95] The harshness of such requirements is modified by the presence of statutory maxima of criminal law detention.

Where, however, the precipitating act is the passing of bad checks, the protective scheme need not be stringent. Confinement of the person concerned in an institution should be permissible only on the basis of a positive showing by the prosecution either: (a) that the likelihood of repetition is rather high and that no fair substitute measure is available which, though it might afford no similar assurance against relapse as does confinement, warrants a fair degree of community protection; or (b) that there is a fair likelihood of a relapse and that treatment with a view to prevention can be better secured in confinement.[96] Conditional release may be granted on a mere showing of therapeutic advantage. Risks may be taken in this instance, where the harm that may occur is not as irremediable as it is in cases involving a threat of grave bodily harm.

A personality evaluation may show that, though the precipitating crime was not violent, a great likelihood exists that the person concerned will in future turn to violence. To justify detention or more protracted detention than may be otherwise warranted by the nature of the crime committed, a finding of

---

[94]The phrase "convincing evidence" is used to denote more than a preponderance of the evidence.

[95]As to this see Hough v. United States, 271 F.2d 458, 462 (D.C. Cir. 1959). Unless adequately supervised, a person released conditionally can cause as much harm as one released unconditionally. If the purpose of confinement in a mental institution of a person acquitted solely by reason of insanity is treatment and not prevention of harm to the community, or if the former purpose overrides the latter, then, by all means, there ought to be a procedure available to take the person concerned out of such detention and transfer him to a different type of detention serving protective needs.

[96]For examples of measures short of confinement that might be used to avert danger, see *infra*. Measures of this type are common in penal codes of civil law countries. In this country they are often imposed as conditions of probation.

such likelihood ought to be based upon specific convincing evidence. In no event should such finding justify excess over the maximum period allowed in cases of crimes such as the crime charged.

The court should have power to order measures short of confinement, appropriate to the nature and degree of the harm to be averted. Upon a showing by the prosecution that the particular measure is rationally adapted to the type of incapacity from which the actor suffers, the court should be able to order: that he submit to psychiatric treatment or to periodic psychiatric checks or to supervision by a psychiatric social worker; that his license to possess or carry arms, to engage in a given profession, occupation or trade, or to drive a car be suspended; that he abstain from engaging in a certain profession, occupation or trade; that he abstain from frequenting certain places or from maintaining certain professional or social contacts; that he change his place of residence; that he make an effort to secure and maintain a regular occupation; etc.

3. Special Categories of the Mentally Incapacitated: The "Habitual Offender" and the "Offender Not Susceptible to Punishment"

A. THE "HABITUAL OFFENDER"

In the foregoing discussion, crime committed prior to that which gives rise to acquittal by reason of mental incapacity was viewed as an indicium of dangerousness. Previous acquittal on the ground of mental incapacity was said to be a particularly strong indication of such state. But neither factor alone ought to lead to a finding that the actor is a "habitual offender" subject to a special type of measure. The "habitual offender" has been suggested by the writer to designate an offender type sui generis, contrasted with the "recidivist."[97]

"Recidivism" is used by the author as a punitive category, a special "crime type" upon which an aggravated punishment is imposed.[98] "Habitual criminality" is used in the sense of a pattern of crime repetition followed by a person suffering from a mental

---

[97]On this see Silving, *"Rule of Law" in Criminal Justice, supra* note 6, at 142.

[98]Discussion of "recidivism" as a punitive category and its appropriate treatment would exceed the scope of this paper.

illness. As stated in a previous publication,[99] it is senseless to inquire whether a criminal act committed by a mentally ill person is or is not the "product" of his disease; for every act of any individual emanates from his total personality rather than from any single trait, such as mental disease. In a similar sense, the problem of habitual criminality should not be cast in terms of crime repetition "produced" by disease. Rather, such criminality ought to be defined as a state determined by commission of a series of criminal acts by a person who in all probability, as evidenced by the repeated conduct itself or other symptoms and by a psychiatric personality evaluation, when committing each or some of the acts within the series, suffered from a mental incapacity, and who is very likely to continue engaging in criminal conduct against which protection is needed. Neither the precipitating incident nor the prior criminal conduct need have led to an acquittal by reason of mental incapacity; each or any of these acts may have resulted in a conviction. Though there has been a conviction for the precipitating act itself, this does not render imposition of a punitive sentence mandatory, since a finding of mental incapacity may still be made in the course of a post-conviction "pre-sentence investigation." In fact, when repetition of the crime pattern is disclosed after conviction—the issue of recidivism should not be permitted to be raised prior to this stage[100]—it may lead to a reconsideration of the prior finding of mental capacity reached without knowledge of the actor's previous criminal activities, for such repetition is itself an important indicium of mental illness.

Often the acts within the habitual criminality series follow a pattern of minor crime. Persons bent on commission of such acts, particularly petty thievery, are, in the words of Norval Morris, "nuisances rather than serious dangers to society."[101] Yet, even

---

[99]See *Mental Incapacity in Criminal Law, supra* at 113–116, 118–120.

[100]Compare *supra* text and note 23; see also *Note, Other Crimes Evidence at Trial: Of Balancing and Other Matters,* 70 YALE LAW JOURNAL 763 (1961), on distinctive treatment of "recidivism" as a sui generis unit. The writer believes that recidivism constitutes such unit for substantive purposes, but this does not necessarily imply that it must be treated as such procedurally, where the accused might be prejudiced.

[101]Morris, *op. cit. supra* note 46, at 296.

in these cases, the constant repetition of the pattern, because of its impact on public morale, represents a danger that should be averted by appropriate measures. Of course, there is also reincidence in serious crime. There is hence a particular public interest in a special device for coping with a phenomenon that, were it not for the subject's mental incapacity, would constitute the special crime figure of "recidivism."

The court should declare the actor a "habitual criminal" if the circumstances of crime repetition, evidenced by either convictions or acquittals by reason of mental incapacity, would, had the actor been punitively responsible, constitute recidivism subject to punishment aggravation, provided that he suffers from a mental incapacity and probably suffered therefrom at the time of some or all of the previous acts, and provided further that he is found to be "dangerous." This declaration should render him amenable to a maximum in measures corresponding to the punishment maximum that may be imposed upon recidivism. In the event of repeated petty crime, such limitation would frustrate any effort at constructive preventive rehabilitation. The court should hence be empowered to extend the measure beyond such maximum in order to make adequate treatment possible, but not beyond a certain additional maximum period. However, where the criminal activity habitually engaged in is minor, detention need not be imposed at all. Other measures, for instance ambulatory psychiatric treatment or supervised liberty, may be found more effective for producing a permanent cure and hence more likely to afford a long-range protection of society.

Detention in cases of "habitual criminality" ought to be utilized for treating the offenders. Release on probation should be available where it promotes therapy without endangering the community. Where toward the end of the ultimate maximum period the psychiatrists in charge of treatment certify that the person concerned has not recovered from his mental incapacity and is still "dangerous," in the sense of being likely to commit further criminal acts, he should nevertheless no longer be detained as a "habitual offender," except by way of an emergency measure which would enable the authorities to pursue and terminate civil commitment proceedings. Where within the maximum period such psychiatrists certify that the person concerned is not treatable and the court so finds, he should be assigned for the rest of the period to a workhouse or agricultural colony, with the proviso that toward the end of the maximum period the same type of proceedings are to be instituted as in the case of the "uncured."

It is extremely important that "criminal law measures," particularly those which deprive a subject of his personal freedom, not be unduly "indeterminate" or, indeed, extend to a period that bears no proportion whatever to the gravity of the crime in issue. The aggravation provided for cases of "recidivism" permits extension of confinement proportionate to the gravity and number of the crimes committed by the offender. The maxima thus permissible and additional maxima for repeated misdemeanors should suffice even in cases of mentally ill persons to afford a reasonable period of treatment with a view to prevention of reincidence. Where a person's "dangerousness" cannot be averted by such "criminal law measures," considerations of public safety must be judged by general standards applicable to the mentally ill, whether of the criminal or the noncriminal type. Unless proportionality to "crime" is safeguarded even in the scheme of measures, there is danger that crime definitions will lose their meaningfulness as guarantees of "legality."

B. THE "OFFENDER NOT SUSCEPTIBLE TO PUNISHMENT"

This category, known in Danish law,[102] designates there a

---

[102]The principal Danish provision on the mental incapacity exemption is § 16, DANISH CRIMINAL CODE 1930, reading thus: "Acts committed by persons being irresponsible owing to insanity or similar conditions or pronounced mental deficiency are not punishable."

There follows a supplementary provision, § 17, reading as follows:

"(1) If, at the time of committing the punishable act, the more permanent condition of the perpetrator involved defective development, or impairment or disturbance of his mental faculties, including sexual abnormality, of a nature other than that indicated in sect. 16 of this Act, the court shall decide, on the basis of a medical report and all other available evidence, whether he may be considered susceptible to punishment.

"(2) If the court is satisfied that the accused is susceptible to punishment, it may decide that a penalty involving the deprivation of liberty inflicted on him shall be served in an institution or division of an institution intended for such

wastebasket category comprising persons suffering from any borderline mental incapacity.[103] The terms used to define this category, "disturbance of mental faculties," "abnormality," are extremely vague and uncertain.[104] They are interpreted as intentionally formulated in this manner, so as to allow for judicial

---

persons. If appropriate, the Prison Commission may alter the decision as to where
the penalty of imprisonment shall be served. If, during the term of imprisonment,
it becomes evident that a continuation of such imprisonment will be useless or
will be likely seriously to aggravate the condition of the convicted, then, at the
request of the Director of Prison Service, the case shall again be brought before
the court which passed sentence in the last instance. This court shall decide, on
the basis of a medical report, whether the penalty shall continue to be served
or not.

"(3) If a person in respect of whom preventive measures are taken under sect.
70 of this Act (cf. subsect. (1) of this section) for an offence committed by him
has committed another offence, and if he is considered susceptible to punishment
for offences of that nature, then, where the latter offence is of minor importance
in relation to the offence in respect of which preventive measures are applied, the
court may decide that no penalty shall be imposed."

Section 70(1), referred to above, provides that "where an accused is acquitted
under sect. 16 of this Act or where punishment is considered inapplicable under
sect. 17 of this Act, while having regard to public safety it is deemed necessary
that other measures be applied to him, the court shall decide on the nature of
such measures."

DANISH CRIMINAL CODE 1930 (Giersing & Grünhut transl., Copenhagen:
G. E. C. Gad 1958). Section 70 and following deal with pertinent measures.

In an answer given by Denmark to an "Inquiry on the Treatment of Abnormal
Offenders in Europe" conducted by the United Nations, § 17 of the Danish
Criminal Code has been interpreted as follows: "Under section 17 certain abnormal conditions other than those mentioned in section 16 may justify a sentence
to special treatment in lieu of punishment. It is stipulated, however, that the
condition must be of a more permanent nature. Section 17 covers in particular
persons having a low degree of mental deficiency and psychopaths; it may also
be applied to persons suffering from severe neurosis or being in a psychically
abnormal condition, e.g., in connexion with the menopause or as a result of abuse
of alcohol or narcotics." 12 INTERNATIONAL REVIEW OF CRIMINAL POLICY 3, 4-5
(United Nations St/SOA/Ser. M/12 1957).

[103]Even as regards the principal incapacity provision, § 16, the Danish court
has a wide discretion. The basic term of this provision, "irresponsible," though
historically associated with the notion of "free will," has been interpreted as at
present conveying merely the idea that mental disease, even a psychosis, does
not *per se* justify exemption and that applicability of the latter is ultimately a
matter of judicial discretion reached on policy grounds. See HURWITZ, *op. cit.
supra* note 67, at 435-36.

[104]On the various meanings of these concepts see *id.* at 163.

policy-making. This intention is inferred from an interesting additional provision[105] permitting imprisonment to be discontinued where it appears in its course "that a continuation of such imprisonment will be useless or will be likely seriously to aggravate the condition of the convicted person."[106] But, contrary to appearances, in administering the pertinent provisions, courts are said to be guided more by considerations of public safety than by those of individual capacity for resocialization by means of punishment.[107] The advantage of the total scheme, of purposive vagueness, is said to lie in the indeterminateness and flexibility of measures applied to persons found to fall within the pertinent provisions.[108] But the same scheme has been criticized as failing to give adeqate consideration to the need for a certain proportion between the precipitating crime or crimes and freedom deprivation, necessary "even in the case of abnormal offenders."[109]

Subject to qualification imposed by the considerations of this criticism and, generally, of "legality," the concept of "offenders not susceptible to punishment" is heuristic. Of course, in the writer's view, punishment serves ends other than deterrence and reformation, to which that concept is geared in Danish law. Within a "law-assertive" and "guilt-oriented" punishment scheme, an offender "not susceptible to punishment," that is, a person who shows considerable deviation in his response to punishment from the response to this sanction of the average community members, is very likely to satisfy the terms of the recommended mental incapacity exemption and thus to qualify for measures rather than for punishment. Within the protective scheme, such "non-susceptibility to punishment" may warrant application of special types of measures. Two groups are submitted to be com-

---

[105]DANISH CRIMINAL CODE 1930 § 17(2), *supra* note 102.

[106]Flexibility of measures, particularly transfer from a penitentiary to a special institution and vice versa, however, applies only if the person concerned has been classified by the original sentence as falling within § 17. On this see Denmark's answer to the United Nations "Inquiry," *supra* note 102, at 88.

[107]See HURWITZ, *op. cit. supra* note 67, at 438-439; Waaben, *Introduction* to DANISH CRIMINAL CODE 1930, *supra* note 102, at 13.

[108]Compare *supra*, note 106.

[109]See Denmark's answer to the United Nations "Inquiry," *supra* note 102, at 88.

prised within the category of "offenders not susceptible to punishment": (a) the so-called "non-deterrable offender"; and (b) the offender whose mental condition is likely to deteriorate as a result of imprisonment.

"Non-Deterrable Offenders." Much energy has been wasted in the administration of the *Durham* rule in determining on a case-to-case basis whether or not "psychopaths" or "sociopaths" qualify as suffering from a "mental disease,"[110] as if the name given to the mental condition of such persons—a condition itself most indeterminate[111]—were a matter of scriptural hermeneutics. No such mental gymnastics are noticeable in Denmark, though the Danish definition of the pertinent concepts is just as vague as that of the *Durham* terms. This is because Danish courts are given the power to shape the sanctioning policy in regard to persons initially deemed "susceptible to punishment," provided that the pertinent Code section[112] has been found in the original sentence to be applicable to them. While, in the light of "legality" demands, the vagueness of the Danish operational terms is as dubious as is that of the *Durham* terms, there is considerable merit in the availability in Danish law of a variety of methods for dealing with the psychopathic offender. Such an offender may be treated initially either punitively or by special measures, and even in the course of sentence execution it is possible to reevaluate his response to a given method and adjust his treatment in accordance with new findings. The Danish special institutions for psychopaths, in which new treatment techniques are being

---

[110]For criticism see Judge Burger's concurring opinion in Blocker v. United States, 288 F.2d 853, 857 (D. C. Cir. 1961); and see particularly the searching analysis of this problem by Chief Judge Biggs in United States v. Currens, 290 F.2d 751, 761-63 (3d Cir. 1961).

[111]O'Beirne v. Overholser, 193 F. Supp. 625 (Dist. Ct., D. C. 1961). "Neither the clinical characteristics nor the clinical limits of these personality maldevelopments are sharply defined." NOYES & KOLB, *op. cit. supra* note 69, at 545. "The extent to which aggressive-destructive and other dynamic impulses may be acted out in sociopathic form before labeling the personality as pathological is a matter of individual opinion and not determined by definite criteria. Likewise there are no fixed types determined by cause, dynamic process or result so that any classification depends upon what manifestations one wishes to stress." *Id.* at 548.

[112]DANISH CRIMINAL CODE 1930, § 17, *supra* note 102.

206 ESSAYS ON MENTAL INCAPACITY AND CRIMINAL CONDUCT

developed for this group of "untreatable" persons, are looked upon as models in other countries.[113]

It is possible to combine abidance by legality principles with provision for a distinctive treatment of particular offender groups. When a psychopath has qualified for exemption from punitive responsibility by reason of mental incapacity, he need not be assigned to a general mental institution. Evaluation in the psychiatric and sociologic examinations center should include a treatment proposal. In the case of a psychopath, such proposal may indicate the desirability of assignment to a special institution for psychopaths patterned after the Danish model. In the event that a person has been convicted and thus not adjudged to have committed the crime in a state of mental incapacity, it may still be possible to transfer him to such special institution upon a finding that he is not "susceptible to punishment," in the sense of not being susceptible to motivation by punishment or by imprisonment in institutions designed for the general class of offenders, for this feature may be taken to constitute "mental incapacity" for the purpose of execution. Such mental incapacity should be defined with a view to the purposes of execution.

Offenders Whose Mental Condition Is Likely to Deteriorate as a Result of Punishment. The second group of offenders "not susceptible to punishment" consists of persons whose illness, by contrast to that of the first group, lies in an excessive conscience. In psychoanalytic literature this group is designated as "criminals from a sense of guilt."[114] Far from being deterred by a threat of punishment, such persons commit crime precisely because they unconsciously desire to be punished. Psychoanalysts have accordingly pointed out that punishing such persons aggravates rather than improves their condition. However, there is no need for a special provision for this group of persons, since within the definition of "mental incapacity" that has been recommended, they will probably qualify for measures rather than for punishment. The appropriate measure to be applied must depend on

---

[113]See DRAFT OF A GERMAN PENAL CODE, 1960, *op. cit. supra* note 49, § 82 (2), and comment at 200-201.

[114]Freud, *Der Verbrecher aus Schuldewusstsein, supra* note 35.

the seriousness of the crime in issue and, within the limits imposed by reason of the nature of such crime, on protective and therapeutic needs.

B. Constitutional and Procedural Problems

In *Ragsdale v. Overholser*[115] the petitioner contended that the District of Columbia provisions for automatic assignment of a person acquitted solely on the ground of insanity[116] are unconstitutional, since such acquittal requires merely reasonable doubt as to sanity, whereas in a habeas corpus proceeding for release the petitioner is required to prove that he is not "dangerous to himself or to others." This contention raised an issue of considerable significance, but its disposition in decisional law is not satisfactory. In fact, the total area of our procedural "law of insanity" is marked by a lack of consistent policy orientation, which is bound to have serious constitutional law implications.

First, there is no agreement among the judges on the purpose of the mandatory automatic detention. Judge Burger has stated that such detention pursues two purposes: "(1) to protect the public and the subject; (2) to afford a place and a procedure to rehabilitate and restore the subject. . . ."[117] Judge Fahy has rather stressed "the necessity for treatment of the mental condition which led to acquittal."[118] In *Overholser v. Russell*[119] Judge Bazelon pointed out that detention being

invoked only in connection with criminal proceedings, its reach must be limited to the purpose of criminal law. Clearly, the

---

[115]281 F.2d 943 (D. C. Cir. 1960).

[116]*Supra* note 43. The wording of the majority view in Starr v. United States, 264 F.2d 377, 382-83 (D. C. Cir. 1958), may be taken to mean that the individual could be released if he showed that he no longer suffered from an "abnormal mental condition." For such reading of the majority view see Judge Bazelon's dissent, *id.*, 383, at 384; also Krash, *supra* note 28, at 946. The situation visualized in this instance, namely, that a person whose mental disease has "caused" the criminal act subsequently recovers his mental health and yet preserves his dangerousness, sheds doubt on the "but for" factor in the original causation.

[117]Ragsdale v. Overholser, *supra,* note 115, at 947.

[118]Judge Fahy's concurring opinion, *id.* 949, 950.

[119]283 F.2d 195 (D. C. Cir. 1960).

needs of such purpose do not encompass the confinement of those who are not dangerous.[120]

Second, there is no clear notion of the type and degree of danger against which the protective measure of continued detention in a mental hospital may be used. In the per curiam opinion in *Russell* it was said that danger of commission of "any criminal act" is a sufficient ground for denying release;[121] but, as pointed out by Judge Bazelon, this issue remains open since it was not raised by the record and need not have been considered. It is also uncertain that the "danger'" must be one of crime commission, for apparently suicide, which is not a crime, is included in the term "dangerous to himself."[122]

Third, there is no agreement on the degree of proof imposed upon the petitioner in habeas corpus proceedings for release. In *Ragsdale*, Judge Burger thought that there must be proof "beyond a reasonable doubt,"[123] but Judge Fahy demands merely that "on the evidence and in the circumstances as a whole the District Court should be able to reach a sound judgment one way or the other on the question of release."[124]

Fourth, no satisfactory explanation is offered of wherein exactly consists the "rational relationship between mandatory commitment . . . and acquittal by reason of insanity,"[125] upon which all the judges insist. This relationship apparently justifies classification of a person thus acquitted as a member of "an exceptional class of people,"[126] assumed to be at least prima facie mentally ill and dangerous, although "the standards and tests for . . . exculpation from criminal responsibility . . . and . . .

---

[120]Judge Bazelon, concurring in the result only, *id.* 198, 199.

[121]The court said, *id.* at 198: "[T]he danger to the public need not be possible physical violence. It is enough if there is competent evidence that he may commit any criminal act, for any such act will injure others and will expose the person to arrest, trial and conviction."

[122]This is not all. The court also pointed out that there "is always the additional possible danger not to be discounted even if remote—that a nonviolent criminal act may expose the perpetrator to violent retaliatory acts by the victim of the crime." *Ibid.*

[123]*Supra,* note 115, at 947.

[124]Cited by Judge Bazelon in Overholser v. Russell, *supra,* note 119, at 199.

[125]Ragsdale v. Overholser, *supra,* note 115 at 947-948, 950.

[126]Overholser v. Leach, 257 F.2d 667, 669-670 (D. C. Cir. 1958).

release from hospital custody" are " separate and distinct."[127] Judges concerned with the constitutionality issue advance the view that in the area of constitutional doubt a reasonably prompt shifting to civil commitment proceedings affords the proper solution.[128] But it is rather dubious that the lack of proper legality safeguards in the original criminal law confinement, or failure to assure a realistic positive substantive relationship between the nature and degree of the danger and imposition of confinement, can be justified by the mere fact that such confinement may be soon replaced by commitment proceedings.

To afford a rational relationship between ends and means, systematization is necessary. This can be afforded only in a planned statutory scheme which reflects a consistent policy giving due comparative weight to public and individual interests. Such systematization must proceed from a diversified notion of "danger" and a discerning scheme of relative "danger-response," and must assign to each "danger-situation," depending on its nature and degree, a measure appropriate to meet that danger. Such coordination of measures and protective needs must be safeguarded by a strict scheme of procedural guarantees of due process.

As pointed out by Judge Fahy, the seriousness of the precipitating crime is an extremely significant item of consideration in determining whether a measure of freedom deprivation is constitutional.[129] Judge Fahy was concerned with continuation of a measure which he thought could properly be imposed merely because of the acquittal by reason of insanity. But even the initial imposition of the measure may be highly dubious where the crime in issue is minor, though the same doubt can be readily dismissed where the person concerned has demonstrated his serious dangerousness by committing a felony against the bodily integrity of a person, though in a state of mental incapacity.[130]

---

[127]*Id.* at 670 n.4.

[128]See Judge Fahy's opinion in Ragsdale v. Overholser, *supra*, note 117, at 950; and see Judge Bazelon's opinion in Overholser v. Russell, *supra*, note 119, at 199.

[129]Ragsdale v. Overholser, *supra* note 128, at 950-51.

[130]In Overholser v. Lynch, *supra*, note 13, 394, at 396-397 Judge Fahy, dis-

Even where the precipitating act is grave, the evidentiary situation is apt to arouse serious preoccupation. It has been stressed that "[i]nherent in a verdict of not guilty by reason of insanity are two important elements: (a) that the defendant did in fact commit the criminal act charged; (b) that there exists some rational basis for belief that the defendant suffered from a mental disease or defect of which the criminal act is a product."[131] Presumably, then, the jury ought to be instructed that unless they find proof beyond a reasonable doubt that the defendant committed the act charged they cannot acquit solely by reason of insanity. But when presented with the alternative of acquittal on the ground of insanity, will the jury take the requirement of proof of commission of the act charged "beyond a reasonable doubt" as seriously as it would were such proof to result in a conviction?

Since "dangerousness" is not an element of the "insanity test," it would seem that acquittal by reason of insanity does not imply even prima facie a need for detention. "Dangerousness" rather evinces from the commission of the act charged. Such "dangerousness" varies in nature and degree depending on that act. Certain types of acts warrant detention, while others do not, either because measures short of detention may suffice to avert the danger or because the anticipated harm is small, so that the defendant's interest in liberty outweighs the public interest in protection. Moreover, the symptomatic value of the commission of a criminal act may be substantially affected by the surrounding circumstances. Given certain conditions, the inference that

---

senting, expressed the view that the release procedures for persons acquitted solely on the ground of insanity in the District of Columbia were not intended by Congress to apply to "persons who have engaged in any kind of conduct, however minor, but only [to] persons who have engaged in unlawful conduct of a dangerous character," particularly crimes of violence. But it is somewhat puzzling that Judge Fahy does not at the same time object to the provision for the automatic assignment of such minor offenders to a mental institution, rather assuming that they are sufficiently protected by means of habeas corpus proceedings. The basis of the writ in such cases would seem to be the illegality of the original detention. Is a statute constitutional when it provides for a detention that is *ab initio* illegal?

[131]Ragsdale v. Overholser, *supra*, note 115, at 948.

the actor is likely to commit a similar act in the future is not very strong. In such cases, whether or not taking a risk is constitutionally required depends on the gravity of the harm feared. Detention of a person on the basis of a small probability of serious harm may be justified, whereas detention on the basis of a small probability of moderate harm may be constitutionally improper.

The injustice implicit in an initial imposition of detention subject to later release upon habeas corpus petition is magnified by the shifting of the burden of proof to the petitioner. Additionally, the degree of proof which some judges believe the petitioner must meet, namely, proof "beyond a reasonable doubt," is impossible to meet in matters involving mental life, and particularly where prognosis is in issue. Again, shifting the burden of proof to the petitioner may be justified in some situations but not in others. Where crimes endangering human life and health are involved, such shifting of the burden of proof may be warranted, but where crimes other than these are anticipated, it is extremely objectionable. Whoever has the burden of proof cannot be expected to adduce more than convincing proof.

If measures applied to persons acquitted by reason of mental incapacity are to be deemed constitutional, certain basic requirements must be fulfilled. It is important to keep in mind that, though not "punitive," such measures are "penal."[132] No purpose other than protection against a danger of future crime commission by the defendant must be the ultimate object of such measures. This means that averting suicide or a threat of provocation of crime of third persons[133] is not a proper object of criminal law detention, except in the form of an emergency measure to be replaced without delay by appropriate means of civil protection.

Although the criminal act charged is of such nature and gravity as to give rise to an irrebuttable presumption of dangerousness justifying detention, a hearing should be granted upon defendant's request on the issue of the imposition of measures. In such a hearing it should be possible to challenge the court's choice

[132]See Silving, *"Rule of Law" in Criminal Justice, supra* note 6, at 145.
[133]See note 122, *supra.*

of the place of detention or the finding of proof beyond a reasonable doubt of the commission of the criminal act adduced during trial. A formal finding of "dangerousness" should be required even where dangerousness is irrebuttably presumed by virtue of the act committed, the court stating the basis of the finding and its evaluation of the evidence at the hearing, if any. As mentioned before, an irrebuttable presumption of dangerousness should obtain where the precipitating act would but for the defendant's mental incapacity be a felony against the bodily integrity of a person; commission of such an act is believed to warrant detention for a minimum period, varying in length depending on whether the act is a homicide or another felony. The presumption of dangerousness in such cases ought to be rebuttable only if a very long time has elapsed since commission of the act,[134] and in such event a hearing should be required. Where a felony against the bodily integrity of a person is not involved, there ought to be a hearing in which the prosecution must prove dangerousness. If the prosecution succeeds in establishing, for example, on the basis of the defendant's antecedents, that he is likely to turn to crimes of violence, confinement may be warranted. It may likewise be warranted where the prosecution shows that there is danger of commission of other serious crime and that no measure short of detention can avert it. Any measure other than detention must also be proved by the prosecution to be appropriate to avert the type of danger threatened. In no case should more than convincing proof be required where prediction of future human conduct is in issue. In all cases in which dangerousness or choice of an appropriate measure is in issue, psychiatric testimony ought to be mandatory.

Before lapse of the minimum period of detention in cases of felonies against the bodily integrity of a person an adversary hearing ought to be held regarding extension or termination of the measure. In this hearing the presumption of dangerousness

---

[134]In Italian law dangerousness is required to be specifically established by the judge in a formal finding even where it is presumed by law from frequent crime repetition, if the conviction or acquittal by reason of insanity is pronounced after ten years since the day of crime commission in cases involving mentally diseased defendants. ITALIAN PENAL CODE art. 204, par. 2, no. 1.

ought to be rebuttable by appropriate evidence. Provisions ought to be made for mandatory periodic examinations of the issue of continued dangerousness, both in cases involving crimes against the bodily integrity of a person after lapse of the minimum detention period and in those involving other crimes as well as measures other than detention.

III. CONCLUSION

In legal fields other than the criminal law the method of "trial and error" characteristic of the common law has produced results which, on the whole, should not evoke particular concern. Although it is not always clear against what "truth" error is tested, different individuals may well find it possible to reconcile these results with their divergent "truth" concepts. But in the area of criminal law this method is highly objectionable, inasmuch as criminal law is authoritarian law *par excellence,* where "man rules over another to the latter's hurt."[135] "Error" is "tested" at the expense of the subject's most vital interest, his personal freedom. "Trial" at such cost is immoral. Rather, there ought to be a clear policy established in advance, setting forth the legitimate objectives of law in a differential discriminatory manner. There must be no freedom deprivation at all unless it is warranted then and there by a legitimate purpose. Nor must there be deprivation in excess of that justified by the particular purpose and the social needs as pertaining to the type of situation involved. Abuse cannot be justified just because it is remediable, particularly when the person concerned has been found to suffer or to have suffered from a mental incapacity, for such person can hardly be expected to possess those mental qualities upon which effective pursuit of available legal remedies is predicated.

---

[135]Eccl. 8: 9.

INTOXICANTS AND CRIMINAL CONDUCT

Once, not too long ago, considering the relative stability of cultural patterns, it was believed that mental illness was the product of sin. For example, melancholia was causally attributed to masturbation, and this was taken to indicate that the illness was due to the accused's own fault and hence did not excuse criminality.[1] It would be exaggeration to ascribe judicial statements of this type exclusively to the judges' ignorance. In no case where the defense of insanity has been raised has its determination been wholly unaffected by the degree of social toleration or condemnation of the type of criminal conduct involved[2] or the adjudicators' contemplation of the consequences of a given decision. In the famed *Durham* case,[3] Judge Bazelon, in a somewhat puzzling argument considering his obvious desire to respond to the demands of psychiatric experts, admitted and accepted the fact that in passing upon the issue of "insanity" the jury renders and, indeed, ought to render a "moral judgment."[4]

There are several impediments to an effective elimination of the "moral" element from the judgment on "insanity." One lies in the fact that social conceptions of "sin" may actually be involved in phenomena of mental illness; they are reflected in the defendant's "superego," which may play a significant role in the breakdown of his personality balance, so that understanding such conceptions is a requisite of comprehending his state of mind. "Mental disease" is a relative notion; it is a deviation from a minimum of that which is deemed "normal" in a given setting;

---

[1]State v. Harrison, 36 W. Va. 729, 15 S. E. 982, 18 L. R. A. 224 (1892); compare *Mental Incapacity in Criminal Law, supra* at 51.

[2]*Query:* Would Judge Brannon in the *Harrison* case have adopted the same "scientific" position had the case involved a less emotionally charged "moral" issue than that of a killing of a fifteen-year-old girl by a youth who had for years enjoyed affectionate hospitality in the house of her parents?

[3]Durham v. United States, 94 U. S. App. D. C. 228, 214 F.2d 862 (1954).

[4]*Supra* at 876.

it is thus relative to the prevailing "moral" patterns. A further obstacle to purging "insanity" of "moral" implications inheres in the dependence of all the disciplines that may help to determine the legal "insanity" issue—psychology, psychiatry, cultural anthropology and sociology, as well as law—on verbalization and verbal communication, which carry "moral glosses" rooted in the use of identical language also in "moral" contexts. In "insanity" cases one such "gloss" seems to run approximately along the following lines: " 'Insanity' exempts from punishment because the person concerned has no choice as regards its causation. If he had such choice—as in the above cited melancholia case—the exemption would not lie." It is not clear when exactly the position was adopted that no one can help becoming "insane," so that one *cannot* be "guilty" of his "insanity." The view that illness is always "involuntary" is wrongly assumed to express a medical or psychiatric insight. Indeed, "involuntary" is a precarious concept belonging to a border area of fact and norm, the demarcation line not being clearly discernible. Mostly inarticulate and inconsistent "moral judgments" pervade with special force treatment of commitment to intoxicants as within or outside the law of insanity.

As regards irreparable alcoholic conditions such as delirium tremens (which—whatever definition of "insanity" one might posit consistently with some socially acceptable usage—could hardly be alleged not to be included in it[5]), the attitude prevailing in law is rather that such condition should qualify as exemption ground in spite of the fact that it was brought about by guilt—

---

[5]Notice some courts' insistence that only a "fixed or settled insanity," which quality has been conceded only to delirium tremens, would excuse. See for citation and discussion of some such cases, *Note, Intoxication as a Criminal Defense*, 55 COLUMBIA LAW REVIEW 1210, at 1219-1220 (1955). This is especially interesting since, according to the modern medical view, all so-called "alcoholic psychoses" with the exception of delirium tremens may occur in individuals who do not drink. HAGGARD & JELLINEK, ALCOHOL EXPLORED 220-221 (Doubleday, Doran & Company, Inc., Garden City, 1942, hereinafter cited HAGGARD & JELLINEK). But see Easter v. District of Columbia, 361 F.2d 50 (D.C. Cir., 1966), differentiating "sickness" in chronic alcoholics from "mental disease" in Durham, *infra* at 238.

the "guilt of an evil life conduct" (*Lebensführungsschuld*).[6] The argument in this instance seems to be that though "delirium tremens" is caused by the patient's life conduct of dissipation and sin, this guilt no longer matters in the face of his total collapse.

In *Robinson v. California*[7] it was held that "being a drug addict" could not constitutionally be made a crime, but the majority opinion left it uncertain whether the reason of such unconstitutionality was that "being an addict" is a "status" rather than an "act" or that it is a specific status, namely, one of "illness." Much importance has been attached to the deterministic feature of drug addiction, a feature which, in the Justices' opinion, necessarily excludes responsibility. Constitutional prohibition against the criminality of "being an addict" on the ground that this is an "illness" was further supported by findings that addiction occurred in newborn infants where the mother was addicted.[8] This insistence on drug addiction being a fate seems to be the Justices' answer to potential allegations of "guilt of a life conduct."

Because of the specific determinism introduced by the *Robinson* decision into the problem of drug addiction—the stress on the possibility of "being an addict by birth," no clear indication is afforded in the case what attitude the Supreme Court might take toward the concept of "guilt incurred by an evil life conduct." In Germany the *Lebensführungsschuld* has been the object of much controversy incident to repudiation, after the collapse of the National Socialist regime, of its favorite idea—that of the so-called "criminal law of the actor" (*Täterstrafrecht, derecho penal del autor*).[9] The latter type of law subjects persons

---

[6]In some cases it is not made clear whether, notwithstanding an actor's insanity, he might not be held responsible if at the time of the act he had been intoxicated. Thus, in United States v. Drew, 5 Mason 28, 25 Fed. Cas. 913, Case No. 14, 993 (Circuit Court, D. Mass. 1828), Circuit Justice Story emphasized that the defendant in the case had committed the homicide with which he was charged in a period of abstinence. Did Justice Story mean to say that even though Drew suffered from delirium tremens, a recognized "insanity," he would nevertheless be responsible for the crime he committed if at the time of commission he had been intoxicated? Compare also Easter v. District of Columbia, *supra*, discussed below, 238–240, 327, 329, 342.

[7]370 U. S. 660 (1962).

[8]See Mr. Justice Douglas's concurring opinion, *supra* 668 at 670.

[9]On the development and breakdown of the latter idea in Germany see Silving,

to criminal sanctions for what they "are" rather than for what they "did" in a specific case ("criminal law of the act"—*Tatstrafrecht, derecho penal del acto*); it punishes a "status," namely, using Heidegger's awkward style, the status of "being thus"— "*so-sein.*" The "criminal law of the actor" violates fundamental democratic tenets such as *nulla poena sine lege, nulla poena sine actu,*[10] and *nulla poena sine culpa.* The concept of "guilt incurred by an evil life conduct" is one step removed from the idea of the "criminal law of the actor." The requisite of a socially harmful conduct, as described by statute, is not necessarily abandoned. But the mental element is not pinned down to this particular conduct; "guilt" rather lies in the defendant's previous total life management, in his "having permitted himself to become thus."[11] In Germany, after a vigorous debate, this concept was in principle repudiated, not alone because German scholars claim that determinism can be "scientifically" proven to be false, but mainly on the basis of the ethical philosophy of modern democratic law.[12]

"Rule of Law" in *Criminal Justice,* in Mueller, ed., ESSAYS IN CRIMINAL SCIENCE 77, at 97-104 (Sweet & Maxwell, London; Rothman, South Hackensack 1961).

[10]This phrase has been suggested by Ryu & Silving, *Nullum Crimen Sine Actu,* SEOUL NATIONAL UNIVERSITY LAW REVIEW (1964), to denote a complex of principles intended to limit crime constructs in which intent is punishable beyond the scope of criminal harm.

[11]This concept is by no means new and may, indeed, be found in ARISTOTLE, THE NICHOMACHEAN ETHICS, Book Three, Chapter V, in THOMPSON, THE ETHICS OF ARISTOTLE, at 74 (1953), formulated thus: "And punishment follows also when the ignorance is thought to have been due to carelessness, it being held that the guilty party need not have shown this ignorance. He should have noticed what he was doing—it was his duty to notice. You may say that very likely he could not help it, he is just that sort of man. But there is an answer to that. Such people have only thelmselves to blame for having acquired a character like that by their loose living, just as they have only themselves to blame for being unjust, if they make a practice of unjust behavior or, intemperate, if they spend their time in drinking or other forms of dissipation. It is their persistent activities in certain directions that make them what they are."

[12]In the famous decision declaring error of law to be a general defense to a charge of crime (2 BGHSt. 194, 1952; discussed in Ryu & Silving, *Error Juris: A Comparative Study,* 24 UNIVERSITY OF CHICAGO LAW REVIEW 421, at 450-452, 1957), the Great Senate in Criminal Matters of the Bundesgerichtshof justified adoption of the so-called "theory of guilt" (*Schuldtheorie*) in preference to the "theory of intent" (*Vorsatztheorie*) on the ground, among others, that the latter

In dealing with conduct connected with intoxicants, it is important to be aware of the pitfalls of the "criminal law of the actor" and understand the problem of the *Lebensführungsschuld,*

---

compels acquittal where the actor, by his own choice of a wrong life conduct, forfeited sensitivity to wrong. The court said (*supra,* at 208-209): "The confirmed habitual criminal forfeited by a criminal life conduct sensitiveness to ethical values and thus the ability to reach by exertion of his conscience realization of the wrong. His guilt is a guilt of a [bad] life conduct." But German law has traveled a long way since this decision was rendered. In the comments to the Draft of a New German Penal Code, ENTWURF EINES STRAFGESETZBUCHES (StGB) E 1962 MIT Begründung, Bundesrat Drucksache IV/650, Bonn 1962, at 94 (hereinafter cited as GERMAN DRAFT 1962), we read the following significant words: "In connection with the *criminal law based on guilt* the recognition has gained ground that, contrary to the opinion of former drafts, the dangerousness of the actor cannot by itself afford a basis for aggravation of punishment. Making the dangerousness of the actor a basis for aggravation of punishment when such dangerousness has been brought about by guilt, is precarious because of the fact that the judge is hardly in a position to ascertain this so-called *Lebensführungsschuld.* From this trend of thought the demand has been derived that the standard of punishment be only the guilt constituted by the act and not the blameworthy life conduct of the actor, that has not been reflected in the act itself." As may be seen, the draftsmen of the German Penal Code Project of 1962 were trying to resolve a difficult philosophical doctrinal controversy by shifting the issue to a procedural level. It is not difficult at all to establish a *Lebensführungsschuld* unless complex psychoanalytic notions are introduced into the evaluational process. Obviously, the draftsmen, in this awkward manner, gave preference to the dominant opinion (MAURACH, DEUTSCHES STRAFRECHT, ALLGEMEINER TEIL [2d enlarged ed., Verlag C. F. Müller, Karlsruhe 1958], hereinafter cited as MAURACH, at 328) rejecting that type of guilt. Certain crime types of the penal codes, however, reflect acceptance of notions of personality types developed by life habits. These, it would seem, are questionable, if the criminal law reaction to them is expressed in punishment rather than in measures. In the Anglo-American law the *Lebensführungsschuld* has never been conceptualized. But the principle derived from this notion of guilt has been often followed by courts, particularly in intoxication cases. In such cases courts have often pointed out that a man cannot use his own wicked life conduct as an excuse for crime or in mitigation of punishment. Thus, in an early case, the judge said: ". . . [M]en who degrade themselves below the ordinary level of social morality, by bad conduct or habits, do not thereby relieve themselves from having their acts and duties judged by the ordinary rules of social action. They cannot set up their own vices as a reason for being set into a special class that is to be judged more favourably than other persons." Keenan v. Commonwealth, 44 Pa. St. 55 84 Am. Dec. 414 (1862). However, where insanity is present, even early cases, ever since admission of insanity as a defense, held that exemption from responsibility is not excluded on the ground that the insanity was brought about by a wicked habit such as drinking.

so as to avoid them. The former may lead to inadvertent acceptance of "pre-delictual criminal law security measures," that is, measures which may be imposed not on the basis of a specific socially harmful conduct described by statute as criminal, but because of an undesirable personality of a given subject, such as "being a drunkard," "being an addict" or "being a vagrant." Whether a "status" of such type may be subject to administrative government intervention by reasonable public health measures, is not in issue in criminal law context. Such intervention is limited by sui generis constitutional terms and restrictions. The problem in criminal law is rather whether it is constitutionally permissible to utilize the machinery of criminal law and procedure for achievement of administrative public health goals where there is no specific criminal conduct as defined by statute and adjudicated in accordance with due process of law as applicable to criminal matters. Confusion of criminal and administrative institutions and procedures is dangerous to individual liberty. Simply substituting "civil" for "criminal" law constructs in order to salvage an otherwise constitutionally objectionable criminal law notion, as attempted by Mr. Justice Clark in his dissent in the *Robinson* case, is not admissible in a democracy.[13] Nor are the deals made by agents of criminal law administration with addicts, where the latter consent to be institutionalized for treatment in order to avoid prosecution, constitutionally unimpeachable. The question is whether it is permissible for the government to secure a waiver of a constitutional right by a threat of prosecution.

The concept of a "guilt incurred by an evil life conduct" is implied in statements such as that a defendant cannot rely on his own "vice" in defense to a charge of crime. It is also reflected in the derogatory use of the term "habitual drunkard." It is precarious, not alone because it tends to disrupt the orientation of democratic criminal law toward a particular act and toward an intent specificially directed to such act, but also because it

---

[13]*Supra* note 7, at 679-685. For a similar argument in relation to the crime of "possession"—*nota bene* of one marijuana cigarette—see Martinez Rodríguez v. Delgado, decided by the Supreme Court of Puerto Rico, June 30, 1965 (Puerto Rico Colegio de Abogados Ref. 1965, No. 115).

impedes inquiry into the potential presence of mental incapacity in cases of offenders substantially affected by alcohol or drug habits. Surely, such offenders are more likely to suffer from such incapacity than offenders not so affected.

In the "moralizing" approach toward alcohol and drug consumption, belief that they are direct causes of serious crime plays an important role. This belief has been discredited by results of recent research. Experts tell us that when a person affected by intoxicants engages in criminal conduct, the latter is not directly referable in a causal sense to the impact of the intoxicant. Rather, the criminal conduct and the commitment to or consumption of the intoxicant are both results of the total personality structure of the offender; they are parallel phenomena, both attributable to the same source and the criminal conduct is not related to the intoxicant by a *propter hoc* nexus.[14] This insight would seem to call for reexamination of our total approach to inebriate criminal conduct.

In attempting to resolve policy issues posed by phenomena of alcohol and drug use in criminal law, we must try not to permit ourselves to be guided by "moralizing" considerations. The law should not be made a *custos morum*. Nor should we conceive of the law as a system serving perpetuation of given cultures, for "cultures" very often express preconceptions and prejudices. On the other hand, we must accept, as part of the total factual situation to be considered with a view to legislative or judicial evaluation, the fact that a given "moral" judgment prevails and that certain "cultural patterns" obtain in the given society, for in a complex sense they may well play a role in the offender's conduct. Only thus is Judge Bazelon's acceptance of the fact that in passing upon the issue of "insanity" juries will "continue to make moral judgments"[15] methodologically and constitutionally admissible. The "moral judgment" in this context ought to be understood as a "judgment of fact," finding the defendant's conduct or state of mind to be or not to be consistent with pre-

---

[14]Noyes & Kolb, MODERN CLINICAL PSYCHIATRY 167 (6th ed., W. B. Saunders Company, Philadelphia 1963, hereinafter cited as Noyes & Kolb). For further authorities see *infra* at 251–254.

[15]*Supra* note 3, at 876.

vailing morality or culture, as part of an evaluation of his adaptive or integrative functioning within the community. It should not be an expression of an autonomous censure or tolerance measured by the jury's own moral standards, except to the extent that the latter may reflect community standards. For example, when a man is charged with cannibalism and the issue of his "insanity" is raised, the adjudicator may take account of the fact that cannibalism is so unusual in the given society as to afford at least one indicium of defendant's "insanity" or "social abnormality" under the circumstances. But the adjudicator should not simply find him to be "insane" or "sane" because that adjudicator has himself a strong revulsion against cannibalism.

In this sense it is necessary for purposes of sound legislation to consider the moral and cultural significance within a given society of alcohol or drug consumption. This significance, derived from long-forgotten tradition, enters into the consumers' unconscious motivations, which, rather than the amount consumed, determine the consequences of the consumption.[16] A most impor-

---

[16]Authoritative students of alcoholism, Haggard & Jellinek, 11-12, state: "Whether a man is a moderate drinker or not depends less upon any actual standards set for amounts drunk than upon his motives for drinking and the control of the amounts he drinks by these motives. Thus the effects desired and produced by alcohol become criteria of moderation and excess." But, of course, the determining motivations, according to psychoanalytical schools of thought, are the unconscious ones. Psychoanalytic writers try to explain psychoetiologically (causally) why people drink, whereas proponents of other theories merely describe what more or less immediately provokes drinking, Another important psychoanalytical finding is that motivations, e.g., of habitual so-called "social drinkers" are not remote from those of the frankly intemperate drinkers. Glover, *The Etiology of Alcoholism*, in ON THE EARLY DEVELOPMENT OF MIND (International Universities Press, Inc., New York 1956), at 85, states: "Social drinking habits have the same etiological relation to alcoholism as a pandemic of mild itch would have to acute eczema."

There is an elaborate psychoanalytical literature on the etiology of alcoholism. See ABRAHAM, *The Psychological Relations Between Sexuality and Alcoholism*, in SELECTED PAPERS (Hogarth Press, London 1927); Glover, *op. cit. supra*, 81-90; Knight, *The Psychodynamics of Chronic Alcoholism*, 86 JOURNAL OF NERVOUS AND MENTAL DISEASE 538-548 (1937); *Treatment of Chronic Alcohol Addiction*, 1 BULLETIN OF THE MENNINGER CLINIC 233-250 (1937); FENICHEL, THE PSYCHOANALYTIC THEORY OF NEUROSIS (W. W. Norton & Company, Inc., New York 1945); MENNINGER, MAN AGAINST HIMSELF (Harcourt, Brace, Inc., New York 1938); Lorand, *A Survey of Psychoanalytical Literature on Problems of Alcohol:*

Bibliography, 1 YEARB. PSYCHOANAL. 359-370 (1945).

As pointed out by Lisansky, *Psychological Predisposition in Alcoholism*, 21 QUARTERLY JOURNAL OF STUDIES ON ALCOHOL 314, at 317 (1960), one must "choose between a theoretical conceptualization of alcoholism by orthodox psychoanalytic thinkers or no conceptualization at all."

For criticism of the psychoanalytical theory of alcoholism see Landis, *Theories of the Alcoholic Personality*, in ALCOHOL, SCIENCE AND SOCIETY 129, at 134-135 (QUARTERLY JOURNAL OF STUDIES ON ALCOHOL [1945]).

Psychoanalytical writers are not in full agreement as to the exact etiology of alcoholism except that they all relate it to oral fixation and homosexual tendencies. But, contrary to the assertions of their critics that these explanations are meaningless since they refer to either manifest (orality) or not specific features (homoeroticism being prevalent) (for this criticism see Landis, *supra*, at 134-135), psychoanalysts do offer explanations of the dynamics of acquisition and maintenance of the alcohol habit. Thus, Radó, S., *Psychoanalysis of Pharmacothymia* (drug addiction), 2 PSYCHOANALYTIC QUARTERLY 1-23 (1933), traced the childhood experiences which generate the individual's feeling of inability to solve his life problems through his own initiative and thus lead to a longing for satisfaction coming from the outside, as is characteristic in infancy. Knight, *supra*, expressed the view that any neurotic conflict may lead to alcoholism, which then creates, by way of a neurotic vicious circle, new conflict, frustrations leading to hostility, the latter to guilt feelings, destructive masochism, to be appeased in turn by indulgence as proof of affection. MENNINGER, MAN AGAINST HIMSELF, *op. cit. supra*, sees alcohol addiction as a form of self-destruction used to avert a greater self-destruction deriving from aggressiveness, excited by ungratified eroticism and a sense of guilt related to the aggressiveness.

While psychoanalytically oriented students delve into deep-seated conflicts rooted in childhood experiences (see also, e.g., NOYES & KOLB, 165-167), adherents of learning theory are satisfied with observation of immediate reactions. They believe that drink is a response learned, because it reduces fear, in life situations involving approach-avoidance conflicts. See, e.g., DOLLARD & MILLER, PERSONALITY AND PSYCHOTHERAPY (McGraw-Hill Book Company, Inc., New York 1950). There is a variety of sociological approaches to the problem, some of which may be found represented in ALCOHOL, SCIENCE AND SOCIETY, *op. cit. supra*, par. 4. It would lead us too far afield to deal with these and other interpretations of alcoholism.

Some writers assume, on the very basic level, physiological, psychological and sociological factors combining to produce alcoholism, all of as yet unknown degrees of importance, but query why many such suffering persons do use alcoholic beverages and do not become alcoholics while others (well under 10% of users) do succumb to the disease. These writers suggest that there may be social and cultural terrains that are more or less favorable for the emergence of alcoholism, and that the background psychological factors considered important for alcoholism may not mature into that condition if the cultural conditions are negatively structured for such a development. Bacon, *Social Settings Conducive to Alcoholism, A Sociological Approach to a Medical Problem*, 164 JOURNAL OF THE AMERICAN MEDICAL ASSOCIATION 177-181 (1953). NOYES & KOLB, at 165-166, suggest that the causes of alcoholism are the same as are those which are productive of neu-

tant factor in the Western World's approach to alcohol is the role of alcohol in Jewish and Christian rites, representing ancient, perhaps prehistoric ideologies. Symbolization of the "blood of Christ" by wine leads to alcohol's toleration. For symbolization typically works in reverse: Wine, by serving as such symbol, is being itself sanctified and its use is thus condoned.[17] A compromise is struck: As in primitive customs the gift of alcohol to the gods,[18] so in our modern religious customs the alcohol ritual functions as a medium of achieving condonation; likewise, as in primitive customs, so in our modern religious ones, limitations imposed upon drinking serve as the price of toleration. In the Bible we find condemnation limited to excessive drinking, and this policy is maintained by most Christian denominations. Only

---

rosis in the nonalcoholic. If an individual with a low anxiety tolerance lives in a social setting which imposes heavy social penalties on intoxication, he may take recourse to other frankly neurotic escapes.

[17]This type of mental process is also noticeable in other areas, particularly that of sex and marriage taboos. Marriage serves as a symbol of the relationship of the Lord to the children of Israel as well as that of Christ to the Church. By virtue of its function as such symbol, marriage itself is sanctified. See Ephesians 5:32. In the *Decree for the Armenians*, published by order of the Council of Florence (1439), it is said: "*Septimum est Sacramentum matrimonii, quod est signum conjunctionis Christi et Ecclesiae, secundum Apostolum dicentem: Sacramentum hoc magnum est, ego autem dico in Christo et in Ecclesia.*" When Christ attended the marriage of Cana, He, significantly, turned water into wine, thus purifying both marriage and alcohol (John 2).

[18]Since alcohol is a depressant and thus an anxiety-reducing agent and since it is available wherever agriculture is practiced, it has been used since time immemorial by primitive societies. Its consumption is widely accepted among primitive men, although there are a few primitive tribes that are abstinent. Primitive men drink for the intoxicating effect of alcohol, although they rationalize the drinking habit in various ways. The uniform pattern among primitive tribes is to drink to a state of full intoxication. While the profound motive for drinking lies in its anxiety-reducing quality, drinking also evokes anxiety, for by eliminating inhibitions it releases sex drives and aggression, so that sex taboos are transgressed and antisocial acts occur, which in turn produces guilt feelings. The ensuing ambivalence toward alcohol is resolved by various methods of institutionalization and limitation of drinking habits. The primitive man is never a solitary drinker. Drinking is a social occasion and follows an established pattern. In some tribes women are excluded from drinking parties; in others they serve as watchmen over the conduct of the drunken men. A frequent phenomenon is relaxation of normal sex taboos for the occasion. Provisions are made for avoidance of excessive harm in the course of aggression incident to anticipated intoxication.

very few sects advocate complete abstinence.[19] Moreover, there is a tendency to sublimate the drinking need. The drinking orgy is replaced by "orgiastic" experience in the higher spiritual values. The pattern for this is also set in the Bible.[20] This sublimation potential may be one of the bases for an attitude of leniency toward the primitive prototype of the higher spiritual experience. In both the primitive and the religious pattern there are noticeable a spirit of rationalized condonation and tolerance for the alcohol consumer alongside with a deeply rooted condemnation, no doubt charged with personal guilt feelings, of the sin or crime committed in drink, that is somehow sensed to be fused with the drink into a single experience, prompted by motives that are antecedent to drinking. Modern laws reflect these phenomena of our Western culture.

Presumably, our attitude toward drug use is similarly rooted in the ancient history of our culture. But we know less about that history than we do about that pertaining to alcohol consumption. The Bible does not directly deal with drugs. But an indication that some form of a drug habit was in existence might

---

Weapons are hidden. Rules of proper conduct while in a state of institutionalized intoxication develop. The notion gains ground that "you can be aggressive, provided you do not use weapons and provided it does not go too far." Thus, frequently, the drinking bouts end up in a brawl in which, however, no appreciable harm is done. A tacit convention is adopted not to hold a grudge against the man who assaulted you, because it is understood that this is one of the effects of the particular drink, and perhaps also because everybody was a party to the drinking. Alcohol consumption is rationalized on the ground that alcohol is a gift of the gods, and the gods are appeased by being offered the first few drops of the valuable alcohol, apparently on the theory that the gods also enjoy it. See Horton, *The Functions of Alcohol in Primitive Societies*, in ALCOHOL, SCIENCE AND SOCIETY *op. cit. supra* note 16, at 153-177.

[19]See Bainton, *The Churches and Alcohol*, in ALCOHOL, SCIENCE AND SOCIETY, *op. cit.* note 16, at 287-298. In the Old Testament priests are prohibited from drinking alcohol while in service (Leviticus 10:8, 9). This is interpreted as a means of "differentiating between the holy and the profane and between the contaminated and the clean" (Leviticus 10:10). There may be some relation between this prohibition and the priests' eating of the sacrifice which is in turn connected with their function of "bearing the sins of the community and atoning for them before the Lord" (Leviticus 10:17).

[20]"And be not drunk with wine, wherein is excess, but be filled with the Spirit" (Ephesians 5:18).

be found in the institution of sacrifice to the Lord, in which the scent of burning, pleasing or displeasing the Lord, played an important role.[21] There seems to have been a preference for blood sacrifice,[22] and this type of manifestation of extreme aggression, peculiarly enough, appears to be the ancient prototype of drug consumption which in our culture is the choice of the nonaggressive, peace-loving, contemplative individual,[23] while alcohol, a product of nonaggressive agricultural activities, is the choice of the openly aggressive. Psychoanalytically oriented cultural anthropologists might find in these biblical phenomena a clue to the divergent contemporary community reactions to drug and alcohol use. The fact is that the Western World's social attitude toward alcohol consumption is both disapproving and permissive, so that in sum total it amounts to but a mild criticism, whereas there is an overwhelming and vociferous disapproval of, and indeed contempt for, drug use. It has been observed that this imbalance of attitudes toward alcohol and drug use is unfounded, in the light of the fact that drug addic-

---

[21]Genesis 4.

[22]The Lord preferred Abel's animal sacrifice to Cain's agricultural one (*ibid.*) Notice particularly the sacrifice of one's own children such as Jephta's sacrifice of his only daughter (Judges 11:29-40), Abraham's attempt to sacrifice his only son (Genesis 22:1-18).

[23]Indeed, one theory sets forth "avoidance of aggression" as motivation for drug addiction. Wikler and Rasor, *Psychiatric Aspects of Drug Addiction,* 14 AMERICAN JOURNAL OF MEDICINE 70–89 (1929). According to this view, the choice of intoxicant by a person psychologically tending toward addiction is determined by the manner in which that intoxicant alters behavior. The alcoholic chooses alcohol because he unconsciously yearns for release of his aggressiveness and because alcohol, by removing inhibitions, produces this effect. The drug addict, on the other hand, "who desires in his inmost self to be quiet, untroubled and contemplative, chooses the drug which will facilitate such an effect," opium or opium derivatives, such as morphine, heroin. NYSWANDER, THE DRUG ADDICT AS A PATIENT 67 (Grune & Stratton, Inc., New York 1956). Opium, in fact, reduces aggressive criminal tendencies, and it has been shown that criminals with a history of violence abandoned all violent activity as part of their behavior pattern after becoming addicted (Kolb, *Drug Addiction and Its Relation to Crime,* 9 MENTAL HYGIENE 74 (1935), cited in NYSWANDER, at 67). The number of arrests of addicts for violent offenses against the person, such as rape and aggravated assault, is remarkably small; indeed, it constitutes only a fraction of the proportion of such arrests among the population at large. Finestone, H., *Narcotics and Criminality,* 22 LAW AND CONTEMPORARY PROBLEMS 69, at 71 (1957).

tion is socially much less harmful than is alcoholism.[24] An international study group of the World Health Organization suggested that the drug taboo "affords possible outlets for social hostility and satisfaction of need for guilt feelings,"[25] precisely because the drug addict, in contrast to the alcoholic, is allegedly unconsciously motivated by a desire to avoid sex and aggressiveness. Whether it is this "purity" of the addict that affords the basis for his being chosen as the white scapegoat destined to atone for the guilt originating in forbidden wishes and aggressive desires of others,[26] or whether it is rather a deeper-seated uncon-

---

[24]As pointed out by MENNINGER, THE HUMAN MIND (3d ed., Alfred A. Knopf, Inc., New York 1955): "[t]he public has many erroneous ideas about drug addiction. There are not nearly so many cases as is generally supposed . . ." ELDRIDGE, NARCOTICS AND THE LAW 66-103 (American Bar Foundation 1962), has shown flagrant methodological errors in statistics of narcotic crimes, which result in a completely misleading picture of the social problems presented by these crimes. WILLIAMS, DRUGS AGAINST MEN 129-134 (Robert M. McBride & Co., New York 1935), speaks of "the 'dope fiend' bugaboo whereby the public is being misled to believe that a devastating army of 'dope fiends' is threatening the moral and mental stability of the nation." He answers the question of what actually is the harm produced by drug consumption, saying: "It all depends on what you mean by 'harmful.'" Overeating kills far more people than are killed by overdrinking, and too much sugar may be worse for the body than a good deal of alcohol. The argument that any of the drugs, alcohol, caffeine, nicotine and the drugs officially dubbed narcotics, of which opium and its derivatives are the chief, are poisons is a mere quibble. So are, for example, proteins, the essential constituents of all tissue-building foods, if introduced undigested into the blood stream. What delimitates dangerous drugs is, according to the author, that all these drugs: "(a) produce characteristic effects on the brain and nervous system; (b) produce changes in the organism which permit their tolerance in larger and larger doses with continued usage; and (c) by virtue of these changes, acquire such hold on the organism that their discontinuance is resented." See Williams, op. cit. supra, 21, 23, 85-87. Alcohol has an adverse effect on the brain, and narcotics are "harmful" because they are addictive. The author points out (ibid., 132-133) that for the year 1932 there is no record of any automobile accident ascribable to morphine addiction and invites the reader to compare this with the incidence of accidents in which alcohol was at least a contributing factor. Addiction, however, creates such dependence of the person concerned on the drug that he would do almost anything to obtain it, and in this sense it is crimogenic.

[25]See TREATMENT AND CARE OF DRUG ADDICTS, REPORT OF A STUDY GROUP, World Health Organization Technical Report Series, No. 131 (Geneva 1957, abbreviated World Health Org. Techn. Rep. Ser., 1957, 131), at 14.

[26]It may be important to stress that he does not engage in aggressive acts or

scious recollection of a tradition of aggression that invites the community's counteraggression, is an intricate problem which merits study that might shed further light on the conflicts of the drug user and on community reactions to him. At present, legislators must proceed from the fact that, in contrast to the alcohol addict, the drug addict seldom shows antisocial behavior or aggression[27] other than violations of narcotic drug laws and crimes committed in order to secure the needed drug supply, that cannot be obtained by lawful means.

---

in sex crime. The motivations of the drug addict are controversial (on this see Glover, *op. cit. supra* note 16, at 187-215).

Of course, the attitudes toward drug addiction vary geographically and change in time. The World Health Organization Study Group (*supra* note 25, *ibid.*) observed that while the Koran proscribes the use of substances that alter the state of consciousness, interpretation has limited this to alcohol and by inference allowed narcotics. Indian religion also forbade the use of alcohol and hence the Brahmin priesthood of India became users of opium as a sublimating substitute (ANSLINGER AND TOMPKINS, THE TRAFFIC IN NARCOTICS [Funk & Wagnalls Company, Inc., New York 1953] 2). Until the turn of the twentieth century the use of opium and its derivatives was generally less offensive to Anglo-American public morals than cigarette smoking. King, *Narcotic Drug Laws and Enforcement Policies*, 22 LAW AND CONTEMPORARY PROBLEMS 113 (1957).

[27]This indisputably applies to the drugs of major use in the United States, that is, opium and opium derivatives, morphine, heroin. The impact of marijuana (hashish) is controversial. In response to alarming sensational newspaper and magazine propaganda against the "marijuana menace," Mayor Fiorello La Guardia, "New York's best-loved and most colorful mayor," requested assistance in ascertaining the truth about marijuana from the New York Academy of Medicine, which appointed a committee to obtain the facts about this drug and its effects. The report of the Mayor's Committee on Marijuana, published in 1944, showed that there was a great deal of exaggeration in the journalistic publicity. According to this report, no direct relationship could be demonstrated between marijuana smoking and crime. But the report was vigorously attacked by sensation-hungry journalists "who saw themselves deprived of a valuable source of material for headlines." On this see DE ROPP, DRUGS AND THE MIND (St. Martin's Press, Inc., New York 1957) 100-109.

Cocaine is a stimulant, whereas opiates are depressants. It produces delusions and when a cocainist carries a weapon, he is quite capable of using it under the impact of such delusions. The view has been expressed that probably the idea of the "dope fiend," so incorrectly applied to heroin addicts, originated from some violent acts committed by cocainists (DE ROPP 165-166). Neither marijuana nor cocaine is addictive. Barbiturates are addictive and they have an ill effect upon the mind, retarding mental processes and, in the event of withdrawal, producing violent epileptic convulsions (*id.* 162-163).

Legal solutions are importantly determined by the needs of enforcement which, in turn, requires drawing clear lines of demarcation for which there may be no support in strict scientific criteria. The law thus attempts to differentiate sharply degrees of commitment to intoxicants, where from a scientific point of view, the demarcation lines between such degrees are blurred.[28] Thus for instance, the transition between "social drinking" and "habitual drinking" is often difficult to perceive, and socioethical evaluations and prevailing social prejudices no doubt play an important role in the pertinent classifications. Yet, the concept of a "habitual drunkard" may carry significant legal consequences, though it is hardly ever legally defined. It might be interesting indeed to make studies for the purpose of determining the ratio of the rich among those suffering legal disadvantages due to being classified as "habitual drunkards." The suspicion of social prejudice is but one of the reasons for the need to define the pertinent concepts for legal purposes, precisely because they are not scientifically defined. There is also an imperative need for establishment of the exact role of such concepts within the scheme of criminal law and evidence.

Among the lesser forms of commitment to intoxicants, acute intoxication followed by criminal conduct plays the most significant role. There is a tendency to ascribe such conduct directly to the intoxication, which is held to be "voluntary" except under the most unlikely conditions.[29] In this situation it is felt that the "guilt of a life conduct" need not be considered, since there is a basis for a direct attack on the state of mind of the offender at the time of "becoming intoxicated." However, there is noticeable in certain laws of civil law countries a marked discomfort regarding the precise object of "guilt" in situations of this type; it is difficult to discern whether these provisions attach "guilt" to the intoxication itself or to the crime committed in drink.[30] These provisions, in fact, seem to point to an emerging concep-

---

[28]Compare *supra* note 16.

[29]HALL, GENERAL PRINCIPLES OF CRIMINAL LAW 539 (2d ed., Bobbs-Merrill Company, Inc., Indianapolis 1960) notes on the basis of case study that *"involuntary intoxication is simply and completely non-existent."*

[30]On § 330a, GERMAN PENAL CODE, see *infra*, at 278–290.

tion in which the intoxication and the criminal conduct in drink form a unit for the purpose of legal evaluation. This corresponds to modern scientific insight into their relationship, as well as to inarticulate, intuitive primitive interpretations.

The mentioned provisions also express realization of the fact that the nature of the conduct in which a person engages while he is intoxicated has an important bearing on the issue of his dangerousness. It was once thought that the type of conduct in which an inebriate person engages is more or less accidental. The now-prevailing scientific position is that this view is incorrect, that the intoxicant merely removes or reduces inhibitions but does not determine the type of unsocialized conduct in which the inebriate person will engage, and that the nature of such conduct rather depends on the latter's general personality. That conduct hence is a most significant factor in the evaluation of the total existential situation in alcoholic criminality. It ought to be assigned a primary role in the determination of the sanctions to be imposed.

Penal codes of civil law countries, many of which consider acute intoxication a general exemption ground included in the provision on the mental incapacity exemption, concern themselves greatly with the attitude of the defendant at the time of incurring intoxication toward his own crime potential in drink. There are various phases of such attitude: The defendant may wish to drink for the purpose of committing crime; he may have accumulated experience pointing to his criminal tendencies in drink; such experience may indicate grave criminality, minor criminality or uncertain, undefined criminality; the defendant may, indeed, desire such criminality to be cloaked as a drunken spree; he may desire it unconsciously; etc. An outstanding problem in any such attitudes arises from the foresight and prediction element, when they refer to a person's own future conduct. As pointed out by Max Planck in his observations on freedom of will, the fact that no one can predict his own future conduct without at the same time influencing it renders both the prediction and the choice elements in such situations particularly precarious.[31] In context with drink or drug consumption ad-

---

[31]Vom Wesen der Willensfreiheit (1939).

ditional complications are often present. These are inherent in the general problem of why people drink or use drugs. For example, is an epileptic equally "free" to abstain from drinking or to pass a rational judgment upon his criminal potential when in drink as is a person of average health? Drinking or drug habits are often unconsciously used as safeguards against graver disorders than commitment to intoxicants or against graver crime than that committed in connection with the intoxicant.

In the above analysis I neglected the difference drawn by law between : (a) the role to be attributed to the impact of intoxicants as factors in provisions exempting from, or reducing, responsibility for conduct that is otherwise criminal, whether it be criminal apart from any connection with intoxicants or specifically defined in terms of such connection; and (b) the problem of specific crimes created by narcotic and alcohol legislation. The first mentioned issue is one of the general part of penal codes, the second one arises within the framework of the special part. The difference is most significant in the light of constitutional law. Democratic due process, prohibition against cruel and unusual punishment and, for example, in Puerto Rico, against impairment of the defendant's human dignity and perhaps also against abusive attacks on his honor, reputation and private or family life,[31a] require that exemptions from responsibility be broad and that crime conceptions be narrow and, indeed, not multiplied beyond obvious, urgent social necessity.

In considering, as we must and want to, constitutional limitations to be applied to criminal law provisions, we ought to concern ourselves with the diverse types of constitutionally protected rights that may be involved: those of the offender against specific narcotics or alcohol laws; those of the offender who is a drug addict, an alcoholic, a habitual drunkard or an acutely intoxicated person against "punitive" treatment whatever may be the offense; those of the physician acting within the scope of his profession; those of the medical expert; perhaps also those of the family of the defendant. Legislators ought also to consider, even should the Judicial Branch refuse to do so,[32] whether

---

[31a] Article II, Sections 1 and 8 of the Constitution.

[32] Mr. Justice Harlan, dissenting in Douglas v. California, 372 U. S. 353, 360,

given crime constructs "operate" essentially equally as regards diverse classes of persons where an express discrimination would be constitutionally barred. Thus, they should take into account in their deliberations, e.g., that wealthy drug addicts are seldom involved in criminal court proceedings; it would be most unfortunate if we were to develop laws—especially criminal ones —which in their practical operation have an impact only on the life of the poor.

This essay will deal mainly with the problem of the proper legislative approach to the treatment of criminal conduct engaged in by a defendant in a state of acute intoxication. Relatively little attention has been lately paid to this problem in comparison to the overwhelming concern with laws on general mental incapacity and drug addiction. Except in matters of petty criminality, no thought has been given to the possibility of subjecting the acutely inebriate offender acquitted on the ground of mental incapacity at the time of the act to a regime of measures; both in countries of the common law and in those of the civil law, such offender is either punished or released entirely. This is especially puzzling in those countries of the civil law where the acquittal is based on qualification of full intoxication as "temporary insanity" or "disturbance of consciousness" enumerated as an excuse within the very provision or, indeed, within the same sentence as general "mental disease."[33] It seems that no attention has been paid to the fact that "temporary" conditions might well be recurring[34] and that, particularly where the criminal conduct engaged in is grave, there is room for concern with the probability of its recurring under similar conditions.

---

at 361-362 (1963), drew a distinction between legislation which discriminates "between 'rich' and 'poor' *as such*" and legislation "of general applicability that may affect the poor more harshly than it does the rich." While it is possible to argue that no legislation ever affects two people alike, so that perfectly equal protection is a utopia, there are limits—I believe—constitutionally set to legislation which, though not discriminating upon its face will, in the light of the prevailing economic and social conditions, in all likelihood have a discriminatory practical effect.

[33]Section 51, GERMAN PENAL CODE; art. 10, SWISS FEDERAL PENAL CODE.

[34]But see, e.g., Decision of the Bundesgerichtshof (German Fed. Rep.) of October 10, 1957 (IV Strafsenat), reported in 11 N. J. W. 266 (1958), and discussed in *Mental Incapacity in Criminal Law, supra,* at 107–109.

Before dealing with this principal topic, I shall devote a section to problems of the qualifications within the general mental incapacity exemption of certain groups of offenders whose life has been more comprehensively affected by alcohol or drugs, that is, addicts, habitual drinkers and drug users, symptomatic and pathological drinkers.

As in cases of the so-called "insane' acquitted by reason of mental incapacity of a criminal conduct charged, so in the case of those who qualify for such classification by reason of alcohol or drug addiction or on the basis of lesser commitments shown to be connected with mental incapacity, there is need for treatment by measures of security and cure. The same principle of a "dual system" would seem to be needed in the case of the acutely inebriate offender, exempted from punitive responsibility on the ground of full intoxication.

The third part is devoted to discussion of "measures," as distinct from "punishment," to be applied in the described situations of intoxicants and criminal conduct, subject to limitations imposed by "legality" demands.

A brief last section will touch upon certain basic constitutional problems posed by special crime constructs pertaining to alcohol and drug consumption.

I. ALCOHOLISM AND DRUG ADDICTION QUALIFYING FOR THE GENERAL MENTAL INCAPACITY EXEMPTION

In the famed New Hampshire case which inaugurated our "mental disease mythology,"[35] the issue of whether or not to exempt from responsibility an alcoholic who had committed homicide[36] was cast in terms of the question of whether "dipsomania" *is* or *is not* a "mental disease." The court held this to be a pure "question of fact," since it assumed that the quality of dipsomania as being or not being a mental disease is immanent in the phenomenon of dipsomania neither laws nor judges having any power to qualify it otherwise. Peculiarly enough, it was a physician rather than a jurist who began doubting the method-

---

[35]Compare Szasz, The Myth of Mental Illness (Hoeber-Harper 1961).
[36]State v. Pike, 49 N. H. 399 (1870).

ology of this argumentation, apparently realizing that by this method the lawyers could, more less consciously, shift the burden of resolving difficult policy questions to physicians.[37]

Whether "dipsomania" is a "mental disease" depends on how these terms are defined, and defining them should be oriented to the purpose of definition and scientific insight so that such purpose be best implemented. The basic issue is a normative one; but sound policy requires that in resolving it psychological and sociological reality be considered.

This insight will be applied when trying to answer the question of what states of mind connected with alcohol consumption and drug use should be deemed included within the general mental incapacity exemption. In some situations there may be no basis for an *ipso facto,* but a sufficient ground for establishing a prima facie, case of inclusion; those are the situations which show features strongly pointing to the presence of "mental incapacity," in that experience shows that, in most cases where such features occur, the underlying mental state is one qualifying for classification as "mental incapacity." In law in such instances it may be convenient to shift the burden of initial coming forward with evidence to the party who alleges that there is no mental incapacity.

It is necessary to point out at the outset certain limitations imposed upon the laws' utilization of scientific knowledge in dealing with the criminal conduct of persons who are affected by or more or less committed to an intoxicant. Scientific interpretations and classifications concerning the impact of intoxicants on human conduct are highly controversial,[38] and the general

---

[37]See Dr. Ray's statement, quoted by Reik, *The Doe-Ray Correspondence,* 63 YALE LAW JOURNAL 183, at 188-189 (1953); discussed *supra, Mental Incapacity in Criminal Law,* at 116, and n. 144.

[38]In science serious difficulties are encountered in trying to define the pertinent concepts accurately. Thus, "alcoholism" is being defined in a variety of ways. Thompson, *Acute and Chronic Alcoholic Conditions,* in 2 AMERICAN HANDBOOK OF PSYCHIATRY 1203 (Arieti ed., Basic Books, Inc., New York 1959, hereinafter cited as Thompson), suggests the following definition of "alcoholism": "From the psychiatric viewpoint, any person who uses alcohol in amounts sufficient to impair his efficiency or to interfere with his occupational, social or economic ad-

"scientific criteria" of differentiation that are suggested are not sufficiently discrete or readily verifiable in specific instances to serve legal purposes. In such cases the law must adopt more discrete, though less profound, differentiations, provided that they are functional, in the sense of facilitating law administration, and scientifically acceptable.

In previous essays I have recommended a definition of "mental incapacity" to be used as a test of exemption from punitive responsibility and of amenability to measures of security and cure. This definition reads thus: Exemption from punishment is accorded to any person "whose integrative functioning was, at the time of the criminal conduct charged and for some time prior thereto, so impaired that he had a very considerably greater difficulty in complying with social demands and rules than does the majority of the members of the community."[39] This test of general mental incapacity will serve as our major premise.

No doubt, persons suffering from irreversible alcoholic deterioration satisfy the terms of this definition. They are classifiable as "insane" or "mentally ill" within much stricter definitions, even the *M'Naghten* rules. But alcohol and drug addicts present a more intricate problem within the prevailing definitions of "insanity." Specifically, with regard to "drug addiction," an authoritative student, Dr. Marie Nyswander, points out that "contrary to popular opinion, morphine's effects on the central nervous system are not such as to interfere with the addict's ability

---

justment is an alcoholic. As an adjunct to this definition, any person who is unable to avoid the repeated use of intoxicating alcoholic beverages is an alcoholic." In the REPORT OF THE WORLD HEALTH ORGANIZATION, Expert Committee on Mental Health, Alcoholism Subcommittee, Second Report (cited World Health Org. Techn. Rep. Ser., No. 48, Geneva, 1952), "alcoholism" is used in the sense of any state in which loss of control over drinking is the central feature. HAGGARD & JELLINEK, 15, 16, avoid the use of the term "alcoholism" entirely, since such usage conflicts with the definition of "chronic alcoholism." They rather use the generic term "inebriates," "inebriety," "comprising all habitual excessive drinkers, regardless of whether they are normal excessive drinkers or addicts or those who have become chronic alcoholics." For the corresponding problem in "drug addiction" see below, at 235–238.

[39]Compare *supra, Mental Incapacity in Criminal Law*, at 138; and see *Criminal Law of Mental Incapacity*, at 141–142.

to work in society nor yet to lessen his moral judgment."[40] Such a person knows the difference between right and wrong in the sense of the *M'Naghten* rules, and whether he suffers from a "mental disease" within the criteria of the *Durham* rule is a nice "question of fact," with the added gloss that it is not even certain as to whether it is to be answered properly by psychiatrists or by courts or by juries. A recent decision deals with this problem, and it may serve us as a background for pointing up more sharply the methodological aspect of the question of whether "addiction" *should or should not, can or cannot,* be classified as a "mental incapacity." Decisions rendered within other recent tests will be compared, and the methodological issue presented in all these tests examined.

Castle[41] was convicted, on proof by statutory presumption arising from possession, of purchasing narcotic drugs without a tax, and facilitating the concealment and sale of drugs, knowing them to have been imported contrary to law. "[T]he crimes charged were purchase, receipt and concealment by appellant in his own bedroom of a quantity of drugs equal to one day's habit."[42] He contended that "1. narcotics addiction can itself be a mental disease which, if it caused criminal behavior, warrants a verdict of not guilty by reason of insanity, and 2. active narcotics addiction is evidence from which an underlying mental disease or defect may be found, also resulting in a verdict of not guilty if causal relationship is established." He also advanced a defense described in the case as one of "duress or compulsion to consume drugs to prevent withdrawal symptoms"[43] which, however, might more properly be denoted as one of "necessity."

There was not a scintilla of doubt in the case that the appellant was an active narcotics addict at the time of crime commission. "On the day after the offense and arrest . . ., he was admitted to the jail hospital suffering from withdrawal symp-

---

[40]Cited *supra* note 23, at 45.

[41]Castle v. United States, 347 F.2d 492 (D.C. Cir., 1964), *cert. denied,* 85 S. Ct. 1568, 1811 (1965).

[42]*Supra,* at 494.

[43]*Supra,* at 493.

toms."[44] And it may be particularly pertinent to note that "[s]even months prior to the offense he had voluntarily submitted himself for examination as a drug user and had been treated for withdrawal symptoms, but was not accepted by hospital authorities for rehabilitative treatment."[45] The conviction was affirmed, the court finding that on the facts "[t]he jury could have concluded that appellant had a mental disability which caused the acts charged. But, on this evidence, the jury need not have done so, nor need it have a reasonable doubt on this issue."[46]

Judge Burger, concurring in the result,[47] took issue with description of addiction as an "illness" within the context of the defense of insanity. He said: "Neither this court nor any other court has ever held that drug addiction is per se a form of mental disease or 'insanity' in the context of assessing criminal responsibility."

The net effect of both the majority and the concurring opinion is that whether a drug addict, by which, within the spirit of common law case reading we must understand an "addict" such as the appellant in the case, Castle, that is, a persistent recidivist drug user who suffers severe withdrawal symptoms when abstinent, qualifies as "mentally diseased" within the *Durham* rule, is a "question of fact" to be determined by the jury. This implies, and has been also specifically expressed by Judge Burger,[48] that, for the purpose of that rule, some addicts may be mentally diseased while others may be mentally healthy.

The fact remains that, however controversial may be the causes of drug addiction, the latter is a well-defined category, in the sense that some of its features do not vary from case to case. In this light, it may be instructive to read Judge Burger's concluding sentence: "The core of the problem since our *McDonald*

---

[44]*Ibid.*

[45]*Ibid.*

[46]*Supra*, at 494.

[47]*Supra*, at 495.

[48]"Certainly some addicts are mentally ill persons and some mentally ill persons are addicts, and in some cases it is difficult for the experts to determine whether mental disorder led to addiction or the addiction brought on mental disorder" (*supra*, at 496–497). The last statement suggests adoption of the ethics of "guilt of life conduct."

holding is not one of labels whether 'disease' or 'addiction' but whether an abnormal condition of the mind has substantially impaired the accused's capacity to control his behavior."[49] Is there any "drug addiction" with symptoms such as Castle's, recurring through long periods of time, which does not fulfill these terms? It occurs that in our zeal to eliminate "labels" we tend to forget that, however "ambiguous" linguistic expressions may be, there are outer limits of their "meaning." Were it not so, language would be meaningless and useless.

In *Blocker v. United States*[50] Judge Burger had justly criticized the majority's conceding "the power of St. Elisabeth's Hospital Staff to alter drastically the scope of a rule of law by a 'week-end' change of nomenclature,"[51] when the majority approved the hospital staff's change of mind on the question of whether or not "psychopathy" was a "mental disease" within a judicial test of mental incapacity. However, the question of whether such abstract determination can be properly made, whoever it may be that should be empowered to make it, would seem to depend to a large extent on the degree of certainty of the definition not only of the term "mental disease" within *Durham* but also of that which one purports to classify as within or outside such term. The issue whether "psychopathy" or "sociopathy," known to be a psychiatric "wastebasket category" so vague as to render its specific use in law constitutionally doubtful,[52] is a "disease" is not comparable to the issue of whether

---

[49]*Supra*, at 497.

[50]288 F.2d 853 (D.C. Cir., 1961).

[51]Concurring in the result only, *supra*, at 857, 860.

[52]The AMERICAN LAW INSTITUTE MODEL PENAL CODE, Proposed Official Draft, 1962, § 4.01(2), provides: "As used in this Article [on responsibility], the terms 'mental disease or defect' do not include an abnormality manifested only by repeated criminal or otherwise anti-social conduct." This is intended to exclude from the mental incapacity exemption psychopaths or sociopaths. The question may be asked whether there is any person thus afflicted who does not also manifest symptoms other than illegal or antisocial conduct, though such symptoms may not be identifiable in terms of present manifest traits. In any event, taking a single trait as defining a personality structure is always dubious except where it favors the defendant. Even where "scientific insight" is relied on, this legal-ethical-political aspect of advantage or disadvantage to a defendant in criminal law is an item of decisive significance.

"addiction" is one, even for the purpose of the *Durham* rule. Vagueness and certainty are matters of degree, and the degree may well be found decisive from the standpoint of sound policy, even where a major premise is rather inarticulate.

Moreover, in the District of Columbia, since *Easter v. District of Columbia*[53] it would seem no longer to be necessary to invoke the *Durham* "mental disease" formula in order to secure an incapacity exemption for users or possessors of drugs who are drug addicts. For the *Easter* case has introduced a new dimension into the exemptions tradition: "sickness" which is not necessarily a "disease" even though it is necessarily chronic. It held that public intoxication *cannot* be a crime when the subject is a chronic alcoholic, since chronic alcoholism is "a sickness which is accompanied with loss of power to control the use of alcoholic beverages." For this proposition the court relied in the first place on an Act of Congress providing for the "Rehabilitation of Alcoholics."[54] It pointed out that this act "does not state that a chronic alcoholic is suffering from a mental disease which causes the loss of control; the defense is not in terms of insanity. The defense is defined as a 'sickness,' and Congress did not find it necessary to specify whether it is mental, physical or a combination of both." Apparently, the exempting faculty of such "sickness" is attributed to the loss of control power accompanying it, so that we are thrown back upon the general test of "involuntariness," which actually makes any other tests or test ingredients dispensable. On this ground also, punishing a chronic alcoholic for public drunkenness was held to be punishing crime without *mens rea* and thus constitutionally untenable.

One might ask whether, as a rule, loss of control power over use of drugs in the case of an addict is lesser than is that of the chronic alcoholic over alcohol consumption. But in *Castle* no such argument was even suggested. In *United States v. Freeman*,[55] in denying automatic exemption to drug addicts within

---

[53]361 F.2d 50 (D.C. Cir., 1966).

[54]61 Stat. 744, c. 472 (1947), now incorporated in District of Columbia Code Sections 24-501 *et seq.*

[55]357 F.2d 606, 625 (1966).

the Model Penal Code "insanity" test, the Court of Appeals for the Second Circuit, indeed, relied on the fact that Congress had imposed severe penalties on use and possession of drugs. It seems odd to attribute this distinction in treating alcoholics and drug addicts to statutory differences when the issues have also constitutional dimensions.

Would the defense of "sickness" be maintainable also if the crime charged had been other than drinking or appearing under the influence of alcohol? An obvious example coming to mind is the case of an alcoholic stealing a bottle of rum. The rationale of *Easter*, that a defendant in such instance "cannot help" acting as he does and thus does not possess a "criminal mind," would fit the case; but so it might well fit more remote situations. Since, within the interpretation of the meaning and scope of the *Durham* rule[56] as well as of those of the Model Code test, the crux of the defense of insanity is "involuntariness"[57] or absence of a "criminal mind," one might wonder what unique function the "defense of insanity" is still performing.

Nor is denial of classifying either "psychopathy" or "drug addiction" or "chronic alcoholism" as a "disease" for purposes of the exemption for mental incapacity in the last analysis attributable either to medical-scientific considerations or to semantic inadequacies. There is an inarticulate sui generis policy behind it, and that policy is best summarized in the court's frequent use of the term "voluntary," in which would-be psycho-

---

[56]See particularly Carter v. United States, 102 U.S. App. D.C. 227, 252 F.2d 608 (1957). Of course, McDonald v. United States, 312 F.2d 847, 851 (1962), interpreting "mental disease" as "any abnormal condition of the mind which . . . substantially impairs behavior controls," is ultimately also a test of "voluntariness."

[57]United States v. Freeman, *supra*, does not verbally suggest such interpretation when adopting that test, as modified by grant of an exemption also to those who appreciate the criminality of their conduct, but, "because of delusion," believe it to be "morally justified." *Supra*, at 622, citing People v. Schmidt, 216 N.Y. 324 (1916). Perhaps, indeed, the Model Code test itself does not necessarily impose such interpretation; only the Comments to § 4.01 (TENT. DRAFT No. 4, at 157-158, 1955) seem to imply it when speaking of "impairment of volition." The rule itself is consistent with State v. Quigley, 26 R.I. 263, 58 Atl. 905, which attributes the defense of "insanity" to inadequacy in the "actor," as well as with the more common view that insanity excludes the criminality of the "act."

logical and normative-theological elements are commingled. When saying that some addicts are mentally ill while others are not,[58] Judge Burger implied that some addictions are incurred "voluntarily" while others in a sense "befall" the person concerned, for surely he does not mean that present addiction, whatever its origin, is not "involuntary." One may well surmise the difficulty of purging the moralizing aspects of the issue to be traceable to persistence of the dubious ethical concept of "guilt of life conduct." And yet, in alcoholic cases that concept was deemed outmoded in 1828[59] and has been expressly rejected in *Easter.*[60] The differentiation between drug addiction and alcoholism in terms of their exempting quality lies clearly in the diversity of attitudes and prejudices towards them. There is, indeed, a touch of humor in the Second Circuit's refusal to hold "narcotics addiction without more . . . the sole evidence of abnormality" within a judicial test of exemption because of the severe penalties imposed by Congress for the possession and sale of narcotics."[61] Obviously, the problem of the meaning of the "insanity" test is no longer one of "labels" but one of unconscious manipulation of terminology to accommodate inarticulate "moral judgments."

Notwithstanding the vast variety of theories on "addiction," it is easy to define it for legal purposes, since there is available in its case at least one uniform objective manifestation. Defining it as a condition of a person where abstinence entails severe withdrawal symptoms, whether physiological or psychological, may not reveal much regarding its nature or essence or origin, but it indicates one significant common feature difficult to simulate, that is, the presence of a psychological "state of

---

[58]Compare Castle v. United States, *supra* note 41, at 496-497, and Blocker v. United States, *supra* note 50, at 867. Notice that in the last-cited case, Judge Burger's criticism was essentially directed at the *Durham* rule's abandonment of the "will" test traditionally accepted. In *Castle* it would seem that Judge Burger, within his own criteria set forth in *Blocker*, ought to have answered whether he believes that Castle at the time of the act possessed the same degree of "will" power as does an average person.

[59]Unitd States v. Drew, cited *supra* note 6.

[60]*Supra* note 53.

[61]United States v. Freeman, *supra* note 55.

necessity." That an addict's conduct is "uncontrolable" and, in this sense, "involuntary," should be taken to mean that the pertinent behavior is hardly ever in fact "controlled" by the patient except under external compulsion or external assistance.

If "addiction" is defined as suggested, it falls squarely within the definition of "mental incapacity" recommended by the writer. Even though an addict may, given certain favorable conditions, function in a socially acceptable manner, his personal integrative functioning is no doubt impaired to a degree where conformance to certain social rules, particularly those which demand abstinence, becomes practically impossible. Though the condition of the alcohol addict is distinguishable from that of the drug addict, it also fits beyond doubt within the chosen definition of "mental incapacity."

It is hence perfectly proper to adopt an irrebuttable presumption that an "addict" as defined is "mentally incapacitated" and hence exempt from punitive state intervention, within the terms of the rules applicable to general mental incapacity. In a "dual system," such as is advocated by the writer for all purposes of criminal law, that is, a system in which sanctions are divided into "punishment," on the one hand, and "measures of security and cure," on the other hand,[62] exemption from punishment does not necessarily mean immunity from all state intervention. A person acquitted by reason of mental incapacity should be subject to "measures of security and cure," provided that the special terms of "legality" applicable to such measures in a system of law governed by the "rule of law" are met. Obviously, in the case of

---

[62]Conscious systematic separation of "punishment" and "measures," as distinctive types of sanctions, is a requisite of a "rule of law," since it helps to avoid confusion of proper criminal law ends, which are assertion of prohibitions (pursuable by the first-mentioned type of sanction) and protection of society (pursuable by the second-mentioned type). This, in substance, is the function of the "dual system." This system also helps to make legislators and judges aware of the need for application of "legality" principles to "measures." However, the system recommended by the writer is not a "dual-track system," in a narrow sense of the term, meaning that it does not permit application of both punishment and detentive measures in the same case. Compare Silving, *The Criminal Law of Mental Incapacity, supra* at 145; also *"Rule of Law" in Criminal Justice*, cited *supra* note 9, at 118–119, 141.

the "addict," such measures which are oriented to protection of society and cure of the individual are better adapted to the needs of both than is punishment. At the same time it is important to stress that, while not "punitive," such measures are "penal" and not "administrative." They are imposed by a criminal court after a trial in which engagement by the defendant in a criminal conduct has been established in accordance with criminal law due process and a sentence reached on the basis of a finding of the defendant's "dangerousness." They are subject also throughout their enforcement stage to "judicial jurisdiction" and judicial supervision.[63] Of course, "civil commitment" in a free society is likewise subject to "legality" safeguards, but the latter have a different orientation. Penal law "measures of security and cure" are not "welfare dispositions" of a paternalistic type; they are social reactions to a criminal conduct.

When turning to other types or different degrees of commitment to alcohol and drug use, legislators should notice the fact that many of its aspects, particularly in regard to motivation, are in part controversial and in part as yet not sufficiently explored.[64] While there seems to be no disagreement regarding the fact that moderation and excess are relative concepts, there is no agreement concerning the factor that determines "excess." Even on superficial observation one might notice that primitive men drink in order to get drunk,[65] and so do by custom people of

[63]The writer recommends a complete reorganization of our courts system, specifically: (a) separation of criminal courts from the rest of the courts; (b) introduction of collegiate tribunals on all levels of criminal law administration; (c) composition of such tribunals to include jurists, psychiatrists and sociologists, each having also a fundamental training in the discipline of the others, and each fully endowed with judicial independence and responsibility; (d) introduction of thus-composed "courts of sentence execution," that is, courts charged with supervising the process of execution, so that a convict would also have access to a court in realistic terms. See Silving, *"Rule of Law" in Criminal Justice, supra* note 9; also *And Let Them Judge the People at All Times,* in SILVING, ESSAYS ON CRIMINAL PROCEDURE 353 (Dennis & Co., Buffalo, 1964).

[64]Notice that in those areas of strange human behavior even elementary factors are as yet unexplored. Thus, e.g., Jellinek, *Effects of Small Amounts of Alcohol on Psychological Functions,* in ALCOHOL, SCIENCE AND SOCIETY, *supra* note 16, at 85, notices that not even the mechanism of the changes that alcohol produces in the central nervous system has been as yet explained.

[65]Compare *supra* note 18.

certain advanced cultures, while in other cultures drinking seems to be closely associated with religious customs and often, regardless of the amount consumed, does not lead to inebriety.[66] On the other hand, there are such phenomena as "pathological intoxication" in which absurdly small amounts of alcohol lead to full intoxication—phenomena of which the causes are obscure.[67]

---

[66]Ascetic and orgiastic features are variously distributed in religions. Sometimes stress is placed on the former; at other times there is a combination of both, so that the latter are permitted to appear only in certain forms or on certain occasions. Institutionalization of otherwise-prohibited indulgence is the usual method of its tolerance, for such institutionalization, perhaps by making guilt collective rather than individual, relieves the burden of guilt feelings, while the Divinity is appeased by rites and made an accomplice to what would be otherwise a sin. Compare Bainton, *supra* note 19.

[67]Two or three drinks (4 to 6 oz. of whisky or its equivalent) may suffice to produce an automatic violent behavior, often criminal conduct (Thompson, *supra* note 38, at 1210); but the individuals concerned do not always react to alcohol with violence. "Sometimes they may be able to consume considerable quantities without showing any consequences except ordinary intoxication," (HAGGARD & JELLINEK, *supra* note 5, at 228). According to Thompson, there must be some pathological physiology of the brain to account for this occasional peculiar reaction to small alcohol amounts, but the precise location of this area in the brain is unknown. Thompson believes that pathological intoxication fits even the strictest definition of "legal insanity." But the description of the phenomenon by other scholars does not necessarily support such contention. Thus, Noyes and Kolb state that it occasionally occurs in "an individual of unstable personality" (*supra* note 14, at 194-195), and Haggard and Jellinek point out that, aside from being frequent in psychopathic individuals, "pathological intoxication may occur in normal persons under exceptional conditions," e.g., in men who have been subjected to extraordinary physical and mental strain. It has thus been reported as occurring in soldiers on the battlefield after forced marches or harassing experiences (228-229). A special feature of pathological intoxication is complete amnesia for the incident (Thompson, *supra*, at 1210).

In some Irish decisions, cited in RUSSELL ON CRIME, vol. 1, at 68 (10th ed. Turner, Stevens & Sons, London 1950), exemption was accorded in situations in which such causes as long watching, want of sleep or deprivation of blood have reduced a person to such a condition that a smaller quantity of drink would make him drunk than would produce such a state if he were healthy. But in other common law jurisdictions such conditions would hardly fit any of the known definitions of general mental incapacity except perhaps the "irresistible impulse" test. For all but the latter require as basis of exemption "a mental disease or defect" as source of the incapacity. The German and the Federal Swiss Penal Codes include a state of this type in their notion of "disturbance of consciousness." "*Bewusstseinsstörung*" in § 51, GERMAN PENAL CODE and "*schwere Störung des Bewusstseins*" in art. 10, SWISS FEDERAL PENAL CODE (here the disturbance is

Psychoanalysts, though not necessarily in agreement among themselves, have in common the principle of seeking etiological explanations for all drinking and drug habits and the tendency of bringing down the various degrees of commitment, including acute intoxication incidents, to common etiological denominators. In the light of their findings, the type of conduct in which an affected individual engages is seldom, if ever, a fortuitous matter. Nor is it necessarily dependent on whether he is fully committed to the intoxicant, e.g., an addict or a so-called "symptomatic drinker" whose drinking is referable to a more or less severe mental illness (a schizophrenia, a manic-depressive psychosis, a paranoia or a neurosis), a habitual or a social drinker, or apparently not committed at all, e.g., a person who has never touched a drop of alcohol before. The criminal conduct in which an affected person engages thus acquires a meaning transcending any more or less specific connection with the use of intoxicants, provided that some connection be found.

In the light of such general uncertainty in scientific approaches and unavailability of clear bases of definition or delimitation, even if legislators were prepared to choose among the various schools of scientific thought, it seems desirable to adopt, tentatively, definitions reflecting certain objectively observable features, for the purpose of facilitating legal disposition. With this end in view, it seems desirable to define: a person using alcohol or narcotic drugs "habitually to excess" as one whose "patterns of conduct or life habits have substantially deteriorated in con-

---

required to be grave), would no doubt include a pathological phenomenon, such as described above. In the test recommended by the writer there is no requirement of "mental disease," but there must be present such a degree of integrative impairment as to make compliance with social demands and rules very considerably more difficult for the person concerned than it is for the majority of the community members. The incapacity must be present at the time of the criminal conduct and for some time prior thereto, so that if a perfectly normal person can be suddenly subject to a pathological attack upon consumption of small amounts of alcohol, the exemption would not be applicable to him. However, even those scholars who assume the possibility of the occurrence of such an attack in "normal persons" stress that this could happen only under very exceptional conditions which are apt to reduce a man's mental balance very substantially, so that an ego impairment must be present for some time prior to the intoxication and the criminal conduct.

nection with alcohol or drug use"; a so-called "symptomatic drinker or drug user" as a person in whose case "an integrative impairment underlies the drinking or drug use preceding the criminal conduct charged"; and a person suffering from "pathological intoxication" as one in whose case "the intoxication at the time of the conduct charged bore no normal relation to the amount of alcohol used." In many, indeed, in most cases concerning persons within these categories there is simply no rational basis for maintaining the presumption of sanity. For this reason, such persons should be relieved of the burden of putting that presumption out of operation. This can best be done by providing that such persons be deemed prima facie to qualify for the exemption for the "mentally incapacitated."

There may be difficulties in securing approval for this position. Such difficulties may arise particularly because of preconceptions implicit in the indiscriminate use of certain legal-ethical symbols. "Voluntary" is one such "normatively ambiguous" symbol, as seen from the variety of uses made of it in our law of constitutional criminal procedure.[68] One need not necessarily object to its use in law, provided that it is given a uniform meaning at least in defined contexts. Nor is legal uniformity a safeguard against future confusion where a term is rooted in the history of ideas which are both fixed and subject to social change. Most importantly, to be functional in law, such a term must be formulated against the background of psychologically relevant discriminations. For example, in a case of "pathological intoxication," one might ascribe "guilt" to a defendant who, on the basis of past experience, knows that he may well under the impact of very small amounts of drink commit a crime. One might argue that such person has the "duty" to abstain from drinking, and that he "voluntarily" chose drinking in "knowledge" that it constituted a risk. Granting that such argument may have some merit, it would still be appropriate to take into consideration the fact that we know very little about the phenomenon of "pathological intoxication" and that certain medical experts refer it to some pathological physiology of the brain, the precise location

---

[68]See on this Silving, *op. cit.* note 63, at 261-265.

of the affected area in the brain being as yet unknown.[69] "Knowledge" may cover various states of consciousness and may be accompanied by a variety of feelings,[70] and prediction of one's own future conduct is a complex process, additionally complicated where the person thus expected to search his own soul is not an individual of "average" health.

Present scientific insight seems to indicate that not only is the amount of the intoxicant consumed not a necessarily decisive factor, but also that where an individual affected by an intoxicant, whatever may be the type or degree of his commitment to it, engages in criminal conduct, it is fallacious and misleading to attribute such conduct causally to that commitment. As stated before, such commitment, regardless of its degree, and the criminal conduct engaged in may be ascribable to a common cause. In fact, it is quite conceivable that the criminal conduct is in a sense the motive of the commitment to the intoxicant and not its consequence. It follows that in law it should never be required to show a "causal nexus" between the criminal conduct and the commitment to an intoxicant.

Whether the exemption from punitive responsibility by reason of mental incapacity should be conceded to the "addict" either *ipso facto* or with support of a presumption to this effect—whatever the nature of the criminal conduct charged, is an intricate question. One might argue that such exemption is inconsistent with legislation prohibiting use and possession of narcotics. It may seem strange allowing a person charged with such possession to allege in defense that he is a drug addict and thus qualifies for the exemption of "mental incapacity." Yet, this is the strongest case that may be cited in support of classification of "addiction" as a mental incapacity. In fact, it may be said to point up sharply the potential unconstitutionality of crimes of possessing drugs in amounts not exceeding the defendant's daily need. In the light of Judge Burger's analysis of the historically developed principles of the bases of criminal responsibility, reduc-

---

[69]*Supra* note 67.

[70]On the varieties of signification this term may import in the M'Naghten "knowledge test," see Hall, GENERAL PRINCIPLES OF CRIMINAL LAW, cited *supra* note 29, at 520-522.

ing them to some concept of "will" or "choice,"[71] whatever meaning might be ascribed to it, the addict should be exempt from punishment, lest these terms lose all meaning. By the same token, holding him "guilty" defies the common law notion of "guilt" as crystallized in "due process."

There are indications that the constitutional philosophy regarding consumption of intoxicants, not fully articulated but certainly suggested in *Robinson v. California*,[72] may be extended, though there are also some signs to the contrary. But in the last analysis there is need for an over-all approach to the problem of the significance of intoxicants in the criminal law. An idea that has been suggested by the draftsmen of the American Law Institute Model Penal Code,[73] though they *nota bene* carefully avoided coping with narcotics crimes,[74] is provocative: "Addiction" might well be viewed in the light of the expanding law of "necessity." Since to the drug addict the drug has the meaning which items of basic human needs have to the nonaddict, one might well argue that crimes committed by an addict for the purpose of securing the drug he needs should be treated as is theft of food committed by a hungry man. Such theft in some civil law countries is subject to special rules of mitigation, even immunity.[75] However, this approach is predicated upon a specific interpretation of the law of "necessity," which I believe to be dubious. It introduces into that law a psychological element that subjectivizes it. "Necessity" should be determined by weighing objective social values and not states of mind. Addiction should be treated rather as a phenomenon of the "mental element." Of course, a neat separation of the "*actus reus*" and the "*mens rea*" is a matter of separate proof rather than a fact of observation. But the requirement of such independent proof is an essential of the "rule of law."[76] The problem of intoxicants and criminal

---

[71]See Blocker v. United States, *supra* note 50, at 867.

[72]*Supra* note 7.

[73]Comment to § 6.12, TENT. DRAFT No. 2, at 31 (1954).

[74]See PROPOSED OFFICIAL DRAFT, Comment, at 241 (1962).

[75]For this type of theft, known in Germanic laws as *Mundraub* (limited to petty theft), see particularly art. 138, SWISS FEDERAL PENAL CODE.

[76]See Ryu & Silving, *Nullum Crimen Sine Actu, supra* note 10.

conduct should be resolved as one of the "mental element" and in large measure as one of "mental incapacity."

The problem of the proper scope of measures to be applied to persons exempted from punitive responsibility because of their commitment to alcohol or drug use will be discussed below. Certain constitutional implications of this problem, however, require present clarification.

Medical opinion not being settled on the methods of treating addicts, indeed even on the appropriateness of institutionalized as against ambulatory treatment,[77] it would seem highly questionable for the law to dictate a particular medical solution,[78] such as that ambulatory treatment shall not be used although the physician may deem it medically indicated. It has been suggested that narcotic drug addiction has affinities with the psychoses and the neuroses (with depressive states and the obsessional neuroses).[79] It would thus seem that a general rule of compulsory institutionalization, as a condition of appropriate treatment, in such case is as dubious as a corresponding rule applied to all psychoses and neuroses would be. Such a general and unqualified rule may be said also to infringe upon the physician's constitutional rights.

However, within the special context of, for example, the treat-

---

[77]For a most instructive debate on this issue see *Medical Views on the Narcotics Problem,* presented at the Annual Judicial Conference of the Second Judicial Circuit of the United States, Sept. 15, 1961, 31 F. R. D. 53-59 (1962).

[78]While some cases suggest the constitutional dubiousness of barring a physician from applying what he believes to be "fair medical standards" in the treatment of an addict (notably Linder v. United States, 268 U.S. 5 [1925]), federal regulations for the enforcement of the Harrison Narcotic Law (Harrison Act, 38 Stat. 785 [1914], Int. Rev. Code of 1954, § 4701 ff.) have interpreted the act harshly. For example, a regulation interpreting § 4705 (c)(1), which enables the physician to dispense and distribute drugs "in the course of his professional practice," provides that "if a physician, pursuant to so-called reductive ambulatory treatment, places narcotic drugs in the possession of the addict who is not confined, such action will be regarded as showing lack of good faith in the treatment of addiction and that the drugs were furnished to satisfy the cravings of an addict."

[79]Glover, *The Roots of Crime,* SELECTED PAPERS ON PSYCHOANALYSIS, vol. 2, at 124 (International Universities Press, Inc., New York 1960). In his paper *On the Etiology of Drug-Addiction, supra* note 16, at 193, Glover remarked that in psychoanalytic literature drug addiction has been treated on the whole as a stepchild of psychoses.

ment of addicts who are acquitted of crimes by reason of mental incapacity, the problem of measures is not limited to purely medical aspects.[80] It is also one of the individual's "dangerousness," evidenced particularly by the type of criminal conduct in which he had engaged and giving rise to the community's right —or "privilege"—to protect itself against recurrence of harmful events. In a democracy the problem of appropriate measures is always reducible to one of the broader policy of balancing interests in social protection against individual interests in freedom. The requirement of "balancing" such conflicting interests precludes a rule of undifferentiated institutionalization, regardless of the nature or of the seriousness of the criminal conduct with which the individual has been charged, as it precludes a rule of unqualified ambulatory treatment. For example, assuming that the crime charged is shoplifting involving minor items and that the danger anticipated is repetition of such conduct, should a physician's opinion that the defendant may be better treatable on an ambulatory basis be necessarily disregarded? On the other hand, assuming that the conduct charged is armed robbery, involving loss or jeopardy of human life, should not a similar medical opinion yield to considerations of community protection? It is hence recommended that the problem of proper disposition be treated as it should be within the context of an acquittal by reason of mental incapacity. The present writer has recommended compulsory minimum detention measures in cases of such acquittal where the criminal conduct involved would but for mental incapacity constitute a felony against the bodily integrity of a human being. Differential treatment depending on the type of criminal conduct involved and the danger anticipated, with maximum periods of detention and of other measures, appears to afford a solution corresponding to demands of rule of law and of legitimate protective needs in a democratic community.[81] Subject to minimum and maximum detention provisions, the question of detention should be resolved after due

---

[80]The measures here in issue arise in the context of criminal law. They are intended to avert reincidence of criminal conduct.

[81]Silving, *The Criminal Law of Mental Incapacity, supra,* at 180–187.

consideration of medical and sociological opinion to be consulted in each case.

II. INTOXICATION AS BASIS OF SPECIAL MENTAL INCAPACITY EXEMPTION

The object in this section is to determine the nature and scope of responsibility of an individual who while affected by an acute alcohol or narcotic drug use engages in criminal conduct. Crime commission under the direct impact of a drug is rare indeed.[82] Crimes of omission are likely to occur, for example, when a person has used a barbiturate. But situations of this type are not sufficiently frequent to constitute a major problem in criminal law. There is thus no reason for their separate treatment; they are adequately covered by pertinent provisions of penal codes on conduct under the influence of intoxicants, without specification of type. In the present chapter discussion will focus on drunken conduct.

Formulation of sound rules on the treatment of criminal conduct in a state of intoxication is predicated upon a scientific rather than lay insight into the relationship between intoxication and crime. Modern psychological studies show that the conduct of an intoxicated person is not unmotivated or "fortuitous," just as the type of conduct in which a generally mentally incapacitated person engages is not "accidental." This finding warrants reexamination of the present legal treatment of criminal conduct in drink as either fully exempt from any type of state intervention or as calling for punishment. Conduct in drink may not be "guilty," yet may evince "dangerousness," justifying application of preventive and/or curative measures. A major problem of a modern approach to the criminal conduct of inebriates is to determine the proper scope of treating them either punitively or by measures.

A rational approach to this problem cannot be reached unless we purge misconceptions rooted in primitive beliefs and prac-

---

[82]Cocaine use may bring about violent criminal conduct, but this drug is rarely used, and since its medical use is now negligible, it may be possible to eliminate it entirely.

tices, consciously and effectively secularize our law and base it on insight of modern science and on principles of the rule of law. It is desirable to deal at the outset with certain fundamental findings of scientific studies that are relevant to the policy to be adopted on the treatment of criminal conduct in drink.

Lessons to Be Derived From Scientific Insight

No doubt, since alcohol tends to reduce inhibitions, it "contributes" to this extent to crime. As reported by Henderson and Gillespie,[83] more than half of the 9028 persons proceeded against in Glasgow for Breach of the Peace (including Petty Assault) were found to be under the influence of intoxicating liquor at the time of the offense. The same writers point out that while few reliable figures are available to show how much alcohol contributes to other offenses or crimes, "authorities agree that it is an important factor in the genesis particularly of sexual and aggressive crimes (including suicide and murder.)" On the other hand, Banay concluded from results of his investigation of 3135 Sing Sing prisoners that, contrary to common belief, the contribution of alcoholism to crime is not very substantial and that it is greater in the minor than in the major crimes.[84] More significant than mere statistics of the apparent relationship between alcohol and criminality is new insight into the meaning

---

[83]HENDERSON & GILLESPIE, A TEXTBOOK OF PSYCHIATRY 58-59 (8th ed., Oxford University Press, London 1956).

[84]Banay, *Alcohol and Aggression,* in ALCOHOL, SCIENCE AND SOCIETY, *supra* note 16, 143, at 147-149. In this study the incidence of inebriety was shown to be 25 per cent, whereas it was formerly estimated to be 60 per cent. The leading offense in this group of 3,135 prisoners, was among the inebriates, assault, while in the control group this crime took only fifth place. Of the acquisitive crimes, burglary was more common among the inebriate prisoners and grand larceny was more common among the noninebriate ones. The most aggressive of all crimes, homicide, constituted 9 per cent of the crimes committed by the inebriate group and 8 per cent by the noninebriate ones. Of the crimes most prominently associated in the public mind with habitual inebriety and acute intoxication, sex crimes, 7.5 per cent of the inebriates were committed to prison because of such crimes, while the ratio among the noninebriates was 5 per cent, so that the contribution of alcohol to this crime category was apparently substantiated. But, as the investigator remarked, criminal inebriates are generally known to be arrested more often for exhibitionism rather than for rape, while in noninebriate criminals the reverse is true.

of "contribution." Banay contends that the mere quantitative relationship between alcohol and criminality, even assuming it to be substantial, would not by itself afford a proof that alcohol is the source of a person's dangerousness. Such proof would rather require establishment of a causal nexus between these two phenomena. As regards the causal problem, "[t]here is now an increasing tendency to consider that both alcohol and criminalism are caused by similar social and psychological factors" and that "[m]ore frequently is the relation of alcohol to crime one of a common cause rather than of cause and effect."[85] It follows that elimination of the practice of drinking would at best afford but a relative reduction of the scope of crime at present connected with alcohol consumption. In individuals disposed toward criminal conduct who are also alcohol consumers it is reasonable to assume that other methods of reducing inhibitions would probably lead to the same criminal results.[86]

Since criminal law must concern itself in the first place with serious crimes, it is of prime importance to notice that alcohol consumption does not determine the nature or gravity of the criminal conduct engaged in under the impact of intoxication. Banay's study has shown that there is "no greater homicidal tendency among inebriate criminals than among noninebriate criminals."[87] Since alcohol is known to reduce inhibitions, the question is posed as to why the release of aggression by drink does not operate in this instance, when it operates where lesser crimes are involved. Banay answers this question by suggesting that "[t]his extreme form of aggression [homicide] is so strongly inhibited that even intoxication does not release it more easily than the factors which account for it in noninebriates." In fact, the prevailing opinion is that alcohol "does not determine the type or form of behavior which follows, but only tends to make the form different from the usual."[88] Alcohol always has the

---

[85]NOYES & KOLB, 167. For this reason one should not attribute too much importance to statistics, and there is no need to engage in an inquiry into the statistical methodology followed by Banay.

[86]On this see Jellinek, *supra* note 16, at 84-86, 91.

[87]Banay, *supra*, at 148.

[88]Dr. Leon A. Greenberg, Director of the Laboratory of Applied Biodynamics

same effect upon individuals, in the sense that it causes "a temporary loss of socialization as a process, rather than any specific types of accident, crime innovation or non-action."[89] But in what manner or form or on what level this desocialization will express itself, in other words, "[t]he specific locus of the socialized behavior [which alcohol will affect] is determined by factors other than the beverage of alcohol."[90] Traits which reveal themselves during intoxication represent the individual's basic personality. Always, the genesis of the crime antecedes the alcoholic indulgence or the alcohol addiction.[91]

Several suggestions regarding legal policy on the treatment of conduct in a state of intoxication may be based on these interpretations advanced by leading students of alcoholism. Obviously, in the light of these interpretations, the person who commits crime in an alcoholic situation or state was "dangerous" before he ever drank, and the nature and degree of the danger he represents must be sought in features other than alcohol consumption or alcoholic habits. It follows that our present focus on the intoxication, whether as an exempting factor or as a basis of punitive responsibility should under given circumstances yield to consideration of that other factor which is common to both intoxication and crime. While the punitive aim of the law may be directed to the factor of drink followed by criminal harm, if the required elements of "guilt" are present, there is in the case of conduct in drink, as in conduct in a state of general mental incapacity, abundant room for operation of the preventive aim focused on the common causes of alcoholism and criminality. In appropriate cases intoxication should be treated as a clue for curative and preventive rather than punitive intervention.

As in the case of the offender suffering from a general mental incapacity, so in that of the offender in a state of acute intoxication, "causation" of the specific criminal act by intoxication

---

and of the Yale Center of Alcoholic Studies, *Address to the American Bar Association Section of Criminal Law,* Third Session, August 30, 1960, 1960 PROCEEDINGS, p. 45, at 50-51.

[89]*Ibid.*

[90]Bowman and Jellinek, *Alcoholic Mental Disorders,* 2 QUARTERLY JOURNAL OF STUDIES ON ALCOHOL 312, at 321 (1941).

[91]Banay, *supra,* at 147.

should not be required to be proven. For it may be difficult to show that had it not been for the intoxication the criminal conduct would not have occurred, as it is impossible to show that had it not been for mental disease the offender would have been law-abiding. Once the causation problem is eliminated there is no basis for a general concept of "crime *caused* by alcohol," although it may be proper to base exemption from punishment and inquiry into the potential applicability of measures on a finding of severe intoxication at the time of the criminal conduct. Also, intoxication introduces a significant aspect into the scheme of sanctions; it has a special bearing on the choice of measures to be applied.

From Banay's observation that inebriety does not produce homicide and that this extreme form of aggression rather proceeds from a personality otherwise disposed toward that crime, it follows that the nature and gravity of the criminal conduct engaged in while under the impact of intoxication should be attributed special significance in measures. For the type of criminal conduct in which the actor engaged in such a state is the best indicium of the nature and degree of his dangerousness.

My submission is that whenever a serious harm has been caused by a criminal conduct in a state of intoxication, either punitive or protective treatment is called for; in such cases there ought to be no exemption from punishment without simultaneous intervention by way of measures of security or cure. No one who kills another in a state of intoxication should be released of all state intervention. There is need for distinguishing between punishment and measures and applying the one or the other depending on the actor's mental attitude at the time of intoxication toward his criminality potential when in drink. Further diversification is necessary regarding the choice and limits of measures, as well as of punishment.

As it is taken to afford the principal ground of intervention in measures, so the crime type in issue should also serve as a basis for limitation of intervention. The scope and duration of measures imposed on the inebriate offender ought to be proportionate to the seriousness of the crime type rather than uniform in nature and time limitation.

Instead of approaching the problem of criminal conduct in a state of intoxication in the light of scientific findings, contemporary law as well as modern reform projects have assumed a purely moralizing attitude, varying, however, depending on the degree of social disapproval of drinking. The doctrinaire arguments advanced in support of the various legal solutions are obvious rationalizations of preconceived notions of the evil of drinking. The defects of the traditional solution can be demonstrated easily.

Three basic approaches to acute intoxication followed by criminal harm are discernible in traditional law. In some legal systems intoxication affords a complete exemption from all state intervention, whether punitive or preventive, relieving the person concerned of all responsibility except for the intoxication itself, if incurred at least negligently. In other legal systems, except in special contexts, the intoxication is simply ignored as irrelevant, so that the person concerned is responsible for the criminal conduct engaged in under the impact of drink, as though the latter did not occur at all. Finally, in some laws intoxication is deemed to constitute an aggravation ground.

Exemption from all responsibility is usually rationalized on a theory of temporary insanity, an insanity assumed to operate in a single discrete moment and to leave the remainder of the individual's life intact, so that there is no reason for curative or preventive measures. This interpretation is unsound in the light of the above described scientific insight into the nature and operation of the unconscious motivations of intoxicated persons. These motivations are shown to antecede the intoxication and to continue after its termination. If the crime is serious, the danger of repetition is sufficiently grave to warrant measures of prevention.

Treatment of intoxication as if it did not exist is utterly unrealistic and, as all unrealistic approaches, unjust. It fails to take account not only of the variety of motivations that may obtain at the time of the criminal conduct when the actor is under the influence of alcohol, but also of the motivations which lead to drinking when drinking constitutes a risk.

The view which qualifies intoxication as an aggravation ground is self-contradictory. It is based on the assumption that a person who voluntarily eliminates his own "free will" is subject to an additional responsibility, whereas this very charge implies that the principal crime was committed in a state of so-called "will impairment." In ultimate analysis, the drunken offender is punished twice for creation of a sole criminal harm. The theory on which this view is based apparently analogizes intoxication to use of a deadly weapon or of poison, which is traditionally aggravating. This theory implies that an intoxicated person is more dangerous, in the sense of being more efficient in pursuing a criminal purpose, than a sober one. As will be later shown, this notion of the increased efficiency of an intoxicated person is based on a popular misconception, contrary to scientific findings: While reducing inhibitions, intoxication impairs rather than increases skill and efficiency.

In recent decades there has been a growing uneasiness about the basic assumptions implicit in these legal approaches. Attempts at their reexamination, however, have been impeded by the deeply rooted ambivalence toward the reduction of inhibitions produced by alcohol consumption, an ambivalence reflected in these assumptions. Because of this ambivalence, approaches to crime committed in drink are often inconsistent, and the legal rules governing such crime frequently have the character of clumsy compromise solutions.

Attitudes to Alcohol Reflected in Legal Development

The ambivalence to alcohol, which may be observed in primitive customs and religious patterns,[92] may be also found in the history of legal attitudes toward crime committed under the impact of alcohol.[93] This history is perhaps best summarized in the famous *Beard* case.[94] There Lord Birkenhead described the original English approaches to alcoholic crime thus:

---

[92]Compare *supra* notes 17 to 22, on primitive and religious patterns for consumption of intoxicants.

[93]See, e.g., for the variety of ways in which French decisional law and doctrine reach the conclusion that intoxication constitutes neither a justification nor an excuse for the criminal act committed under its impact, the summary by Heuermann, *Die Behandlung der Trunkenheit und der Gewohnheitstrinker*, in MATERIALIEN ZUR STRAFRECHTSREFORM, vol. 2, Rechtsvergleichende Arbeiten, 1 Allgemeiner Teil (Lang-Hinrichsen ed., Bonn 1954) 209-227, at 209-210.

[94]Director of Public Prosecutions v. Beard [1920], App. Cas. 479, 14 Crim. App. R. 159 (House of Lords).

... [U]nder the law of England as it prevailed until early in the nineteenth century voluntary drunkenness was never an excuse for criminal misconduct; and indeed the classic authorities broadly assert that voluntary drunkenness must be considered rather an aggravation than a defence. This view was in terms based upon the principle that man who by his own voluntary act debauches and destroys his will power shall be no better situated in regard to criminal acts than a sober man.

Apparently, it has been felt that though drink destroys the "will power," it does not destroy the motivations that prompt the crime of the drunken man, as they prompt that of the sober one. As will be seen, throughout modern legal development it has been persistently maintained that the drunken person, in contrast to the insane one, acts with "intent." According to this view, which has roots in early legal thought, the drunken offender possesses an "intent" but no "will," which contrasts oddly with the frequent definition of "intent" as a combination of "knowledge and will."[95]

In the course of the nineteenth century the rule that voluntary drunkenness is never an excuse for crime was gradually relaxed, but as noted in the *Beard* case, "this mitigation cannot for long time be affiliated upon a single or very intelligible principle." The *Beard* case set out to establish such an "intelligible principle," but failed to do so. It did not explain why "actual insanity [resulting from] alcoholic excess . . . furnishes as complete an answer to a criminal charge as insanity induced by any other cause,"[96] but full intoxication produced by a single drinking bout does not do so. The conventional rationale of this differentiation, that insanity eliminates intent, while intoxication, however grave, does not do so, is incompatible with the rule, accepted by the court, that evidence of intoxication may be adduced to prove that the defendant was "incapable" to form a specific intent. Turning to discussion of "nonspecific" intent, the court abandoned the premise which it had assumed when commenting on specific intent, namely, the premise of full intoxication, and announced

[95]ITALIAN PENAL CODE, arts. 42, 43; SWISS FEDERAL PENAL CODE, art. 18, par. 2.
[96]Compare the *Drew* case, *supra* note 6.

that "evidence of drunkenness falling short of a proved incapacity in the accused to form the intent necessary to constitute
the crime, and merely establishing that his mind was affected
by drink so that he more readily gave way to some violent pas-
sion, does not rebut the presumption that a man intends the
natural consequences of his acts." Does evidence of full drunkenness rebut that presumption? We search in vain for an answer
to this question. The confusion of substantive requirements of
intent and proof requirements, noticeable in the court's decision,
follows the traditional pattern, which impedes a square facing
of the ultimate substantive policy issue, which is, whether a high
degree of intoxication should be taken to exempt from punitive
responsibility.

Our law, allegedly without justification, persists in admitting
the exemption in cases of "specific intent" but not in those of
"general intent." The leading American reform project, the
American Law Institute Model Penal Code adopts this tradition.[97] On the other hand, leading legal scholars of the common
law world base their critique of that tradition on the assertion that
there is no relevant distinction between crimes of specific and
those of general intent.[98] The fact is that there is a relevant structural distinction between these two crime categories, and there
is abundant reason for imposing stricter evidentiary requirements
on a showing of specific intent than on proving general intent.
However, admitting this distinction and its evidentiary implications has no bearing whatever on the question of whether the
policy of barring the defense of intoxication to the charge of
crime, whether one of specific or one of general intent, is sound.
Perhaps this point can be better made if we first dispose of the

---

[97]Section 2.08 (2), PROPOSED OFFICIAL DRAFT (1962); TENT. DRAFT No. 9
(1939), and comment at pp. 7-9. For American authorities to the same effect as
Beard, see Intoxication as a Criminal Defense, Note, 55 COLUMBIA LAW REVIEW
1210, at 1211-1213 and notes 10-15 (1955). Notice that two states, Missouri and
Vermont, refuse by common law to consider intoxication at all, even as to specific
intent (ibid. note 10 at 1211-1212).

[98]WILLIAMS, CRIMINAL LAW, THE GENERAL PART (2d ed. Stevens & Sons Ltd.,
London 1961), at 377-378; HALL, GENERAL PRINCIPLES OF CRIMINAL LAW (2d
ed., Bobbs-Merrill Company, Inc., Indianapolis 1960), at 545.

arguments basing support for such defense on the alleged similarity of crimes of specific and those of general intent.

A crime of specific intent is one in which a portion of the mental element exceeds the *"actus reus,"* that is, the conduct of the defendant (including the attendant circumstances) and the consequence, as described by law.[99] Assuming the definition of such conduct plus result to be represented by the letter X, the accused must intend X, and in addition he must also intend something beyond X, which we may call Y, but to which there need not be any corresponding outward occurrence. Thus, e.g., in burglary the accused must intend to enter the building illegally and he must actually enter it; he must, moreover, intend to commit a felony in that building, but it is unnecessary that he actually commit the felony there. Though, for legal-ethical reasons, I am not prepared to defend the presumption that a man intends the natural consequences of his acts, it is fair to say that this presumption is not wholly arbitrary. It has often been described as a rule of logic and experience; where facts are present, from which in the light of experience intent may be rationally inferred, such intent is presumed. When a man does something which normally has certain results, and these results in fact occur, it is presumed that he intended these results. From the occurrence of X and accused's participation in its causation it is thus inferred that he intended X. But the presumption does not extend beyond X. Since Y does not necessarily occur, there may be no basis in the crime constituent facts themselves from which an intent to produce Y can be inferred: Intent of Y is not presumed, simply because there need not be any Y. Hence, the accused's intention of Y must be proven by the prosecution without the benefit of any presumption. Against this structural and evidentiary situation we must evaluate the accused's attempt to set up his own drunkenness as a defense.

As I did not defend the presumption of intent in relation to "natural consequences," neither do I defend the position which

---

[99]In German law, crimes of "specific intent" are called *Delikte mit überschiessender Innentendenz,* perhaps best rendered in English as "crimes with an overflowing inner tendency."

bars a man from invoking his own intoxication as a means of escaping responsibility. My submission is merely that, whatever its intrinsic merits, this defense in common law countries is inadmissible both in crimes of specific and in those of general intent. Only the results of this rule are different in the two situations. When the issue is whether the accused intended to enter the building (X) and he alleges that he was too intoxicated to entertain such intent, the prosecution may answer: "You cannot set up your drunkenness as a defense." Hence, the presumption that he intended what he in fact did remains in full force. But when the issue is whether he intended to commit a felony in that building (Y), there is actually no need for him to set up the defense of intoxication or any other defense, for the prosecution must prove that intent, since there is nothing in the act itself to prove it. So, if it evinces from the facts that the accused was so intoxicated as to make his entertaining such intent doubtful, the prosecution has not proved its case and will fail even without any effort on the part of the defense. In this country it has thus been held that when, on an indictment of first degree murder, requiring specific intent, there is testimony in the record which if believed might have led the jury to conclude that at the time of the crime the accused was intoxicated to a greater or lesser degree, and the judge fails to instruct the jury on the question of the potential impact of intoxication upon the accused's intent to kill, a judgment of conviction should be reversed "even in the absence of a proper request by the counsel for the defendant."[100] The issue of intoxication simply arises where intent must be proven, but is inadmissible where intent is presumed.[101]

---

[100]People v. Koerber, 244 N. Y. 147, 155 N. E. 79 (1926), citing People v. Van Zandt, 224 N. Y. 354, 120 N. E. 735 (1918).

[101]WILLIAMS, op. cit. supra note 98, at 378, advances the following critique of the rule on specific intent: "The law is sometimes stated in restrictive form, it being said that drunkenness may help to negative a 'specific intent.' Lawyers tend to breathe this phrase with peculiar reverence, but it has already been suggested that the word 'specific' is otiose. . . . If the word means an intent expressly alleged in the indictment, the rule is too narrowly framed, for no intent is specifically alleged in an indictment for murder, yet an intent is involved and drunkenness may help to negate it. It makes no substantive difference whether an intent is required to be expressed in the indictment or is implied in the name

Of course, one might very well argue that this distinctive treatment of "specific intent" is a mode of mitigating the harshness of the crime category characterized by such intent. Actually, that crime category is only one step removed from that of conspiracy, in which the intent need not be directed to a specific criminal act, and which is hence criticized as a crime of "intent alone."[102] The basic doubt regarding the propriety of admitting such crime categories may have been the reason for relaxation of the earlier common law rule which apparently barred exemption of intoxication even where it affected specific intent.

Use in modern law of a doubtful analogy between crimes of general and crimes of specific intent in support of liberalization of the rule on the defense of intoxication in the former is comparable to the type of rationalization utilized to the same end in primitive and early religious systems. Actually, psychoanalytical theory sheds doubt on the propriety of like treatment of general and specific intent. For, according to this theory, there is a great deal of realistic difference between an intent which is materialized by action and by a result (X) and an intent confined to the mind of the person concerned (Y). Let us approach the problem of exempting from punishment conduct engaged in under the impact of intoxication directly as a ra-

---

of the crime." However, the issue is not what is required to be stated in the indictment but whether, according to the legal definition of the crime, any portion of intent need not be accompanied by an outward realization. In this country first-degree murder is a crime of specific intent, since there is no outward occurrence, as described by the definition of that crime, that corresponds to premeditation and deliberation. The latter must be proven, for it is not presumed. With regard to murder in England, according to modern authorities which admit its negligent commission (see Regina v. Ward [1956], 1 Q. B. 351; Director of Public Prosecution v. Smith [1960] 3 Weekly L. R. 546 [H. L.]; on these cases see Collings, *Negligent Murder—Some Stateside Footnotes to Director of Public Prosecutions v. Smith*, 49 CALIFORNIA LAW REVIEW 254 [1961]), there is reason to assume that it is not a crime of specific intent. This total area is somewhat confusing, since—as correctly pointed out by Williams, *supra*, at 78-79—if the presumption of intending natural consequences is not rebuttable, the line between intentional and negligent homicide is obscured. It may well be, however, that something more than intent to kill was required in murder at common law and that though this added qualification has been lost in the course of time it nevertheless left traces in evidentiary rules.

[102]Compare Ryu & Silving, *supra* note 10.

tional policy problem, challenging the crucial moralizing contention that a man must not set up his own "wickedness" as a defense, rather than engaging in technicalities of general and specific intent doctrines.

Recommendation for Adoption of the Principle of Exemption

The state of mind of a seriously intoxicated person may be best described as one of altered consciousness. In some penal codes of civil law countries, for instance, the German and the Federal Swiss Penal Code, intoxication is included in the term "disturbance of consciousness," which is one of the sources of cognitive or conative disability enumerated in the definition of mental incapacity or, in our terms, "legal insanity."[103] In common law countries this assimilation of intoxication to insanity is rejected on the ground that an intoxicated person preserves his intent while, as is mostly believed, an insane person is incapable of possessing one.[104] But modern psychiatric insight shows that only few, if any, mentally ill persons are in fact deprived of the capacity to form an intent.[105] The presence of intent in a psychological sense should not be decisive of the issue of exemption in intoxication cases, as it is only apparently and superficially decisive of that issue in general exemption cases.

The reason for holding persons engaging in criminal conduct in a state of intoxication not responsible for such conduct should be the same as obtains in the case of persons suffering from a general mental incapacity. Such person should not be held punitively responsible if his integrative functioning was so impaired that he had a very considerably greater difficulty in complying with social demands and rules than does the majority of the community members when not under the influence of alcohol

---

[103]Compare *supra* notes 33 and 67.

[104]In *People v. Koerber, supra* note 100, the Court said that "[i]t is common knowledge that intoxicated men, although not in normal control of their faculties, do deliberate and premeditate and form a particular intent." In their *Note, Intoxication as a Criminal Defense, supra* note 5, at 1217, the writers reject making intoxication a defense on the ground that "[t]he psychological studies on the effect of alcohol on the individual's personality all suggest that he may often intend his actions and their consequences as purposively as those of a sober man."

[105]On this see *Mental Incapacity in Criminal Law, supra,* at 59-60, 118-119, 140.

or drugs. Clearly, not every degree of intoxication should be sufficient to constitute an exemption. Rather, the impairment must meet the stated requirements. It might appear that, if thus formulated, the exemption for intoxication is included in the general mental incapacity exemption. However, there is one significant difference. For the purpose of the latter exemption, as recommended by the writer, the integrative impairment must have been present "at the time of the criminal conduct and for some time prior thereto." The last-mentioned clause need not be included in the exemption test for criminal conduct in states of acute intoxication. Where the drunken conduct is very grave, there obtains a high probability of previous impairment.

One might argue that there is an inconsistency in requiring for the "general mental incapacity" test that such incapacity obtain "at the time of engaging in criminal conduct and for some time prior thereto," and dispensing with the last cited clause in intoxication cases. But the reason for relaxation of the incapacity test in such cases is referable to differential sanctioning conditions recommended for them. In intoxication cases there may be situations where the intoxication itself is culpable and deserves punishment, and other ones where the actor's "state of mind" either at the time of intoxication or at the time of the drunken conduct rather warrants security measures.

The basic position adopted in the rule recommended by the writer, namely, that the philosophy underlying the exemption for intoxication is the same as that justifying the exemption for general mental incapacity, is also adopted by a number of penal codes of civil law countries.[106] With formulation of such exemption from punitive responsibility for persons engaging in criminal conduct while in a state of integrative impairment conditioned

---

[106]As to the German and the Swiss Federal Penal Code, compare *supra* notes 33 and 67. Cf. also the POLISH PENAL CODE, 1932, art. 17, § 1 (intoxication included in "other disturbance of mental functioning" in the general exemption definition). The same policy was also reflected in the Spanish provision of the Penal Code of 1932; intoxication states were included in that code in the phrase *transtorno mental transitorio*. The 1944 Code, present text of 1963, however, regards intoxication merely as a mitigation ground (art. 9, 2°); intoxication is no longer deemed included in the above-cited phrase figuring in the general exemption provision (art. 8, 1°).

by alcohol consumption, there is reached a completely non-moralizing social policy approach to the problem of such conduct itself. I must now deal with the question of whether punitive responsibility may attach on grounds different from guilt "at the time of the act." This involves problems of punitive responsibility for the so-called *actio libera in causa,*" that is, for the intoxication itself with intent or foresight of the criminal conduct later engaged in, and for intoxication with a state of mind less directly related to such conduct. Thereafter, I shall discuss the problem of amenability to measures, based on mental states connected with use of intoxicants which do not satisfy the requirements of "guilt."

Actio Libera in Causa

Intoxication for the Purpose of Crime Commission

Practically all laws of civil law countries deny an either exempting or even extenuating effect to intoxication incurred for the purpose of committing a crime, and some codes treat such deliberate intoxication as an aggravation ground.[107] It is difficult to think of any rational basis for aggravation of punishment for an intentional crime because the actor placed himself in a state of intoxication in order to commit it. The rule seems to be based on the theological view that depriving oneself of "free will" is itself a blameworthy deed.[108]

---

[107]Thus, the ITALIAN PENAL CODE, art. 92, § 2 provides: "If the intoxication was purposely incurred in order to (*preordinata al fine*) commit the crime or to prepare an excuse, the punishment shall be increased." The Project of the Bolivian Penal Code, prepared by Professor Manual López-Rey y Arrojo, excludes mitigation otherwise available in intoxication cases if the intoxication was *preordenada al delito*. See LÓPEZ-REY, PROYECTO OFICIAL DE CÓDIGO PENAL, Publicaciones de la Comisión Codificadora Nacional de Bolivia (vol. 1 de la Colección), Gobierno de Bolivia, La Paz 1943, art. 26, par. 2. The total article reads thus: "Intoxication may be considered as mitigation factor only if, while fortuitous, it is not full. It aggravates penal responsibility in the remaining cases and particularly when the actor is a reincident or habitual inebriate or when the intoxication is incurred for the purpose of committing the crime." The same project exempts from responsibility when the intoxication is "full and fortuitous" (art. 20, § 1, par. 2).

[108]Compare Lord Birkenhead's statement that classic authorities refused to grant exemption in intoxication cases because it was thought that "a man who

Since alcohol removes inhibitions, it is often resorted to by those who wish to achieve this effect so as to be better equipped to commit a particular crime. But alcohol also reduces skill in performance, so that the stated device is a double-edged sword. Jellinek points out that, due to this dual effect of alcohol, its consumption works differently in different personality types. A study of men in whom alcohol seems to increase efficiency for the performance of tasks led this expert to the belief that "these men have little confidence in themselves, are so shy, so greatly subject to anxieties, that they are hindered, or, as the psychologists like to say, they are inhibited in doing what they truly are capable of doing. Alcohol may lessen these inhibitions, increase their confidence, and make it possible for them to perform better than they usually can, even though the performance is less than they would be capable of if their inhibitions were removed in some other way."[109]

There is no reason to assume a priori that men who get drunk in order to obtain the courage for committing a crime do not at the same time know, whether consciously or unconsciously, that they are simultaneously reducing their own performance capacity. The significance of such impairment will be discussed later. At this point it is sufficient to note that there is obviously no basis for punishing a man beyond the measure appropriate to the guilt incurred by intentional commission of the crime that is in issue solely because he sought courage to commit it by intoxicating himself. The question of whether distinctive treatment is justified in such cases on other grounds requires a more detailed discussion.

Where intoxication deliberately incurred for the purpose of crime commission is not deemed an aggravation ground, it is generally treated as not affecting responsibility for the crime at all; the intoxication is simply disregarded. There is an express provision to this effect in the Swiss Federal Penal Code[110] and

---

by his own voluntary act debauches and destroys his will power shall be no better situated in regard to criminal acts than a sober man." *Supra* text at note 94.

[109]JELLINEK, *supra* note 64, at 89.

[110]Article 12, stating that the provisions on the exemption from punishment in mental incapacity cases (art. 10) and on reduction of punishment in cases of reduced capacity (art. 11) do not apply "when the severe disturbance or the

in the Polish Penal Code of 1932;[111] in the Austrian and in the Spanish Code the exemption or mitigation clause is expressly formulated in such a manner as not to be applicable to intoxication thus intended.[112] The same principle applies in our law even in regard to specific intent, notwithstanding the fact that, at the time of acting, the accused was so intoxicated as to be allegedly unable to form the intent.[113] This is explained on the theory that the *actus reus* in such cases results from the intent or the deliberation and premeditation preceding the intoxication, the requirement of "concurrence" or "joint operation of act and intent" being understood in the sense of causation rather than in that of a coincidence in time.[114] The latter doctrine, reminiscent of the civil law doctrine of "psychological causation,"[115] has doubtful

---

impairment of consciousness was brought about by the actor himself for the purpose of committing in this state a criminal act." In Germany the same applies by virtue of judicial interpretation (60 RGSt. 29; 73 RGSt. 182; Neue Juristische Wochenschrift 1955, at 1077).

[111]POLISH PENAL CODE, 1932, art. 17, § 2.

[112]AUSTRIAN PENAL CODE (Strafgesetz 1945) § 2 provides that "the act or omission shall not be imputed [to the actor] as a felony where . . . c) it was committed in a [state of] full intoxication incurred without intention directed to that crime . . ." The Spanish Penal Code of 1932 accorded an exemption to a person "in a situation of temporary mental disturbance, provided that it was not purposely sought" (art. 8, 1°). The provision continued thus: "To exempt from responsibility, intoxication must be full and fortuitous." The present Code (1944) text of 1963, art. 9, 2°, which treats intoxication solely as a mitigation ground, also excludes the mitigating effect where the intoxication was brought about for the purpose of committing crime [*con propósito de delinquir*]."

[113]See PERKINS, CRIMINAL LAW (The Foundation Press, Brooklyn 1957, known as PERKINS ON CRIMINAL LAW, hereinafter cited as PERKINS), at 789-790 and cases cited in notes 3 and 4. It may be doubtful whether in such state he could commit any criminal act, other than an omissive one.

[114]PERKINS, at 789-790 and 725-728.

[115]Thus, e.g., the Italian Corte di Cassazione (Sezione II Penale), Jan. 23, 1956, reported in 61 GIUSTIZIA PENALE, Parte Seconda 647 (1956), held that there could be no responsibility within art. 113, PENAL CODE (cooperation in crime of negligence) unless there was proof of psychological causation, meaning unless there was a showing that the harm done is traceable to the negligent state of mind of a particular actor. Where it could not be shown that a spark from the cigarette of a particular actor rather than one from the cigarette of another was the one that started the fire, neither was there a showing that the fire was a product of his mind. Cooperative negligence could be present only where the negligence of each participant was connected with that of the others, for only then could the state of mind of each be deemed "causal."

implications, since it is difficult to visualize a situation in which, given external causation, psychological causation could be excluded or, by the same token, proven.[116] Where a person intends to commit an act and then, whatever period of time or occurrence may have intervened, commits that very act, it would hardly be possible to assert absence of a causative connection between the intent and the act. One might wonder whether any event can rationally be said to be the product of a particular intent, each act being caused by the total life development of the actor; the question is on what principle the particular intent can be singled out as "the cause" of the given act. It may be wiser not to insist on so-called "concurrence" at all, but rather to consider the statutory requirement of correlation of a particular intent with a particular act to be satisfied if it is shown that the actor intended the act and the result, if any, at some not too distant time and then committed that act and produced such result. Assuming this principle to apply to the relationship of intent and act generally, the question still remains to be answered whether in the light of realistic psychological insight it is rational not to attribute any significance whatever to the fact of intervening intoxication.

As pointed out by Perkins, "psychological causation" does not seem to operate where there intervenes between the intent and the act a change of mind,[117] which, of course, would seem to suggest that the intent, to be deemed "causal," must continue

---

[116]In the last-cited Italian case, external causation could not be ascertained; it was impossible to find whose cigarette originated the spark that started the ominous fire. Collective negligence could supply the external causation factor merely by dispensing with the need of specific reference to the particular spark.

[117]Perkins, 726-727, gives the following example: ". . . if X made a murderous assault upon D under such circumstances that D was forced to kill X to save his own life, D is guilty of no crime although he had armed himself and set out to murder X—if D had changed his mind and abandoned his purpose entirely before finding where X was or making any communication to him." State v. Rider, 90 Mo. 54, 1 S.W. 825 (1886). This, in the present writer's view, would not be a crime even had D not changed his mind, for there would be objective self-defense, and thus no *actus reus* of murder. According to the policy adopted by the writer there can be no punitive responsibility for subjective intent alone, and it is irrelevant whether the *actus reus* is absent in the sense that the crime as described by statute has not been fulfilled or in the sense that a factual situation obtains which renders that statute inapplicable.

until and throughout the time of the act. The view that a change of mind interrupts psychological causation but that intoxication, which, though it does not necessarily preclude intent, in any event creates a distinctive state of mind in which the intent operates, does not interrupt such causation, is apparently based on the moralistic ground that a repentence or withdrawal is quite distinctive from voluntary wicked intoxication. It may be argued that an accused might have changed his mind but for his intoxication. There is one case which seems to recognize interruption of the causal nexus by intoxication even when the latter is incurred for the very purpose of committing the crime in issue. In *Sabens v. United States*[118] it was held that even though the defendant formed a deliberate and premeditated design to kill the victim and then "voluntarily made himself drunk for the purpose of nerving himself for the accomplishment of the design," intoxication was a proper subject of consideration in the determination of the question whether at the time of acting he could entertain the specific, malicious intent which the statute says must be present in first degree murder (premeditation and deliberation).

The *Sabens* case has the merit of recognizing the psychological and sociological significance of intoxication even where it is used as a medium of crime. But its underlying policy is, nevertheless, questionable, since it takes no account whatever of the act of intoxication itself as a factor in the total event. Realistically, neither psychological causation nor its interruption should be deemed to afford the proper solution. Rather, we ought to view the totality of the events that culminate in the harmful result as a basis of evaluation in the light of sound policy. If we arrive at the conclusion that the intent as present before the intoxication should be deemed the decisive state of mind, then, instead of engaging in questionable structural discussions, we ought to formulate a rule whereby the actor is "deemed" to have possessed at the time of and prior to the conduct charged, the state of mind with regard to it and the result, which he possessed before he became intoxicated [or influenced by the drug]. This would

---

[118]Sabens v. United States, 40 App. D. C. 440 (1913).

mean that the actor could invoke all defenses that would be
available to him had the relevant state of mind been that preceding the intoxication, e.g., the defense of error. All variations
of intent that might affect degrees of responsibility would be
considered as regards the pre-intoxication state of mind. Of
course, within the total picture of life events leading to the
harmful result, the fact of intoxication should be accorded its
proper relative significance.

The evaluational process must first take into account the fact
that the actor incurred intoxication for the purpose of committing the crime in issue. His state of mind with regard to the
criminal conduct in which he engaged bears this distinctive trait:
He felt a need for encouragement and sought it in alcohol. It
would be difficult to ascertain in most cases whether he knew
of the incapacitating quality of drunkenness or weighed it against
his hope of improving performance by removing inhibitions.
There remains the fact that he committed the act in issue, which
has a significant bearing also on his unconscious attitude toward
that act.[119] Thus, on the whole, no proper foundation seems
to be laid for mitigation of punishment on the basis of the fact
that the actor intoxicated himself in order to commit the crime,
though there is certainly no warrant for aggravation. But a different basis for mitigation might be considered.

In the writer's view, objective probabilities of attaining a desired result—probabilities as obtaining at the time of the intent
and at the time of the conduct aimed at achieving such result—
play an important role in determining degrees of responsibility
even for intentional crime.[120] This approach is based on the assumption that the degree of objective probability of attaining a
desired result cannot fail to affect the intent itself, even if
only by the medium of unconscious response to the actual
chance of success. A man who intends to kill another by stick-

[119]Strong unconscious objections might and probably would have prevented
performance.

[120]Compare SILVING, CONSTITUENT ELEMENTS OF CRIME (Thomas, ed. Slovenko 1966), at 34, 213-214, 224-225. This is contrary to conventional doctrine,
according to which, once a person intends to commit a crime it is irrelevant what
chances he has to carry out his intention, provided that he produces the result.

ing him with a pin should not be held responsible in the same degree as one who intends to do so by using a gun, even though by virtue of a variety of supervening or antecedent circumstances the application of the pin results in death. In this sense it is appropriate to consider reduction of skill in states of intoxication as one of the factors in determining the relevant objective probability that the actor who uses intoxication as a means of crime will in fact succeed in accomplishing the desired end. The court should weigh such impairment of skill against the reduction or elimination of inhibitions that might hinder performance. If the former is found to outweigh the latter, mitigation would seem to be justified. While the relevant state of mind should be that obtaining at the time of becoming intoxicated, the relevant objective probabilities situation should be that which obtains at the time of the conduct, that is, the time when the defendant's skill in performance is decisive. This, of course, bears on unconscious foresight at the time of intoxication, and to this extent the intoxication itself and its degree should figure as factors in the degree of responsibility.

Intention to Commit Crime and Alcohol Consumption (or Drug Use) in Knowledge of Intoxicating Effect

Is there a significant difference between the situation in which a person gets intoxicated for the purpose of committing a crime and the situation in which he also wishes to commit a crime but, though not consciously intending to use intoxication as a means of its commission, intoxicates himself, desiring to do so or in knowledge that he would become intoxicated?

Two aspects bearing on the actor's state of mind ought to be considered. When a person undertakes to commit a crime and then proceeds to get himself intoxicated without there being any provable connection between the two decisions, several possibilities are suggested: that he unconsciously either desired to gain courage in this manner or wished to jeopardize performance by incapacitating himself or that both these conflicting desires were operative in his unconscious simultaneously. Such coexistence of inconsistent wishes is characteristic of unconscious thinking. However, by hypothesis, the actor did commit the criminal act, which indicates an intensity of the criminal desire. When a man decides to commit a crime and then commits it though in a state of intoxication, there is no reason to deny a connection between the sober decision and the act, even though the continuity of the decision may have been broken. Unless we view a human personality as a bundle of disconnected states of mind, we can hardly assume the drunken decision to be a new and separate entity. Since, on the other hand, we cannot prove the existence of a connection between the decision to commit the crime and the intoxication, neither can we exclude the possibility that but for the intoxication the actor might have changed his mind in the last moment. Last moment reconsiderations are well-known in the *"iter criminis."*

It is hence submitted that the rule set forth for the treatment of the actor who uses alcohol (or a drug) as an avowed means of crime performance be also applied to the actor who decides to commit a crime and then gets himself intoxicated and commits the crime while under the influence of the alcohol (or drug); but that the absence of a conscious decision to utilize the intoxicant as a medium in the scheme be deemed a sufficient basis for assumption of a constructive disruption of the connection between the criminal decision and the criminal conduct to justify a considerable reduction of punishment.

A further instance of an *actio libera in causa* obtains where the actor does not intend to commit the criminal act but knows that he might commit it when intoxicated. Conventional doctrine assimilates to this situation that where he merely "should know" of such possibility. In either event, to constitute an *actio libera in causa,* in a true sense, the actor's recklessness or negligence (inadvertent negligence) must be directed to the particular act that he eventually commits. But there are other situations in which such direction does not obtain, but which are probably more frequent in practice. It will be convenient to discuss this last instance of *actio libera in causa* and the last mentioned situations together, at the cost of disrupting the continuity of presentation of the crime construct of *actio libera in causa.*

Reckless *Actio Libera in Causa* and Miscellaneous Other Situations

As stated, an *actio libera in causa* is also present where the actor knows or, according to conventional doctrine, should know that when intoxicated he may commit a particular crime. But this situation is rare and certainly does not deserve the dominant attention it has received in various codes and projects. More frequently the actor knows that he might when intoxicated commit some crime, though without specification of its nature. Foresight of commission of a particular crime may often be hardly distinguishable in practice, and certainly no clear differentiation of these two situations has been made in some new codes and projects.

The Yugoslav Penal Code of 1951, art. 6, par. 3, read thus:

> The offender is criminally liable if by use of alcohol or in another way he had brought himself in a state of temporary mental derangement, although he was aware or should and could have been aware that he might commit a criminal offence in such a state of mind.[121]

The provision upon its face seems to convey the idea that the defendant is punitively responsible for whatever crime he commits while under the impact of intoxication under the penalty provisions applicable to that crime if, at the time when he incurred the intoxication, he was aware or should have been aware of the fact that he might when in drink commit some unspecified crime. If this interpretation is correct, then intoxication is treated as a crime of abstract jeopardy, predicated upon consequences; yet, this crime is apparently assimilated to intentional engagement in the conduct occurring at the time of intoxication. It is highly dubious that such crime construct meets the requirements of the principle of guilt and guilt gradation.

Even in the law of torts culpability is required to be directed

---

[121]English translation published by the Federation of Jurists' Associations of Yugoslavia, Belgrade 1951. The examples used in this paper are chosen on the basis of considerations other than furnishing up-to-date comparative law information.

to the harm for which the defendant is held liable.[122] A policy assuming a less stringent standard—a general concept of free-floating intent or negligence—is hardly acceptable in a criminal law of punitive orientation. It is reminiscent of the medieval notion of *dolus indeterminatus determinatur eventu*.[123] True, the latter notion, whereby indeterminate guilt becomes determinate through, or is reflected in, the result, fits well within the psycho-analytical finding that the result of conduct reflects the actor's unconscious intent. However, unconscious attitudes do not afford a basis for constitution or aggravation of punitive responsibility in democratic law, though they may be taken as basis for liability to measures, provided that there is present a criminal conduct as described by law.

If "recklessness" and "negligence" are defined, as they should be, as referring to specific circumstances and effects, it would seem that a person could not be punished if he had a foresight of or a duty to foresee the probability of committing merely *some* crime, without specification. In a monistic system recognizing no separate scheme of measures, a person who, while becoming intoxicated, thought that possibly he might commit "some" crime in drink and then committed murder, might strictly speaking be held guilty at best of the petty misdemeanor of "drunkenness," if such crime type exists.

As will be shown more fully when discussing § 330a of the German Penal Code and the provisions for which it served as a model, there is a need for careful differentiation of the various states of mind that may be present in intoxication cases and that may justify divergent treatment:

1. The actor is aware or knows of the probability that when intoxicated he may commit the particular crime which he then commits; it would probably be unobjectionable if to this situation one were to assimilate that in which the actor

---

[122]Seavey, *Principles of Torts*, in LANDMARKS OF LAW (ed. Henson, Harper & Bros., New York 1960) 377, at 391-393.

[123]In this, psychoanalytical doctrine might well rely on St. Thomas' sentence *"effectus virtute praeexistit in causa"* (the effect preexists virtually in the cause). On this and on the doctrine of *dolus indeterminatus* see LOEFFLER, DIE SCHULD-FORMEN DES STRAFRECHTS 156 (1895).

is aware or knows of the probability that he may in such state commit a crime of the same category as that in fact committed and not of considerably lesser gravity;

2. The actor is aware or knows of the probability that in such state he may commit some crime of considerable gravity;

3. The actor is aware or knows of the probability that in such state he may commit some unspecified and unspecifiable crime;

4. The actor has no awareness or knowledge of any of the foregoing probability types but a majority of community members in his situation would have possessed such knowledge or awareness.

It should be noted that, in Situations 2 and 3, making the actor responsible for the reckless commission of the crime actually perpetrated in a sense violates conventional notions that the mental element must be related to the particular conduct. Responsibility in such cases constitutes a deviation from the doctrine of guilt—guilt as directed to the specific act charged. However, in Situation 2 there is undoubtedly present at the time of intoxication a highly blameworthy state of mind, so that while it may not be justified to impose upon the actor the full punishment for recklessness in the sense of specific direction of foresight to the actual conduct, there is a sufficient basis for deeming the composite of his attitude and act not to differ considerably in moral evaluation from conduct falling within the technical definition of recklessness. Some reduction may be warranted where the ensuing conduct is a serious one, whereas if it is less serious than is the general type of conduct that has been anticipated, no reduction whatever is justified. If we add to this situation that in which the actor, rather than knowing, "should know" of the probability of grave harm, we have actually described the instances covered in our law by the so-called "depraved mind" doctrine, in which even an inadvertently negligent defendant may suffer as high a punishment as is provided for intentional and premeditated conduct.[124]

---

[124]See, for example, Nestlerode v. United States, 122 F.2d 56 (D.C. Cir., 1941).

In Situation 3 the problem of responsibility is more precarious. Yet, this situation is probably much more frequent than the previously mentioned situations. One should particularly stress in this instance, as in the next mentioned one, the objective gravity of the risk and of the ensuing harm.[125]

A distinctive treatment of Situation 4 is warranted by the postulate that no punitive responsibility should lie unless the actor had knowledge of taking a risk. Assimilation of duty of knowledge to knowledge violates the guilt principle. If it never occurs to a person that by intoxicating himself he may create an unjustifiable risk, whether or not other persons in his situation would have thought or known of such probability, he cannot be held responsible for guilt, since the actor's conscious evaluation of his act is an essential of his guilt. Unconscious factors reflected in choices of modes of intentional conduct may determine a limited differentiation of punitive responsibility.[126] Where the conduct is neither intentional nor reckless but the unconscious attitude reflected in it is danger-boding, a security measure rather than punishment is the appropriate sanction. My submission is hence that in all situations referred to in 4, essentially situations which come within the conventional notion of inadvertent negligence, the actor should not be subject to punitive responsibility, but should be subject to measures.

A further distinction is that between awareness of danger and a mere knowledge of danger. I understand by awareness a present conscious realization that such danger exists, whereas by knowledge I understand a preconscious state of mind, meaning that the actor has previously learned of such danger or its constituent elements and that such information has not been repressed, so that it is susceptible to being brought to conscious-

---

[125]Regarding the distinction between awareness and knowledge of risk, see below.

[126]The writer is recommending such differentiation depending on the objective situation, meaning the degree of objective probability of harm, as determinative of the degree of punishment within the punishment scale. To this extent "dangerousness" may play a role in the punitive scheme. This solution, which somewhat disrupts the neat separation between the punitive and the protective scheme, is accepted as one dictated by the need for considering even in punitive law objective situation variants—as a legality safeguard.

ness at the relevant time. This difference ought to be considered a significant item in the differentiation of conduct as to degrees of its gravity. Conduct is less "blameworthy"—denoting the degree of the limitative function of the mental element—when it is engaged in while the actor merely knows of the danger it entails than it is when the actor is aware of such danger.

On the other hand, I believe that drawing an express distinction between "voluntary" and "involuntary" or "self-induced" and not "self-induced" intoxication, as is customary in our law, projects and writings, or between intoxication based on a "fortuitous case or force majeure" and "voluntary" or "nonaccidental intoxication," as is customary in civil law sources,[127] is unnecessary. The general rules on duress and error are also applicable to cases of intoxication. There is hardly any point in singling out "medical advice" as justifying drug administration.[128] If the actor knows that such administration creates a jeopardy, the mere fact that it is done upon medical advice ought not to constitute a justification that would not otherwise be available to him on the ground that the interest in cure or alleviation of pain in the situation at hand outweighs the social interest in avoiding the danger. Alcohol is hardly an object of medical prescription and among the drugs the most important ones that are in medical use are not crimogenic in a specific sense. Upon administration of any drug that might reduce normal alertness, the physician ought to be required to tell the patient of this quality of the drug.[129] Unless thus put on notice, the patient could in ap-

---

[127]Compare art. 91, ITALIAN PENAL CODE (Compare *ubriachezza derivata da caso fortuito o da forza maggiore* and *voluntaria*); also art. 74 and art. 75, PROGETTO PRELIMINARE DEL CODICE PENALE 1949, Ministero di Gracia e Giustizia, Commissione Ministeriale per la Riforma del Codice Penale (Roma, Istituto Poligrafico dello Stato 1949) (as first above and *ubriachezza non accidentale*).

[128]The A.L.I. MODEL PENAL CODE, § 2.08 (5) (b), Proposed Official Draft 1962, defines "self-inducted intoxication" as "intoxication caused by substances which the actor knowingly introduces into his body, the tendency of which to cause intoxication he knows or ought to know, unless he introduces them pursuant to medical advice or under such circumstances as would afford a defense to a charge of crime."

[129]Crimes that may be committed in a state of reduction of alertness are mostly in the nature of omissions and negligent offenses. Let us assume that the patient

propriate cases plead error, and the latter might be evidentially substantiated by the physician's failure to give the patient the pertinent instruction.

However, a substantive exemption from punitive responsibility in the case of engagement in criminal conduct in a state of intoxication notwithstanding foresight of danger is commendable where the interest in the administration of a drug outweighs the interest in avoiding the danger of crime commission. Once such relationship is established, by definition, there ought to be no responsibility for "recklessness."

A final and perhaps most significant problem, mentioned in previous context, is the determination of the exact meaning of foresight, whether awareness or knowledge, of the probability of one's own conduct when in a state of intoxication. Most people tend to use rationalizations in evaluating their own conduct. Some writers have suggested that in order to charge a person with responsibility on the basis of knowledge of his own dangerous potentialities, there must be present certain outward indicia, such as previous misconduct when in a state of intoxication[130] or the fact that the actor is an "experienced normal inebriate," who at least once prior to the harm in issue has been "intoxicated and dangerous."[131] But unless one assumes a complete discontinuity between the sober and the drunken state, indeed, an amnesia for all mental experiences during intoxication, a person may well know of his own dangerous tendencies when in drink, without having ever before committed any misdeed during such state. On the other hand, the tendency to rationalize a previous misdeed, if any, may bar self-insight, so that objective experience is not necessarily decisive. Even more than in other areas there

---

knows, but the physician does not know, that the patient, as an employee of a railroad company, is charged with the duty of giving certain traffic signals. Let us further assume that the patient knows of the quality of the drug prescribed for him by the physician. Should it be an excuse that the patient took the drug upon medical prescription?

[130]WILLIAMS, *op. cit. supra,* note 115, at 375, suggests that unless the crime charged is "a second misdeed when in drink," punishment of the drunken offender cannot serve as a deterrent in his case.

[131]HALL, *op. cit. supra* note 29, at 555.

is hardly any basis here for equiparation of what one ought to know to actual knowledge.

Despite the precariousness of foresight of one's own future conduct in drink, it would seem that responsibility for recklessness in getting intoxicated with knowledge of the probability of production of grave harm should be in principle maintained. Where there is foresight of but some indefinite harm, or where proof of foresight cannot be adduced, a subsidiary catchall provision patterned after Section 330a, German Penal Code, but with a distinctive imprint, might be found useful. Since this section both introduces a significant departure from conventional law and is highly controversial, a detailed discussion of its history and development might be instructive.

It is mostly assumed that, while it may be justified to hold the actor responsible for recklessness or negligence in incurring intoxication, there is no need for concern with the accused's state of mind when intoxicated, provided that the degree of such intoxication is sufficient to come within the statutory definition of incapacity due to intoxication. But this view is based upon an erroneous conception of the operations of the mind of an intoxicated person, comparable in this instance to the prevailing misconception that an insane person cannot possess intent or has no mind.[132] The Italian Reform Project of 1949 departs from this approach by introducing the doctrinal notion of *"voluntà abnorme,"* corresponding to the German notion of "natural intent," into the law in provisions on differentiation of responsibility and punishment. Such intent should be deemed to afford a ground upon which punishment within the statutory scale may be differentiated as well as an indicium of dangerousness for the purpose of applying measures. For this reason it may be useful to discuss also the pertinent provisions of the mentioned Italian Draft.

Section 330a of the German Penal Code

As stated before, in the German Penal Code exemption from responsibility for criminal conduct in a state of intoxication is

---

[132]On this see *The Criminal Law of Mental Incapacity, supra,* at **188** n. 81.

included in the general provision on the exemption for mental incapacity; intoxication figures in the definition of this exemption as an instance of a "disturbance of consciousness."[133] If the intoxication has been incurred for the purpose of committing the crime, within the judicially developed principle of *actio libera in causa*, the actor is fully responsible for the principal crime. The *actio libera in causa* has been defined as "an act whose decisive cause ['*causa*'] has been set in motion by the actor while he was in a state of imputability [being then a 'free' agent (hence *actio 'libera'*)] but whose effect as described by law occurs at a time when the actor is not responsible [not imputable]."[134] In such cases, says Maurach,[135] the actor utilizes his own person as a tool, having set causation in motion while in possession of insight and self-determination.[136] Whatever the merits of this interpretation, an *actio libera in causa* is not necessarily predicated upon an intentional setting of a cause which later bears fruit while the actor is in a state of incapacity.[137] It may as well consist in a reckless or in the currently prevailing view, even in a negligent, conduct. According to conventional doctrine, to constitute an

---

[133]Section 51, GERMAN PENAL CODE. Compare *supra* at 231, text and note 33.

[134]MAURACH, 349.

[135]*Ibid.*

[136]This interpretation is based on an obsolete conception of the operation of the mind of an intoxicated person. Nor does it fit certain notions of *actio libera* which may be said to lie in the border area of intent and recklessness. For example, in the case of 7 BGHSt. 327 (IV Strafsenat) (1955), the accused, determined to kill her friend, hit her several times with a hammer and by so doing was aroused to a "blood frenzy," in which she killed the victim. She was held guilty of murder, although at the time when she administered the fatal blow she was allegedly in a state of insanity. Of course, she intended to kill the victim, but she was at best reckless with regard to putting herself in the state of frenzy. Can it be said that she used her own person as a tool? Probably not, since she did not intend to kill by means of such frenzy. However, the result is undoubtedly correct, for she carried out her intent to kill, both as regards the fatal result and as regards causation (killing by hitting with a hammer).

[137]Nor is intoxication the only instance in which the principle of *actio libera in causa* applies, as may be seen in the case cited in the preceding note. An instance of a negligent *actio libera*, not involving intoxication, is 60 RGSt. 30. A driver, in knowledge of his exhaustion and of the danger implicit in driving in such condition, continued to drive and later, having fallen asleep at the wheel, ran over and killed a child. He was held responsible for negligent homicide.

actio libera in causa, it is not necessary that the actor know the risk which he incurs by his own act; it is sufficient if he "should have known" that risk, meaning that the "cause" may be set in motion by inadvertent negligence. But the negligence, just as intent, must be directed or referable to the legal interest which is then actually violated. The actor must be negligent at the time of incurring intoxication in regard to this specific interest. This means that he must be aware of, or be in a position where he should be aware of the probability of violating this very interest. The principle of *actio libera in causa* does not apply beyond the described situations.

Because of this relatively narrow scope of this construct, it has been felt that there remained a gap in the law, for no statutory or decisional provision existed for dealing with a person who at the time of becoming intoxicated neither knew nor should have known the specific risk incurred by such intoxication, meaning, the probability of committing in such state the precise type of act which he then committed. Section 330a was intended to fill this gap. This section, introduced into the German Penal Code by the Law concerning Dangerous Habitual Criminals of November 24, 1933,[138] reads thus:

> (1) A person who, intentionally or negligently, by use of intoxicating liquors or of other intoxicants, places himself in a state of intoxication excluding responsibility (§ 51, subdiv. 1), shall be punished by imprisonment or fine if, in such state, he commits an act upon which punishment is imposed.
>
> (2) However, the punishment shall not be more severe in kind or degree than that imposed upon the intentional commission of the act.[139]

According to the terms of this provision, to be responsible, the actor must have incurred intoxication either intentionally or negligently and have committed what would be a crime but for his intoxication and consequent incapacity. The wording of the statute indicates that the intent or negligence is required to be di-

---

[138] [1933] RGBl. 1. S. 995.

[139] Subdivision. (3) reads thus: "Prosecution shall take place only upon private complaint." This provision is of no interest in the present context.

rected only to the intoxication, whereas no mention is made of any *mens rea* with regard to the criminal conduct later engaged in under the impact of intoxication. But the punishment limit is that imposed upon the intentional commission of the crime corresponding to that conduct. The provision lends itself to a variety of interpretations regarding the state of mind related to that conduct as well as the nature of the wrong which it proscribes. There is no certainty as to the basis of the responsibility it imposes: Is the object of proscription the act of self-intoxication or rather the crime committed under its impact? The controversy waged over these problems has brought to light the ultimate incongruity of any punitive treatment of intoxication followed by a criminal conduct unless the former is incurred at least in awareness of the probability of *some* crime.

In Germany, as in other civil law countries, the precariousness of a crime in which intent or negligence need not be directed to the factual circumstances as described by statute (the *Tatbestand, tipo legal*) is magnified by the fact that unspecified intent, such as in our law the intent in conspiracy cases, has been vigorously criticized, as well as by the fact that presumptions, such as that of intending the natural consequences of one's acts, have been vociferously condemned. Hence, Lange, for example, insists that, whatever may be the wording of Section 330a, the crime it creates is by virtue of unwritten law a crime of concrete jeopardy, and the defendant's state of mind must be directed to such jeopardy.[140] This means that the intoxication must constitute a specific danger which the actor, at the time of intoxication, knows or ought to know. Within this interpretation, the crime of Section 330a would be an instance of *actio libera in causa*.

However, Lange's view is exceptional. In the majority opinion, the *mens rea* in Section 330a need not go beyond abstract jeop-

---

[140]LANGE, KOHLRAUSCH-LANGE, STRAFGESETZBUCH (42nd ed., Walter de Gruyter & Co., Berlin 1959), comment to § 330a, 111 at 663-664. Lange infers this from the general doctrine of guilt as well as from external indicia. The latter are: (a) the fact that the provision was introduced by the Law concerning Dangerous Habitual Offenders, indicating that it is a provision on "dangerous persons;" and (b) the fact that the section is included in the title of the Code dealing with "Crimes of Public Danger" (Title 27, entitled *"Gemeingefährliche Verbrechen and Vergehen"*).

ardy, meaning that the intoxication must carry a danger that some crime, without specification of type, might be committed, of which indeterminate danger the actor knows or ought to know.[141] The Fifth Criminal Senate of the Bundesgerichtshof advanced what might be called a third view. While maintaining that the crime of Section 330a is one of abstract jeopardy, this Senate thought that every person, with very rare exceptions, when intoxicated creates such jeopardy and that this fact is so well known that foreseeability of danger implicit in intoxication requires no special finding by the trial judge.[142] Later, the court imperceptibly dispensed with the necessity of actual *mens rea*. It introduced into the area of the law of intoxication a sort of irrebuttable presumption of jeopardy and of *mens rea*, comparable to our law's presumption that a man intends the natural consequences of his acts.[143] As will be seen, the 1962 Draft of a German Penal Code made full use of this trend of thought. When faced with the objection that the scheme of Section 330a, as thus interpreted, violates the guilt principle, the court answered that it has long been recognized that criminal guilt does not consist merely in intent and in the psychological element of negligence, but that blameworthiness must be added to these factors. Such concept of guilt—said the court—does not exclude

---

[141]See MAURACH, 351.

[142]May 7, 1957, 10 BGHSt. 247 (1957).

[143]The court said: "True, there may be people who lack the tendency to commit, when intoxicated, acts upon which punishment is imposed. But there is hardly anyone who can with certainty say of himself that he belongs to this category of persons. Tendencies may be often unconscious and may remain unconscious for a longer or shorter period of time, until one day, upon some occasion, they become apparent. We must, therefore, proceed from the assumption that in general every adult, even though he may not know, can and should take account, of the possibility that he is not free of tendencies of the described kind. It should be added that crimes committed in a state of intoxication are by no means always results of the actor's tendency to commit, when intoxicated, acts of that kind. The dangerousness of a fully intoxicated person often lies in the fact that while lacking the tendency of committing when in drink crimes of a certain kind, he may yield to external temptations to which he would not yield when sober or that he may succumb to lack of diligence or carelessness to which he would not succumb when sober, e.g., that he may by negligence or carelessness cause a fire or a traffic accident, in which many persons lose their lives. This also is or, at any rate, should be known to every adult." Decision of Oct. 29, 1957, reported in Juristische Rundschau (1958), at 28.

the possibility of blaming a person for a consequence which he neither intended nor as regards which he was negligent. This argument, of course, is fallacious: From the fact that guilt calls for blameworthiness in addition to intent or negligence, it does not follow that there can be guilt without either intent or negligence. But this argument also left clear traces in the 1962 Draft.

When trying to comprehend the nature of the wrong proscribed by Section 330a, we are at the outset faced with a number of peculiarities of the provision, which make it difficult to determine whether the crime it creates is deemed a *malum in se* or only a prohibition of convenience. Also difficult to determine is the degree of the gravity of that crime. In a much-criticized decision, the Great Senate in Criminal Matters of the Bundesgerichtshof laid the foundation for the treatment of this dubious crime as a minor offense based on convenience rather than on moral reprehensibleness.[144] The issue before the court was whether conviction on alternative fact findings of either slander[145] committed in a state of considerably diminished responsibility[146] or full drunkenness produced by the accused's own fault and followed by slander (§ 330a) was admissible. Conviction on alternative fact findings (*Wahlfeststellung*), according to German decisional law,[147] is admissible only where the alternative crimes charged are "legally-ethically and psychologically comparable." The Great Senate held that there obtained no legal-ethical and psychological equivalence between slander, even if committed in a state of diminished responsibility, and self-intoxication followed by such slander. The Great Senate's statement in this context has a significant bearing on the evolution of the provision in the Draft of 1962:

---

[144]Oct. 15, 1956, 9 BGHSt. 390 (1956). For criticism see MAURACH, 351.

[145]Section 185, PENAL CODE.

[146]Section 51 (2), *id.*

[147]68 RGSt. 257. Such conviction is permissible in German law, where it evinces from the established facts that the accused has committed one of two (or more) alternative crimes but no proof has been adduced which of these he perpetrated. The punishment may then be imposed only within the range of the more lenient crime. Such conviction was formerly based upon statute, § 2b, PENAL CODE, which was repealed by the Allied Control Council. Today it is admissible by virtue of decisional law.

A person who by drinking guiltily puts himself in a state of intoxication which excludes responsibility and then commits an act upon which punishment is imposed, which act he neither foresaw nor could have foreseen prior to drinking, commits an act that is entirely different—regardless of the similarity of the external event—from the act of a person who, though in a state of considerably diminished responsibility, offends another, endangers traffic, rapes a woman or kills another. The scope of potential criminal conduct extends here from the negligent or intentional self-intoxication up to any other guilt-censure, from public mischief up to murder.

By declaring Section 330a to be a general subsidiary provision, a catchall rule which becomes operative whenever the intoxicated or allegedly intoxicated defendant cannot be punished for his principal crime, the Great Senate made the controversy over the ultimate nature of this section more acute than it ever was.[148] It became settled law, however objectionable it might be to guilt-oriented scholars, that an actor who engages in criminal conduct while in a state of intoxication is always punishable; if no other ground for his punishment is available under any traditional provisions or under judicial construction, Section 330a is ready for use. This in itself shows that this section lacks an independent moral justification and is but an expediency device aimed at combatting the rising tide of alcoholic crime.

Yet, a plain expediency device will never appear satisfactory to German jurists trained in the virtues of systematizing and theorizing. For what exactly, they ask, is the inebriate offender being punished? In 1951, the Second Criminal Senate of the Bundesgerichtshof said that, since the accused, for purposes of Section 330a, need not know that when in a state of intoxication he tends to commit dangerous acts, he is obviously being punished for the guilty lack of moderation in drink, if followed by harmful results.[149] But this view was vigorously challenged on many grounds. Punishing self-intoxication—it was said—is con-

---

[148]This holding reversed earlier law which admitted concurrent application of § 330a and a corresponding crime of negligence (2 BGHSt. 14 at 17-20 [II Strafsenat], Nov. 23, 1951).

[149]2 BGHSt. 17-20.

trary to the community sense of justice in Germany.[150] Such
being the case, making it punishable because it is followed by
harmful consequences reflects the idea of "crimes predicated
upon consequences," against which German jurists have fought
for a long time. Even more objectionable is the fact that the degree of punishment in Section 330a is ultimately determined by
the nature of these consequences, without the actor's state of
mind being required to be directed toward them. This revives
the notion of "crimes aggravated by consequences" not comprised by the actor's guilt—a notion clearly proscribed by Section
56 of the German Penal Code.[151] Finally and most importantly,
the assimilation of negligent to intentional commission of the
criminal act is wholly unacceptable.[152] All these features of Section 330a are objectionable from the standpoint of the guilt-
principle, otherwise prevailing in German law. They also make
it appear highly dubious that the actor is really being punished
for self-intoxication and not rather for the crimes committed
under its impact. When faced with this intricate problem, the
Great Senate found an escape for not resolving it, but pointed
out by way of a dictum that assuming self-intoxication rather
than the crime committed in the ensuing state of irresponsibility
to be the wrong subject to punishment is practically preferable,
since it is more favorable to the defendant.[153] Again the Fifth
Senate offered what seemed to be the redeeming theoretical solution. After pointing out the particular wrongfulness of a man's
depriving himself voluntarily of his "free will," the court said:[154]

The actor in a state of intoxication is distinguishable from
other irresponsible persons by the fact that "he could help

---

[150]See Decision of the Great Senate, cited *supra* note 144.

[151]This section provides that an aggravation of punishment for special consequences of an act must not be imposed upon the actor unless he brought them
about "at least negligently."

[152]See Decision of the Great Senate, *supra* note 144.

[153]*Ibid.* Were these crimes the object of punishment, it would have to be assumed that a person who commits several crimes while intoxicated is responsible
for all of them and that each such crime must be counted in determining the
presence of repeated crime as well as in evaluating an actor as a dangerous
habitual offender.

[154]*Supra, note* 143.

committing the act" [*dass er für die Tat was kann*], as the Great Senate expressed this idea. The conscience of a right-thinking man bothers him because of that which he committed while in a state of intoxication. In this he is distinguishable from an insane person, and the guilt-censure raised by law attaches to this point.

The mistake of those who allege that holding a man responsible for self-intoxication because of an act which he committed in such state is incompatible with the guilt principle—said the court—consists in unjustifiably "tearing asunder a life event which constitutes a unit—intoxication and act." Only thus is it possible "to regard the intoxication as 'not forbidden' and the act 'as not caused by guilt.'" The court concluded that

> . . . intoxication which leads to criminal acts is forbidden and an act committed in a state of intoxication is caused by "guilt" (in the sense of blameworthiness), if the intoxication was brought about guiltily and the actor could foresee that it might lead to any violations of a criminal nature.

Draft of a New Penal Code of Germany of 1962

Thus the matter stood when the draftsmen of the Project of a New German Penal Code were formulating the latest draft—that of 1962. After citing the tremendous increase of alcoholic crime in recent years,[155] they seemed perfectly satisfied with the theoretical foundation for the punishment of persons who commit criminal acts in a state of self-induced intoxication. They avowed firm adherence to the guilt principle, but rejected the view that the latter admits of no punishment unless the actor when getting intoxicated knew of the concrete danger he was thereby creating. Such interpretation according immunity to the actor who realizes his dangerous propensities for the first time —they remarked—would prove disastrous for the administration of justice. They finally rationalized their acceptance of a punitive approach to self-intoxication followed by criminal acts thus:[156]

---

[155]See ENTWURF EINES STRAFGESETZBUCHES (StGB) E 1962, cited *supra* note 12, comment to §§ 351-353, at p. 536. The draft will be cited hereinafter as DRAFT 1962.

[156]*Id.* at 537.

The above described doctrinal view [the view insisting on limitation of punishment to persons whose *mens rea* is directed to a concrete jeopardy] proceeds from the assumption that bringing about intoxication which excludes responsibility does not by itself constitute a criminally relevant wrong. But this view is no longer entitled to recognition in a community in which human beings are herded together within an extremely narrow space. Whoever guiltily places himself in a state of grave intoxication constitutes, as long as this state lasts, a danger to the community; for, as a result of the ensuing removal of inhibitions and lack of self-steering, he may be driven to acts of aggression against legally protected interests or, because of reduction of control of his physical and mental powers, he may be unable to fulfill the duties of care to which he is subject within the community. The actor may diminish such dangers by appropriate safeguards; but he cannot exclude them altogether. Even when a person gets drunk at home, he may for unforeseeable reasons be forced to leave the house and then because of his drunkenness become a danger to others. For these reasons the criminal law must consider the bringing about of a grave state of intoxication which excludes culpability as a sufficient basis for a criminal provision.

The draftsmen, nevertheless, felt that the severity of punishment provided for by Section 330a of the present Code is incompatible with the guilt principle, since it bears no proper relationship to the seriousness of the offense, which is self-intoxication and not the crime committed under its impact. They recommended for that crime a very lenient punishment—detention, which is subject to a maximum limit of six months,[157] or a fine. In this punishment maximum—the draftsmen emphasize—is reflected the slightness of the actor's culpability.[158] This maximum should afford sufficient room for satisfying the "need for atonement" even in cases of unforeseeably grave consequences.

The Draft of 1962 recommends addition of another provision creating an aggravated crime, where the actor "anticipates or could anticipate [literally, 'counts or could count with'] the fact that he would commit illegal acts in the state of intoxication."

---

[157]Section 47 of the DRAFT.

[158]*Id.*, comment to § 351, at 537-538.

In such event, which the draftsmen believe to be the normal one, the punishment provided for is imprisonment up to five years, detention or a fine. Since this "aggravated" crime requires that the actor merely anticipate or "count with" commission of "illegal acts" without further specification, obviously the basic crime of self-intoxication requires no *mens rea* whatever in regard to the criminal act later committed in drink. As admitted by the draftsmen, the guilt of the basic crime simply consists in "guiltily bringing about one's own full intoxication."

The history of the meaning of Section 330a shows the following absurdities: (a) The argument over this provision was begun by stressing that punishment of self-intoxication is flagrantly inconsistent with the community sense of justice and ended by asserting that such punishment is justified even when a man gets drunk in his own home; (b) feverish attempts have been made to rationalize such punishment by reference to the "guilt principle" but in the end the punitive provision has been disclosed to be a sheer concession to expediency; (c) grave concern with the *mens rea* of the crime yielded to an awkward admission that the mental element in it is exactly what it appeared to be on the face of Section 330a, intentional or negligent self-intoxication, not related to the crime potential at all, for if any such relation existed, the aggravated crime would become applicable; (d) Section 330a has been a theoretical misfit, but a practical device of first magnitude.[159] Reducing the punishment to a maximum of six months is likely to deprive the provision of all efficacy in the most important cases, namely, those in which a grave criminal harm has been produced. Where the act perpetrated in the state of intoxication is, for example, a homicide, otherwise punishable by a maximum sentence for life or for twenty years in a penitentiary,[160] imposing detention for six months (the maximum) is obviously but a token gesture. Nor

---

[159]Notice the statistics set forth in the footnote to the comments to the Draft provision at p. 536. In the Federal territory of Germany, 2,711 persons were convicted under § 330a in 1950. The number of convictions has been increasing steadily in subsequent years, and in 1959, that number was 7,551.

[160]Section 135 (murder) of the DRAFT; § 134 (manslaughter) in combination with § 44 (duration of penitentiary sentence).

can such reduction redeem the awkwardness of allegedly punishing self-intoxication, since such punishment presumably now
as before is objectionable to the community sense of justice.

Evaluation of Our Study of Section 330a and the Draft Version

The lesson to be derived from this history of Section 330a is
extremely valuable. It shows that there is a genuine social need
for state intervention in cases where intoxication leads to engagement in criminal conduct, particularly of the grave variety.
It further shows that in order to reach a sound solution to the
problem of crime committed in a state of intoxication, we cannot
engage in purely analytical theorizing but must concern ourselves with the reality of the psychological and social situations
obtaining in such cases. One of the occasional insights of German
courts into this reality is the observation of the Fifth Criminal
Senate of the Bundesgerichtshof that it is a misconception to
tear asunder "a life event which constitutes a unit—intoxication
and act."[161] The courts have treated these phenomena as completely detached occurrences, as though they did not emanate
from one person. The principal argument of German jurists
against Section 330a has been that it makes the degree of punishment dependent on the gravity of the criminal conduct engaged in while in the state of intoxication, although the latter
by hypothesis excludes responsibility. From the standpoint of the
guilt principle, this indeed might be a serious defect. Reform-
ers of German law have accordingly recommended a token punishment for intoxication, which permits an exceedingly narrow
framework for differentiation between a case in which the actor
when inebriated commits a minor misdemeanor and a case in
which in a similar state he kills a man. But is it really true that
the nature and gravity of the consequences of crime committed
in a state of intoxication are practically meaningless? If so, why
does the conscience of a right-thinking man bother him because
of that which he did while in a state of intoxication, to use
again one of the Fifth Senate's phrases? How, then, can the
need for state intervention varying in scope depending on the

---

[161]*Supra* note 143.

nature and gravity of the harm caused by the inebriate be reconciled with the guilt principle?

The net result of our learning acquired by study of this phase of the German jurists' excursion into the field of public welfare crime is that the criminal conduct involved, while undoubtedly calling for state intervention, does not lend itself to adequate punitive treatment but calls for treatment by measures. Indeed, the proper basis of state intervention in cases of this type is not guilt at all, but the actor's dangerousness;[162] the degree of his dangerousness depends upon a number of circumstances, among which the nature and gravity of the criminal conduct in which he engages while he is intoxicated are the most important ones.

Basic Suggestions

As pointed out by Bowman and Jellinek, the traits which reveal themselves during intoxication represent the individual's basic personality.[163] Banay, noticing that there is no greater homicidal tendency among inebriate criminals than among noninebriate criminals, explained that "[t]his extreme form of aggression is so strongly inhibited that even intoxication does not release it more easily than the factors which account for it in noninebriates."[164] As the conduct in which the actor engages while intoxicated, so are the consequences of that conduct very seldom accidental. Freudian psychology has shown that the nature and gravity of such consequences depend in large measure on the actor's unconscious mental attitude toward these consequences. True, alcohol reduces inhibitions. Yet it does not eliminate them entirely. When grave consequences occur, there is a strong indication that they were unconsciously intended by the actor and that the countervailing forces were not strong enough to inhibit the actor's efficient realization of his unconscious intention.[165]

---

[162]As stated in KOHLRAUSCH-LANGE, op. cit. supra note 140, comment 111 to § 330a, "[t]he illegality content of the misdemeanor [that of § 330a] is not fully characterized by the external action; its crux is rather the actor type of a person who when in a state of intoxication presents a public danger."

[163]Bowman & Jellinek, Alcoholic Mental Disorders, QUARTERLY JOURNAL OF STUDIES ON ALCOHOL 312, 321 (1941).

[164]Banay, supra note 84, at 149.

[165]When recommending a narrow framework for differentiation between an act

The very intoxication may have been part of this unconscious scheme to bring about such consequences.

Thus, if in the case of criminal conduct in a state of intoxication, there is no basis for punitive responsibility for the act of intoxication itself, that criminal conduct ought not to be disregarded, though it should not be punishable. In such case the appropriate criminal law approach should be preventive, operating by the medium of measures of security and cure.

The following situations are within the potential purview of a scheme of measures:

1. The actor is aware or knows of the fact that when intoxicated he may commit some unspecified crime;
2. The actor does not know of the probability that when intoxicated he might engage in the particular criminal conduct in which he eventually engages or a conduct of

---

of intoxication resulting in commission of a homicide and such act leading to a minor disturbance of peace, the German draftsmen of 1962 proceeded on the assumption that the act of intoxication itself, unless consciously directed to potential criminal conduct, is a substantially uniform crime type, not subject to differentiation depending on the criminal conduct engaged in while the actor is intoxicated. If such is the case, one might well query what function that conduct performs in the structure of the crime of self-intoxication. The draftsmen's answer is that such conduct has been made a "condition of punishability" on grounds of "a policy of criminal law expediency which is not related to the wrongfulness of the act but prevents involvement of courts in adjudication of meritoriously meaningless events" (DRAFT 1962, comment, at 538). This answer is not satisfactory, for it does not explain why that conduct has been chosen as a limitative condition or why, having been so chosen, such small margin has been left for differentiation depending on its nature. If harm to the community is used even as a limitative principle, why should not the gravity of that harm also constitute a significant differential factor? Obviously, the present § 330a, which originated in the Law concerning Dangerous Offenders, has been better structured in permitting such differentiation; this section expresses the view that differentiation, depending on the type of conduct thereafter engaged in, is justified since that conduct reflects the personality of the actor, particularly the degree of his dangerousness. That it does reflect this factor, however, is scientifically ascertainable only on the basis of psychoanalytic interpretation. While that interpretation has been consistently ignored by German jurists, legal provisions often reflect intuitive understanding of mental phenomena, the scientific explanation of which is afforded by psychoanalysis. To some extent, § 330a expresses such intuitive understanding of the connection between intoxication and the criminal conduct engaged in under its impact, though this section utilizes this understanding in a wrong context, namely in the context of punishment.

the same category and not of appreciably lesser gravity; but the majority of community members in his situation would have possessed such awareness or knowledge;

3. The actor does not know of the probability that when intoxicated he might engage in criminal conduct of considerable gravity; but the majority of community members in his situation would have possessed such awareness or knowledge;

4. The actor does not know of the probability that when intoxicated he might engage in some unspecified and unspecifiable criminal conduct; but the majority of community members in his situation would have possessed such awareness or knowledge;

5. The actor has no awareness or knowledge of any of the foregoing probabilities, but neither would other community members have possessed it in his situation.

Situation 1 occupies a border area of the "guilt principle" (knowledge of abstract jeopardy). Situations 2, 3 and 4 are those in which it is conventionally said that the actor "should have known" the respective probability. These are "inadvertent negligence" situations, which according to the scheme proposed by the writer are always deemed to imply that there is no "guilt" and hence no punitive responsibility but to call for treatment by measures. In Situation 5 there is no negligence; this is the situation in which, according to the doctrine of civil law countries, the harm is deemed "merely accidental" (*caso fortuito*). Clearly, in all the enumerated situations the risk taken must be objectively unjustifiable.

Another classification that should be considered in judging whether measures or what type of measures ought to be made applicable to all or to some of the situations described above is that dividing the criminal conduct engaged in under the impact of intoxication according to degree of gravity. This classification might be cast in terms of: (a) homicide; (b) other felonies against the bodily integrity of a person; (c) all remaining felonies; (d) misdemeanors.

A combination of the first mentioned classes with those mentioned second affords the proper framework for determining differentially whether measures are to be applicable and, if so, what should be the scope of such measures as to any given combination. In measures, as in punishment, proportionality is a requirement of basic legality; measures which bear no rational relationship to the nature and degree of the actor's dangerousness have no place in a democratic criminal law, just as excessive punishment is "cruel and unusual." But the rationality of the relationship in measures is judged by the appropriate standard, the actor's dangerousness, and not by his guilt, whereas in punishment the reverse situation obtains. The intricate problems raised by the special German provision on the crime of full intoxication predicated upon specific crime commission (§ 330a) have resulted from the confusion of these standards in conventional law and a failure to realize that these standards are frequently conflicting.

Before submitting specific recommendations on the treatment of the diverse combinations of factors in given situations, it is necessary to introduce another variant, suggested by the Italian Draft 1949–50.

Italian Draft 1949–50

The present Italian Penal Code (1930) briefly provides that "[i]ntoxication that is not brought about by accident or superior force neither excludes nor diminishes responsibility."[166] Doctrinal writers point out that this provision does not indicate the nature of the actor's responsibility or for what exactly he is held responsible.[167] A controversy developed regarding the proper construction of the provision. There are, according to conventional doctrine, three possible interpretations that might be considered.

Some believe that the responsibility of an actor who commits a crime in drink is objective, meaning that he is responsible for

---

[166]Article 92, par. 1: "L 'ubriachezza non derivata da caso fortuito o da forza maggiore non esclude ne diminisce la imputabilità."

[167]BETTIOL, DIRITTO PENALE (4th rev. ed., G. Priulla Editore, Palermo 1958, hereinafter cited as BETTIOL) 336. The following presentation of the controversy over the nature of that responsibility is mostly based on Bettiol's discussion at 336-339.

intentional commission of the crime thus committed, regardless of his state of mind toward that crime when he incurred the intoxication [provided that he either intended to incur the latter or was at least negligent in regard to it]. Such interpretation, apart from being objectionable to civil law authorities who admit absolute responsibility only very exceptionally, leads to the following absurd result: When a sober driver negligently kills another, he is subject to a maximum imprisonment of five years, but if the same driver were intoxicated, he would be subject to a minimum punishment of twenty-one years.

A second view is hence advanced, whereby the inebriate offender is responsible for intentional or negligent commission of the offense, depending on his state of mind with regard to it at the time of its commission. In fact, this view is prevalent.[168] But since, by hypothesis, the actor was intoxicated at the crucial time, the question has been raised as to whether it is at all possible to differentiate his state of mind at the time of the act into an intentional and a negligent one. Bettiol submits that "it is improper to speak of intent or negligence with reference to psychological connections that might tie a factual occurrence to a subject who is in a state of intoxication. Intention or negligence for these purposes presupposes normality of the psychological relationship—a normality that must be deemed excluded if the agent is in a state of incapacity at criminal law."[169]

A third view hence transfers the focus from the actor's state of mind at the time of his engagement in the inebriate criminal conduct to his state of mind at the time of intoxication, as is done, for example, in the Yugoslav Penal Code of 1951 and in punitive context in the approach of the present writer. The latter state of mind is—apart from the situation in which the actor intoxicates himself for the purpose of engaging in the criminal conduct[170]—at best a state of mind of "negligence" [colpa], in the

---

[168]Manzini, Ranieri, Saltelli and Romano; see on this Heuermann, *supra* note 93, at 210. This article will be cited hereinafter as Heuermann.

[169]BETTIOL, 337.

[170]The possibility which was visualized in the second-mentioned type of *actio libera in causa, supra,* is hardly ever considered.

conventional sense of the term.[171] The difficulty arising within this construction is that in the law of civil law countries only a few types of conduct specifically enumerated in codes or statutes constitute "crimes of negligence." Rigid abidance by this principle results in limitation of the responsibility of the inebriate actor to situations in which the ultimate criminal conduct falls within one of these enumerated negligence types. In fact, this construction is said to be imperatively imposed by the principle of *nullum crimen sine lege* wherever the crime engaged in is specifically predicated upon intention, e.g., larceny, slander.[172] This view advanced by Paoli has been challenged by Vannini, who submits that the actor might still be responsible for intentional commission of the eventual inebriate crime if he incurred the intoxication voluntarily and at that time not only considered the risk of committing the crime in issue but also took it into the bargain should it occur.[173] However, this extension of responsibility to *dolus eventualis* is hardly sufficient to satisfy the need for an over-all regulation of the criminal responsibility of intoxicated offenders. Nor is it acceptable, on the other hand, to rigid adherents of the conventional Italian interpretation of the *actio libera in causa*.[174]

Bettiol, anxious to preserve rules of systematic precision in preference to following policy considerations, submits *de lege ferenda* that intoxication itself should be subjected to a higher penalty but that responsibility of the actor for the criminal conduct engaged in while thus intoxicated should be limited to situations in which he intoxicated himself for the very purpose of engaging in such conduct.[175]

This doctrinal situation raises several questions in the mind of a student of Italian trends of criminal law thought. One of these questions is why the Italians, though imposing treatment

---

[171]According to the conventional view, there is no differentiation between recklessness and negligence (which term the present writer uses only for inadvertent negligence).

[172]These are, to use common law terminology, crimes of specific intent.

[173]Cited in BETTIOL, 337-338.

[174]Negligent *actio libera in causa* is mostly rejected by Italian writers. On this see Heuermann, 211 n. 21, 217.

[175]BETTIOL, 338.

exclusively by measures on several conduct categories which are not subject to punishment,[176] do not admit such treatment in cases of criminal conduct of the voluntary inebriate, although that conduct would but for the intoxication constitute a punishable act as described by statute. Prescribing measures rather than punishment for inebriate criminal conduct would dispose of most of the described controversies. For within this treatment there would be no objection to consideration of the state of mind of the inebriated actor with regard to the conduct in which he engages. The Draft of 1949–50, following the dominant doctrinal view, while outlining a strictly punitive scheme for crime in drink nevertheless considers that state of mind as a significant differential quality determining punishment. Article 75 of this Draft, which was proposed to replace the present article 92, 1°, reads thus:[177]

> Where the [criminal] act is committed in [a state of] full, nonaccidental intoxication, the actor is responsible for negligence, and the punishment is determined by the following provisions:
> 1° If the [criminal] act is formulated [by law] as an intentional and as a negligent crime, the penalties provided for the negligent variety shall be applicable. However, if the act was directed to producing the result [se l'azione era diretta alla produzione dell'evento], the penalties for the intentional variety shall be applicable, but there shall be substituted for imprisonment in a penitentiary simple imprisonment from eight to fifteen years; other penalties shall be reduced by not exceeding three fourths of their amount. If the [criminal] act is formulated [by law] only as an intentional crime, the second part of this number shall be applicable.[178]

The crime type of Article 75 is described as "negligent," "neg-

---

[176]Article 49, PENAL CODE (putative crime); art. 115 (agreement to commit crime and solicitation not received by the principal).

[177]Cited *supra* note 127, hereinafter cited as ITALIAN DRAFT 1949-1950.

[178]Number 2° and 3° of this article read thus: "2° if the result that actually occurs is graver than the one to which the action is directed, the reduction provided for in number 1° shall be applied to penalties prescribed for preterintentional crime; 3° if the (criminal) act is formulated (by law) as a misdemeanor (contravvenzione), the penalties prescribed for the latter shall be applied."

ligence" apparently referring to the state of mind of the actor at the time of intoxication and consisting in his knowledge or duty to know of the probability of his committing some crime.[179] Thus the draftsmen seemingly thought to satisfy the "guilt principle," which in their view is being severely violated by the present provision of Article 92.[180] But the provision for treatment of this crime of "negligence" (under certain conditions) after the pattern of intentional crime, though with a considerable reduction,[181] shows this insistence on abidance by the "guilt principle" to be largely verbal. What is the functional meaning of describing a crime as one of "negligence" but attaching to it legal consequences which are normally attached to intentional crime? At best, one might say that, in view of the reduction of punishment and its consequent position between the punishment prescribed for intentional and that prescribed for negligent commission, there is in fact created an intermediate type of crime, occupying a border area between intent and negligence. In this border area is the situs of intent of an intoxicated offender. Though the punitive approach assumed by the Italian Draft is objectionable, significance attributed to the "intent" of the intoxicated offender is for our purposes most heuristic. Notice that without recognition of such intent, unless the actor intended the crime at the time of intoxication, a large number of crimes could never be charged against him, namely, all crimes of specific intent, as well as crimes of general intent in systems which do not adopt presumptions of intent. Nor could, strictly speaking, any reckless crime be charged against an offender, except where his state of mind at the time of intoxicating himself was directed to such crime.

The intoxicated actor's state of mind is described in the quoted provision as "direction of the act to the production of the result." In the Report which accompanies the Draft this intent is described as "*volontà abnorme*," abnormal intent,[182] and such in-

---

[179]Report accompanying the Draft, Relazione 1, at 56, hereinafter cited as Relaz.

[180]See Relazione 1, at 54.

[181]Second and Third Sentence 1° and 2°.

[182]Relaz. 1, at 55-58. Where the conduct in issue is not punishable if it is negligent and the actor does not possess a *volontà obnorme*, he is immune from punishment.

tent is contrasted in Italian doctrine with *"negligenza semplice,"* perhaps best translated as *"de facto* negligence." *"Volontà abnorme"* is known in German doctrine as *"natürlicher Vorsatz,"* while *"negligenza semplice"* is sometimes referred to as *"hypothetische Fahrlässigkeit."*[183] The idea underlying this use of terminology, which might seem puzzling to the lawyer of common law tradition, is that the state of mind of the inebriate is by no means irrelevant and is susceptible of legally significant variations. Nor is this attributable to a disregard of intoxication in evaluating the acts of the inebriate, as is obtaining in our law; it is rather due to recognition of the actual psychological relevance of an inebriate's state of mind. In fact, the same type of phenomenon is recognized in insanity cases.[184]

Evaluation of the Doctrine of the Italian Draft

In the Italian Draft, as seen, the inebriate actor's state of mind is determinative of the degree of his punitive responsibility. This position is most controversial. However, there seems to be no reason to deny this state of mind any effect whatever within the scheme of the punitive responsibility of the inebriate offender, although it may not be appropriate to accord it significance in formulating the punishment scale for the offense.[185] Perhaps recognition of the relative importance of the varieties of state of mind in drink may be best expressed in the form of a general directive to courts to take into consideration in meting out punishment within the pertinent punishment scale whether the actor, when engaging in the criminal conduct, possessed a natural intent, was reckless or possessed no knowledge of the risk.

A considerably greater significance should be attributed to the mental state of the actor while intoxicated in the scheme of measures. In this scheme, it may determine the crime type where the latter depends on the actor's state of mind, as well serve as

---

[183]Heuermann, 210.

[184]On this see *The Criminal Law of Mental Incapacity, supra,* at 190-191.

[185]As will be more fully discussed below, that mental state is first and foremost an indicium of the actor's dangerousness and thus is predominantly relevant in measures. However, in a limited sense it should be also deemed relevant in the punitive scheme, since there may be twilight zones between "intent" and "no-intent" or "knowledge" and "no-knowledge" (or "awareness").

indicium of the actor's "dangerousness," which is the decisive element in preventive law. It may well be that this state of mind is a stronger indicium of "dangerousness" than is the actor's attitude prior to intoxication toward such intoxication and toward his own crime potential when under its impact.

Final Policy Scheme

To arrive at a rational scheme of measures, we must now consider the three variables in all combinations in which they may appear. Special consideration of these three variables does not mean that other factors may not afford other variables. However, I shall use these three variables to demonstrate what type of analysis may serve as a basis of determination. The following are examples of types of situations that may evince from a trial:

Situation I: The accused killed another in a state of intoxition; at the time when he incurred the intoxication he was aware of the probability that he would become intoxicated and that when intoxicated he might commit some unspecified crime; at the time of the killing he possessed a natural intent to kill;

Situation II: This situation is identical with the above described one, except that, at the time of the killing, the accused was only reckless with regard to it.

Situation III: The accused killed another in a state of intoxication; at the time when he incurred the intoxication he was aware of the probability that he would become intoxicated but did not know that he might if intoxicated engage in killing or in conduct of the same category (maiming or serious wounding); yet, other community members in his situation (his life experience) would have possessed such awareness or knowledge; at the time of the act, he was reckless.

Situation IV: The accused wounded another in a state of intoxication; at the time when he incurred the intoxication he was aware of the possibility of committing a grave crime when in drink; at the time of the act he possessed neither intent nor knowledge of the nature of his conduct.

It would be difficult, of course, to list all the permutations, given the three variables; clearly, no legal provision could conceivably list differential maximum measures as regards all possible situations. Only a general guide may be suggested.

In cases of general mental incapacity the writer recommended that where the defendant in such state had killed another he should be confined in an institution for a minimum period of two years. This recommendation was justified by the extreme gravity of the social harm created by the defendant and the high degree of dangerousness demonstrated by the very fact of killing. Where the killing occurs in a state of intoxication rather than in one of general mental incapacity, the comparative law picture is striking indeed. In those countries in which intoxication constitutes an exemption ground and responsibility attaches in principle only to the act of intoxication itself, if the defendant did not know and "could not have known" at the time of becoming intoxicated that he might when intoxicated commit some crime, the killing is deemed "accidental" and, except within the framework of provisions such as that of Section 330a, German Penal Code, which are treated as anomalies, such killing is not subject to any sanctions. On the other hand, in countries of common law tradition, since the intoxication is disregarded and the presumption of general intent applies, such defendant is subject to conviction for second degree murder, which in Puerto Rico, for example, is punishable by an indeterminate sentence, the minimum of which must not be less than ten years and the maximum of which may not be more than thirty years in a penitentiary.[186] Despite such discrepancies in basic approaches, there is a sufficient basis in present law, both in civil law countries where provisions of the type of German Section 330a are in force, and in common law countries, for acceptance of a minimum period of restraint in cases of a killing even if it was neither foreseen nor foreseeable at the time of intoxication. Nor

---

[186]Art. 202, PENAL CODE, 33 L. P. R. A. Sec. 634, and Rule 178, Rules of Criminal Procedure.

can objections be raised in cases where the intoxication itself is inadvertently negligent, that is, where the defendant at least should have known that he is becoming intoxicated. In cases where the defendant incurs intoxication "accidentally," that is, not even by inadvertent negligence, there is no support in present law for any detentive measure, indeed, for any measure, for the intoxication itself is deemed to be "involuntary." Although in the light of psychoanalytical thought killing under such circumstances might not be regarded as necessarily fortuitous, neither the legal nor the lay public may be expected to accept a rule consistent with such interpretation. However, there ought to be no objection in this type of case against imposition of a measure consisting in a judicial prohibition against drinking. Perhaps no opposition ought to be voiced against suspension of licenses for engagement in activities in which drinking constitutes a hazard, e.g., driving. Finally, should findings of psychiatric experts indicate that such actor needs treatment, indeed, hospitalization to prevent further harm to the community, it would seem that a court order imposing such measures under proper legality safeguards ought to be acceptable.

If we vary the described situation, substituting for killing another felony against the bodily integrity of a person, it may be expected that provisions for measures of the suggested type but of lesser gravity (e.g., reduced minimum detention period) would encounter no greater objections, for the crimes in this category include, for example, maiming. But, beyond the area of felonies of this type, it would seem that measures will hardly be tolerated by either lawyers or laymen unless the intoxication is at least inadvertently negligent. Where either the intoxication is inadvertently negligent or where it is incurred in ignorance of a potential commission of some unspecified crime, under circumstances where the majority of community members would have possessed the respective knowledge, measures other than mandatory minimum detention might be acceptable even in cases of misdemeanor.

Once the limits of "accidental" and "inadvertently negligent" conduct are exceeded and the problem of "recklessness" is posed, objections against imposition of sanctions may still be raised within civil law doctrine in cases where the actor's knowledge or awareness is directed to some unspecific and unspecifiable crime, that is, a crime of abstract jeopardy. In common law countries, of course, differentiation of knowledge of abstract and that of concrete jeopardy has always been rather vague. While this is not the type of situation in which, within the proposed scheme, no punishment could be thought appropriate, the basis for punitive intervention is rather tenuous. Society can hardly expect a person to abstain from intoxicating himself merely because he knows that he might in a state of intoxication commit *some* crime. Since drunkenness itself should not be made a crime, punitive responsibility for intoxication in such situations is far-fetched. But where the actor engages in criminal conduct while in such a state of intoxication, measures are called for; they should vary depending on other factors present in the case, foremost among these, the type of criminal conduct engaged in and the state of mind of the actor at the time of commission.

In the following section I shall suggest a scheme of meaures which seems appropriate in cases of general mental incapacity connected with alcoholism or drug addiction and in cases of inebriate criminal conduct.

III. MEASURES APPLICABLE IN CASES OF ACQUITTAL BY REASON OF MENTAL INCAPACITY CONNECTED WITH ALCOHOLISM OR DRUG ADDICTION OR BY REASON OF INTOXICATION

Bases of Measures

The classical school of criminal law proceeded from the idea that the basis of state intervention at criminal law is the actor's guilt and that the proper reaction to such guilt is punishment geared to the particular offense that has been committed rather than to the offender. By contrast, the positivistic school assumed that guilt is a theological concept, proceeding from the unscientific notion of "free will," and hence has no place in a scientifically oriented law;[187] that the sole justification for state interven-

---

[187]It is important to distinguish this claim of the *scuola positiva* that the law

tion into a man's life is the "social necessity" for protection of the community against his "dangerousness," which may, but need not, evince from the "symptomatic act" of his having committed a crime; and that such intervention should not be vengeful punitive retribution but ought to be a preventive, curative or eliminative measure, varying in scope depending on the special features of the actor's personality rather than on the type or gravity of his crime. Both the classical and the positivisitic schools were "unitary" or "monistic," that is, utilized a single type of reaction to crime: That single exclusive type of state intervention was, according to the classical school, punishment and, according to the positivistic school, the measure.

Although since time immemorial, predominantly punitive legal systems admitted certain "measures," there has been until relatively recently no doctrinal consciousness of the distinctiveness of the latter. Indeed, such lack of consciousness of a systematic disparateness of punishment and measures is still noticeable in countries of common law tradition, which have introduced into criminal law a number of institutions that in some civil law countries would be qualified as protective and curative measures,[188] integrated in a sui generis system and governed by a distinctive concept of "legality."

With growing realization of the insufficiency of punishment to cope with certain situations in which a grave danger exists

---

ought to be "scientific," meaning based on insights of the sciences of men such as psychology, sociology, anthropology and the claim of certain civil law jurists that the law is a "science," by which they mean that it is by its "nature" organized in a systematically consistent manner. Often this systematic consistency claim is carried ad absurdum when legal rules are deduced not from a legislative will or from appropriate policy considerations but from purely conceptual categories which were not originally intended to be applicable to situations other than those for which they were created. On this see Ryu & Silving, *Toward a Rational System of Criminal Law*, 32 UNIVERSITY OF PUERTO RICO LAW REVIEW 119 (1963).

[188]See OLESA MUÑIDO, LAS MEDIDAS DE SEGURIDAD (Casa Editorial Bosch, Barcelona 1951) 21-27. The Germanic outlawry, called *Friedlosigkeit* or forfeiture of peace, the Roman *relegatio* (expulsion), etc. were "measures" intended to protect the community against the offender rather than retributive devices. Today, laws providing for assignment of the criminally insane to mental institutions, inebriates' laws, etc. are protective laws, the sanctions of which often have the character of "measures."

but in which the mark of guilt is believed to be absent, for example those involving an acquittal by reasons of insanity of a dangerous offender, there has developed in countries of the civil law a so-called "dualistic" approach, which—as is usual in these countries—was systematically formulated and justified. According to this approach, state intervention at criminal law must be divided into punitive intervention, which is a reaction to guilt, and intervention by measures, which are a reaction to dangerousness of the offender. This dualistic approach is highly controversial, in particular where dangerousness is also thought to be a basis of punishment or of its gradation, where punishment is conceived of as a reformative device and where the indeterminate sentence, depending in length upon actor qualities rather than upon the nature of the act, prevails; for the stated features of punishment assimilate it to a measure. Yet, in a growing number of penal codes the dualistic doctrine is being introduced in practice. In most of these the dualistic system takes the form of a "dual-track" system (*Zweispurigkeit*), which permits application of punishment and measures successively in the same instance.

The dualistic system is largely predicated upon the view that punitive responsibility is the appropriate reaction to the guilt of a responsible person, meaning one who enjoys "free will," the average, normal individual, whereas the measure is the proper device to be applied to the abnormal, nonaverage individual, and that both approaches are needed, each operating within its particular sphere. In the case of persons of diminished responsibility, to be sure, it has been found apparently that they belong to both categories, so that to them most laws have applied both punishment and measures. Apart from instances in which the same individual may be thus subject to both punishment and measures,[189] there are also instances in which a type of conduct, as described by statute, is sanctioned only by measures, as is the case in Italian law in putative crime[190] and in agreements to commit crime.[191] There is thus noticeable a departure from the

---

[189]This is the case also with regard to habitual offenders, persons who tend toward idleness, etc.

[190]ITALIAN PENAL CODE, art. 49.

[191]*Id.* art. 115; also solicitation not received by the principal.

principle of "punishment for the normal, measures for the abnormal." This fact has led to grave uncertainties in doctrine.[192]

In the two last mentioned situations there has occurred an apparent departure from the neat separation of the principles of "guilt" and "dangerousness," the punitive and the protective principle. This departure calls for reflection in regard to a need for introduction of distinctions other than that into "normal" and "abnormal individuals." As is well known, in the life of an individual who is otherwise classifiable within the "normal" group and hence does not qualify for a general mental incapacity exemption, situations might occur in which his state of mind is one of altered consciousness. Such is the case when such individual is intoxicated. When in such state he commits what would otherwise be a crime, progressive legal systems hold him exempt from punitive responsibility except perhaps for the act of intoxication itself. But should he be subject to measures? The answer to this question is not an easy one. Generally, laws do not provide for measures in cases of this type. Assignment to an institution may be ordered under the German or the Federal Swiss Penal Code only when a person who committed a crime when in a state of intoxication is a chronic alcoholic or a generally mentally incapacitated person. Other measures also are in principle applied only to persons who are chronic or habitual alcoholics. But, for example, the provision of the Swiss Federal Penal Code, which authorizes the judge to impose upon a person who committed a major or minor crime "attributable to an excessive use of intoxicating drinks," in addition to punishment, a prohibition to frequent localities in which alcoholic drinks are served,[193] lends itself to an interpretation which makes the provision also applicable to situations where the actor has never before drunk to excess.

Thus, while laws which exempt from punitive responsibility the perpetrator of an offense committed in a state of acute intoxication do not in general impose upon him any measures

---

[192]On this see OLESA MUÑIDO, op. cit. supra, 108-116.
[193]Article 56.

unless he is a chronic inebriate,[194] there is a marked feeling of uneasiness about the resulting gap in the law. To this feeling is attributable the growing trend to follow the pattern of the German Section 330a, imposing punitive responsibility for the act of intoxication itself. Similar provisions have been adopted by the Federal Swiss Penal Code,[195] the Austrian Penal Code,[196] the Greek Penal Code[197] and the Czechoslovakian Penal Code of 1950.[198] But all these provisions undoubtedly constitute serious departures from the guilt principle, and rationalizations such as those advanced in Germany are felt to be clumsy. The reason for state intervention in cases of this type simply cannot be the actor's "guilt" in getting himself intoxicated—an act that could not conceivably merit six months' imprisonment (Draft of 1962) —but must be the danger emanating from the intoxicated actor. The submission of the present writer is hence that measures rather than punishment are the appropriate reaction in such cases.

---

[194]In the GERMAN PENAL CODE, § 42 b assignment to an institution in the case of commission of a criminal act in a state of mental incapacity or diminished responsibility, is conditioned upon such assignment being "required for purposes of public safety," and this condition is deemed not to be fulfilled in the case of a temporarily disturbed normal person, even if he is an addict, unless the addiction itself is based on a mental disease. 73 RGSt. 44, BGHSt., reported in JURISTENZEITUNG 1951, at 695. For further authorities see Kohlrausch-Lange comment to § 42 b, comment at 124-125. Section 42 c (assignment of a person who "consumes alcohol or intoxicating matters habitually to excess" to an institution for alcoholics or a withdrawal institution, if such person committed a crime in a state of intoxication or was sentenced under § 330a) obviously requires that the person concerned be a habitual alcoholic. The same applies under the SWISS FEDERAL PENAL CODE, art. 14 (assignment of nonimputable actor or actor of diminished responsibility to a mental institution) and art. 44 (assignment of habitual drunkard to an institution for alcoholics).

[195]Article 263.

[196]PENAL LAW, 1852, text STRAFGESETZ 1945, as amended in 1952; § 523 has been introuced by this amendment.

[197]PENAL CODE OF AUGUST 17, 1950, art. 193 (German transl. by Karanikas in *Sammlung ausserdeutscher Strafgesetzbücher in deutscher Übersetzung* [Walter de Gruyter & Co., Berlin 1953]). Notice the interesting feature of a differential maximum punishment depending on whether the criminal conduct engaged in while in drink is a major crime (2 yr.) or a minor crime (6 mo.).

[198]PENAL CODE OF JULY 12, 1950, art. 186 (punishment up to five years, but if the crime committed in drink is punishable less severely, that punishment sets the standard) (TRESTNI ZAKON ZE DNE 12. CERVENCE 1950, c. 86 Sb).

This position raises a significant doctrinal issue regarding the standard of separation of law into the scheme of punishment and the scheme of measures: Must this separation be based exclusively on the principle of "punishment for the normal" and "measures for the abnormal"? The person who engages in criminal conduct in a state of acute intoxication, without being otherwise an alcoholic, is presumably "normal" and merely finds himself temporarily in an "abnormal state." The question of whether, if such person commits homicide in a state of intoxication, he can still be classified as "normal" but not punitively responsible since acting in an "abnormal state," may be left aside. For it is submitted that the separation between the scheme of punishment and that of measures must be placed on a broader basis. It should follow the distinction between the "normal" and the "abnormal individual," as well as that between the "normal" and the "abnormal state," between "situations" in which considerations of "guilt" are decisive and "situations" in which the paramount policy concern is averting "danger," as is the case, for instance, in inadvertent negligence. Finally, there may be "situations" in which there is no sufficient specificity of harm to warrant punitive intervention, but sufficient danger to justify a measure. The last cited situations are not in issue in the present context, though doctrinally they may bear on it.[199] The present concern is with action in an "abnormal state," the "state of intoxication" and with inadvertently "negligent" or even "accidental" self-intoxication, as bases for measures.

I shall deal first with measures to be applied to those persons who qualify for the general mental incapacity exemption (Title 1) and then with measures to be applied to the intoxicated but otherwise sane offender (Title 2).

Title 1: Measures Applicable in Cases of Alcoholism and Drug Addiction Qualifying for the General Mental Incapacity Exemption

The writer has recommended that alcohol and drug addicts

---

[199]These are situations, such as obtains in conspiracy or in a serious threat, where one might hesitate to assume punitive intervention because of the lack of

(as defined above) be irrebuttably deemed to satisfy the requirements of the general mental incapacity test. Habitual alcoholics, persons whose alcohol or drug use is symptomatic of
another disease, and persons in whom alcohol activates another
disease should be *prima facie* held mentally incapacitated. In
the case of individuals within the first mentioned groups, *ipso
facto* qualifying for exemption, and in that of individuals within
the second mentioned groups, if found by the court to come
within the exemption, the provisions on the treatment of the
mentally incapacitated should in principle apply. However, certain additional provisions are needed to take account of special
problems presented by the alcohol and drug cases, as contrasted
with other general mental incapacity cases. This should not be
understood to imply that either alcoholics or drug addicts present homogenous groups; it merely indicates that these groups
have in common the attempt of resolving mental conflicts by
resort to chemical means; they also have certain common features relevant to treatment that may not be in issue in other
mental incapacity cases.[200] Also, there are differences between
the alcohol and the drug cases which are specifically relevant to
the issue of their respective treatment.

One of the most important among the special issues presented
by these groups is the question of whether the person concerned
should be at all submitted to compulsory medical treatment. In
this respect, a substantial difference obtains between alcohol
addicts and drug addicts.[201] Alcohol is very often connected with
crimes of violence, whereas the use of addictive drugs does not
promote, but on the contrary, reduces such crime incidence.
Moreover, alcohol has a deteriorating effect upon the human
mind, whereas the most frequently used narcotic drugs do not

---

specificity of the direction of the conduct [not of the intent] toward the criminal
goal, but sufficient danger exists to justify preventive intervention. Notice ITALIAN
PENAL CODE, art. 115.

[200]E.g., assignment to an institution of persons deemed of diminished responsibility because of chronic alcoholism (art. 219, ITALIAN PENAL CODE).

[201]As stated by Nyswander, *Drug Addiction*, in I AMERICAN HANDBOOK OF
PSYCHIATRY, *op. cit. supra* note 3, 614, at 617: "[w]hereas dynamics of addiction
formerly grouped narcotic addiction with alcoholism, pharmacological and psychological data now available warrant a clear line of demarcation between the two."

have such effect. Informed students of drug addiction are opposed to compulsory cures for drug addicts.[202] They insist that cures, to be effective, must be voluntary. The British law,[203] often set up as a model, permits no compulsory cures, but allows the doses needed by the addict to be dispensed to him by a qualified physician. Adherents of this system submit that if possession (and consumption) of a reasonable supply of the drug to which a person is addicted (meaning a supply not indicating destination for sale) ceases to constitute a crime and if qualified physicians or clinics are assigned the task of administering to an addict, properly found to be one, the doses he is found to need, the bulk of crimes committed by narcotic addicts, *viz.*, crimes created by the legislation on narcotics, may be expected to decrease very substantially. Since the criminal law of measures is concerned with specific prevention of future crime, it may justifiably insist on curing alcohol addicts, shown to be dangerous, whereas a compulsory treatment of drug addicts is not warranted by any special statistically demonstrated connection between drug addiction and the most serious types of crime. One might hence argue that a compulsory withdrawal cure should be permissible in the case of alcohol addicts, if such cure without the patient's consent is recommended by a psychiatric and sociological examinations center,[204] but that no compulsory with-

---

[202]The New York Academy of Medicine found that "[p]hysical dependence on drugs can be removed by the withdrawal treatment. The mental and emotional fixations, however, are to be overcome only through the individual's own efforts and desires. Psychotherapy cannot be forced upon him with any hope of lasting benefit." The New York Academy of Medicine, Committee on Public Health, Subcommittee on Drug Addiction, *Report on Addiction*, 31 BULLETIN OF THE NEW YORK ACADEMY OF MEDICINE 592-607 (1955). Though this may also apply to alcoholics, society may insist on abandonment of a practice which may seriously affect the safety of others, even though this abandonment does not promise durability.

[203]Dangerous Drugs Act of 1920, 10 & 11 Geo. 5, c. 46, as amended. On this legislation, see Lindesmith, *The British System of Narcotics Control*, 22 LAW AND CONTEMPORARY PROBLEMS 138 (1957); also THE ADDICT AND THE LAW (Indiana University Press, Bloomington, Indiana 1965).

[204]The writer has suggested the establishment of such a center for the diagnosis and treatment recommendations to be used by courts. See *The Criminal Law of Mental Incapacity, supra* at 146, 161.

drawal cure should be admissible in the case of drug addicts. A second highly controversial issue confronting legislators is whether ambulatory treatment ought to be permitted or whether the law ought to insist on institutionalization. Most codes which adopt measures for alcoholics and drug addicts contemplate placement of these persons in special centers devoted to withdrawal cures.[205] On the other hand, many medical experts, particularly in the narcotics field, are opposed to rigid adherence to the rule of institutionalization[206] or, indeed, to a principle of invariable withdrawal.

The writer's submission is that in order to resolve these and similar issues rationally, legislators must first determine what type of issues they are. The controversies concerning compulsory as against only voluntary withdrawal cures and concerning institutionalized as against ambulatory treatment have a medical aspect, on the one hand, and a legal-social one, on the other hand. Whether compulsory treatment can be effective and whether institutionalized or ambulatory treatment is medically preferable are medical questions, on which "reasonable" medical experts may differ and on which any given expert may change his mind in the course of time and, above all, regarding which the same expert may have divergent views depending on the needs of a particular patient. These are questions which a code ought not to presume to resolve.[207] Indeed, one may well argue that if a code attempted to resolve such questions it would en-

---

[205]See GERMAN PENAL CODE, § 42c; FEDERAL SWISS PENAL CODE, art. 44; GREEK PENAL CODE (1950), art. 71.

[206]Daily, *The Case for the Voluntary Out-Patient Method of Handling Narcotic Addiction*, in MEDICAL VIEWS ON THE NARCOTIC PROBLEM, Lectures delivered at the Annual Judicial Conference of the Second Judicial Circuit of the United States, Sept. 15, 1961, 31 F. R. D. 53, at 74-88 (1962).

[207]Compare *supra* text at notes 77-81. See also *Report of the New York Academy of Medicine* of April 4, 1963, urging the Federal Bureau of Narcotics that it "gracefully bow out of the practice of medicine." The *Report*, based on a six months' study headed by Dr. Bernard J. Pisani, criticized the Bureau for not recognizing that "addicts differ" and for demanding that "one mode of treatment be applied to all addicts." The *Report* continued saying: "It [the Bureau] has had a rigid, one track stereotyped policy for a situation that demands judgment and flexibility. This is what happens when revenue agents become dictators of medicine." See NEW YORK TIMES of April 5, 1963, pp. 1 and 24.

croach upon constitutional freedoms of the medical profession. On the other hand, since the problem of proper disposition arises within the framework of criminal law, being precipitated by a criminal conduct, the protective end of criminal law is invoked. That end may, on a balance of interests of the community and of the individual, justify certain measures, whether or not such measures appear to be indicated or are preferable to others from a purely medical point of view. Thus, e.g., institutionalization may be required on the basis of grave danger, even though ambulatory treatment may be the medically proper or preferable therapeutic device.

To the extent that proper protective considerations permit, the law should abstain from passing medical judgment. The choice of measures should be made by the court on a case-to-case basis upon the advice of a psychiatric and sociological examinations center. Subject to paramount protective considerations, ambulatory as well as institutionalized treatment should be legally authorized. Compulsory treatment or institutionalization should not be authorized even if it is recommended by the psychiatric and sociological examinations center except where the danger to be averted by such treatment is very serious.

In the case of persons acquitted by reason of general mental incapacity, the writer has recommended that the type and restrictiveness of measures to be imposed ought to depend on the actor's dangerousness and that the latter be taken to be in the first place indicated by the nature of the criminal conduct engaged in. In cases of felonies against the bodily integrity of a person, minimum detention periods, subject to extension where dangerousness continues, have been recommended as safeguards of the community against danger of irreparable serious loss.[208] On the other hand, it has been suggested that maximum periods of detention as well as of other measures be imposed, corresponding to the maxima of punishment for the pertinent crimes, except that where these maxima are so low as to render any treatment effort futile, a limited extension ought to be allowed. These rules ought to be correspondingly applicable to persons

---

[208]Compare *The Criminal Law of Mental Incapacity, supra* at 197-198.

acquitted by reason of mental incapacity connected with alcohol or drug use. Of course, in the latter cases, distinctive problems may arise, for instance, so far as the proper places and terms of detention are concerned. There may be no need for placement of a detainee of this class in a mental hospital, so that it may be appropriate to place him for a compulsory minimum period in a work colony, an agricultural colony or a training center. Also, transfers from and to mental hospitals and from one detention place to another ought to be made possible, provided that such transfers are judicially authorized, preferably by a court supervising sentence execution.

Where the deterioration of an alcoholic has reached a stage of complete hopelessness, treatment of alcoholism may be pointless. When such person is specifically found to be dangerous or is subject to detention for a minimum period, he may be assigned to an institution of care or, if this is still possible, to a work colony or an agricultural colony. After lapse of the maximum detention period, however, such persons must be released from criminal law intervention on legality grounds. But the proper civil authorities ought to be advised of their continued dangerousness, so that steps might be taken for their civil commitment.

Release or release on trial ought to be predicated upon cessation of dangerousness rather than upon a "cure." But a cure may well be a significant factor in determining a judgment that a person is no longer dangerous. It hence becomes pertinent to inquire into what should constitute a cure. Psychiatric authorities assert that a mere successful withdrawal treatment is not a cure and affords no safeguard whatever against relapse, for it does not reach the profound motivations that have led the person concerned to adoption of the alcohol or drug habit.[209] A reasonably durable cure requires, in addition to a withdrawal treatment, an intensive psychiatric treatment. No person should hence be deemed "cured" unless a psychiatrist testifies that a reasonably successful psychiatric treatment has been given to the patient.

---

[209]See NOYES & KOLB, 477–479. Cf. also HAGGARD & JELLINEK, 172–176.

In cases in which minimum detention periods are not or no longer applicable and the court finds that the person concerned is dangerous but not to an extent as to require detention, it may order probationary release subject to appropriate terms and supervision.

Appropriate terms of probation might be one of the following or a combination of these:

That the person concerned receive or continue a psychiatric treatment or be subject to periodic psychiatric checks;

That he be placed under supervision of a social work agency;

That he abstain from drinking or drug use;

That he abstain from frequenting certain establishments, such as taverns;

That he not reside in a certain district;

That he abstain from engaging in a certain occupation, such as that of a bartender;

That he not carry a weapon;

That he not drive a car;

That he report periodically to a probation office.

Some of the enumerated terms constitute in laws of certain civil law countries special measures, for example, the prohibition to frequent taverns. This measure is known in Italy, Brazil, Switzerland and Rumania.[210] In Switzerland it bears the character of a collateral punishment. In Italy such prohibition is not absolute but rather permits an occasional visit to the barred establishment.[211] It should be possible to impose any one or a combination of the above prohibitions either as independent measures or as terms of probation. Where they are the latter it is not necessary to regard every breach of a prohibition as a ground of forfeiture of the probation benefit. Other sanctions may be imposed in most situations, e.g., contempt of court, and a forfeiture provided for only in those cases where the breach or breaches are not compatible with the meaning and purpose of probation.

---

[210]ITALIAN PENAL CODE, art. 234; BRAZILIAN PENAL CODE, art. 98; FEDERAL SWISS PENAL CODE, art. 56; RUMANIAN PENAL CODE, art. 77.

[211]On this see Heuermann, 227.

Title 2: Measures for Persons Who Commit Crime When in a State of Acute Intoxication

When a person who does not know that he might become intoxicated or that if intoxicated he might engage in criminal conduct, under circumstances in which the majority of other persons would have possessed such knowledge (inadvertent negligence), becomes intoxicated and commits a homicide in drink, he may not be "guilty" in the sense attributed to this term by the present writer, but he is undoubtedly dangerous. A recent estimate is that 68,000,000 persons in the United States drink alcoholic beverages.[212] The number of homicides committed in states of intoxication certainly bears no appreciable proportion to the probable number of persons among those 68,000,000 who drink to a state of intoxication or had intoxicated themselves on some occasion. Obviously, commission of homicide in a state of intoxication is not attributable to the alcoholic state itself. At best, alcohol facilitates its commission. It is not the ultimate source of homicide or of homicidal danger. That danger lies rather in the personality of the offender. It is probable that this offender might have killed even if he never intoxicated himself, provided that his inhibitions were reduced in some other manner. Such offender may kill again, and the danger he represents can hardly be averted by imposing upon him a term of imprisonment for negligent homicide or involuntary manslaughter or even for murder.

When finding an offender, who in a state of intoxication engages in serious criminal conduct, to be sane, one is merely stating that he does not qualify for the general mental incapacity exemption, as defined by law. He may be, nevertheless, in need of a psychiatric treatment aimed at discovery and cure of the deep-seated roots of the criminal conduct in which he engaged while in drink. Such need may be found in the course of a psychiatric examination in a psychiatric and sociologic examinations center. If so, such treatment might then be imposed as an ap-

---

[212]Estimate of Zeller and Efron, cited in Zwerling and Rosenbaum, *Alcoholic Addiction and Personality,* in AMERICAN HANDBOOK OF PSYCHIATRY, *op. cit. supra* note 38, at 623.

propriate measure. If the person concerned is a habitual drug or alcohol user, other than an addict, but the prima facie case of mental incapacity has been overcome, so that he has been found not to come within the general mental incapacity exemption, he may nevertheless require psychiatric assistance in order to abandon the drug or alcohol use. Since, addicts being excluded, abandonment of the habit involves no severe withdrawal symptoms, it may undoubtedly be required. Such abandonment may be ordered to be carried out with or without psychiatric guidance. Other potential measures are those enumerated above as terms of probation. Perhaps the most important measure short of detention and psychiatric treatment is supervised liberty. This measure should always be imposed unless the person is detained or under psychiatric treatment.

When the criminal act committed by the intoxicated offender was of a type which but for the intoxication would have constituted a felony against the bodily integrity of a human being, he should be subject to a minimum detention period such as provided for in cases of mentally incapacitated offenders who engage in similar conduct. Likewise, extension of this minimum period should be possible, under terms similar to those obtaining in cases of mentally incapacitated offenders. Finally, the same maximum periods should apply.

In situations in which the actor did not know that he might become intoxicated or that if intoxicated he might commit a crime and neither would a majority of the community members have possessed such knowledge, in conventional law the intoxication and the consequent crime commission are deemed not to be even "negligent." According to conventional phraseology, they are "accidental," and I am using this term merely as an artificial construct summarizing the total situation as described and not as implying exclusion of a causal relationship between the defendant's unconscious state of mind and the criminal harm. Imposition of measures in such cases of "accident" or "misfortune" cannot be supported unless the act involved is a most serious one. It is submitted that in situations of this type measures should not be imposed unless the conduct in drink would but for the intoxication have been a felony against the bodily integrity of a human being.

The measures applicable in the described situation of "accident" should be considerably more limited than those provided for in cases of conduct which in conventional terms is "negligent" or "reckless." Detentive measures should not be imposed except on a showing of a concrete danger. For, in principle, in conventional law in those countries which admit a general defense of intoxication, the person concerned would be completely absolved of all criminal liability. Reflection on so-called "accidental occurrences" in the light of modern psychological interpretation suggests modification of this legal approach. Indeed, in law an "accident" merely means that in the defendant's situation most people would have possessed no greater knowledge or foresight or would have exercised no greater care than the defendant. If such is the case, where the conduct results in serious harm, it would seem that this standard of the reasonable or prudent or average man is no longer adequate. In fact, it is necessary to re-educate the reasonable, prudent or average man. Using various disguises, our laws are actually more or less unconsciously pursuing this end. In common law countries the intoxication is simply disregarded and the intricate system of presumptions becomes operative. German law, though with abundant excuses and rationalizations, imposes upon the inebriate actor a punishment, the maximum of which is that applicable to the crime committed in drink.[213] Some laws admit such punishment only if this crime is at least a misdemeanor.[214] Contraventions are excluded.

The suggestion advanced by the present writer is that we abandon our "moralizing" approach to criminal conduct in drink, take into consideration scientific insight, and above all try to be honest with ourselves. What is it that preoccupies us in cases of "accidents" preceded by intoxication? It is the fact that, outside of very rare cases, these "accidents" are not "accidental" unless

---

[213]Compare *supra* text at note 139. In fact, the German § 330a admits a farther-reaching interpretation.

[214]This is the case in Switzerland (FEDERAL PENAL CODE, art. 263) and in Greece (PENAL CODE, art. 193).

we posit the "reasonable man" test, which is outmoded because in the light of scientific insight an average man is no longer believed to be motivated exclusively by "rational" considerations, as was the eighteenth and nineteenth century's "reasonable man." Today's "reasonable man" needs to be understood and perhaps also counseled. But this cannot be accomplished by putting him in jail. In fact, he does not "deserve" such treatment, within a democratic concept of "guilt." In his case, if he engages in criminal conduct in drink, measures rather than punishment are appropriate.

Although it is recommended that the punitive policy of the laws concerning conduct in a state of intoxication be replaced by a protective one, the lead of some of these laws may be followed by predicating imposition of measures in the case of such conduct upon its being at least a misdemeanor. There is no sound reason for submitting a person to measures when his inebriate act was but a petty misdemeanor.

As has been noted above, though in insanity cases in our law intent is deemed to be absent, no corresponding position is maintained regarding the intent of an intoxicated person. There is hence no reason, even under present law, to disregard the intent or the recklessness of the intoxicated offender. It is submitted that, as in the case of punitive responsibility, so *a fortiori* in measures the court should consider, in estimating the degree of permissible intervention, whether the defendant acted with "natural intent," "*de facto* negligence" or without any pertinent knowledge whatever.

Among the procedural problems that may arise in connection with crimes of intoxicated offenders there is one which deserves special consideration, since it is possible to argue that it should be treated differently from the corresponding problem in general mental incapacity cases. It is the problem of who should be permitted to raise the intoxication issue. In general mental incapacity cases, the writer submits that the insanity issue ought to be treated as affirmative defense in misdemeanor cases but that in felony cases the prosecution and the court, as well as the defendant ought to have authority to raise the issue of defendant's insanity at "the time pertinent to the act."[215] The same principle should apply where the integrative impairment of the alcoholic or drug user may be of such nature as to qualify him for a general mental incapacity exemption. But the problem is distinctive where the issue is an otherwise sane defendant's state of intoxication at the time of the crime.

On the whole, in the punitive area, within the rules recommended by the writer, intoxication is a factor which is advantageous to the defendant. Even in the case of intoxication for the purpose of crime commission, the probability of achieving the intended result is judged as of the time when the defendant was intoxicated, which, considering the general reduction of skill due to intoxication, is a factor favorable to him. Permitting both court and prosecution to raise the issue of intoxication cannot be said to prejudice him. Where the punitive approach is inapplicable, that is, where the actor was not at least reckless when he incurred the intoxication, the problem presented is most intricate, for while the defendant's liability to measures may be based on a state of mind at the time of intoxication that does not normally afford a ground of responsibility [not even negligence or abstract jeopardy], the prosecution might, if intoxication does not become an issue, prove criminal intent or recklessness at the time of the act. In this event the defendant's responsibility might be considerably higher than that which he would incur in the event of a treatment on the assumption of intoxication. Thus, it is submitted that both in felony and in misdemeanor cases the court and the prosecution as well as the accused should have authority to raise the issue of intoxication.

IV. SPECIFIC CRIMES CREATED BY NARCOTICS AND ALCOHOL LEGISLATION

In this section I shall deal with the problem of the legitimacy and, indeed, constitutionality of 1. the "use" and "possession"

---

[215]See The Criminal Law of Mental Incapacity, supra at 149-151. Lynch v. Overholser, 69 U.S. 705 (1961), holding that permitting the court to raise the issue of insanity at the time of the act would be unconstitutional, is inapplicable, since it was geared to provisions permitting an indefinite detention of a defendant acquitted solely by reason of insanity. In the scheme proposed by the writer the

clauses of narcotics legislation[216] and 2. the crimes of "being under the influence of a drug" or "driving under the influence of alcohol" or "appearing in public in a state of intoxication."

1. Holding that, under the Constitution, "addiction" cannot be made a crime[217] and nevertheless, punishing one of its typical "incidents," namely use and possession for personal limited use of otherwise proscribed drugs, is so highly unrealistic as to be constitutionally questionable within provisions against "cruel and unusual punishment" and against deprivation of rights without "due process." To be sure, if the reason for outlawing the "crime of being an addict" is that the latter is a status and not a conduct type, then punishing the conduct types of "use" and "possession" may not be improper within a formalistic notion of law. So, in the last analysis, the issue posed would seem to be reducible to the question of whether it is possible to determine generally that an addict "cannot" abstain from using drugs or possessing them for his own use. Otto Fenichel said that "addicts represent the most clear-cut type of 'impulsives.'"[218] Affinities have been found to the psychoses and neuroses. But since involvement in arguments which might ultimately reduce themselves to "free will" debates should be avoided so far as possible, it may be desirable to approach the subject from a different angle. I shall thus try to answer the question of whether, apart from the issue of the degree of psychological stress that might be held to put "free will" out of operation, the crimes of "using" narcotics

---

maxima of punishment and those of measures are coordinated. Only to a very limited extent can the period of a measure exceed that of punishment.

[216]See, for example, Title 24 § § 973 et seq., PUERTO RICO ANNOTATED (1964) [Health and Sanitation, chapter known as the "Narcotics Act of Puerto Rico" of 1959]; § 220.05 of NEW YORK REVISED PENAL LAW to become effective September 1, 1967; and 26 U. S. C. (I. R. C. 1954), § 4704 (a); Narcotic Drugs Import and Export Act, § 2 (c,f), 21 U. S. C. A. § 174, the federal statutes applied in the Castle case, *supra* note 41, at 493. Notice also the use in a criminal case of presumptions of knowledge arising from possession of facts other than such possession itself—a factor which practically eliminates the constitutional requisite of proving "guilt" and the constitutional presumption of innocence.

[217]Robinson v. California, *supra* note 7.

[218]THE PSYCHOANALYTICAL THEORY OF NEUROSIS 375-16 (W. W. Norton & Company, Inc., New York 1945).

or "possessing" them in amounts not exceeding personal need are constitutionally maintainable.

Throughout many ages ethical philosophies of various cultures have struggled to free mankind from the absurdity of the criminal law notion of "self-murder," *felo de se*. It took a revolution, a mass uprising against the shackles of a decadent obstinate social morality, to abolish the crime of suicide in Europe.[219] In countries of common law tradition, development of the idea that suicide is not an appropriate crime construct has penetrated into legal systems less abruptly. But, in the United States, punishing attempted suicide has been on the whole felt not to conform to "the spirit of our institutions."[220] In any event, whatever may be the psychological interpretation of the phenomenon of self-destruction, there is no doubt that no civil law country today and no common law jurisdiction in which attempted suicide is not at present a crime would even remotely consider reintroducing it into its penal legislation. Yet, suicide and suicidal attempt are presumably most harmful to the individual concerned as well as highly contagious to others.[221]

An eminent psychiatrist, Dr. Karl A. Menninger, believes alcoholism and drug addiction to be forms of "indirect self-destruction," actually, indirect suicide.[222] This interpretation is particularly apposite in the present context, since one significant rationale of the law's maintaining specific alcohol and drug

---

[219]See on this Silving, *Suicide and Law*, in CLUES TO SUICIDE 79 (ed. Shneidman & Farberow, McGraw-Hill Book Company, Inc., New York, Toronto, London 1957).

Psychologists might well inquire into the psychological significance of the fact that this amendment of the law in France was moved by the famed "Docteur Guillotin," the man who thought of himself as a humanitarian when he devised the "*guillotine*" as an instrument of capital execution allegedly less painful than hanging, but which in effect facilitated mass executions and turned them into bloody spectacles of mass appeal. *Id.* at 84. However, the outcome of any such studies ought not to affect the legal immunity of suicide based on the political ideal of self-determination.

[220]Burnett v. People, 204 Ill. 208, 68 N. E. 505, 510 (1903).

[221]On "epidemics of suicide" see SZITTYA, SELBSTMÖRDER 351-370 (Weller & Company, Leipzig 1925).

[222]A PSYCHIATRIST'S WORLD 347-349; and see 353-356 on the "riddle of indirect self-destruction" (Viking Press, New York 1959).

crimes is that abuse of intoxicants is self-destructive and causes damage to those depending on the person concerned. But, surely, such unconscious indirect self-destruction ought not to justify government intervention when an attempt at a direct and immediate suicide is thought not to afford an appropriate basis for such intervention.

The argument that drug use is contagious and should not be tolerated on this ground is more persuasive. But a similar argument referring to the contagiousness of suicide has not been successful, it being felt that in a "free society" the individual's right of self-determination as regards his own body and mind overrides the community's interest against contagion. True, society has the right to protect itself against the spread of contagious diseases. But is addiction contagious in the same sense as is typhoid fever or rather in a sense comparable to the contagiousness of suicide? Undoubtedly, contagiousness in this instance, as in that of suicide, consists in a danger of imitation. It is thus pertinent to ask: Would any legislator today suggest punishing or otherwise sanctioning attempted suicide, even if a suicide wave were to occur, as such waves are known to have occurred frequently in the history of mankind in various cultures?

Further factors to be considered are that drug use is the individual's chosen method of "pursuing his happiness" and that an unwarranted interference with such use is actually an undue privacy invasion.

In recent years, our courts have shown extraordinary courage in sacrificing enforcement of penal provisions involving high criminality such as murder, armed robbery, gang activities to principles of "due process." The objection once raised by Judge Cardozo, that "under our constitutional exclusionary doctrine '[t]he criminal is to go free because the constable has blundered,'"[223] as well as the more significant concern with the indubitably serious danger to the community entailed in leaving at large persons who have directly and immediately offended against the bodily integrity of others, are increasingly yielding

---

[223]People v. Defore, 242 N. Y. 13, 150 N. E. 585 (1926), cited in Mapp v. Ohio, 367 U. S. 643 (1961).

to an implied recognition that the crux of the matter is not such blunder *per se,* but assertion of the dignity of the accused who has suffered an indignity by such blunder and of the overriding value of his privacy interest that has been violated. In a free society the community's interest in protection against the serious danger of reincidence must yield to these primary values.

When risking the safety of our innocent neighbors to preserve the dignity and privacy of the "guilty" in matters of procedure, should we not ask ourselves whether considerations of "human dignity" and privacy ought not a fortiori to compel examination of substantive crime concepts which *per se* involve denial of such human rights. Is it proper to assume the crime in *Castle v. United States,*[224] whereby a man may be convicted for possession *in his own bedroom* of drugs in an amount not exceeding his own immediate use, to be constitutionally unchallengeable, while the conviction in *Mapp v. Ohio* is reversed[225] because the evidence used in the trial against the accused was obtained under conditions of indignity to her?

Nor can a punitive sentence of six to ten years with forced labor in the case of *Martínez Rodríguez v. Delgado,*[225] precipitated by the accused's smoking one marijuana cigarette, be justified on the ground that imprisonment afforded him an

---

[224]*Supra* note 41, at 493.

[225]Cited *supra* note 223. This case marks a turning point in the total philosophy of constitutional criminal procedure, shifting the weight formerly placed on the state's immunity vis-à-vis the federal power to the individual's immunity vis-à-vis all government power. To be sure, in Linkletter v. Walker, 381 U.S. 618 (1965), the majority minimized this value of the *Mapp* case by interpreting its rule of exclusion from state courts of evidence obtained by unreasonable searches and seizures to be but a device of deterring the police from such practices in future cases. But even apart from the forceful argument advanced by the dissent in *Linkletter,* the very majority admitted the substantive rule prohibiting unreasonable searches and seizures to be established for the protection of the individual's —even the guilty defendant's—civil right to privacy. Notice particularly in contrast to Castle, Massiah v. United States, 377 U.S. 201 (1964), where a member of a large and well-organized ring of illegal wholesale drug dealers was set free because after his indictment a government agent had used a secret radio transmitter (installed in a car owned by Massiah's accomplice with the latter's consent) to procure from him a self-incriminating statement without his knowledge.

[226]Decided by a five to four majority of the Supreme Court of Puerto Rico on June 30, 1965 (Colegio de Abogados Ref. 1965, No. 115).

opportunity for treatment.[227] Consolations of this type disregard the social meaning of a punitive sentence and, by confusing punishment and treatment, promote a criminal law philosophy fit for an authoritarian welfare state.

The issue we are facing is ultimately one of choice of a form of government in criminal matters: May the government in a democracy treat a man against his will when the danger of contagion consists in a probability that his conduct will be imitated by others? May it do so under the guise of criminal law prosecutions, the crimes in issue being specifically devised indirectly to compel treatment? May it force people under threat of criminal prosecutions for such crimes (or, indeed, for any other crimes) to bargain away their freedom of disposition over their own body and mind? May it make such deals in advance of conviction?[228]

Even if it were found that the need for avoiding "contagion" is so overwhelming as to override considerations of individual freedom, it might not be necessary to assign to narcotics crimes as broad a scope as they possess at present. The danger could be met where it is actually operative, and prohibition need not take the form of absolutes. Use and limited possession of narcotic drugs could be made criminal provided that they occur "in public," i.e., where there is opportunity for others to observe and imitate the indulgence.

Having used the analogy to suicide in the context of the "principal's" conduct, it is appropriate to consider certain aspects of this analogy also regarding complicity. Aiding and instigating suicide has been made a crime in some countries and jurisdictions which do not regard the principal's conduct as criminal.[229] "Complicity" in such situations differs *toto genere* from the principal's conduct. Notice, however, that French and German jurists have, mostly as a matter of systematic consistency, rejected

---

[227] This was the ultimate argument for upholding the sentence.

[228] See "The Arrested Narcotic Addict Commitment Act" of New York (Chap. 204, LAWS OF 1962), 211.

[229] On this and the following discussion see Silving, *Euthanasia: A Study in Comparative Criminal Law*, 103 UNIVERSITY OF PENNSYLVANIA LAW REVIEW 350, 369-378 (1954); also *Suicide and Law, supra* note 219.

a special crime construct of this type where the principal's conduct is not a crime.[230] Even apart from questionable "dogmatic" considerations, one might hesitate to create such special crime of complicity in a conduct whose motivations are as yet to a large extent obscure, so that it would seem to be an almost insuperable task to explain the type of psychological interaction that may obtain between the principal and his accomplice.

Notwithstanding such doubts, there are sufficient grounds for maintaining an independent criminal construct of complicity in suicide. These grounds are magnified in cases where the accomplice is a physician and the principal is his patient. Unless the physician is trained to understand his own motivations, the specific relationship of physician-patient in penumbra situations is instinct with danger.

Similar though perhaps greatly modified considerations may justify introduction into the law of an independent concept of criminal conduct of aiding, instigating and facilitating the "use" or "possession" of a narcotic drug except as authorized by law. The special problem of self-determination obtaining in the case of the user or possessor himself does not apply to the accomplice. Indubitably, such complicity should be criminal where the principal is not an addict. Where he is an addict, a distinctive medical and social-ethical situation obtains also in regard to the accomplice. This is particularly the case where the accomplice is a physician and the addict is his patient.

By established tradition—which may, indeed, be found to constitute a principle recognized by all civilized nations—a physician has the duty not only of curing but also of alleviating pain.[231] I submit that where a physician finds attempting to cure

---

[230]Often the borderline between such complicity and homicide is rather vague. Compare Silving, *Euthanasia, supra,* at 373-376.

[231]Compare on this duty of a physician the case of *Ministère public et Noinin v. Dunand,* decided by the Cour d'appel of Bordeaux on October 28, 1953, reported in Dalloz, *Recueil de Doctrine, de Jurisprudence et de Legislation 1954,* JURISPRUDENCE 13. Dr. Dunan was convicted for refusing to render assistance to a person in peril under art. 63, par. 2 of the FRENCH PENAL CODE (establishing everyone's duty of assistance when the person concerned can give it without risk to himself or third persons). In his appeal he alleged that the patient (notice, a regular patient of another doctor) could not be saved even if the defendant had

an addicted patient of his addiction not to be promising or to be medically or psychiatrically unwise, such physician has a constitutional right to administer to or prescribe for such patient amounts of an otherwise proscribed drug as are absolutely needed to alleviate the patient's pain for a period rationally related to the circumstances of the particular case. This is part of a physician's "freedom" of the exercise of his chosen profession as recognized in the leading case of *Butchers' Union Slaughter-House Co. v. Crescent City Co.*[232] The same applies a fortiori where a physician, in good faith and rationally as judged by medical standards, administers or prescribes controlled narcotic drugs in the process of attempting the cure of an addict.

There is need for establishing a record of such administration or prescription of controlled drugs by licensed physicians, which, however, should not under any circumstances stigmatize the patient-addict. If it had this effect, its constitutionality might be dubious. I should like to emphasize that the record should be one of drug administration and not one of forced registration of addicts. Such record should be accessible only to the patient and persons authorized by him, as well as to any physician showing that the information is pertinent to the medical treatment of the patient concerned, that he refuses to grant authorization and that the information is needed to prevent frustration of the purposes of the law.

I hope that, in the future, our courts will realize increasingly the significance of bringing the constitutional standards of our substantive criminal law closer to those of our procedural law. In a rational legal system the spirit that dominates the latter is equally applicable to the former. The "drug user" may be the

---

responded promptly to the call. In upholding the conviction, the appellate court said: "[I]n fact, under the terms of art. 63, par. 2, Penal Code, there is no need to inquire whether the omitted intervention would have necessarily produced salutary results; . . . the duty to intervene is not predicated upon the efficacy of the assistance; . . . the physician's duty is not only to prescribe the most appropriate treatment but also, where a cure cannot be produced, to care, assist, give relief to, the sick person and try to save him."

[232]111 U. S. 746 (1880).

first in whose case the need for such coordination might be recognized.

2. Analysis of the most common crimes connected with alcohol consumption discloses certain elements of incongruity, which ought to lead to their abandonment in some instances and revision in others. In the crimes of "appearing in a public place under the influence of alcohol"[233] and "driving under the influence of alcohol," the person concerned is presumably sufficiently drunk to render his appearance in public offensive or his driving dangerous.[234] Yet, he is being held punitively responsible for such "appearing" or "driving." If we assume that punishment in such cases is aimed at the actor's intoxicating himself rather than at his appearing in public or driving under the influence, difficulties are raised by the nature of self-intoxication. A man does not get drunk on a single drink; self-intoxication is rather a process in the course of which the person concerned gradually loses control over his faculties, so that he is progressively less mentally capable in regard to additional imbibing. Self-intoxication could be thus conceived of as committed in a state of mental normality only where the person concerned not only purposely "drinks" but actually puts himself in a state of intoxication with the purpose of reaching that stage. Considering these precarious aspects of the mental state in the crimes mentioned, it would seem that these crimes should be abandoned as punitive categories. The question remains whether they ought to be maintained as preventive entities or types of criminal conduct sanctioned by measures.

---

[233]In 1959, out of 2,612,704 arrests reported for 1789 cities in the United States having a population of over 2500, 1,011,427 (30%) were for drunkenness. Considering that "disorderly conduct" is often but a guise for a charge of drunkenness and that "vagrancy" is sometimes taken to mean drunkenness, the number of total arrests for drunkenness seems overwhelming indeed. Statistics cited in AMERICAN LAW INSTITUTE MODEL PENAL CODE, art. 250, comments, note 1, at p. 2 (Tent. Draft No. 13, 1961).

[234]In general, most writers agree with the standards recommended by the Committee on Tests for Intoxication of the National Safety Council, according to which persons with a concentration of 150 mg % of alcohol in the blood are not safe drivers. See Thompson, op. cit., supra, note 38, at 1207. As physiological and psychological faculties are affected at this point, judgment is also impaired. See Jellinek, Effects of Small Amounts of Alcohol on Psychological Functions, supra, note 64, at 87-88.

Undoubtedly, driving under the influence of alcohol creates a grave public danger—a danger so serious as to deserve criminal law reaction. The most adequate measures ought to be suspension of a driving license or, if the person concerned does not hold a license, disqualification for receiving one temporarily. If an actual damage occurs, measures should be adequate to the gravity of the corresponding crime. Other potential measures that might be imposed on driving under the influence are compulsory education in public safety; in serious cases, as when a person drives at high speed in disregard of traffic rules in high traffic, even psychiatric examination and therapy as a condition for restoration of a driving license.

By contrast to "driving under the influence," the criminal conduct of "appearing in a public place under the influence"—the notorious crime of "public drunkenness"— is one of the many types that should be jettisoned in an enlightened free society. The problem of such drunkenness should be handled by public health authorities rather than by criminal justice. The harm of such appearance is not sufficiently grave to justify criminal law intervention.[235]

The provisos and caveats which the courts see fit to insert into decisions advancing more enlightened treatment of drug addicts and alcoholics[236] appear not to be encouraging. One hundred and thirty years ago a ship captain killed a mate in a fit of delirium tremens. He was acquitted on the ground of insanity, the court emphasizing that before the act he had thrown overboard all the liquor in his possession, so that he was not intoxicated at the time of the act. No opinion was expressed on the hypothetical question of whether he would have forfeited his defense had he been drunk then.[237] The *Easter* case stops short of the expectable concession to an "alcoholic addict" such as Easter of the "defense of insanity." The reason is obvious. Such concession would put an end to most instances of public drunk-

[235]Compare Silving, *Philosophy of the Source and Scope of Criminal Law Prohibition,* in Slovenko, ed., CRIME, LAW AND CORRECTIONS (Thomas, 1966), 232, at 243-245.

[236]See United States v. Freeman, *supra,* note 55; Easter v. District of Columbia, *supra,* note 53.

[237]United States v. Drew, *supra,* note 6.

enness. Perhaps qualifying chronic alcoholism as a "sickness" accompanied by a loss of self-control will have the same result. But the novelty of the approach—rather a revival of an ancient one—will make acceptance of such treatment of alcoholism more palatable.

The *Freeman* case,[238] which afforded the background for the Second Circuit's introduction of a broader "insanity" test, involved a narcotics addict. That the court broadened the test in such context shows an open-mindedness toward the phenomenon of drug addiction beyond expectation. The case involved selling, so that there was no occasion to rule on "use" and "possession." Yet, the court made sure not to be understood as affecting congressional legislation on possession and sale of narcotics.[239]

American lawyers are trained to read cases in a distinctively "American way,"[240] especially to concentrate on what "courts do" rather than on what "they say." In this light *Easter* and *Freeman* are most encouraging even though their rationalizations are faulty.[241]

CONCLUSION

In comparison with the tremendous volume of legislative, decisional and doctrinal efforts expended on the study of the problem of the "nature" of the insanity exemption in criminal law, until very recently little attention has been paid to the equally intricate general topic of rational dealing with the criminal conduct of chronic alcoholics and drug users. Criminal conduct in a state of acute intoxication has been treated in a confused manner, partly moralizing and partly dogmatically legalistic. The misconceptions prevailing in law regarding the relationship of the use of intoxicants and criminal conduct are comparable to those which in former times obtained in regard to "insanity." As the latter was once referred to wickedness, so today drug

---

[238]*Supra*, note 55.

[239]Compare *supra*, text at note 61.

[240]See on this Silving, *"Stare Decisis" in the Civil and in the Common Law*, 35 REVISTA JURÍDICA DE LA UNIVERSIDAD DE PUERTO RICO 195 (1965).

[241]Reference is made to the critique of the Model Code test in *Mental Incapacity in Criminal Law, supra*, at 97-101.

addiction, alcoholism and even sporadic full intoxication are widely believed to be more or less direct products of a bad life-conduct, calling for a punitive response.[242] This is further supported by a prevailing belief that the criminal conduct in such cases is the direct product of the intoxication or broader commitment to an intoxicant. A similar belief concerning the criminal conduct of the "insane" led to the dubious "product" portion of the *Durham* rule.

Recently, the described attitude has been considerably revised concerning drug and alcohol addiction and chronic alcoholism. Increasing interest has been shown in the problem of the proper treatment of drug addicts. But even this interest has been centered on the circuitous debate over the question of whether drug addiction is or is not a "disease," as though by the magic of such ontological characterization one could functionally resolve a profound social policy issue, also involving intricate constitutional problems. Nevertheless, whatever may be the ideology underlying the "finding" that chronic alcoholism is a "sickness" or drug addiction a "disease," its naively realistic implications are helping to pave the way to social recognition that, in this area, treatment by measures is preferable to punishment.[243]

As a matter of sound policy oriented to the operational consequences of a disposition rather than merely to its semantic implications, addiction ought to be included within the general mental incapacity exemption. Indeed, the latter should be formulated in such a manner as to permit no doubt regarding inclusion of addiction. The definition of the "mental incapacity" exemption recommended in former essays clearly applies to both alcohol and narcotic addicts, for beyond doubt such persons' integrative functioning is always impaired to a degree making it considerably more difficult for them than for average persons to abide by social demands and rules, especially those barring access to the chosen intoxicant. The classification within the exemption does not free them of all state intervention. It merely makes

---

[242]But see Easter v. District of Columbia, *supra*, note 53, expressly discarding the notion of "guilt of life conduct."

[243]Compare Robinson v. California, *supra*, note 7, which originated a more liberal approach to addiction.

them amenable to measures of security and cure rather than to punishment.

It has been observed that alcoholism and commitment to narcotic drugs, even short of addiction, very often occur in persons who independently qualify for exemption from punitive responsibility by reason of mental incapacity. In fact, the frequency of such concurrence is so great as to justify adoption of a presumption that an alcoholic or a habitual drug user is thus exempt and at the same time potentially subject to measures.

Even when an addict engages in criminal conduct other than possession or use of drugs for the purpose of satisfying his craving for a drug, the opinion is increasingly voiced that he should be treated leniently or, indeed, by measures rather than punitively. But when a person engages in criminal conduct while under the impact of drink, the dominant legal opinion relates it directly to the single act of intoxication and interprets it exclusively as a product of willful self-inflicted incapacity, with the result that at law the intoxication is either disregarded (the common law solution) or punished beyond proportion to guilt (§ 330a, German Penal Code).

Neither of these legal solutions takes account of contemporary scientific insight into the nature of criminal conduct in drink. Both assume a moralizing attitude which tends to conceal unconscious reactions of decision-makers to both the indulgence in the intoxicant and the conduct engaged in under its impact. Further anthropological, psychological and sociological studies might throw more light on the unconscious motivations of the criminal conduct of alcoholics, drug users and acutely intoxicated persons, and on the interacting attitudes of contemporary decision-makers to such conduct. Abandonment of preconceived notions and assumption of an enlightened approach, based on scientific insight, is a condition of truly impartial judgment.

A general exemption for addicts from punitive responsibility for drug use or possession, based on the proposition that they suffer from a "mental disease" within the *Durham* rule, has been declined. Judge Burger said that this would constitute rule by "labels." But this statement seems to disregard the significant fact that to the extent that the law is governed by "language," it is always governed by "labels," the question being whether the respective "label" has any meaning at all or, if so, to what extent is its meaning determined or, in some instances, determinable. A "label" is not always used in a completely arbitrary manner. Also, its meaning and scope may be vague and uncertain for one purpose but not for another. An otherwise vague label may yet unambiguously cover or not cover certain things. There is a clearly discernible common behavioral element in certain cases of commitment to intoxicants, and this element might well be used to define "addiction" for legal purposes. There is no comparable community between all instances of "psychopathy," so that analogy to this phenomenon is not pertinent. The question in regard to addiction is then whether this element common in all addiction fits it within the "mental incapacity" exemption. Such may be the case even if the test of the exemption is otherwise vague. When stating that "some addicts are mentally ill persons and some mentally ill persons are addicts . . .,"[244] Judge Burger, of course, implies that the "label" "mental disease" has developed into a relatively functional determinant, even if a scientifically wrong one, and that the label "addiction" has some, however vague, meaning. An explanation is outstanding as to why Judge Burger believes that whatever is denoted by the label "addiction" does not *per se* fit within such a determinant label.

I have tried to avoid dealing with the issue of "free will," permeating the "mental incapacity" debate of today just as magic had governed it in former times. This issue is not answerable by law except arbitrarily and apparently is not expected to be answered by any rational legal fiat. Inserting into the "mental disease" definition an issue of that type renders practical solutions necessarily inegalitarian. Despite the uncertainty of the "mental disease" concept, one might expect that it would be made more definite in the course of the common law judicial process of inclusion and exclusion. But the judicial task is rendered almost impossible when the issue is converted into one of theology, that may be, furthermore, questionable within the constitutional "wall of separation" between Church and State.

---

[244]Judge Burger in Castle v. United States, *supra*, note 41, at 496-497.

Even a metaphysical issue may be resolved by law in operational terms and thus endowed with a practical meaning, provided that the original concept is not constantly being reactivated, jeopardizing law development. Such reactivation of the metaphysics of *Durham* occurred when its "mental disease" notion was interpreted in *McDonald v. United States*,[245] as "any abnormal condition of the mind which substantially affects mental or emotional processes and substantially impairs behavior controls." That addiction was held not to be *per se* included within this test, shows that the latter has jeopardized rather than enhanced the survival of *Durham*.

The problem of the addicts' qualification for the general exemption for the "insane" raises an additional issue within a judicially formulated "insanity" test. Whether addicts such as Castle ought to be conceded punitive immunity within such test, is a priori not a question of word-use or "labels." Where courts assume the legislative task of defining legal "insanity" in abstract terms, it is difficult indeed to comprehend their disclaiming authority to determine the question of whether addiction qualifies as "insanity."

Experts assert that the motivations in sporadic and in chronic intoxication as well as in addiction may be similar in kind. Again, whether the element of such similarity is the crucial one in the classification of these conditions as within or outside of the mental incapacity exemption is a question that can be answered by law. In Germany and Switzerland, as shown, this question has been answered. True, it may be asserted that in the light of present scientific knowledge there is no sound policy basis for including "inebriates" within the "mental incapacity" exemption. The next question would then be whether there obtains an independent basis for exemption of such persons under all or under some circumstances. The submission of this essay has been that such a basis exists in some situations and that it is related to the basis underlying the general mental incapacity exemption.

The main object of this essay has been to submit a fresh ap-

---

[245]312 F.2d 847, 851 (D.C. Cir., 1962).

proach to the problem of criminal conduct in drink. Conventional criminal law solutions are unrealistic and hence unjust. This is true both of the solution obtaining in common law countries, whereby the intoxication phenomenon is disregarded, as well as of the solution prevalent in civil law countries, whereby the conduct in drink is immunized but punitive responsibility invariably attaches to the act of intoxication. Both solutions are incompatible with the guilt principle and take no account of the unconscious motivations of either the conduct in drink or the drinking phenomenon itself. The submission presented in this paper is that a "dual system" of punishment for the "guilty" defendant, and measures of security and cure in the case of the "dangerous" though not or not predominantly guilty one, is appropriate for conduct in drink, as it is in many other criminal law situations which are at present dealt with exclusively punitively. Punitive responsibility ought to be imposed where the accused has been reckless in becoming intoxicated. In cases where his intoxication was incurred "accidentally" or in inadvertent negligence regarding his criminality potential or in foresight of unspecific criminality, he ought not to be deemed guilty; yet, he has proved to be dangerous and ought to be subject to measures, just as a person acquitted by reason of insanity is today subject to measures. We have traveled a long way before reaching this solution in insanity cases. Indeed, in common law countries this solution is still handled confusingly; there is no distinctive systematization of measures, and this bars formulation of a consistent body of legality principles governing them, for example, in cases of acquittals by reason of insanity. In the case of conduct in a state of acute intoxication there is still outstanding both in common law and in civil law countries recognition of the need for a preventive and curative approach, that is, for treatment by measures responsive to the type of dangerousness evincing from the respective conduct.

Nor should such recognition necessarily result in adoption of measures identical with or analogous to those developed in insanity cases. A "dual system" ought to be adopted throughout the area of criminal law and not only in certain disparate situations; appropriate measures should be introduced systematically.

There are ample grounds for applying them not only in cases of the mentally ill, drug and alcohol addicts but also in those of inebriate offenders, inadvertently negligent offenders and many others. The principle of the "rule of law," requires more than a case-by-case inquiry into the question of why particular measures are being introduced. Only a comprehensive inquiry directed to the ends of criminal law will permit conscious, planned systematic application of "legality" tenets to criminal law measures.

Apart from cases involving "addicts," "use" and "possession" in private of narcotic drugs in amounts which do not indicate purported sale cannot be made crimes under the Eighth Amendment, also incorporated or repeated in the Fourteenth Amendment to the Federal Constitution and the respective provisions of the Bills of Rights of State Constitutions and Section 12 of Article II of the Constitution of the Commonwealth of Puerto Rico, as well as Section 1 of the latter ("Man's dignity is inviolable"). This follows a fortiori from the constitutional bar against unreasonable searches and seizures and against any other procedural privacy invasions. It is clearly irrational to the point of being unconstitutional also within the due process clause of both the Fifth and the Fourteenth Amendment to the Federal Constitution, while not admitting in evidence fruits of privacy invasions to make an individual's use of the respective privacy rights criminal. "Privacy," of course, does not denote in this context a matter contrasted with "public,"[246] but rather refers to the intimate, partly unconscious "personality" sphere in regard to which the individual ought to be "let alone" in a democracy. I do not mean to say that in all situations in which a search would be unreasonable, the individual is free to engage in any conduct he pleases however it may be harmful to others. I am rather asserting that there are spheres of human privacy immune from government encroachment by substantive criminal law, by the same token by which procedural encroachment would be obnoxious to principles of the "rule of law" in a free society.

To reach persons whom the government intends to "cure,"

---

[246]Mr. Justice Black assumes it to be so used. See his dissent in Griswold v. Connecticut, 381 U.S. 479, 507 (1965).

legislation is at times interpreted as being designed to meet the "act" requirement of criminal law while at the same time making persons amenable via "punishability" to "cure." Such persons are, in fact, being "blackmailed" to submit to a cure by a threat of criminal prosecution or of execution of a penal sentence.[247] "Use" and "possession" clauses of narcotics legislation occasionally have been construed as serving such more or less disguised welfare purposes. Crimes thus conceived indirectly to serve ends other than those professed or other than those properly sanctionable by punitive criminal law are constitutionally dubious.

Allegedly, the issue of such "criminality" and that of the constitutional bar against making "addiction" a crime are not related to one another. But this approach is unrealistic to the point of being clearly unfair to the defendants concerned and violative of the constitutional principles barring "cruel and unusual punishment" and deprivation of rights without "due process."

This book deals with problems of "criminal law," which comprises both "punitive criminal law" and "protective or preventive criminal law," functioning by means of "punishment" in the former instance and "measures" in the latter. These two types of "penal law methods" are distinguishable from each other, but have certain common features which in turn separate them from other methods, the "civil law methods." The present book does not deal with the latter. But this should not be misunderstood to carry the implication as though any topic or method that cannot be constitutionally treated in terms of "crime" or "criminal conduct" or by "punishment" or "measures of security and cure" at criminal law can be controlled by the "civil" or "administrative" law. In a free society there are many items which are not accessible to government intervention by any means. Certainly, in such a society the government has no power to obviate a constitutional prohibition against treatment of a condition as "criminal" simply by giving it a "public health and welfare" imprint.[248]

Given the fact that "being an addict" cannot be made a crime,

---

[247]Compare "The Arrested Narcotic Addict Commitment Act" of New York (Chap. 204, Laws of 1962, § 211).

[248]See the recent New York narcotic law signed by Governor Rockefeller on April 6, 1966, Laws of New York 1966, Chapter 192.

may a legislature pursue an identical policy by cloaking the criminal sanction as a public health measure? May it, however bona fide, assume unlimited power over addicts on the mere ground of their "being addicts," or even on the additional ground that addicts are "harmful" to the community or that their sight has certain undesirable consequences?

True, it has been said that addiction is a "disease" and for this reason cannot be made a crime, and "diseases," no doubt, are proper subjects of "public health and welfare" concern. But *Baxstrom v. Herold*[249] has made it abundantly clear that illness does not warrant indiscriminate government intervention and that "legality" limitations, though distinctive ones, are applicable also to "civil" measures. This is, of course, true of "substantive legality" demands as it is of procedural safeguards.

If, indeed, addiction is a "disease," whatever this may mean, does this necessarily imply that the government can place addicts in concentration camps just as it establishes quarantines for cholera patients or as it provides for vaccination against smallpox? Should it assume the power of treating addicts against their will, although it may not impose compulsory treatment against other "diseases"? Would it not be pertinent to inquire first if there are any distinctive features of drug addiction as compared to cholera or smallpox that may be relevant to legitimate purposes even of civil law measures? Since in a democracy the crux of policy decisions lies in an adequate weighing of the negative value of deprivations to be suffered by the individual against the positive value of the end to be attained by the community, should the government be deemed to have the right to subject addicts to long-term confinement and compulsory treatment without ascertaining: (a) Since the evil of addiction consists in its spreading, how exactly, by whom, to whom, under what conditions the drug habit spreads; (b) what is the degree of probability of a cure; (c) does such probability of cure, if any, apply to some addicts, to many addicts, to a vast majority of addicts; (d) what is the relation of the number of addicts in a community to its spreading.

---

[249]383 U.S. 107 (1966).

An initial question the government in a democracy should be called upon to answer is what role the legislative bar against access to drugs has played in the case of those who would not otherwise become a source of contagion to others. Its first duty is to go back to fundamentals of the philosophy upon which such bar is based. Such reexamination, to be rational, is predicated upon understanding of the unconscious motives of popular attitudes toward addicts.

Autocratic welfare legislation is the line of least resistance, particularly when it is applied to persons who are not likely to engage in public protests or exert pressures. Typically, such legislation utilizes a system of "spies and informers,"[250] more pernicious in a free society than addiction can ever be.

---

[250]Notice in the New York Law (Section 200 of Mental Hygiene Law, as amended, § 206, 2a, 1966), "anyone who believes that a person is a narcotic addict" can start court proceedings to have him sentenced to a three-year stay in a hospital for treatment. No doubt, New York will became an informers' paradise. Even so-called "good faith" is not a safeguard against the obvious evil of this legislation which, by its fiat, presumes to turn anyone into a medical expert on addiction. This writer believes that this "informers' clause" by itself renders the statute unconstitutional. It would be difficult, indeed, to enumerate all other sources of its unconstitutionality.

Eventually the Supreme Court of the United States will have to answer the basic question whether a statute which offers an opportunity of civil rather than criminal treatment to one person charged with crime but denies such opportunity to another person in a closely similar situation except that the latter is not medically treatable for reasons not referable to his guilt satisfies the demands of equality. See National Narcotic Addict Rehabilitation Act of 1966 (80 Stat. 1438, 28 U.S.C.A. §§ 2901–2906; 18 U.S.C.A. §§ 4251–4255.) Indeed, should "guilt" be made to depend on capacity to be treated?

CONCLUSION

EXEMPTION from punishment by reason of "insanity" or "mental incapacity" should be treated as one of the mutually interrelated topics comprised in the complex of "responsibility." The latter should be defined as a normative connection of conditions and consequences of attribution of answerability for an act or an event or a combination of such phenomena to a person.

Structuring criminal law, including assignment of meaning and scope to constructs such as "insanity," "guilt," "responsibility," is a policy disposition rather than a discovery of factual relationships, although sound policy requires orientation of norms to insight into reality. This normative or decision-making process is obscured by an often inarticulate belief that facts by themselves have the power of emanating norms. Such belief may produce operational consequences. But these consequences are not necessarily desirable from the standpoint of rational judgment. Above all, since the decision-making process in such instances is not a conscious one, it escapes the censorship of reason and realism, permitting intrusion into the law of unconscious ancient obsolete traditions—carriers of prejudice.

Thus, statements such as "insanity eliminates guilt" or "absence of guilt [innocence] precludes responsibility," are often formulated in such a manner as to induce a belief as though they were conveying information about phenomena of nature which decision makers are unable to alter. When it is said that dependence of guilt on sanity and of responsibility on guilt is a constitutional tenet, there seems to obtain a tacit expectation that these terms are defined by the constitution or interpretative constitutional decisions. Actually, in constitutional usage they are rather treated as referring to ontologically given phenomena to be found by methods similar to those which a natural scientist uses in discovering phenomena in his discipline.

As in all other branches and ramifications of contemporary law, so in modern criminal law our first task is to "purge its symbols" of all implications beyond those consciously intended to be conveyed. Our methodological aim is not necessarily to eliminate ultimately ontological interpretations; it is rather to eliminate those among them which are not deliberately adopted with awareness of their implications. The purpose is to avoid unconscious self-deception. I have chosen to call the operational significance of such self-deceptive interpretation of a symbol— a significance which is not the result of a rational policy choice but rather a by-product of a fallacious unconscious methodology —an "incorrect meaning" of the given symbol.

To be able to verify whether any meaning attributed to a symbol is "correct," in the above described sense, we must proceed from an initial critical minimum meaning, not implying any political-philosophical commitment. In this sense, "sanity," "guilt," "responsibility," as well as other legal symbols, may be said to possess a general "correct meaning." "Guilt" and "Sanity" represent constructs or are abbreviated expressions signifying fulfillment of certain postulates upon which the law predicates ascription of answerability to a person. Legal "sanity" or "mental capacity" at criminal law denotes fulfillment of those postulates within the "responsibility" concept which pertain to the mental condition of the person charged. Such postulates are not limited to the substantive "sanity" notion but also comprise procedural and jurisdictional demands. Defining the specifics of such postulates, of course, is a policy problem.

In a democracy this policy, in turn, is defined by constitutional objectives and limitations. Some of the applicable constitutional tenets may be summarized thus: Abandonment of the exemption for "insanity" is constitutionally barred. An appropriate definition of exempting "insanity" is constitutionally imposed. It is constitutionally required that this exemption be integrated in a comprehensive democratic law of mental incapacity, including proper rules of procedure and of evidence and proof, as well as of proper disposition regarding the individuals concerned.

Of course, the first mentioned proposition would be deceptive unless there obtained a proper minimum definition of "sanity" at constitutional criminal law and procedure. In fact, the order of enumeration of the stated constitutional requisites should not be understood to imply that there obtains a rank hierarchy among them or an order of importance. These requisites are mutually interdependent. The "law of insanity," to be democratic, must be viewed in its totality bearing on each and every one of its issues. There can be no just solution of any of them apart from the total plan.

Thus, meaningfulness of a definition of "insanity" is predicated upon the scope and import of fitness to proceed, specifically, the defendant's fitness to raise, and personally conduct the litigation of, the issue of his former insanity. *Vice versa,* the scope of the definition of "fitness to proceed" should be geared to that which in most cases is at stake when this issue arises — "sanity" at the time pertinent to the conduct charged. The defendant must possess a certain measure of insight into his own former insanity as well as into his present relationship to it and, of course, such former insanity is no longer in realistic terms independent of its present reflection. The definitions of both fitness to proceed and insanity should be geared to the treatment prescribed by law for offenders found "unfit" or "not guilty by reason of insanity." That treatment, in turn, must be adjusted to the characteristics of those to be treated, and what these characteristics comprise depends on the scope of unfitness and of the exemption for insanity.

Defining the exemption for "insanity" as well as "fitness to proceed" constitutes a major problem of constitutional law, comparable — but not parallel — to that of defining "voluntariness" for the purpose of the "confession rule."[1] As is generally the case with issues of "due process," it is not even settled whether the proper constitutional definition is a historically established or rather a contemporary one. It has been assumed in this book that it is the latter, since "due process" no doubt requires such definition to be rational, that is, formulated in

---

[1]Compare SILVING, ESSAYS ON CRIMINAL PROCEDURE 256-269 (Dennis & Co., Buffalo, 1964).

the light of present rather than an obsolete scientific insight. Of course, this involves introducing into the law of "mental capacity" a "natural law" rather than a "positivistic" approach, if indeed such differentiation which has been the subject of debate among Justices of the Supreme Court of the United States[2] can be said to be itself sharply definable.[3] "Natural law," in the sense of a law adaptable to the changing insight and not merely to altered circumstances pertinent to decision making, is particularly apposite to solutions of problems which involve the mental element of crime.[4]

Today there obtains an urgent need for substituting psychologically, psychiatrically and sociologically realistic notions for the outmoded concepts of the quasi-psychology which dominates our law. That "psychology" is perhaps best described by the symbol used to represent the "mental element of crime" in French law — "elément moral," indicating a confusion of psychological and moral features. A comparable conception of "mental phenomena" as part of a "moral" discipline is reflected in our

---

[2]On this see particularly the controversy between Mr. Justice Frankfurter and Mr. Justice Black in Adamson v. California, 332 U.S. 46, 60-68, 69-92 (1947); Rochin v. California, 342 U.S. 165, 171-172, 175-177 (1952).

[3]Whether an argument is "positivistic" or one of "natural law," depends to a large extent on how one interprets "interpretation"—a feature which no law, however "positive," can eliminate. The difference between "positive" and "natural law" is just as relative as is that between "law" and "fact," "procedure" and "substance," etc. Compare Silving, *The Twilight Zone of Positive and Natural Law*, 43 CALIFORNIA LAW REVIEW 477 (1955); *Positive Natural Law*, 3 NATURAL LAW FORUM 24 (1958); *In re Eichmann: A Dilemma of Law and Morality*, 55 AMERICAN JOURNAL OF INTERNATIONAL LAW 307 (1961); also Introduction to DERECHO POSITIVO Y DERECHO NATURAL (Eudeba, Buenos Aires 1966), which is a Spanish translation of the two first-cited articles.

[4]One might argue that the appropriateness of a "natural law" or a "positivistic" approach should be deemed to depend on the type of issue that is involved. One could also contend that the "moral" framework of constitutional law pertinent to such issues as "responsibility," "guilt" or "sanity" is fixed and that only the social, psychological or psychiatric interpretations of factual phenomena should be regarded as changing. This contention, however, would disregard the fact that constitutional principles are themselves affected by changing interpretations of mental and social life, as has been perhaps best demonstrated in the famed desegregation cases. Brown v. Board of Education, 347 U.S. 483 (1954). This should not be taken as a denial that there are contexts which call for "more positivistic" treatment than others.

law's assignment to the jury of authority, when deciding upon
the "defense of insanity," to pass a "moral judgment."[5]

No pretense is advanced that there is any social issue — the
problem of "insanity" in a criminal case is such an issue —
which does not involve a "moral judgment," in the sense that a
"political judgment" is a type of "moral decision." The misleading aspect in assigning such decision making on the "insanity" issue to juries consists in categorizing the "moral" aspect
involved as part of the jury's "fact finding." Nor does the present
criticism imply denial that the difference between law and
fact is a relative one. This criticism is rather aimed at the un-
disclosed features of manipulating the symbols "moral" and
"mental," law and "fact" in decision making. By its medium
there are intruding into the law not only openly "moral issues"
but also disguised unconscious prejudices. Nowhere is the
described phenomenon more marked than in qualifications of
alcoholism and addiction as within or outside the exemption
for "insanity." Conceding or denying to these phenomena classification as "insanity" is mostly in ultimate analysis dependent
on the degree of the adjudicators' unconscious "moral" tolerance
or condemnation of the alcohol or drug habit. Evidence of
this may be found in the judges' reliance, in categorizing alcoholism or addiction as a "disease" or not "per se a disease," on
legislative action, either imposing upon those affected by the
intoxicant severe penalties or treating them as "ill."[6] A recently
invented notion of a "sickness" that is something other than a
"disease" is apparently intended to facilitate exceptional treatment in cases of particular minor crimes.[7] Even when commitment to an intoxicant is legislatively recognized to be a "disease,"
and thus immune from punishment, the unprincipled character
of our law of civil measures permits dubious methods guised as
welfare state action to suppress civil liberties.[8] The over-all picture is incoherent and limitations imposed upon man's power

---

[5]Durham v. United States, 214 F.2d 862, at 875-876 (D.C. Cir., 1954).

[6]United States v. Freeman, 357 F.2d 606, at 625 (2d Cir., 1966); Easter v.
District of Columbia, 361 F.2d 50, 51-53 (D.C. Cir., 1966).

[7]Ibid.

[8]Compare Intoxicants and Criminal Conduct, supra, at 334-337.

over man are not clearly drawn, so that there is ample opportunity for making the most defenseless individuals the victims of unconscious sadistic public aggression.

Purging the symbols of both criminal and administrative law and going back to fundamentals of legal thinking are not but matters of *elegantiae juris*. They are essential requisites of administering equal, even and balanced justice under a "rule of law." There is need not only for reformulation of definitions but, indeed, for a total reorientation of law, starting with a reconsideration of its ends. Rules and definitions, which are but parts of rules, must be so conceived as to serve operationally the chosen ends.

Thus, the exemption for "mental incapacity" must be derived from the function it is to perform within a system of criminal law oriented to given ends and not from a preconceived notion of "insanity" or from a confusing conception of "intent" which is allegedly negatived by "insanity." Modern psychiatry has found that "insanity" *per se* does not exist, but is rather a matter of qualification by others of a person's functioning with regard to others. "Intent" within the jurisprudential view set forth above, is itself a legal construct to be shaped on the basis of a sound policy choice. Indeed, if the conventional position that "insanity excludes intent" means what it appears to say in common language, it is false; in the light of realistic psychology, "insanity" more often releases than eliminates intent. On the other hand, if intent is not a psychological concept, there is no clarity even as to the type of concepts to which it belongs. Decision makers are trapped in a circuitous reasoning: they are deducting from their own constructs meanings which they had themselves put into them without conscious realization of the mechanism of jurisprudential exegesis that is involved.[9] In the light of a critical philosophy of law, neither "insanity" nor "intent" are existentially fixed realities; they are constructs shaped to meet either conscious or unconscious policy objectives.

In a rational policy scheme, the question, Whom should we

---

[9] Compare Ryu and Silving, *Toward a Rational System of Criminal Law*, 32 UNIVERSITY OF PUERTO RICO LAW REVIEW 119 (1963).

exempt? Must be derived from the answer to the query, Why should we exempt? The latter should be geared to the end of punishment, as that from which the exemption is to be made. It is the submission of the writer that neither reformation nor deterrence can be taken to be a primary end of punishment or of any other criminal law sanction so long as we do not know how to reform or how to deter offenders. The goal of punishment is symbolical; its aim is to assert and differentiate legal rules. Punishment is a means of documenting the "validity" of laws. Hence, exemption ought to be granted in those situations in which this goal is not applicable. A democratic community is a partnership in law, based on a constructive social contract. It is a community of those with a view to whom laws are made. Thus, anyone whose psychic organization deviates so considerably from that of other community members that law abidance is not actually expected of him should be exempt from punishment. The exemption is defined by the writer thus: "No punishment shall be imposed upon a person if at the time of engaging in criminal conduct and for some time prior thereto his integrative functioning was so impaired that he had a very considerably greater difficulty in complying with social demands and rules than does the majority of the members of the community."

One might argue that the proper standard of comparison should be the functioning of the "normal" or the "average community member," so that the exemption be granted to the "abnormal" or "nonaverage." But these are vague concepts, and there may be no concrete individual that might be realistically described as an "average person." I have hence chosen as a standard the functioning of the "majority of community members," but adjusted the discrepancy between the "average" and the "majority" standard by requiring the deviation to be very great.

The term "difficult" is used in an objective sense. It is not meant to indicate any endeavor to comply. A psychopath who does not attempt to observe the law may be included as well as a neurotic who yields despite utmost effort to conform. Nor does "difficult" imply a standard measured against a background of "free will." It is rather directed at the expectability of a conduct in the light of experience. A person is exempt if he belongs to a category of persons who in fact do not in most situations conform to social demands and rules.[9a]

The proper method of establishing a test of mental incapacity is to proceed from operational propositions oriented to a chosen policy and thereafter attempt to find for them the most appropriate verbal expressions. When it appears not feasible to draft a general rule that would unambiguously apply or not apply to given significant situations, a rational drafting technique requires resolution of the ambiguity by a further express specification of the legislative policy disposition rather than by analysis of more or less fixed terminology. Even in legislation in force there should be no objection to extension of the "mental incapacity" test in reliance not necessarily on its words but on statutory purpose where this benefits the defendant. *Nullum crimen sine lege* is intended to favor the defendant and thus does not bind the law of exemptions.

Where the "insanity" test is judicial rather than statutory, resort to hermeneutics as well as disavowal of any guiding principle under the motto of opposition to a "rule of labels" — both of these attitudes may be observed in the administration of the *Durham* rule,[10] even as interpreted in *McDonald* v. *United States*[11]—are wholly unjustified. In cases of alcoholism and drug addiction the ultimate issue is not whether the defendant's condition fits the term "disease," as thus interpreted,[12] but whether it can be included within the purpose or rationale

---

[9a]It has often been pointed out that even a psychotic patient complies with hospital rules. However, such rules are given directly and compliance is closely supervised. Even an animal obeys rules in this form. When I speak of "social demands and rules," I am referring to abstract norms rather than concrete immediate orders.

[10]*Supra*, note 5.

[11]312 F.2d 847, 851 (D.C. Cir., 1962).

[12]In Castle v. United States, 347 F.2d 492 (D.C. Cir., 1964), *cert. denied*, 381 U.S. 929, 953 (1965), though the "rule by labels" was vigorously criticized, no evidence appears of analyzing the addict's qualification for exemption within the ultimate "purpose" of the "insanity" rule. The decision was rather reached on the basis of a strict interpretation of the term "disease" as construed in the McDonald case.

of the exemption for insanity. The pertinent method in common law tradition is not but a process of "inclusion and exclusion" but also analogy. If need be, the exemption for "insanity" should be deliberately enlarged to cover persons of the mentioned category. Such judicial extension of the test involves no greater law-creativeness than was assumed by the Court of Appeals for the District of Columbia when it substituted *Durham* for *McNaghten* or by the Court of Appeals for the Second Circuit when it replaced the latter by the American Law Institute Model Penal Code formula.[13]

Neither the available tests nor their abundant criticisms permit expectation that clarity and consistency will be reached in the near future. The criticisms themselves are often "mislabeled," so that it is difficult to discern the precise ground of censure in issue. Frequently a much criticized term is maintained or even newly introduced with modifications which only slightly affect the point for which it has been criticized. Thus, for example, both the "product" notion and the "disease" concept, which underwent a devastating criticism under the *Durham* rule, occur in the American Law Institute Model Penal Code test, now adopted by the Court of Appeals for the Second Circuit.[14] In the Model Code test, the "incapacity" must be the "result [product] of the disease" — a proposition which except in narrowly defined situations a psychiatrist can no more assert than he can answer whether the conduct is a "product of the disease." Since in all dual tests the incapacity, however defined, must be one related to the act charged, one may well argue that there is implicit in this total structure a double "causation" requirement: between the "disease" and the "incapacity" and between the latter and the "act" charged.

Durham's use of the term "disease" has been criticized as having introduced a "rule by labels." The Court of Appeals for the District of Columbia hence proceeded to clarify that term in the following manner: "[A] mental disease . . . includes any abnormal condition of the mind which substantially affects

---

[13]United States v. Freeman, *supra,* note 6.

[14]*Ibid.* For the pertinent part of the Model Penal Code test see *infra,* text at note 16.

mental or emotional processes and substantially impairs behavior controls."[15] The Court of Appeals for the Second Circuit rejected the *Durham* test and adopted the American Law Institute Model Penal Code formula,[16] which in the part pertinent in the present context reads thus: "A person is not responsible for criminal conduct if . . . as a result of mental disease . . . he lacks substantial capacity . . . to conform his conduct to the requirements of law." Should the Second Circuit seek for a recent interpretation of the term "mental disease" — a term left undefined in the Model Code test—it might wish to consult the quoted construction of the same term within the *Durham* rule. The resulting formula would be "substantially" tautological: "A person is not responsible . . . if as a result of any abnormal condition of the mind which substantially impairs behavior controls, he lacks substantial capacity to conform his conduct to the requirements of the law."

The *Freeman* case involved an addict. Since within any conceivable definition of "substantial incapacity to conform" it would be difficult indeed to disqualify the addict, it may well be expected that future arguments will focus on the question of whether or not addiction is a "disease." Apparently, this is not believed to have been resolved by *Robinson* v. *California*,[17] though an explanation of the difference, if any, between "disease" or "illness" in the latter case and "disease" within either the *Durham* or the *Freeman* rule is outstanding. The salient fact in this regard is that in 1962, the year when the Model Penal Code's "responsibility" test appeared in the Official Draft, with the experience of the administration of the *Durham* test before them, the draftsmen of the Model Code should have squarely faced the issue of whether or not addiction ought to be deemed included in the term "disease" within the test which they advanced. But they expressly declined to deal with the difficult problem of the legal treatment of "addiction,"[18] even though they had shown admirable courage in dealing without

---

[15]McDonald v. United States, *supra*, note 11.
[16]Section 4.01, Proposed Official Draft (1962).
[17]370 U.S. 660, 667 (1962).
[18]Comment to § 6.12, Tent. Draft No. 2, at 31 (1954).

prejudgment with other sensitive issues such as that of homo-sexuality.[19]

The issue of the addict's "sanity" has recently come up in the context of "fitness to proceed"[20] which — it has been submitted by the writer — is closely related to the problem of exemption for "mental incapacity." It appeared that such fitness may be excluded either as a result of drug use [if the latter produced a brain syndrome] or as a result of abstinence [withdrawal being a medically recognized "disease"], which would seem to indicate that an addict's fitness is generally suspect. The United States Supreme Court has implicitly held that fitness to proceed need not amount to fitness to waive the assistance of counsel.[21] Yet, where the defendant is an addict, the District of Columbia Court of Appeals thought even such moderate degree of fitness as is required to enable the defendant to stand trial to be precarious.[22] It may be significant to note that in the conventional view, "capacity to commit a crime" requires a higher degree of mental health than does "fitness to proceed,"[23] although one might argue—wrongly, I believe—that the difference is one in kind and not in degree. In any event, there seems to be enough basis in contemporary interpretations of addiction as well as in legal authority to postulate an addict's qualification *per se* for the "mental incapacity" exemption.

The test recommended by the writer clearly applies to alcohol and drug addicts, and it presumptively applies also to habitual excessive users of intoxicants. This is so because it was deliberately devised to have a broad coverage, so that the defendant obtain the benefit of any doubt. Nevertheless, as a matter of special caution, it seems advisable to provide expressly for application of the "mental incapacity" exemption to such categories of persons. In borderline situations, the question should be not whether the persons concerned *are* "insane" or "diseased"

---

[19]Notice Sections 213.2 and 213.3, which do not comprise consensual deviate intercourse between adults.

[20]Hansford v. United States, 365 F.2d 920 (D.C. Cir., 1966).

[21]Westbrook v. Arizona, 384 U.S. 150 (1966).

[22]Hansford v. United States, *supra,* note 20.

[23]See *The Criminal Law of Mental Incapacity, supra,* at 161-167.

or "ill" but rather whether they should be treated in criminal law context *like* "mentally incapacitated" persons.

Undoubtedly, in the case of alcoholics and drug addicts treatment by measures is more appropriate than punishment. The rationale of the exemption for "mental incapacity" applies also to them. Rationally, laws should not be made with a view to being observed by persons thus handicapped; their punishment is not in a democratic country a proper means of asserting the law. Their treatment should be geared to their "dangerousness," if any, and to the type and degree of "danger" they represent, rather than to their "guilt."

In the case of drug addicts, such "dangerousness" is very often the product of legislation that bars their access to the drug which has become a necessity to them. The initial task in such situations is to reconsider that legislation, where the person concerned is an adult and would not but for such legislation cause harm to others.

In the complex of institutions and rules which I have chosen to call the "criminal law of mental incapacity" and which is an integral part of the over-all structure of "criminal law," special consideration is due in our law to the institution of "penal law measures," to be distinguished from "punishment," on the one hand, and from "civil law measures," on the other hand. Considerable effort, time and expense, as well as a substantial cost in human suffering can be spared by adopting this institution known in the civil law world. It is based on the view that "dangerousness" evincing from "criminal conduct" not attended by guilt is a *sui generis* social phenomenon. While punishment is not applicable, neither is a civil law measure the appropriate response, since the probability of future criminal activity when substantiated by a finding that the defendant had engaged in a criminal conduct in the case at hand imports into the situation an element of objectivity not shown to be present in civil commitment cases. Some civil law countries have recognized this differentiation of criminal law sanctions into "punishment" and "security measures." The advantage of such "dual system" may be realized by comparing the treatment of persons acquitted by reason of insanity in our law with that of such persons in countries adhering to a "dual system." The incoherence of our "monistic" approach, which actually recognizes only a "civil commitment" as an alternative to criminal punishment, has cast the law of the District of Columbia into chaos. In recent bills before the Congress of the United States it has become apparent that this approach may create new conflicts of Federal-State jurisdiction, if a person acquitted by reason of insanity in a Federal court must be referred to State authorities for "civil commitment," the latter being a matter of State law.[24]

In a "dual system" penal law "measures" are subject to *sui generis* legality safeguards and limitations. The awkward and probably unconstitutional devise of automatic commitment regardless of the type of criminal conduct in issue and subsequent habeas corpus, as well as the alternative of civil commitment proceedings after termination of a criminal trial are avoided. The criminal court in which the trial has been held decides also upon the "measures" to be imposed, if any, but it does so subject to special legality standards prescribed by statute for the administration of criminal law measures.

As in the case of persons acquitted by reason of insanity, so in cases of alcoholics and drug addicts involved in criminal proceedings, the criminal court imposes the pertinent measures, as provided for and limited by law.

As may be readily seen, this system has distinct advantages, among them particularly that of the trial court's special competence to judge the need for measures or for given types of measures as of the time of the termination of the trial. In the course of the latter, the court has had an opportunity to learn

---

[24]Two bills were submitted to the United States Senate, both purporting to provide for the commitment of certain individuals acquitted of Federal criminal charges solely by reason of insanity at the time of the alleged crime. The bill authored by Senator Tydings (S. 3753, 89th Congress, Second Session, Congressional Record, vol. 112, No. 140, August 23, 1966, p. 2) visualizes commitment of the persons concerned to the Federal Attorney General for hospitalization. Another bill, authored by Senator Robert Kennedy (S. 3689, see *ibid.* for discussion of differences), contemplates transfer of dangerous persons other than those who also endanger the safety of officers, property or other interests of the United States, to proper State authorities for commitment proceedings, if any, by the respective State.

what type of danger, if any, the defendant presents. While this should not be taken as a substitute for consulting experts, it certainly adds an important element to the court's qualification to pass judgment regarding the type of treatment proper for the defendant.[25] The writer has recommended adoption of a "dual system" in this country.[26]

It is possible to argue, to be sure, that the classification of offenders into those "guilty" and those "not guilty but dangerous," as postulated by a "dual system," is not warranted in the light of psychological insight into the varieties and multiple levels of motivations of action in each individual. No attempt is made to deny the fact that such classification would be wrong in a legal system oriented exclusively to psychological considerations and guided solely by the aim of protecting the community; in such a system a principle of complete individualization of sanctions would afford the appropriate solution. But this would require adopting an approach of total "psychoauthoritarianism" which cannot be tolerated in a "free society." The "dual system" aims at striking a balance between stress on individual freedom and legal certainty, on the one hand, and emphasis on community protection and welfare, on the other hand, subject to an over-all demand of maintaining a maximum degree of "rule of law."

However, the "dual system" in those civil law countries which adopted it has not been consistently applied. "Dangerousness" is often deemed a factor in determining the degree of punishment, which tends to blur the distinction between this personality trait and "guilt."[27] "Measures" are used in lieu of punish-

---

[25]Where the need for additional or substitute measures arises in the course of sentence execution, jurisdiction to impose them should be vested in a "court of sentence execution," which ought to supervise the process of execution of both punishment and measures. Availability of such a court is particularly important in the case of "measures," which must be administered more flexibly than punishment but which, nevertheless, should be surrounded by all guarantees of legality, including imposition and supervision by a court and not by a board or other administrative agency.

[26]Compare SILVING, CONSTITUENT ELEMENTS OF CRIME (Slovenko ed., Thomas, 1966).

[27]See Silving, *"Rule of Law" in Criminal Justice,* in Mueller, ed., ESSAYS IN CRIMINAL SCIENCE 77, 107, 117-119 (1961).

ment in certain types of cases but not in others in which they would be equally or even more warranted. A significant example of this feature of the "dual system" as operating in civil law countries may be found in the fact that in them punishment continues to be imposed on inadvertent negligence, though where it never occurs to the defendant that his conduct might constitute a risk punishing him is clearly inconsistent with the "guilt principle." Another instance, which is especially pertinent to the subject of this book, is the approach to criminal conduct in drink.

In Anglo-American law in cases of criminal conduct in a state of acute intoxication, the latter is disregarded except if it affects "specific intent." On the other hand, in many civil law countries full intoxication, unless incurred with intent or at least negligence as regards the ensuing criminality, constitutes an exemption ground. But there are special crime constructs which feature "inebriate conduct" (Rauschtat) as a separate punitive category without clear basis in criminal law theory. Nowhere has an attempt been made to deal with this type of conduct by "measures" rather than punitively. The reason for this lies in the fact that a defendant who engages in a criminal conduct while in a state of acute intoxication but is not a habitual alcoholic or an addict is not considered to be "dangerous." The criminal act is causally attributed exclusively to the intoxication, and the type of conduct engaged in is considered fortuitous.

To reach a rational policy decision on the treatment of inebriate conduct, it is necessary to reexamine the scientific assumptions, whether express or tacit, on which its present treatment is based. Contemporary insight into the phenomenon of such conduct, though by no means complete, has at any rate destroyed the belief that intoxication is an immediate and exclusive "cause" of the criminal conduct in which an affected individual engages. The present view is that intoxication merely reduces inhibitions permitting the individual's basic personality to express itself more freely than it does when he is sober. The criminal conduct, its nature and gravity, are determined by his total personality, and the very intoxication may be an incident of the operation of that personality. An individual who commits crime when in drink was "dangerous" before he ever drank.

The nature and gravity of the criminal conduct in which he engaged in drink afford a clue to the type and degree of his dangerousness. Unless in incurring intoxication he was at least reckless with regard to the ensuing criminal conduct, "guilt" — conceived democratically, in the sense of being geared to psychological reality—does not lie. Punishment is inappropriate. However, in the criminal conduct in which the defendant engaged, he has demonstrated his "dangerousness," and the latter warrants application of criminal law "measures of security and cure" aimed at protecting society against future criminality. The nature and degree of restrictiveness of the measures that may be imposed ought to be determined by the seriousness of the danger to be averted and the latter, as suggested, is best indicated by the gravity of the criminal conduct, though that conduct occurred while the actor was intoxicated. In this respect, considerations of scientific insight and those of legality point in the same direction. A "law of the act" has a basis in both.

It seems fitting to conclude this collection of essays with a forecast. The Supreme Court of the United States has shown "increasing concern during the last decade with the constitutional dimensions of the problem of competence to stand trial."[28] It has manifested no comparable interest in the problem of "mental capacity" pertinent to the conduct charged. This is regrettable, since there is noticeable a growing demand for abandonment of the exemption for "insanity."[29] I submit that such abandonment would be unconstitutional. The sooner the Supreme Court announces this, the less opportunity will be available for increase of the confusion surrounding the exemption.

The constitutional dimensions of the exemption are rooted in the philosophy of criminal justice in a "free society," basically, in its justification of the demand for law abidance. In this philosophy there is also implicit recognition of a realistic connection between competence to stand trial and "capacity" pertinent to the conduct charged. To be fit to stand trial, the de-

---

[28]Hansford v. United States, *supra*, note 20, n. 7 at 923.

[29]For a recent recommendation to this effect see Roche, *A Plea for the Abandonment of the Defense of Insanity*, in Slovenko, ed., CRIME, LAW AND CORRECTIONS 405 (Charles C Thomas, 1966).

fendant must have some basic insight into his own former insanity, but at the same time also be able personally—and not merely by his attorney—to dissociate himself from it if his former act was performed in a state of altered consciousness. On this depends his being a "subject" and not a mere "object" of the proceedings, hence the meaningfulness of the adversary system of our litigation.

The Supreme Court's increasing insistence on genuine, and not but formal, competence to stand trial[30] thus permits the prediction that it will soon also face the constitutional aspects of "mental capacity" pertinent to the conduct charged. If it holds a total abandonment of the exemption for "mental incapacity" to be unconstitutional, it must also deal with its minimum scope. When it does, it will no doubt in due course confront the vital issue of whether such exemption may be constitutionally denied to addicts.

---

[30]Thus, the Court recently noted that "it is contradictory to argue that a defendant may be incompetent, and yet knowingly and intelligently 'waive' his right to have the court determine his capacity to stand trial." Pate v. Robinson, 383 U.S. 375, 384, 86 S. Ct. 836, 841 (1966). Of course, there is no way to completely overcome the paradox of the defendant's competency to argue his own present or past insanity. Undoubtedly, within our system of law the defendant has the right to argue his own case even if he has no capacity to waive counsel. Where his competence to stand trial is challenged by the prosecution or the court, it would seem that the defendant cannot be denied the right to cross-examine opposing expert witnesses—the psychiatrists who claim, e.g., that he is now insane.

TABLE OF PENAL CODES, PENAL CODE DRAFTS, STATUTES AND OTHER GENERAL SOURCES*

Pages

AUSTRIA

Penal Code

Intoxication
  Crime in a state of — 306
  — as a defense 266

BOLIVIA

Penal Code Bill, 1943
  Actio libera in causa 264

BRAZIL

Penal Code

Prohibition to frequent certain places 313

CZECHOSLOVAKIA

Penal Code of 1950

Intoxication, Crime in state of — 306

DENMARK

Penal Code

Mental Incapacity
  Test of — 74, 77
  Treatment of the Mentally Incapacitated 202-205
Sociopaths, Special institution for — 75-76

---

*References are to pages of this book. Comprehensive sources, such as constitutions, codes, are italicized.

Pages

ENGLISH SOURCES**

Dangerous Drugs Act of 1920 309
Homicide Act of 1957 127
Mental Health Act of 1959 128
Royal Commission on Capital Punishment
  Critique of "Irresistible Impulse" Test 59, 93
  Mental Incapacity Test 127
Royal Medico-Psychological Association of Great Britain and Ireland (1924)
  Objective trial 168
Wolfenden Report
  Recidivism, Specificity of — 172-173
  Sanctioning limited to harm to others 31, 41, 178

FRANCE

Penal Code

Duty of Assistance 324-325
Mental Incapacity Test 104

GERMAN SOURCES

Dangerous Habitual Offenders, Act concerning 104, 280-281, 291

Penal Code

Alcoholics
  Assignment to institution 306, 310
Alternative fact findings, Conviction on — 283
Attempt 129
Crimes of Public Danger 281
Crimes in State of Intoxication,
        See Intoxication
Diminished Responsibility 129, 283, 306
  Assignment to institution of persons of — 306
Drug Addicts
  Assignment to institution of — 306, 310
Intoxication
  Crimes in State of —
    (§ 330a, Penal Code) 228, 278-286, 300, 306, 316, 330
  — as a defense,
        See Mental Incapacity

**The term "English" is used here informally. The sources included in this list would justify use of a broader term. The informal designation was chosen, because of changes of status of respective countries after the dates of the pertinent sources.

Pages

Mental Incapacity
   "Disturbance of consciousness" 243-244
   "Free will determination" 30
   Intoxication as a defense 231, 243, 279
   Test of — 101-111
Pandering 19
Slander 283
Unintended Consequences 285

Penal Code Draft 1956

Diminished Responsibility 129
Guilt 33-34
Mental Incapacity 111-112
— and Error 103

Penal Code Draft 1960

Diminished Responsibility 129
Guilt 34
"Illegal Act" 175
Mental Incapacity 103-104
— and Error 103
Sociopaths 205-206

Penal Code Draft 1962

Diminished Responsibility 129
Error 103
Guilt 33-34
— of Life Conduct 218
"Illegal Act" 175
Intoxication
   Actio libera in causa 287-288
   Crime in a State of Intoxication 282-291
Manslaughter 288
Mental Incapacity 103, 109, 111-112
Murder 288
Sentence 288

GREECE

Penal Code

Alcoholics, institutional treatment 310
Crime in State of Intoxication 306, 316

ISRAEL

Law concerning the Mentally Ill 1955
  Mental Incapacity
    Measures, Appeal 171
    Raising the Issue of — 148

Pages

ITALIAN SOURCES

Penal Code of 1930

Agreement to commit crime 296, 304, 308
Alcoholics,
 Assignment to an institution 305
Drug addicts,
 Assignment to an institution 308
"Intent," definition of — 257
Prohibition to frequent taverns 313
Putative Crime 296, 304
Solicitation not received by principal 296, 304

Penal Code Draft (Progetto Preliminare) 1949-50

Intoxication
 Sanctions for crime in state of — 276, 293-299
Report accompanying Draft 1949-1950 ....190, 297
 De facto recklessness 190, 298
 "Natural intent" 190, 297

POLAND

Penal Code of 1932

Actio libera in causa 266
Intoxication as a defense 263
The "Unreformable Offender" 77-78

RUMANIA

Penal Code

Prohibition to frequent taverns 313

SPANISH SOURCES

Penal Code of 1870

Mental Incapacity test 123

Penal Code of 1932

Actio libera in causa 266
Intoxication 263

Penal Code of 1944 (1963)

Actio libera in causa 266

Pages

Intoxication 263
Mental Incapacity test 120-125, 134

Siete Partidas

Mental Incapacity 123

SWEDEN

Penal Code

Mental Incapacity test 112-113

SWISS SOURCES

Federal Swiss Penal Code

Actio libera in causa 265-266
Alcoholics
  Assignment to an institution 306, 310
Diminished Responsibility 129, 265-266
  Assignment of persons of — to an institution 306
Drug Addicts
  Assignment to an institution 310
"Intent," definition of 257
Intoxication
  Crime in State of — 306, 316
  — as a defense 231, 263
Mental Incapacity 265-266
  Assignment to an institution 306
  "Disturbance of consciousness" 243-244
Petty Larceny in "State of Necessity" 247
Prohibition to frequent taverns 305, 313
Recidivism 192

Penal Code Project of 1893

"Dual System" in Sanctions 32

UNITED STATES JURISDICTIONS' SOURCES
American Law Institute Model Penal Code

Model Penal Code (Tentative Drafts are included)

"Abnormal Offender" 144
Critique of
  "Irresistible Impulse" test 93
  M'Naghten 92
"Culpability" 58
Drug Addicts, "state of necessity" 247
Drunkenness 326

Fitness to Proceed *Pages*
Test 161-162
Unfitness, Commitment 169, 171-172
Homosexual Offenses 348
Incapacity to have a specific state of mind 128
Intoxication 258, 276
Mental Incapacity (Insanity)
Affirmative defense 146-147
Psychiatric Examination in advance 153
Constitutionality 155
Psychiatric testimony
Qualification, Scope 152-153, 158-159
Test of — 94-102, 104, 130, 346-347
"as a result of" 97-98
"Free will" formula 142
Incapacity
"to appreciate" 94-97, 102
"to conform" 94, 96-100, 102
"Involuntariness" 239
"Mental disease or defect" 94, 98, 130-131
"Sociopaths" excluded 237
"Substantial" 98-99, 104

California

Penal Code
Adult Authority, discretion 22

Federal Sources

Bills in Congress
Bills for commitment of persons acquitted of Federal criminal charges
solely by reason of insanity 350

Constitution of the United States
Acquittal by reason of insanity
Assignment to an Institution 207-211
Other measures 211-213
Release 172
Addicts 216, 319
Alcoholics 215, 238
Cruel and unusual punishment 216, 319
Fitness to proceed 348, 353-354
Test of — 162-165, 353-354
Trial of unfit person 162, 168, 172
Mental Incapacity (Insanity) 353
Test 42-45
Physician's freedom to exercise his profession 324-325

Pages

Privacy rights 321-322, 334-335
Procedural rights 321-322, 336
Prohibition of "status crimes" 216, 319
Separation of Church and State 331, 334

District of Columbia Code

Acquittal solely by reason of insanity
  Commitment 147
  Release after commitment 172, 185
Doctor-patient privilege 160
Murder, definition 126
Rehabilitation of Alcoholics 238

Federal Laws

Harrison Narcotic Law 248, 319
Narcotic Addict Rehabilitation Act 337
Narcotic Drug Import and Export Act 319

Massachusetts Sources

Briggs Law
  Pre-trial psychiatric examination 153-154
Massachusetts Judicial Council
  Objective trial 168

New York Sources

Arrested Narcotic Addict Commitment Act of 1962 ....323, 335
Mental Hygiene Law, as amended 1966 ....335, 337
New York Academy of Medicine
  Committee on Public Health, Subcommittee on Drug Addiction (1955)......309
  Report (1963) 310
Revised Penal Law (effective 1967) 319

PUERTO RICAN SOURCES

Code of Criminal Procedure

Indeterminate sentence 300

Constitution of the Commonwealth

Honor, reputation and family life protected 230
Man's Dignity, inviolability of — 230, 334
Narcotics Act of Puerto Rico of 1959 319

Penal Code

Murder in the Second Degree 300

YUGOSLAVIA

Penal Code of 1951

Intoxication 272, 294

TABLE OF CASES *

Pages

AUSTRALIA

Attorney-General for the State of South Australia v. Brown 158

ENGLAND

Arnold's Case 81
Bellingham's Case 82
Director of Public Prosecutions v. Beard 256-258, 264-265
Director of Public Prosecutions v. Smith 261
Earl Ferrers Case 81
Hadfield's Case 114
M'Naghten's Case......4, 6, 79-93, 113, 127, 130-131, 142, 159-160, 189, 234, 235, 248
Regina v. Ward 261
Rex v. Charlson 184

FRANCE

Ministère public et Noinin c. Dunan 324

GERMANY

Reichsgericht:
    60 RGSt. 29, 30 (actio libera in causa) 266, 279
    68 RGSt. 257 (conviction on alternative fact findings) 283
    73 RGSt. 121 ("mental debility") 112
    73 RGSt. 182 (actio libera in causa) 266
    RG DR 1939 ("moral insanity") 110
Bundesgerichtshof:
    2 BGHSt. 14, 17-20 (interpretation of § 330a, Penal Code 284
    2 BGHSt. 194 (defense of legal error) 27, 102, 106, 217
    3 BGHSt. 195 ("disturbance of consciousness") 109
    BGHSt., Neue Juristische Wochenschrift 1953, 513 (error of law) 96-97
    6 BGHSt. 46 (moral reference terms) 19, 31, 41
    7 BGHSt. 82 (mandatory expert evidence) 151
    7 BGHSt. 327 (actio libera in causa) 279
    BGHSt., Gotdammers Archiv 1955, 269 ("disturbance of consciousness")....107
    BGHSt., Neue Juristische Wochenschrift 1955, 1726
      ("disturbance of consciousness") 112

---

*References are to pages of this book. Where a case is not identified by names of the parties the subject-matter is indicated.

Pages

9 BGHSt. 390 (interpretation of § 330a, Penal Code) 283, 285
10 BGHSt. 247 (interpretation of § 330a, Penal Code) 282
BGHSt., Neue Juristische Wochenschrift 1957, 1484 ("natural intent").......191
BGHSt., Neue Juristische Wochenschrift 1958, 266
  ("disturbance of consciousness") --108-109, 231
BGHSt., Juristische Rundschau 1958, 28
  (interpretation of § 330a, Penal Code) ---------------------------282, 285, 289

ITALY

Corte di Cassazione, 61 Giustizia Penale II, 183 (mental incapacity test)......122
Corte di Cassazione, 61 Giustizia Penale II, 647 (psychological causation)....266

POLAND

Supreme Court, Collection of Supreme Court Decisions 1952, Item 67, at 228
  (notion of "unreformable offenders") ---77-78

SPAIN

Tribunal Supremo, October 5, 1944, Quintano Ripolles (mental incapacity)....123
Tribunal Supremo, 15-4-948, Aranzadi 1960, 572
  ("temporary mental disturbance") --125
Tribunal Supremo, 24-1-949, Aranzadi 1960, 46 (mental incapacity).......124, 125
Tribunal Supremo, 9-5-949, Aranzadi 1960, 662
  ("temporary mental disturbance") --124

UNITED STATES JURISDICTIONS

Adamson v. California --341
Ashley v. Pescor --162
Baxstrom v. Herold --47, 336
Blackburn v. Alabama --64
Blocker v. United States--------------------------48, 54, 69, 188, 205, 237-238, 240, 247
Boardman v. Woodman --115
Bostic v. United States --126
Brown v. Board of Education ---341
Bullock v. United States --126
Burnett v. People --320
Butchers' Union Slaughter-House Co. v. Crescent City Co.-------------------------325
Carter v. United States --------------------------43, 49, 98, 119-120, 121, 187, 188, 239
Castle v. United States -----------------------------------235-238, 240, 322, 331, 345
Diaz v. Campos --145
Douglas v. California --230-231
Durham v. United States.........42-43, 48-49, 64-70, 79-80, 89, 97-98, 116-121, 123,
    131-134, 142, 159, 187-188, 295, 214-215, 220, 235-237, 330-332, 342, 345, 347
Dusky v. United States --165
Eagles v. Samuels --145
Early v. Tinsley --155

Pages

Easter v. District of Columbia................................215-216, 238-240, 327, 329, 342
Fisher v. United States 126-128
Griswold v. Connecticut 42, 334
Hansford v. United States 348, 353
Holloway v. United States 63-64, 121, 133
Hough v. United States 183, 186, 198
Isaac v. United States 185
Jackson v. Commonwealth 137
Jessner v. State 155-156
Jimenez v. Jones 165
Keenan v. Commonwealth 218
Leland v. Oregon 43, 60, 121
Linder v. United States 248
Linkletter v. Walker 322
Lyles v. United States 68
Lynch v. Overholser 147-148, 318
McDonald v. United States 43, 237, 239, 332, 345, 347
McNally v. Hill 145
Mapp v. Ohio 321-322
Martinez Rodriguez v. Delgado 219, 322
Massiah v. United States 322
Nestlerode v. United States 274
O'Beirne v. Overholser 205
Overholser v. Leach 185, 208-209
Overholser v. Lynch 147, 162, 209-210
Overholser v. Russell 207-209
Parker v. Ellis 145
Pate v. Robinson 354
People v. Burson 153
People v. Defore 321
People v. Koerber 260, 262
People v. Van Zandt 260
Pueblo v. Alsina 84, 96
Pueblo v. Sanchez Maldonado 64, 152
Ragsdale v. Overholser 187, 207-210
Robinson v. California 42, 216, 219, 247, 319, 329, 347
Rochin v. California 341
Rosenfield v. Overholser 197
Sabens v. United States 268
Sinclair v. State 11
Starr v. United States 207
State v. Harrison 51, 214
State v. Jones 65, 95, 114-116, 187
State v. Lange 11
State v. Livingston 155
State v. Lucas 153
State v. Myers 155, 160

Pages

State v. Pike 65, 113-115, 120, 185, 232
State v. Quigley 239
State v. Rider 267
State v. Strasburg 11
State v. Swinburne 155
Tayler v. United States 159
Turner v. Commonwealth 126
United States v. Ballard 142
United States v. Currens 159, 188, 205
United States v. Drew 216, 240, 257, 327
United States v. Freeman 6, 238-240, 327, 328, 342, 346-347
United States v. Naples 158, 167
United States v. Pound 170
United States v. Wilson 126
Westbrook v. Arizona 168, 348
Wagner v. Jauregg 104
Williams v. New York 46

INDEX OF CITED AUTHORS*

Abraham, K., 221
Alexander and Healy, 97, 172
Alexander and Ross, ed., 135, 189
Alexander and Staub, 20, 22, 75, 139
Andanaes, 77
Anslinger and Tompkins, 227
Arieti, ed., 233, 243, 308, 314, 326
Aristotle, 217
Arnold, Thurman, 63-64
Aschaffenburg, 104

Bacon, S., 222
Bainton, 224, 243
Banay, 251, 252, 290
Beling, 26
Bentham, 19, 56
Bettiol, 293-295
Bockelmann, 19, 31
Bowman and Jellinek, 253, 290
Bridgman, 54
Bromberg and Cleckley, 137

Cahn, 32
Carnap, 65
Carrara, 124
Cleckley, 93
    See also Bromberg and —
Collings, 261
Collinson, 82

Daily, 310
Darwin, 29
Davidson, 74, 93

de Ropp, 227
Devlin (Lord Justice), 32, 41, 61, 178
Dohna, 26
Dollard and Miller, 222
Donnelly,
    See Lasswell and —

Eaton, 168
Edwards, 127, 128
Efron,
    See Zeller and —
Eissler, ed., 87-88
Ellison and Haas, 80
Engel and Metall, ed., 12
Engisch, 13

Farberow,
    See Shneidman and —, ed.
Fenichel, 163, 221, 319
Ferri, 28, 81
Finestone, 225
Flower, 153
Frank, Ph., 10
Frank, R., 25-26
Freud, S., 19, 40, 51, 80, 90, 163-164,
    167, 206
Freudenthal, 26

Garofalo, 28, 44, 181
Gillespie,
    See Henderson and —
Glover, 191, 221, 227, 228, 248
Goldschmidt, J., 26

*References are to pages of this book.
Author's initials are included where necessary for purposes of identification.

Goldstein and Katz, 172
Greenberg, L., 252-253
Grimm, H., 182
Gross, H., 167
Guttmacher, 21, 92, 151-152
  See also Guttmacher and Weihofen
Guttmacher and Weihofen, 159-160

Haas,
  See Ellison and —
Haggard and Jellinek, 215, 221, 228,
  234, 243, 312
Hakeem, 22, 172
Hall, J., 59, 92, 228, 248, 258, 277
Harno, 137
Hartmann, H., 88
Hegel, 29-30, 56
Heidegger, 217
Heldmann, 113
Henderson and Gillespie, 184, 251
Heuermann, 256, 294-295, 298, 313
Hoch and Zubin, ed., 74, 151-152, 153
Horton, 224
Hughes, 127
Hume, 115
Hurwitz, 183, 203

Jacobson, E., 164
Jellinek, 242, 252, 265, 326
  See also Bowman and —;
    Haggard and —
Jescheck, 19
Jiménez de Asúa, 181

Kant, 26, 29-30, 56
Katz, J.,
  See Goldstein and —
Kaufmann, F., 36-37, 71-72
Kelsen, 12, 23, 51-52, 71, 115
King, R., 227
Knight, 221, 222

Kohlrausch-Lange, 111, 190, 281, 290,
  306
Kolb, L., 6, 225
  See also Noyes and —
Krash, 160, 170, 172, 207

Landis, C., 222
Lang-Hinrichsen, ed., 256
Lange,
  See Kohlrausch-Lange
Lasswell and Donnelly, 32
Lewin, K., 121
Lindesmith, 309
Lisansky, 222
Loeffler, 273
Lombroso, 28
López-Rey, 192, 264
Lorand, 221-222
Lorenz, 29

MacDonald, 91, 173
Macdonald, ed., xii, 51
MacNiven, 74, 168, 182
Manzini, 294
Maurach, 107, 110, 190, 218, 279, 283
Mayer, M. E., 62
Menninger, K. A., 22, 87, 181, 221, 222,
  226, 320
Metall,
  See Engel and —, ed.
Mezger, 30, 33, 66-67, 107
Michael and Wechsler, 74-75
Miller, N. E.,
  See Dollard and —
Mira y López, 181
Miranda, A., xi, 138
Mittermaier, 167
Morris, N., 83, 84, 172, 200
Mueller, 164
  See also Mueller, ed.
Mueller, ed., 20, 56-57, 83, 127, 129,
  142, 146, 154, 159, 174, 176-177, 184,
  188, 192, 199, 211, 217, 241, 351
Mulder, 184

Nice, ed., 168
Noyes and Kolb, 136, 184-185, 205, 220, 222, 243, 252, 312
Nyswander, 225, 234, 308

Olesa Muñido, 179, 181, 303, 305
Overholser, 91, 151, 154

Perkins, 83, 126, 266-267
Pisani, B. J., 310
Planck, 229
Prevezer, 127

Quintano Ripolles, 82, 123-125

Radó, 222
Radzinowicz and Turner, ed., 74, 168
Ranieri, 294
Rapaport, 221
Rasor,
    See Wikler and —
Ray, Isaac, 116, 125
Reid, 65
Reik, L. E., 116, 117, 233
Reik, Th., 20, 75
Reiwald, 20
Roche, 54, 59, 64, 87, 118-119, 137, 143, 353
Romano, 294
Rosenbaum,
    See Zwerling and —
Russell-Turner, 81, 82, 188, 243
Ryu, xi, 16
    See also Ryu and Silving
Ryu and Silving, 24, 27, 28, 33-34, 58, 73, 81-83, 85, 175, 217-18, 247, 261, 303, 343

Saltelli, 294
Scheler, 29
Schneider, K., 104-105
Schneider, W. R., 67
Schönke-Schröder, 107, 110
Schwarz, O., 164
Schuster, C., 12
Seavey, 273
Seelig, 30, 59, 104-107
Shneidman and Farberow, ed., 320
Silving, 4, 14, 20, 32, 46, 56-57, 66, 72-73, 83, 97, 129, 141-142, 146, 154, 159, 162, 174-177, 188, 192, 199, 200, 211, 216-217, 241-242, 245, 249, 262, 269, 309, 311, 318, 320, 323-324, 327-328, 340-341, 348, 351
Skolnick, 162-164
Slovenko, vii-ix
Slovenko, ed., xi, 73, 327, 351, 353
Staub,
    See Alexander and —
Stevenson, 12
Stoos, 32
Storch, 29
Szasz, 48, 232
Szittya, 320

St. Thomas, 273
Thompson, 233, 243, 326
Thomson, 217
Tompkins,
    See Anslinger and —
Turner, ed., 81
    See also Radzinowicz and —, ed.;
    Russell-Turner

Vance, 67

Waaben, 204
Waelder, 22
Watson, 21

Webster, 97
Wechsler, 105
  See also Michael and Wechsler
Welzel, 26-29, 30, 33-34, 39, 182
Wertham, 22
Whitehead, 5
Whitehorn, 91, 135, 189
Wikler and Rasor, 225
Williams, G., 184, 258, 260-261, 277
Williams, H. S., 226
Wisdom, J., 65, 89
Wittels, 75
Wittgenstein, 12, 13, 65

Zeller and Efron, 314
Zwerling and Rosenbaum, 314

Collective Authorship:
Corpus Juris Secundum, 155
Council of Florence (1439), 223
Law Review Notes:
  Columbia Law Review, 215, 258, 262
  Yale Law Journal, 153, 167, 200
United Nations, 203, 204
World Health Organization, 226, 227, 234

SUBJECT INDEX *

A

Abnormal, 305, 344
  Offender, 144
  state, 307-308
Accidental, 167, 184-185, 229, 232, 244,
  259, 315-316
  Intoxication, See Intoxication
Acquittal by reason of mental
  incapacity, 146, 171-213, 241
  Automatic commitment, 172, 197,
    207-213
  Constitutionality, 209-213
  Commitment after finding of danger-
    ousness, 212-213
  Measures, 171-213
    Dangerousness, see latter title
    Maximum and minimum periods,
      187, 197-198
    Measures other than detention, 199
    Periodic examination, 213
    Proportionality of measures to dan-
      ger, 182-187, 196-199
  Release, 185, 207
  See also Addiction; Alcoholism
Act
  as indicium of dangerousness, 179-
    196
  as legality safeguard, 174-178
  "Criminal Law of the Act," 217, 353
  "Voluntary act," 184
Actio Libera in Causa, 264-290, 295
  Intoxication followed by crime, 270-
    271
  Intoxication for the purpose of crime
    commission, 264
  Negligent —, 271
  Psychological causation, 266-268
  Reckless —, 272-274, 279

Addiction
  Acquittal by reason of mental inca-
    pacity, 235, 249, 311-313, 339
  Addict by birth, 216
  and crime, 220, 227
  and mental disease, 233
  and suicide, 323-324
  as an "illness," 216, 336, 347
  Addictive drugs, 227
  Biblical clues to —, 225
  Causes of —, 236
  Commitment
    Civil or criminal, 186, 219, 242,
      350
    Compulsory, 248
    Consideration for commitment or
      ambulatory treatment, 248, 310-
      311
    Maximum and minimum periods,
      311-313
  Complicity in —, 324-325
    See also Physicians
  Compulsory treatment, 308-311, 336
  Constitutional issues, 216, 219, 230,
    246, 248, 334-337
  Culture impact, 221, 224-225
  Cure, 312
  Dangerousness, 242, 249, 311, 349
  Definition, 240, 241
  Drugs
    Addictive —, see above
    Consumption of drugs, 220, 233
    Purchase of drugs, 235
    Use and possession of drugs, 246,
      319-326, 334-335
    Use and possession of drugs in
      public, 323
  Durham rule, applicability to addicts,
    235-238, 330-332, 347
  Fitness to proceed, 348

---

*References are to pages of this book.

371

Free will, 238-239, 245-246
Guilt in —, 247
Guilt of Life Conduct (Lebensfüh-
rungsschuld), 216-219, 240
Harm of —, 226
Informers, role of —, 337
Labels, role of — in classification of
addiction, 240, 330-331
M'Naghten, applicability to addicts,
234, 235
Measures for addicts, 241, 248, 312-
313, 349-350
Maxima and minima, 249
Mental disease, issue of its inclusion
of addiction, 236-238, 245-246,
330, 347
Mental incapacity (insanity), appli-
cability to addiction, 232-241,
246-248, 308, 330-333
Presumption of mental incapacity,
233, 241, 246, 308
Model Penal Code, views on addic-
tion, 238, 239, 347
Moralizing approach to —, 220
Necessity, "state of necessity" in ad-
diction, 235, 240, 247-248
Physicians
Complicity in addiction, 324
Duty to alleviate pain, 324-325
Freedom of profession, 230, 248,
325
Treatment, ambulatory or institu-
tionalized, 248-249
Poverty, role in crimes of addicts,
231
Privacy, right of addicts, 42, 332, 334
Psychological and sociological inter-
pretation of —, 225-227, 233-234
Status crime, 216, 219, 319
Use and possession, see Drugs, above
Voluntary or involuntary activity,
240-241
Withdrawal, 348
Compulsory, 309-310
Withdrawal symptoms, 235-236,
240-241
World Health Organization views on
—, 226-227, 234

Alcohol
addicts, 234, 241
and crime, 227
as cause of crime, 220
legislation, 326-328
Appearing in public under the in-
fluence of —, 239, 326-327
Bible, attitude toward —, 223-224
Culture patterns, 221, 243
Driving under the influence of —,
327-328
Impact of — consumption, 251-256
Jewish and Christian rites, 223-224
Primitive customs, 223, 242
Religious customs, 243
Alcoholic
criminality, 229
deterioration, 234, 312
Alcoholism
Acquittal by reason of mental inca-
pacity, 311-313
as a "sickness," 238, 328-329
as a "mental disease," 232-233, 329
Causes of —, 230
Commitment
Maximum and minimum periods,
312-313
Considerations for commitment or
ambulatory treatment, 248, 311
Compulsory treatment, 308-313
Cure, 312
Dangerousness, 311
Dipsomania, 232-233
Dual system of sanctions, 312-313,
330
"Excess," 221-222, 242-243
Guilt of Life Conduct, 240
Habitual drinker, 228, 244
Habitual drunkard, 219, 228, 230
Measures for alcoholics, 312-313, 330
Mental incapacity, applicability to
alcoholism, 329-330
Presumption of mental incapacity,
233, 308
Prohibition to frequent taverns, 305
Psychological and sociological inter-
pretations of —, 221-222
Withdrawal, compulsory or consen-

sual, 308-309

World Health Organization views on —, 284

Amens (Id Est) Sine Mente, 188-189

Amnesia, 167, 277

Animal Psychology, 29

Appearing Under the Influence, see Alcohol

"As a Result of," 97-98, 346

Assertion of Law, see Ends of Criminal Law

Automatism, 184-185

B

Bible

Alcohol, attitude toward, 223-224

Drugs, attitude toward, 224-225

Free will, 105

"Good and evil" test of responsibility, 81-82

Insanity

as Divine inspiration, 83

as evil spirit, 111

as possession by devils, 111

Knowability of law as condition of responsibility, 86

Man's power over man, 213

Meaning of name, 52

Blameworthiness, 26-30, 61-71

Community judgment on blameworthiness, 62

See also Guilt

C

Canon Law, 82

Capacity

to appreciate, 95-97, 103-107

to commit crime, 59-60

to conform, 95-98, 103-107, 147

Substantial —, 59-60, 98-100

Causation, 115-120, 207

Alcohol and drugs, "causal" relationship to crime, 220, 227, 246

Causes of addiction, see Addiction

Causes of drinking, see Alcoholism

Psychological —, 266-268

See also "As a result of"; "Product of"

Commitment, 47-48, 170, 174, 201, 208, 209, 242, 312, 336

Communication

Interdisciplinary —, 5-9, 43, 53, 132

Labels, rule by, 48-50, 237, 240, 346-347

Language, see latter title

Meaning, see latter title

Community

judgment, 62

standard, 73, 221, 234

disobedience to the —, 73

Consequences of Conduct

Accidental —, 195, 273

Crimes aggravated by —, 285

Constitutional Law, 40-45, 209, 211, 220, 230, 232, 238, 245, 248, 318-328, 339-340

Cruel and unusual punishment, 230, 319, 334

Dignity of Man, 230, 322, 334

Due Process, 230, 247, 319, 335

Equality, 231

Honor, reputation and family life, 230

Privacy, 42, 332, 334

Procedural parallel, 321-322

Separation of Church and State, 331

See also Crimes Created by Alcohol and Narcotics Legislation

Courts' System, 7-8, 159, 176, 242, 312

Crimes Created by Alcohol and Drug Legislation, 318-328

"Criminal"

contrasted with "civil," 174-175, 201-202, 207-208, 211, 219, 242, 349

"Criminal conduct," 242

as indicium of dangerousness, 174, 178, 249

as legality safeguard, 174-177, 195

"Criminal law of the act," 176-178, 217, 353

"Criminal law of the actor," 176-177, 181, 216-220

Culpability, 58

Culture, Perpetuation of, 220

Custos Morum, State as, 220

D

Dangerousness, 45-50, 149, 178, 209-210, 249, 303, 333, 349, 353
Finding of —, 212
Indicia of —, 180-196
Criminal "act" as indicium of —, 180-187, 197
Conduct in drink, 229
Mental state of the insane as indicium of—, 189
De facto recklessness, 190-191, 317
"Natural intent," 190-191, 317
Mental state of the intoxicated as indicium of —, 297, 298
De facto recklessness, 298, 317
"Natural intent," 278, 297-298, 317
Plurality of criminal conduct as indicium of —, 191-195
Hearing on —, 197, 211-212
Irrebuttable presumption of — in certain crimes, 197, 211-212
Measures, Proportionality to —, see Measures
Periodic reexamination of —, 213
Proof of —
Burden of proof, 197, 212
Degree of proof, 198, 199, 212
Separation of — and guilt, 304
De Facto Recklessness, 190-191, 298, 317
Defense of Insanity
Abandoning it, 44-45, 339
Affirmative defense, 147-149, 353
Delirium Tremens, 215-216
Determinism, 181, 216
Deterrence, see Ends and Means of Criminal Law
Diminished Responsibility, 112, 128-130, 174
"Disease," see Mental Disease
"Disturbance of Consciousness," 107-109, 231, 243-244, 262
" 'Dope-Fiend' Bugaboo," 226
Driving Under the Influence of Alcohol, see Alcohol

Drugs
Ancient history, 224-225
Attitudes to drug use, 224-227
Narcotic drugs
Barbiturates, 250
Cocaine, 250
Heroin, 227
Marijuana, 227
Morphine, 234-235
See also Addiction; Crimes Created by Alcohol and Drug Legislation
Dual System of Sanctions, 32, 40, 46-47, 145-146, 173-179, 232, 241, 303-333, 349-352

E

Ends and Means of Criminal Law, 17-23, 41-42, 145, 343
Assertion of Law, 77-78, 204, 344
Community Protection, 46-47, 145, 147, 303, 314, 335
Deterrence, 74-76, 100-101, 204
Non-deterrable offenders, 205-206
Reformation, 76-77, 204
Unreformable offenders, 76-77
Retribution, 20
Error, Law of, 3-4, 39, 73, 81-86, 95, 102-103, 106
Exemption from Responsibility
Exemptions other than those for mental incapacity, 3-4
Philosophy underlying —, 56-57
Rationale of exemption for
addicts and alcoholics, 232-250
intoxicated offenders, 250-256, 262-264
mentally incapacitated (insane) offenders, 57-79, 134-137, 142-143
Experts
Experts' views on the treatment of drug addiction and alcoholism, 308-312
Personality evaluation to ascertain dangerousness, 195-196, 200
Psychiatric examination
Assignment to a mental hospital for examination, 155-156
Constitutional issue, 155-156

Pre-disposition examination, 161, 200
Preliminary examination, 153-157
Procedure in recidivism cases, 154-155
Psychiatric and Sociological Examinations Center, 146, 154, 161, 180, 208, 309
Psychiatric Court Clinic, 156
Psychiatrist, appointed, 156-157
Psychiatric testimony, 133, 157-161, 212

F

Fact, 220-221
Question of —, 232-233, 236
See also "Law-Fact" Dichotomy
Fitness to Proceed
Constitutional dimensions of problem of—, 353-354
Doubt regarding —, 151-157
Evidence regarding —, 156-157
Measures for persons unfit to proceed, 169-171
Objective trial, 168-169
Relation of unfitness to proceed to mental incapacity as regards the act charged, 144-146, 151
Trial of defendant unfit to proceed, 162-164
Test of —, 161-168
Freedom, Freely, Free, 21, 187, 230
Free society, 8, 39-45, 47-48, 73, 242, 334, 353
Free will, 29-30, 49, 106, 121, 142, 187-188, 203, 229, 230, 264, 302, 319-320, 345
"Free determination of the will" (freie Willensbestimmung), 30, 104-105
Free will and prediction of conduct, 229

G

"Good and Evil," 81
Guilt, 9-15, 23-45, 245, 247, 304, 338-339, 341, 353

as blameworthiness, 26-30, 61-71
as directive of punishment, 57-74
as "intent," 58-61
of becoming intoxicated, 306
of life conduct, 42, 216-219, 228, 240, 247
principle, 49, 297
No punishment in excess of —, 145-146, 305
No punishment without — (nulla poena sine culpa), 353
Normative theory of —, 24-28, 32
Phenomenological notion of —, 36-39, 71-74, 174
Psychological theory of —, 24-28, 32
Separation of — and dangerousness, 304

H

Habeas Corpus, 145, 210
Habitual
drinker, 230, 232
drug user, 232
drunkard, 219, 228
offender, 192, 199-202
"Habitually to Excess"
Definition, 244-245
Harm
Crime predicated upon —, 177-178, 217
Homosexuality, 347
and alcoholism, 222

I

"Illness"
that is not necessarily a "disease," 216, 236, 342, 349
Integrative Functioning, 138-139, 221, 234, 241, 245, 262
Intent, 34-35, 189, 343
Evil —, 121
as knowledge and will, 121-122
in mental illness, 59-61, 118-119
Guilt as —, see Guilt
Malice aforethought, 126
Intoxication
Accidental —, 276, 301, 315-317, 333

Actio libera in causa, see latter title

Causation in the relationship of alcohol and crime, 228, 246, 250-256, 352

Causes of drinking, 221-223

Crime commission while in a state of intoxication, 228, 231, 244, 246, 352

Comparative law, 255-256, 258-264

Exemption from responsibility by reason of "disturbance of consciousness," 107, 231, 243-244, 262-264

Measures suggested as sanctions, 231, 250, 301-302, 314-318, 352

Maximum and minimum measures, 315-316

Special mental incapacity exemption, 250, 332-333

Crime of self-intoxication (special crime), 273, 278-290, 306

Intent but no will, 257, 262

Intoxicated offender

Dangerousness of intoxicated offender, test, 275, 353

Dual system, 232, 253-255

Guilt of intoxicated offender, 228, 253

Measures for intoxicated offender, see above

Mental state of intoxicated offender, see Dangerousness

Punishment of intoxicated offender, 230, 256-258

See also *Actio libera in causa;* special crime of self-intoxication, above

as aggravation ground, 255-256

as exemption ground, 229, 231

as mitigation ground, 263

excluding specific intent, 257-262

Involuntary —, 228, 238, 276, 301

Pathological —, 243, 245-246

Public —, 238

Scientific studies of druken conduct, 250-256

Involuntary, 238, 239, 240

intoxication, see Intoxication

conduct, 241

Irresistible impulse, 93-94

J

Judge of Sentence Execution, 46

Jury

Insanity as a question of fact, 236

Law-fact dichotomy, 63-69

Insanity as a matter of moral judgment, 69, 221

Judging senseless questions, 63-65

K

Knowledge

and will, 101, 121-124, 134

of law in insanity tests, 73, 82-85, 94-97

test in M'Naghten, 81-88:

of law, 82-83

of nature and quality of the act, 83

test in Model Penal Code, 94-97

L

Labels, See Communication

Language

Philosophy of —, 52-55

Psychoanalytical communication, 90

Verbalization, 90-92, 158

See also Communication

Law-Fact Dichotomy, 55, 63-67

Manipulating the —, 342

See also Jury

Laymen

Scope of legal knowledge, 85

View of insane conduct, 151-153

Legality, 69-70, 167, 174, 178, 180, 194, 195, 204, 205, 232, 241, 247, 301, 303, 304, 336

Lie Detectors, 162-164

M

Meaning, 5-15

Incorrect usage, 8-9, 339

of ascertaining —, 9-15
of the symbols
  Dangerousness, 45-48
  Guilt, 23-45
  Responsibility, 15-23
See also Addiction; Alcoholism; Disturbance of Consciousness; Illness; Intent; Mental Debility; Mental Disease; Mental Incapacity
Measures
  Applicability of — predicated upon offender's dangerousness, 171, 173, 195-199, 208-213
  Applicability of — to
    Abnormal persons, 305
      Addicts, 232, 241, 307-313; see also Addiction
      Alcoholics, 232, 303-313; see also Alcoholism
      Mentally incapacitated (insane) offenders, 150, 171-213, 232, 330
      Persons unfit to proceed, 169-171
    Abnormal situations
      Inadvertently negligent conduct, 25, 275, 292, 301, 315
      Intoxicated offender's conduct, 232, 250, 352-353; see also Intoxication
    Certain criminal conduct types, 304
  Contrast of — and punishment, 46-48, 304-307
  Court of sentence execution, 46, 242
  Differentiation of civil and criminal —, 46-48, 304-307; see also Commitment
  Judicial supervision over —, 145, 242
  Legality in regime of —, 46, 150-151, 171-179, 195, 204, 232, 241-242, 351
  Maximum periods, 151, 186, 195, 198-199, 201; see also Addiction; Alcoholism; Intoxication
  Minimum periods, 183, 197, 212; see also Addiction; Alcoholism; Intoxication
  Philosophy of regime of —, 302-307
  Predelictual —, 176-177, 219

  Proportionality of — to dangerousness, 145, 173, 196-199, 209-210, 249-250; see also Dangerousness
  Separation of Dangerousness and Guilt, 304
  Types of —: for
    Alcoholics and drug addicts, 248-250
    Insane offenders, 196-199
    Intoxicated offenders, 314-318
    Persons unfit to proceed, 169-171
"Mental Debility," 110-111
"Mental Defect," 94-95, 117
"Mental Disease"
  Culture impact, 215
  Intent in —, 59-61, 118-119, 120-122
  Jury finding on —, 68-69, 220-221
  Moral judgment in finding on —, 121, 214, 220-221
  as possession by devils, 114
  in Durham, 97, 116-117
  in M'Naghten, 83
  in Model Penal Code, 94-101
  in New Hampshire rule, 113-116
  Ontological view of —, 51-52, 114-116
  Psychoanalytic view of —, 118, 189
  Psychopathy and —
    Durham solution, 237
    Model Penal Code solution, 94
  See also Addiction; Alcoholism; Illness; Sickness
Mental Incapacity (Insanity)
  Acquittal by reason of mental incapacity, see latter title
  Applicability to addiction, see Addiction
  Applicability to alcoholism, see Alcoholism
  Definition of —, 133, 143-144, 149, 234, 241
  Diminished responsibility, see latter title
  Doubt regarding —, 151-157
  Evidence of —, 157-161
  Expert testimony, see Experts
  Exemption for —, 55-79

Measures for the mentally incapacitated, see Measures, Applicability to, Types of,
Constitutional issues, 239, 246, 353-354
Tests
ALI Model Penal Code tests, 94-101, 130, 142, 192, 238-239
Author's test, 134, 141-144
Durham test, 116-122, 142, 235, 239
German tests, 101-112
Irresistible impulse test, 93-94, 105-106
Italian test, 121-122
M'Naghten, test, 80-112, 142
New Hampshire test, 94, 113-116, 130
Policeman-at-the-elbow test, 93-94
Royal Commission test, 105-106, 127
Seelig's test, 106-107, 131
Spanish test, 122-125
Methodological problems, 5-15, 51-56, 121, 214, 220-221, 234
Partial responsibility, 126-128, 174
Psychiatric examination, see Experts
Raising issue of —, 146-151, 340
Relation of — to guilt, 149
Moral
Elément moral, 341-342
judgment, 234, 240
reference terms, 31-32
Moralizing Approach, 4, 220, 240, 316, 329

N

Natural Intent, 190-191, 278, 297-298, 317
Natural Law, 8, 341
"Nature and Quality of the Act," 83
"Necessity," State of, 3, 235, 240, 247-248
Non-Deterrable Offenders, 100, 205-206
"Not Guilty," 174-175

O

Objective Trial, 168-169
Offenders Not Susceptible to Punishment, 202-205
Offenders Whose Condition Will Deteriorate by Punishment, 206-207

P

Parens Patriae, State as, 21
Partial Responsibility, 126-128, 174
Paternalism of State, 21, 46, 242
"Pathological Disturbance of Mental Functioning," 109-110
Pathological
drinkers, 232
intoxication, see Intoxication
states, 109-111
Personality Evaluation, see Experts
Phenomenological, see Guilt, Phenomenological notion of,
Physicians, see Addiction
Pleasure Principle, 87
"Pleasure-Unpleasure" principle, 19
Plurality of Criminal Conduct, 192-195
Policeman-at-the-Elbow Test, 93-94
Predelictual Measures, 176-177
Prediction of One's Own Conduct, 229-230, 246, 277-278
Preliminary Examination, see Experts
Presumption of Sanity, 245
"Product of Mental Disease"
Durham test, 120-122, 200, 207, 346
New Hampshire test, 113-116
Psychiatric and Sociological Examinations Center, see Experts
Psychoanalysis, 18-23, 25, 90, 166-167, 181-182, 189, 191, 206, 218, 221-222, 225, 244, 290-291
Psychopaths, 97, 101, 110-112, 196, 205, 206, 301, 344
Public
Appearing in — under the influence of alcohol, 327
Defender of the Rights of the Mentally Ill, 169
Use of drugs in —, 323

Punishment
  Contrast of — and measures, see Measures
  Purpose of —, 55-79
  See also Non-deterrable offender; Offender not susceptible to —; Offender who will deteriorate by —

R

Reality Principle, 87
Reasonable Man, 317
Recidivism, 154, 172-173, 182, 193-194, 199
Record, Criminal, 192-193
Reformation, see Ends and Means of Criminal Law
Responsibility, 9-23, 247, 338-339, 341; see also Diminished Responsibility; Partial Responsibility
Retribution, see Ends and Means of Criminal Law
"Right-Wrong" Test, 6, 81-88, 187, 235
Roman-Canon Law, 83, 88
Science of Criminal Law, 33-37

S

Schools of Criminal Law Thought, 302-303
Scottish Law, 128
Self-Defense, 3
Sentencing
  Guide, 180, 196
  Trial, 146, 154, 161
"Sickness," 236, 342
Status Crime, 216, 219, 338-339
Suicide, 208, 211, 320-321
  Addiction as —, 323-324

Complicity in — and complicity in addiction, 324-325
"Symptomatic Drinkers," 232, 244-245
Symptoms of Mental Disease, 89-90

T

Talmud, 82
Temporary Mental Incapacity
  Temporary insanity, 231
  "Temporary mental disturbance," 101
Treatment, 21
  Ambulatory or institutionalized, 169-171, 196-199, 248-249, 310-311
  Compulsory or consensual, 248, 308-313, 336

U

Unconscious, 4, 25, 154, 162-163, 182, 206, 221, 227, 229, 230, 255, 269, 272, 273, 275, 320, 339, 342-343
Use and Possesion, see Addiction

V

Vagrancy, 178, 326
Vagueness or Certainty, 48, 97, 99, 203, 238, 331
Voluntary, 239-240, 245

W

Will, 112, 121-125, 188, 239, 240, 247
  Vicious —, 188-189
  See also Intent; Knowledge, Knowledge and Will
Withdrawal, see Addiction; Alcoholism